PAUL CELAN'S UNFINISHED POETICS
READINGS IN THE SOUS-OEUVRE

LEGENDA

LEGENDA is the Modern Humanities Research Association's book imprint for new research in the Humanities. Founded in 1995 by Malcolm Bowie and others within the University of Oxford, Legenda has always been a collaborative publishing enterprise, directly governed by scholars. The Modern Humanities Research Association (MHRA) joined this collaboration in 1998, became half-owner in 2004, in partnership with Maney Publishing and then Routledge, and has since 2016 been sole owner. Titles range from medieval texts to contemporary cinema and form a widely comparative view of the modern humanities, including works on Arabic, Catalan, English, French, German, Greek, Italian, Portuguese, Russian, Spanish, and Yiddish literature. Editorial boards and committees of more than 60 leading academic specialists work in collaboration with bodies such as the Society for French Studies, the British Comparative Literature Association and the Association of Hispanists of Great Britain & Ireland.

The MHRA encourages and promotes advanced study and research in the field of the modern humanities, especially modern European languages and literature, including English, and also cinema. It aims to break down the barriers between scholars working in different disciplines and to maintain the unity of humanistic scholarship. The Association fulfils this purpose through the publication of journals, bibliographies, monographs, critical editions, and the MHRA Style Guide, and by making grants in support of research. Membership is open to all who work in the Humanities, whether independent or in a University post, and the participation of younger colleagues entering the field is especially welcomed.

ALSO PUBLISHED BY THE ASSOCIATION

Critical Texts
Tudor and Stuart Translations • New Translations • European Translations
MHRA Library of Medieval Welsh Literature

MHRA Bibliographies
Publications of the Modern Humanities Research Association

The Annual Bibliography of English Language & Literature
Austrian Studies
Modern Language Review
Portuguese Studies
The Slavonic and East European Review
Working Papers in the Humanities
The Yearbook of English Studies

www.mhra.org.uk
www.legendabooks.com

GERMANIC LITERATURES

Editorial Committee
Chair: Professor Ritchie Robertson (University of Oxford)
Dr Barbara Burns (Glasgow University)
Professor Jane Fenoulhet (University College London)
Professor Anne Fuchs (University College Dublin)
Dr Jakob Stougaard-Nielsen (University College London)
Professor Annette Volfing (University of Oxford)
Professor Susanne Kord (University College London)
Professor John Zilcosky (University of Toronto)

Germanic Literatures includes monographs and essay collections on literature originally written not only in German, but also in Dutch and the Scandinavian languages. Within the German-speaking area, it seeks also to publish studies of other national literatures such as those of Austria and Switzerland. The chronological scope of the series extends from the early Middle Ages down to the present day.

APPEARING IN THIS SERIES

1. *Franz Grillparzer's Dramatic Heroines*, by Matthew McCarthy-Rechowicz
2. *Sebald's Bachelors: Queer Resistance and the Unconforming Life*, by Helen Finch
3. *Goethe's Visual World*, by Pamela Currie
4. *German Narratives of Belonging: Writing Generation and Place in the Twenty-First Century*, by Linda Shortt
5. *The Very Late Goethe: Self-Consciousness and the Art of Ageing*, by Charlotte Lee
6. *Women, Emancipation and the German Novel 1871-1910: Protest Fiction in its Cultural Context*, by Charlotte Woodford
7. *Goethe's Poetry and the Philosophy of Nature: Gott und Welt 1798–1827*, by Regina Sachers
8. *Fontane and Cultural Mediation: Translation and Reception in Nineteenth-Century German Literature*, edited by Ritchie Robertson and Michael White
9. *Metamorphosis in Modern German Literature: Transforming Bodies, Identities and Affects*, by Tara Beaney
10. *Comedy and Trauma in Germany and Austria after 1945: The Inner Side of Mourning*, by Stephanie Bird
11. *E.T.A. Hoffmann's Orient: Romantic Aesthetics and the German Imagination*, by Joanna Neilly
12. *Structures of Subjugation in Dutch Literature*, by Judit Gera

Managing Editor
Dr Graham Nelson, 41 Wellington Square, Oxford OX1 2JF, UK
www.legendabooks.com

Paul Celan's Unfinished Poetics

Readings in the Sous-Oeuvre

Thomas C. Connolly

LEGENDA
Germanic Literatures 16
Modern Humanities Research Association
2018

Published by Legenda
an imprint of the Modern Humanities Research Association
Salisbury House, Station Road, Cambridge CB1 2LA

ISBN 978-1-78188-565-9 *(HB)*
ISBN 978-1-78188-566-6 *(PB)*

First published 2018

All rights reserved. No part of this publication may be reproduced or disseminated or transmitted in any form or by any means, electronic, mechanical, photocopying, recording or otherwise, or stored in any retrieval system, or otherwise used in any manner whatsoever without written permission of the copyright owner, except in accordance with the provisions of the Copyright, Designs and Patents Act 1988, or under the terms of a licence permitting restricted copying issued in the UK by the Copyright Licensing Agency Ltd, Saffron House, 6–10 Kirby Street, London EC1N 8TS, *England, or in the USA by the Copyright Clearance Center, 222 Rosewood Drive, Danvers MA 01923. Application for the written permission of the copyright owner to reproduce any part of this publication must be made by email to legenda@mhra.org.uk.*

Disclaimer: Statements of fact and opinion contained in this book are those of the author and not of the editors or the Modern Humanities Research Association. The publisher makes no representation, express or implied, in respect of the accuracy of the material in this book and cannot accept any legal responsibility or liability for any errors or omissions that may be made.

Trademark notice: Product or corporate names may be trademarks or registered trademarks, and are used only for identification and explanation without intent to infringe.

© *Modern Humanities Research Association 2018*

Copy-Editor: Birgit Mikus

CONTENTS

	Acknowledgments	ix
	Introduction: Celan's Sous-Oeuvre	1
1	Learning to Read in the Pre-Text	30
2	Engaging Mallarmé	85
3	Poetry After Frankfurt	137
4	Rembrandt, Mandel'shtam, and the Limits of Ekphrasis	196
	Conclusion: Reading Poetry, Reading Celan	218
	Bibliography	227
	Index	244

For Gabriel, Yaël, and Helena

ACKNOWLEDGMENTS

I owe thanks to more people than I can name for their kindness, patience, intelligence, and support during the writing of this book. I thank Eric Celan and Bertrand Badiou of the 'Unité de recherche Paul Celan' at the 'École normale supérieure' in Paris for years of generous support. I am especially grateful to Judith Ryan, Christopher D. Johnson, and Susan R. Suleiman for their expert guidance and encouragement when this book project was in its early stages. I am grateful to the librarians and staff of the German Literature Archive at Marbach am Neckar for their hospitality and helpfulness during the course of three research visits. I thank Ritchie Robertson, Graham Nelson, and Birgit Mikus at Legenda — as well as the anonymous reader — for their careful reading of the manuscript and for their extremely useful commentary. Heartfelt thanks also to my colleagues in the Department of French at Yale University who have provided a stimulating and sympathetic environment in which to complete this work. Thank you to everyone at Old Bridzor, especially to Anthony C. Connolly, who created the etching reproduced on the cover of the book.

For permissions to reproduce various translations, I thank Ian Fairley and Stanley Moss at Sheep Meadow Press, Susan Gillespie and Sam Truitt at Station Hill Press, and Barnett Zumoff and Shira Atwood at Ktav Publishers.

A version of chapter one recently appeared in *Compar(a)ison* as "Keine Schönschrift für Schulkinder': Towards a Poetics of the Pre-Text in Paul Celan's *Eingedunkelt*'. A version of chapter four appeared in *Modern Philology* (© 2014 by The University of Chicago) as 'Oils, Psalms, and Scum: Anadyomene Paint and the Limits of Ekphrasis in Paul Celan's "EINKANTER: Rembrandt"'.

This book was published with the assistance of the Frederick W. Hilles Publication Fund of Yale University. It was also subsidized in part by Harvard Studies in Comparative Literature. The research for this book was made possible by the A. Whitney Griswold Faculty Research Grant at Yale University, the Harvard University Graduate Society Dissertation Completion Fellowship, the Deutscher Akademischer Austausch Dienst Short-Term Research Grant, the Harvard University Graduate Student Council Summer Scholarship and, on two occasions, the Summer Study and Research Fellowship for Modern Hebrew Language Training in Tel Aviv from the Center for Jewish Studies at Harvard.

T.C.C., Bethany, Connecticut, January 2018

La jeunesse n'aime pas les objets parfaits.
Ils lui laissent trop peu à faire, et l'irritent ou l'ennuient.

Paul Valéry

INTRODUCTION

Celan's Sous-Oeuvre

> Or perhaps
> the Turkish lilac passes by,
> questioning, it obtains
> more than just scent.[1]

Postmeridian

It could be argued that nothing will substantially change the way we read, understand, and think about the work of Paul Celan (1920–1970), one of the foremost European poets of the postwar period. The contours of his poetic project seem to have been definitively laid out for us by the collective and highly skilled labors of half a century of readers, archivists, editors, commentators, translators, theorists, and philosophers. Although Celan was fearful of what George Steiner called the 'exegetic industry'[2] and the 'industry of clerical elucidation',[3] it is this that has facilitated the passage of certain parts of Celan's work into the cultural vernacular. The poet, whose writing has created more confusion and posed the greatest challenges to comprehension than perhaps anybody since Stéphane Mallarmé, would find that today his work is — to a surprising degree — not only read, but accommodated, appreciated, and understood. We could be forgiven for thinking that there are no longer reasons to be surprised by Paul Celan's poetry.

This book stems from a sense that interpretations of Celan's work continue to draw on a relatively narrow set of primary texts. One of the most striking examples of this can be seen in the fact that, regardless of the perspective of individual critics and of the text in question, studies of Celan's poems are almost uniformly structured and justified with reference to the handful of theoretical texts in prose that Celan himself wrote. It is rare, for example, to come across a critical interpretation of a poem by Celan that does not quote a passage from the Georg Büchner Prize acceptance speech, delivered in Darmstadt to the German Academy of Language and Literature in October 1960, and subsequently published as 'The Meridian'.[4] It is true that this speech contains the poet's most extended theoretical and poetical exploration of the tasks and possibilities of poetry. At no other moment does Celan express himself 'more precisely, openly, and explicitly'[5] than he does here. Many will agree with Leonard Olschner when he writes that the speech provides 'a context and a vocabulary from which critical discourse and hence enhanced understanding become possible'.[6] And yet there are also reasons to be wary of such a critical consensus.

In this book, I ask whether appealing to the authority of the poet's own public pronouncements on poetry will continue to be as indispensable to readers of these poems as it has been in the first fifty years of scholarship. Reference to these works has repeatedly been fruitful, allowing readers to orient themselves in what is a difficult oeuvre. But this critical habit may now be preventing readers from considering new, and perhaps less evident, ways of reading and creating meaning. Here, I ask if readers can continue to justify referencing poetological texts conceived in the late 1950s and early 1960s when reading and seeking to better understand poems composed some years later, in the mid to late 1960s. I also explore how our reading of Celan's poems changes when we structure and strengthen our readings of his poems without automatically turning to these central poetological statements. More broadly, I am interested in examining whether the study of difficult poetry is served best by our recourse to external prose texts as we pursue understanding, or if instead we should attempt to look to each individual poem for the unique things it teaches about poetic expression. As Steiner concludes when faced with Celan's posthumously published poems: 'each poem stands by itself. The patterns we make out are probably fallacious'.[7] This book attempts to extend this sentiment to the work as a whole.

I do not ignore the canonical prose texts habitually referenced in readings of Celan's work, but I do seek to move the discussion away from them and onto less familiar ground, perhaps what Michel de Certeau calls the 'textual suburbs'.[8] I attempt to address those parts of Celan's work considered less attractive to readers, commentators, literary historians, and literary theorists. I aim to familiarize the reader of this book with certain of the more unfashionable and inconvenient traces left by Celan after his premature death in April 1970. Beyond a desire to persuade readers to re-assess the way Celan is read and understood, I hope that what follows will encourage readers to devote more of their readerly attention to literary texts that have been neglected either because of their perceived inadequacy or because they constitute those marginal parts of the oeuvre that conventional critical frames tend to keep out of the picture.

The novelist J. M. Coetzee notes that 'there are plenty of incompletely achieved poems in Celan, and, more to the point, plenty of moments of near total obscurity'.[9] Many of the primary texts discussed in this book are drawn from this obscure part of the oeuvre. They might be said to constitute the unconscious of Celan's work, the benighted regions of an otherwise celebrated corpus, what we might call the oeuvre's under-belly, or the sous-oeuvre. In contrast to the oeuvre, which defines all known parts of an author's work, by sous-oeuvre I intend all traces of scriptural activity, whether published or unpublished, visible or invisible, linguistic or super-linguistic, desirable or undesirable.[10] The French 'sous', under, comes from the Sanskrit root 'ubh' or 'umbh' meaning to gather or bring together, so that the sous-oeuvre might be said to bring together multiple contradictory dynamics, dimensions, and intensities that the conventional oeuvre cannot contain.[11] The notion of the sous-oeuvre is designed to promote those texts and textual traces that are generally thought to be underwhelming and disappointing, if not dangerous.

The sous-oeuvre is meant to draw our attention to what Geoffrey Hartman once called 'rhythms and words that come unbidden'[12] to see if they have the capacity to challenge and maybe even change our reading habits and critical assumptions. I ask if these unfinished, overlooked, or forgotten parts of the oeuvre are sufficiently integrated into our understanding of what constitutes literature, and how their inclusion might transform not only our ways of reading literature but also the sorts of texts we as readers are willing and able to read and understand.

Indarkened

Paul Celan's Unfinished Poetics mostly examines various of the poet's later works, dating from the mid to late 1960s. These include a number of texts from the unfinished and critically neglected cycle of poems called *Eingedunkelt* [indarkened].[13] Although not the sole focus of this book, this cycle betrays many of the characteristics of the sous-oeuvre, and will be examined in some detail to identify and define Celan's unfinished poetics.[14] *Eingedunkelt* was composed between 25 February and 2 May 1966 in Prof. Jean Delay's psychiatric clinic at the Sainte Anne hospital in Paris.[15] Celan had been forcibly hospitalized there after a failed attempt to stab Gisèle Celan-Lestrange in November 1965.[16] Following his release from hospital the following June, no reference was made, either in his correspondence or in his personal diaries, to poems composed during his incarceration.[17] In July 1967, Celan returned to re-read and edit a small number of the poems in the *Eingedunkelt* cycle. When, in January 1968, Siegfried Unseld, the editor-in-chief of the Suhrkamp publishing house, asked for a contribution to an anthology of unfinished works, Celan was able to select eleven poems from the *Eingedunkelt* cycle and dispatch them to him within a week.[18] The selection of poems was published a few months later alongside similarly unfinished or abandoned texts by authors including Samuel Beckett, Peter Weiss, Nelly Sachs, and Martin Walser.[19] An editorial note indicated that all other materials relating to the *Eingedunkelt* cycle had been destroyed.[20] But in the months following Celan's death in 1970, an envelope was discovered that contained extensive drafts for the eleven poems published in 1968, as well as genetic documents relating to a further twenty-four poems, amounting in total to over two hundred pages of manuscript and typescript. This body of documents — prematurely consigned to oblivion in the public imagination — constitutes a significant example of that part of Celan's oeuvre that is not commonly considered part of the oeuvre. The notion that the poems in *Eingedunkelt* represent part of the sous-oeuvre is strengthened when we consider that the eleven *Eingedunkelt* poems published in 1968 appeared in a book that was never meant to be sold, and that was instead a complimentary gift for Suhrkamp customers, given out during a two-week period, to celebrate the company's founding eighteen years previously.

In 1991, shortly after Paul Celan's archive had been acquired by the German Literature Archive at Marbach am Neckar, versions of all thirty-five poems were published for the first time.[21] In contrast to all other publications of Celan's work, the poems in *Eingedunkelt* did not readily lend themselves to the modes of publication conventionally used to present poems to the public. It was in certain cases difficult, if not impossible, to identify a definitive version of a given poem, either because of competing definitive versions of the same poem, or because a definitive version of the text could not be identified as such and had to be 'constituted'. As a result, a number of variants were included alongside the definitive or constituted versions of each of the thirty-five poems. The inclusion of variants in this 1991 edition not only disturbed the usual practice of publishing definitive and authorized versions of poems without traces of their genesis. It also pointed to a growing trend in Celanian textual scholarship toward the exhaustive transcription and publication of documents relating to published collections of poems. The transcribed documents relating to *Eingedunkelt* — and which constitute the primary material for much of the work undertaken in this book — were first published in 2006 by the 'Bonner Arbeitsstelle für die Celan-Ausgabe', a research team assembled to publish all traces of Celan's 'Nachlass', that is, work unpublished during the poet's lifetime.

Following the publication of the thirty-five poems in 1991, a flurry of reviews in the German language press showed that critics seemed unsure if these poems offered new ways of approaching Celan's poetry and poetics, or if they were inferior to those in the established oeuvre, being both unfinished and unauthorized. Harald Hartung, writing in the *Frankfurter Allgemeine Zeitung*, took exception to the publication of *Eingedunkelt*, asking 'But do these texts actually add anything to Celan's oeuvre?'[22] Writing three days later in *Die Zeit*, Rolf Michaelis disagreed, saying: 'The poems themselves assert their own value' and 'should not — at any point in time — be stashed away in the apparatus of a critical edition'.[23] In a radio program, Wolfgang Emmerich was also more generous in his appraisal of the poems, saying that they 'were definitely worth reading, as was of course to be expected'.[24] But in addition to this notion of the poems being 'worth reading', there was the qualification that they essentially offered nothing new for us to understand: 'They follow the same poetics which inspired Celan from the 1967 collection of poems entitled *Atemwende* [Breath-Turn], and basically since his great 1960 Büchner prize speech, "The Meridian"'.[25] Much of the critical response in the German language press was marked by just this sense of relief that there was nothing in this unexpected exposure of the sous-oeuvre to disturb established critical assumptions pertaining to Celan's oeuvre. As Hartung writes, 'paradoxically enough, the exciting thing is that there are no surprises'.[26]

In such company, it is easy to forget that the purpose of poetry is to surprise, to reveal things through language that have never previously been revealed, to express what cannot otherwise be expressed. In the case of Paul Celan's poetry, the surprise that inheres in every poetic statement, whether authorized and published or not, has been somewhat overshadowed by the perceived critical hegemony of the 'Meridian' speech. There has been a significant degree of what Certeau calls 'philosophical impatience'[27] in attempts to explicate Celan's poetics with almost exclusive reference to this poetic and poetological statement. Charlie Louth illustrates something of this tendency when he states that 'Celan's speeches are essential, really, to reading the poems'.[28] This is despite the fact, as Leonard Olschner notes, that 'The Meridian' 'makes no claims to be exhaustive or particularly systematic' and 'is not a manual for unraveling the secrets of the poetry'.[29] Once a reader is exposed to the sous-oeuvre, as opposed to the published oeuvre, the authority of 'The Meridian' will appear less obvious. The theoretical and philosophical highways that have been carved through Celan's established oeuvre help only incidentally in understanding the under-belly of the oeuvre. Instead of confirming critical assumptions, this book invites readers of Celan to slow down the speed with which they read and interpret, and to entertain the notion that there are features of Celan's poetics and philosophy that are yet to be uncovered and understood. 'The Meridian' tends to have been used not to 'follow yourself into your own-most straits'[30] as it calls us to do, but to expand art, to mitigate differentiation, to invade and contaminate almost every critical pronouncement on Celan's poetry. As Philippe Lacoue-Labarthe notes about art, so we might say about the artful way critics have approached Celan's oeuvre, namely, that they do so not through the counter-words ('Es ist das Gegenwort')[31] or the steps ('Es ist ein Schritt')[32] that are its poems, but through its speeches: 'Art is, if we can risk the term, a generalized "estrangement": the head of the Medusa, the automatons, the speeches — never ending'.[33] We cheat ourselves of the opportunity to read, and to learn through reading, if we read with the assumption that a poem or set of poems constitute the embodiment, the continuation, and the confirmation of a poetics formulated by the poet most explicitly during the summer and fall months of 1960. For the poet to perceive the need to continue writing throughout the 1960s and up until the days before his death in 1970, there must have been the need to express something that had not yet been expressed, to say something that had not yet been projected.

Throughout this book, I read poems by entering into and exploring the unique manifestation of their internal logic, even where this logic appears hermetic or only partly implemented. Each poem contains a new way of looking at the world that is not so much waiting to be discovered as formed in the event of reading. It is an approach that undercuts the notion of a uniform, explicatory poetics, through which readers are expected and encouraged to approach poetic texts. A poetics is by nature unfinished, multiple, and contradictory. It is always in the process of developing, as new readers encounter and create meaning with the oeuvre. A poetics should be an invitation to continue to explore, challenge, and transform the ways we think about a particular poet's work and thought, rather than a template within which to regulate readings. As Hans-Georg Gadamer explains: 'a poem is not a discovery [Befund] that one can explain as the particular instance of a more generalized tendency, in the way that a scientific discovery reveals an instance of the laws of nature'.[34] Each time a poem is read, it attempts to become reality in the unrepeatability of the reader's encounter with the text. Peter Szondi notes in his explication of Celan's poem 'The Straightening' or *Engführung*: 'the text itself refuses to serve reality, to continue to play the role that has been assigned to it since Aristotle. Poetry ceases to be *mimesis*, representation: it becomes reality. Poetic reality, of course, text which no longer follows a given reality, but which projects itself, constitutes itself as reality'.[35] Here, Szondi is teaching us to read each text as

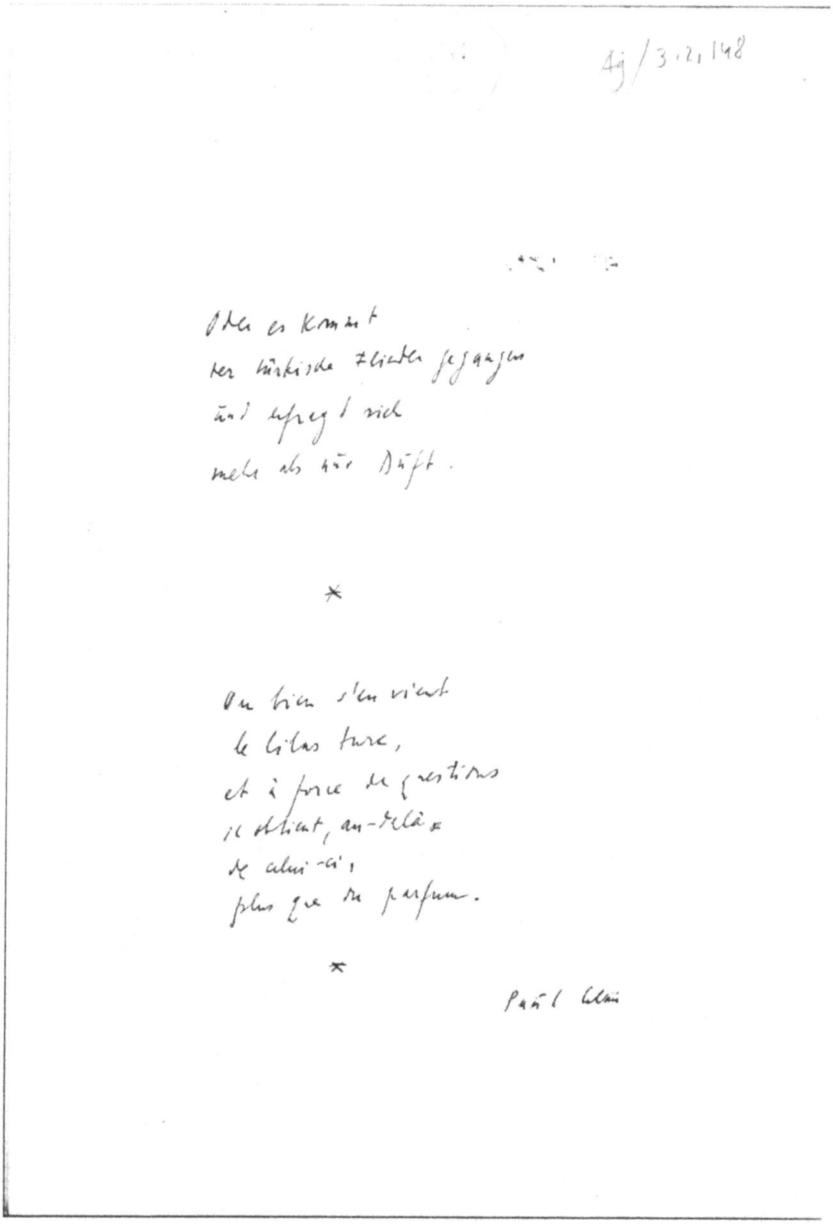

Ag / 3.2, 148

Oder es kommt
der türkische Flieder gegangen
und erfragt sich
mehr als nur Duft.

*

Ou bien s'en vient
le lilas turc,
et à force de questions
il obtient, au-delà
de celui-ci,
plus que du parfum.

*

Paul Celan

FIG. I.1. 'Oder es kommt', with translation into French, 'Ou bien s'en vient'. Blue ink. Ms (Ag / 3.2, 148). © Deutsches Literaturarchiv, Marbach a. N.

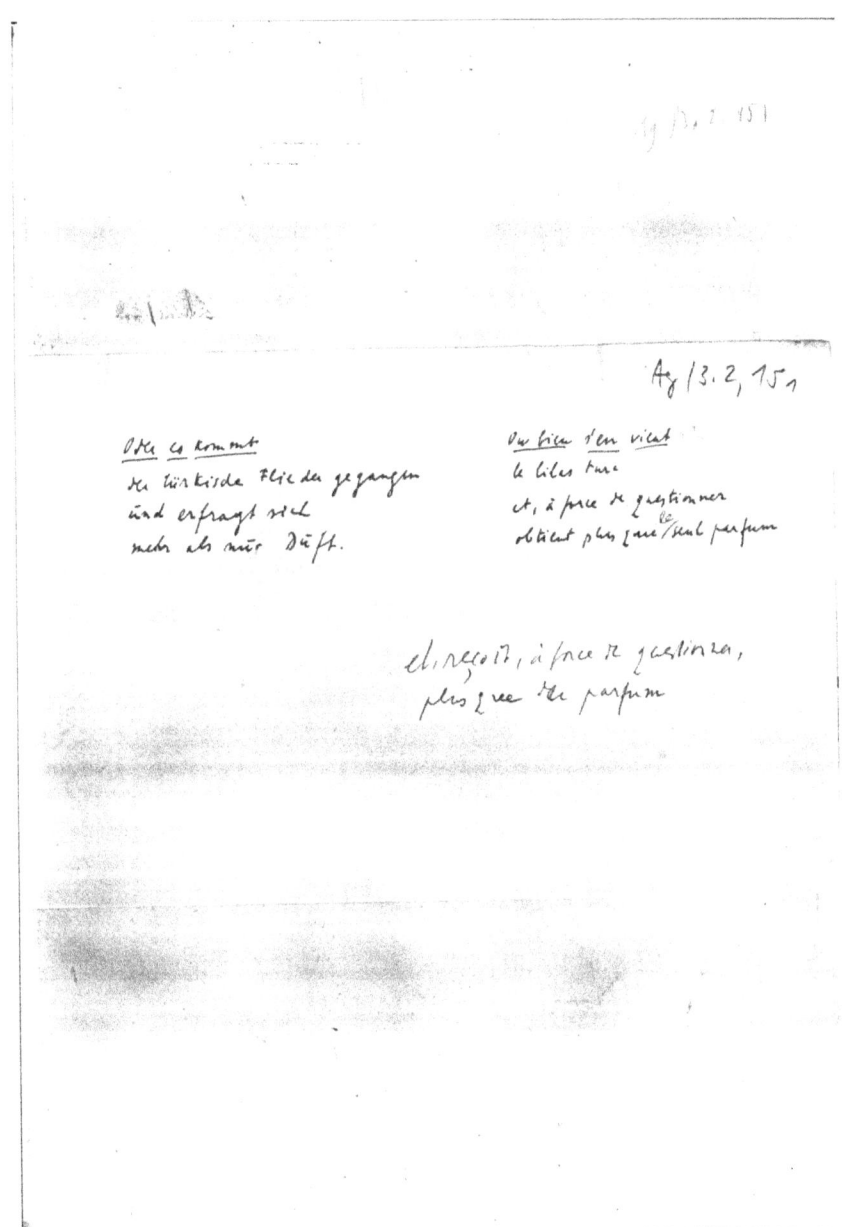

Fig. I.2. 'Oder es kommt', with translation into French, 'Ou bien s'en vient'. Blue ink and pencil. Ms (Ag / 3.2, 151). © Deutsches Literaturarchiv, Marbach a. N.

it asks uniquely to be read, not as the local manifestation of an external, superior, and theoretical source, which would here be the official expression in prose and in public of a poetics. Instead, he encourages us to grasp the way each poem projects and invents reality in the intimacy of its unique textual configuration. To quote a speech given in 1958 on the occasion of Celan's acceptance of the Bremen Prize, and often referred to in readings of Celan's poetry, the poem is both wounded by and seeking reality, 'wirklichkeitswund und Wirklichkeit suchend'.[36] Gadamer expresses a similar idea in less bloody terms when he says that 'each poem is its own topos, [...]: its own world, which never repeats itself, which occurs only once, like the world itself'.[37] The poem asks its reader, at every encounter, to struggle for new realities and new meanings, to invent new constructions of knowledge rather than to deploy modes of comprehension developed previously or in encounters with other texts. As we explore the sous-oeuvre and read neglected fragments of text for the unique ways in which they teach us to read, we will see that Celan's poetics cannot be reduced to the 'already thought' and 'already said', even that said and thought in 'The Meridian'. The sous-oeuvre continues to expand the boundaries of how poetry thinks, and how a reader might learn to think through poetry.

One way in which the sous-oeuvre will fail to conform to conventional expectations is that it is often not clear if the texts concerned are difficult or not. Celan's established oeuvre is commonly perceived to resist many of the conventional modes of understanding poetry, such that its difficulty has itself become a convention, something that readers expect. As Steiner notes, the extreme difficulty of Celan's published work 'is neither contingent nor acrobatic, as it sometimes can be even in Mallarmé, but of the essence'.[38] Two years later, this category of difficulty, in which it is not so much the poet who speaks as language itself, will be called 'ontological'.[39] In the case of the sous-oeuvre, it is often not clear whether a text can be considered ontologically or essentially difficult. A number of critics reacting to the publication of the thirty-five *Eingedunkelt* poems in 1991, for instance, appear pleasantly surprised by the poems' accessibility. Alexander von Bormann said in a radio broadcast: 'these poems demand effort, but they are by no means as impenetrable and sealed as many might expect when they hear the name Paul Celan. [...] There is no doubt that these late poems offer a point of access to the complete works; the interweavings are striking and illuminating'.[40] Rolf-Ulrich Kunze goes so far as to say: 'that most of the poems in the ambit of *Eingedunkelt* are not particularly difficult, much less hermetic. They are rather immediately accessible. And they are beautiful'.[41] Sven Sagé writes that these poems 'will not surprise the connoisseurs, but will initiate anybody who does not already know Celan's work'.[42] Andreas Härter explains the poems' difficulty as imminent rather than immediate, suggesting that these are poems 'that seem to still be waiting for their hermetic compaction; which seem to be on the point of setting out toward hermeticism, but which are still intelligible'.[43]

The notion that *Eingedunkelt* presents fewer difficulties in comprehension than most of Celan's poetry is contested by one of Celan's most prominent advocates in the English-speaking world. John Felstiner has little to say about Celan's 'nearly seven months in the clinics'[44] or about the *Eingedunkelt* poems, but what he does say is at odds with the prevailing view expressed in the German language press:

> From February to May 1966, Celan's poems are so cryptic as to seem like signals from another planet. / / Pour the wasteland into your eye-sacks, / the call to sacrifice, the salt flood, / / come with me to Breath / and beyond. / / Some inner listener is roused to vision — scrotumlike sockets filled with Biblical adversity — and led to 'Breath / and beyond'.[45]

The claim that *Eingedunkelt* presents the reader with a difficulty that is nothing less than interplanetary may be hyperbolical, but it does indicate a strain of difficulty that runs through the cycle, and that Celan fully intended to deploy. Whilst in the clinic at Suresnes, in the weeks before his transfer to Sainte Anne and the composition of *Eingedunkelt*, Celan inscribed the following in a book of Paul Éluard's poems,[46] one of the few books he had with him at the time: 'Whoever does not endow the poem with the resisting force of the immediate, has not written a poem'.[47] In this he echoes the early André Gide — still a Symbolist of sorts — who writes to Paul Valéry: 'Some believe themselves to be greats because they create verses as easily as they breathe — but we, on the other hand, understand the excellence of a poem by its resistance, when we want to extract it from the virtual. [...] Things must be "hardened" [éprouvées]'.[48] Poetry is not a puzzle to be solved and explained. Instead, poetry exposes the reader to a harder way of thinking, to an intransitivity, which has the force to change the way the reader thinks, and how he or she lives according to that thought. The poem can only really be approached through its resistance to comprehension. The reader's task is to find a way of accommodating him or herself within this resistance, and to achieve understanding according to the unique law that governs the poem.

The poem's singularity is an important element of its resistance to comprehension, as Martin Heidegger's notion of the 'holding-back-of-self' [Sichzurückhalten] demonstrates.[49] The self that draws itself back is what makes poetry possible, and what allows it to achieve the 'luminosity' of being: 'The more essentially the work opens itself, the more luminous becomes the uniqueness of the fact that it is rather than is not. The more essentially this thrust comes into the open, the stranger and more solitary the work becomes'.[50] It is for many critics not certain that the poems in *Eingedunkelt* arrive at this same uniqueness of existence, that they penetrate the confines of the world to exist supplementarily, on the outside, excessively with respect to the world. One of the *Eingedunkelt* poems not published in 1968 — and discussed in chapter one — articulates what is at stake here when it says: 'The rope, [...] reaches,[...] for the Eternal Outside' [Das Seil, [...] langt, [...] nach dem Ewigen Draussen].[51] It is unclear whether *Eingedunkelt* succeeds in reaching the Eternal Outside for which it strives. It is unclear whether these poems interrupt the self-sameness of the world, thereby refusing to be implicated in the world's self-identity. It is unclear whether they succeed in breaking into an open place, where everything is other than it usually is. In short, it is unclear whether these texts constitute moments of poetry or 'Dichtung'.

The ontological ambiguity of these poems — the fact that we can't decide whether they are difficult or easy to read, or even if they qualify as poems — appears to have unsettled readers of these poems in their critical habits and expectations. I suggest that this ontological ambiguity — also a form of resistance — should encourage us to persevere in our reading of these poems, and of the sous-oeuvre more generally. I therefore align this study of the sous-oeuvre with Felstiner's initial sense of alienation and incomprehension, rather than with the comprehensive and comprehending tendencies of other critics. An avowal of initial incomprehension should, at the very least, forestall the impatient reader in us who wishes to offer quick and convenient conclusions, so that he or she can then move onto other, unrelated matters. In the best case, this sense of alienation might allow a reader to approach these poems free from the preconceptions usually deployed before reading. He or she will then be in a position to approach these poems in their uniqueness, without haste and without fear at what may or may not be uncovered, and to learn something new about literature in the process. The desire of critics around 1991 to both acknowledge the presence of these poems and to immediately habilitate them into the confines of the established oeuvre, without critical inquiry or imagination, should perhaps be seen as a collective attempt to avoid the truly 'poetic'. It points to the ways that *Eingedunkelt* specifically — and the sous-oeuvre in general — unsettles its rare readers and leaves them exposed.

In contrast to the reader of the oeuvre, who is a consumer of text prepared for his or her consumption, the reader of the sous-oeuvre will be required to define his or her reading object. Besides reading, the reader must become an explorer, a pioneer, an entrepreneur. When reading among *Eingedunkelt*'s unfinished texts, it quickly becomes clear how important the readings Celan undertook at the moment of composition were to the creation of the poems themselves. A number of the poems clearly take their word-matter from the texts Celan read, thereby extending the object of reading beyond the poem and its genetic documents, and into the published texts of other authors. For instance, 'For shame' ['Vor Scham'],[52] relies heavily on a German translation of Thomas Wolfe's 1935 novel *Of Time and the River*, which Celan read regularly during his hospitalization at Sainte Anne, and from which he inscribed copious notes in notebooks.[53] The poem 'Shackled by seaweed jewels' ['Mit Seetang-Geschmeide gefesselt'][54] draws much of its vocabulary directly from Georg Goyert's translation of James Joyce's *Ulysses*, another book that Celan had with him at Sainte Anne, and whose small print he found almost impossible to make out.[55] 'DO YOU TURN' ['WIRFST DU'][56] is built almost exclusively from vocabulary found in Book Nine of Wolfgang Schadewaldt's translation of *The Odyssey*.[57]

Jacques Derrida says that the poem speaks, and that is how we should listen to it.[58] In the sous-oeuvre, however, things are often less clear-cut. As the texts in *Eingedunkelt* remind us, a poem in the sous-oeuvre is rarely alone in speaking. Each poem is surrounded by other, related voices, the voices of past (but still present) iterations, and the voices of foreign, published texts that the poem has in some way co-opted into its own voice. The identification of intertextual sources need not be regarded as contaminating the reader's engagement with the text. The reader should be free to listen to these other voices, to read or recall other texts, even as he or she engages with and responds primarily to the poem. In this respect, Gadamer distinguishes somewhat arbitrarily between information that the reader should 'immediately forget', and 'primary textual findings, which it is good to know precisely'.[59] There are, though, many possible degrees of intensity to which external information can usefully contaminate a reader's reading of a text. Gadamer is perhaps right to warn us of the ways a reader might begin to close him or herself off to the work under consideration. Perhaps the poem's unique voice is heard with slightly less clarity and force than would otherwise be the case. But there should be no restriction of the multiple and varied ways in which the poem might be encountered — sometimes in pure and isolated dialogue as Derrida and Gadamer propose, in which the text speaks directly to the reader's situation in time and space, sometimes with an ear bent to other voices and foreign turns of phrase that might just nudge understanding of the text in directions and into dimensions which, previously, there was no reason to suspect as being possible.

In its original state, the sous-oeuvre will often be monolingual. It is characteristic of texts that originate in the sous-oeuvre that few receive sufficient attention to require translation into other languages. Furthermore, the irregular and unpredictable form of the sous-oeuvre means that its texts may not naturally lend themselves to the conventional critical and interpretative practices of translation.[60] As most of the texts considered in this book were originally composed in German, some parts of the sous-oeuvre — particularly those drawn from manuscript and typescript documents — will be translated here for the first time. In the case of *Eingedunkelt*, however, English translations of less than half of the poems in the cycle already exist.[61] Susan H. Gillespie includes thirteen *Eingedunkelt* poems in her translation of Celan's poems,[62] and Ian Fairley has translated fifteen of the cycle's thirty-five poems.[63] These translations provide rare opportunities for dialogue with fellow interlopers in Celan's sous-oeuvre, although both translators appear to translate these poems as if they were definitive texts, comparable to those in Celan's established oeuvre. I maintain that when translating poems from the sous-oeuvre, the weakened autonomy of the poem as unit of text requires translators to be conscious of the poem's continuing dialogue with the intertext from which it draws language and meaning. By illuminating something of the intertextual network in which the *Eingedunkelt* poems have come into being, I aim to cast light on new possibilities and challenges in the reading and translating of Celan's poems.

By way of example, I examine a short poem written by Celan on 31 March 1966, alongside translations by Fairley and Gillespie respectively.

> FÜLL DIE ÖDNIS in die Augensäcke,
> den Opferruf, die Salzflut,
>
> komm mit mir zu Atem
> und drüber hinaus.[64]

WITH DESOLATION pump the eye,
call to sacrifice, salt tide,

enter with me into breath
and out of it.[65]

FILL THE WILDERNESS in the eye-bags,
the call to sacrifice, the salt-flood.

Come with me to breath
and beyond.[66]

I limit my examination of these two translations to two words.[67] First, let us look at the compound noun 'Opferruf', which combines the noun 'Opfer' ['victim' or 'sacrifice'] and 'Ruf' ['call' or 'cry', but also 'reputation']. Both Fairley and Gillespie break 'Opferruf' into its constituent nouns to give the idiomatic and familiar English phrase, the 'call to sacrifice'. It is easy to overlook that in doing so they both re-invent the way the two words relate to each other. If the implied genitive construction inherent in the juxtaposition of two nouns in German is maintained, then we might more properly deduce something like the 'call of sacrifice'. At this point, an awareness of the texts that Celan was reading on the day of this particular poem's composition might encourage and justify a less familiar expression in English translation. The word 'Opferruf' is used by Wolfgang Schadewaldt in *The Odyssey* to translate the Greek 'ὀλόλυξαν' ['cried in a loud voice', 'ululated'] as it appears in the following passage:

> And when they had prayed and scattered the barley, the great-hearted son of Nestor, Thrasymêdês, instantly drew near and drove home the blow. The axe cut the two neck tendons and released the vigor of the heifer, and Nestor's daughters and the wives of his sons and his own honored wife, Eurydikê, the eldest daughter of Klymenos, cried out in holy ululation [Und es schrien den Opferruf die Töchter und die Schwiegertöchter...].[68]

Crucially, the 'Opferruf' here designates not so much a call *to* sacrifice, that is to say, a call, which recognizes the need for sacrifice, and which pre-empts the sacrifice. Instead, it constitutes a call or a cry *of* sacrifice, a cry uttered by the women only once the bull's nuchal sinews have been hacked open and the sacrifice has begun. The call does not so much announce the sacrifice to come as constitute the acoustic manifestation of the sacrifice in the moment of its occurrence. It is the echo and amplification of the sound of the axe-blow that kills the sacrificial victim, and perhaps also of the sudden gush of hot blood. As such, the cry allows the sound and significance of the blow and the blood to resonate and be sustained beyond the fleeting moment of the blow's impact and the blood's appearance. The cry is, in other words, an integral part of the sacrificial proceedings not as a future event, but as a present and still resonating past event. Fairley's and Gillespie's 'call to sacrifice' re-inscribes the poem in recognizable English idiom. But in doing this, the translators perceive a relation between the two parts of the compound noun that is presumed rather than established, and that removes the 'call' or 'cry' from the sacrifice itself to that which precedes and announces it. The context provided by *The Odyssey* at least allows for the introduction of another possible — and not entirely arbitrary — frame of reference, where before there was none. It permits us to challenge the translation of this compound noun into hard and fast English idiom, and to preserve some of its original uncertainty and ambiguity.

Challenging the conventional translation of 'Opferruf' is not an empty exercise, but allows us to more fully understand the significance of this brief poem. The incorporation of the 'cry' or 'Ruf' into the event of the sacrifice itself means that we can now hear not only the cry of those who commit and celebrate the sacrifice — that is the cry of Nestor's daughters, daughter-in-law, and wife — but also the

> 4. 727—767
>
> hinwieder ohne Kunde aus den Hallen hinweggerafft, und ich habe nicht gehört, daß er aufgebrochen! Ihr Schlimmen! auch von euch ist keiner einzigen in den Sinn gekommen, mich von dem Lager aufzuwecken, und ihr wußtet doch genau im Herzen, wann jener auf das hohle schwarze Schiff ging! Denn wenn ich erfahren hätte, daß er diese Reise vorgehabt, so wäre er gewiß entweder geblieben, so sehr es ihn mit dem Wege drängte, oder er hätte mich als Tote zurückgelassen in den Hallen. Doch rufe mir eine geschwind den alten Dolios, meinen Diener, den mir der Vater damals schon gegeben, als ich hierher gekommen, und der mir den baumreichen Garten pflegt: damit er dieses alles auf das schnellste dem Laertes berichte, sich zu ihm setzend: ob dieser vielleicht irgendeinen Plan im Herzen weben und hinausgehn möchte und einen Jammer vor dem Volk erheben, daß sie seinen und des gottgleichen Odysseus Stamm zu vernichten streben.»
>
> Da sagte zu ihr hinwieder die Pflegerin Eurykleia:
>
> «Liebes Kind! töte mich denn mit dem erbarmungsglosen Erze, oder auch: lasse mich in der Halle! doch will ich dir die Rede nicht verhehlen! Gewußt habe ich dies alles und ihm alles geschafft, soviel er auch verlangte: Speise und süßen Wein. Doch nahm er mir den großen Eid ab, daß ich es dir nicht früher sagen sollte, ehe der zwölfte Tag gekommen oder du selber ihn vermissen und hören würdest, daß er aufgebrochen, damit du nicht mit Weinen deine schöne Haut entstelltest. Doch wasche dich und lege dir reine Kleider an und bete mit deinen dienenden Frauen, ins obere Stockwerk hinaufgestiegen, zu Athene, der Tochter des Zeus, des Aigishalters! denn diese vermöchte ihn alsdann wohl gar von dem Tode zu erretten. Doch plage den Alten nicht, den schon Geplagten! Denn ich denke, den seligen Göttern ist das Geschlecht des Sohnes des Arkeisios nicht ganz verhaßt, sondern noch wird einer wohl nachbleiben, der die hochbedachten Häuser und die fetten Äcker draußen besitzen wird.»
>
> So sprach sie und beschwichtigte ihren Jammer und tat ihren Augen Einhalt in dem Jammer. Und sie wusch sich und legte sich reine Kleider an und stieg in das obere Stockwerk mit den dienenden Frauen, tat Opfergerste in einen Korb und betete zu Athene:
>
> «Höre mich, Kind des Zeus, des Aigishalters, Atrytone! Wenn jemals dir der vielkluge Odysseus von einem Rinde oder einem Schafe die fetten Schenkel verbrannt hat in den Hallen, so gedenke mir jetzt dessen und bewahre mir meinen Sohn und wehre die Freier ab in ihrem bösen Übermut.»
>
> So sprach sie und schrie den Opferruf, und die Göttin hörte ihr Gebet.
>
> 60

FIG. I.3. '... und schrie den Opferruf...', Homer, *Die Odyssee*, p. 60. Blue ballpoint pen. © Deutsches Literaturarchiv, Marbach a.N.

cry of the here nameless victim [Opfer]. In short, the opportunity to translate a single word through a known intertextual reference opens up the poem to echoes of human suffering perpetrated by other men. It dislocates the discourse of the master who calls us to sacrifice to his pagan gods. It asks us instead to hear the almost imperceptible echoes of the human victim's cry, shifting the notion of sacrifice from bull to human, and from mythical Greece to contemporary Germany. When read in the conventional confines of the published and visible oeuvre, these discreet but crucial echoes are not provided with the dimensions required for them to resound and be noticed. It is only when the word 'Opferruf' is considered in the more fluid, less predictable context of the sous-oeuvre that its defining echoes of human suffering can be gently amplified and brought to the reader's attention.

The second instance in this poem where a familiarity with the sous-oeuvre in the form of Schadewaldt's translation from the Greek might inflect the reading and translation of the poem occurs in the word 'Salzflut'. Although this compound noun literally translates as 'salt-flood' (this is the solution proposed by Gillespie and adopted elsewhere by Felstiner), Fairley's choice of 'salt tide' is a more idiomatic rendering of the German. 'Flut', beyond its English cognate 'flood', means 'tide', for which the German cognate would in turn be 'Zeit' [time]. It might be said that there is not much to distinguish salt-flood from salt tide. Both are slightly awkward in English, and where one favors a shared etymological root, the other prefers the shared abstract notion of the daily flood as constituting a naturally occurring measure of time. It is this symmetrical and repeated movement of time that seems to be intimated typographically by the word 'Salzflut' itself. Here, each part of the compound noun — 'Salz' and 'Flut' — is not only equal in terms of the number of letters and syllables each employs. In addition to this, the position of the vowel and the letter 'l' in each word seems to suggest the presence of an invisible and reflective wall between the two words, in which each word is an imperfect reflection of the other. Although relatively rare in contemporary German, the term 'Salzflut' occurs repeatedly in Schadewaldt's translation of Homer's text, and means nothing other than the 'open sea' [θάλασσα]. The translator, however, claims not to be entirely satisfied with this solution: 'I did not avoid unfortunate solutions to translating certain words', he writes in the preface, 'if they were at least able to make the character of the Greek notion visible'. And he gives the example of 'Salzflut' to illustrate his point: 'e.g. 'Salzflut' [Saltflood] as opposed to 'Meer' [sea], 'See' [sea], 'offenes, hohes Meer' [open, high sea]'.[69]

Without an awareness of Schadewaldt's translation — and of the translator's misgivings — an important point of reference is lost that allows us to understand the context in which a 'salt tide' or a 'salt-flood' is also, simultaneously, something much more readily understandable, namely the open sea which is Odysseus's decadal place of exile, the salty wasteland or 'Ödnis' upon which he wanders for ten years. Celan therefore adopts a term that is not only central in Schadewaldt's reconfiguration of the Greek text in German, and which allows us to draw parallels between Odysseus's wandering and Celan's incarceration in a psychiatric ward. The word also represents a dissatisfying compromise between capturing the sense of the Greek term, and preserving its particular verbal form. 'Salzflut' is — perhaps appropriately given the largely unfinished nature of many of *Eingedunkelt*'s texts — a translation that remains forever unfinished, a stopgap that Schadewaldt is unable subsequently to modify. The term is in a perpetual state of becoming and unbecoming, upon which publication has circumstantially conferred a definitive status and sense of completion that the translator's avowal of dissatisfaction continues to undermine. It is only through a precise contextualization of the appearance of the word in Celan's composition, that we can begin to unfold some of the many implications of its slightly unusual expression.

When reading Celan's published oeuvre, Gadamer maintains that everything required to understand the individual poem is already within the poem: 'In principle I believe myself to be in full agreement with [Celan], that everything is in the text and that all instances of the biographical and the occasional should be kept to the private sphere. As they are not in the text, they do not belong to the text'.[70] If this additional information is provided, Gadamer maintains, then the reader must return to the text as if he or she were ignorant of this information: 'Whoever wishes to correctly understand a poem must, at any rate, completely forget the personal and incidental that inheres in external information. It is not in the text. [Reading a poem] depends solely on understanding what the text itself says, regardless of any information that might come from without'.[71] Gadamer's formulation supposes both that what is poem and what is not poem can be clearly identified, and that there are correct ways to understand poems. The examination of these two translations reminds us that enhanced understanding of a text can require recourse to information that erodes the limits of the text and weakens its autonomy. Throughout this book's examination of Celan's work, attention will be drawn to the need to interrogate the boundaries commonly ascribed to a given text. An intertextual source already constitutes an integral part of the text, part of the way it lives and breathes, although it is not usually considered part of that text. Similarly, the process of the poem's composition is also a part of the text that — for the sake of convenience and out of convention — is still largely ignored. The poem is most individual — most itself — not in the idealistic isolation from which Fairley and Gillespie translate it, nor in the respectable context of its initial and mostly conventional publication in 1991, nor in the theoretical isolation in which Gadamer conceives of it, but when present among the inconvenient tangle of its intertextual and genetic sources.

All in the Mind

The concept of the sous-oeuvre should allow for the restitution of information that has in certain circles been considered secondary, if not anathema, to critical reading and interpretation. As Samuel Beckett writes: 'What matter who's speaking'.[72] Instead of positing the text in a biographical void into which 'the writing subject endlessly disappears'[73] and in which the text alone carries the information necessary for understanding, the sous-oeuvre is a sufficiently disorganized domain for elements of biography to be re-accommodated, particularly where these are not easily separable from the text under consideration. In the case of *Eingedunkelt*, few critics writing at the time of the first full publication of the poems in 1991 are aware of the circumstances in which Celan wrote the poems, as they make no mention of his hospitalization for depression and psychosis during the spring of 1966. Hartung was alone among critics responding to the cycle's publication in 1991 to suggest that the discovery of these poems might cast a new light on Celan's biography. The poems, he said, were important 'not as the expansion of an oeuvre, whose significance has long been established, but as evidence of a deep mental disturbance, which the poet apparently wanted to make known to us'.[74] How much does the reader need to know about Celan's life in order to read these poems in their singularity? How much weight should be placed on the so-called facts of Celan's personal history at the time, beyond the texts he was reading and annotating, as mentioned above?

Given that Celan struggled with mental illness during at least the final decade of his life, surprisingly little has been written about this and its potential impact on his poetic output. Celan was first hospitalized in a psychiatric clinic between 31 December 1962 and 17 January 1963, at Épinay-sur-Seine. Between 8 May and 21 May 1965 he was voluntarily hospitalized at a private psychiatric clinic at Vésinet. This book focuses in part on poems composed during his subsequent hospitalization, which took place between 28 November 1965 and 11 June 1966 in three separate establishments at Garches, Suresnes, and Sainte Anne in Paris. On 30 January 1967, Celan attempted to strangle Gisèle Celan-Lestrange and to commit suicide, by stabbing himself in the left lung with a paper knife.[75] Hearing about this episode from Gisèle a few months later, Emil Cioran noted in his diary: 'Description of hell. Impossible to sleep after such revelations'.[76] It was as a direct result of this attack that Celan was re-hospitalized at Sainte Anne from 13 February through 17 October. From 15 November 1968 he was again interned, this time in the psychiatric hospital at Vaucluse, Épinay-sur-Orge, until 3 February of the following year. This followed an unprovoked attack on a passer-by whom he wrongly suspected of harming his son, Eric.[77]

Among the few critics who have touched upon Celan's struggle with mental illness, there has been a tendency to glamorize its ugly realities. Felstiner, for example, does not discuss Celan's illness in any depth, and when he does allude to it, it is in relation to the poet's creative talent. 'Although malaise could stifle Celan', Felstiner notes, 'it could otherwise stimulate him'.[78] Elsewhere we read: 'Celan's lines sever the psyche from the science of it, as Kafka doubted that spiritual malaise was curable'.[79] The poet Peter Horn is one of the rare recent critics to take issue with the tendency of scholars to euphemize Celan's illness, and provides an objective account of the poet's struggle with mental illness in his recent book.[80] Horn remarks that Felstiner demonstrates a 'total lack of understanding of the reality of psychosis' by dressing up mental illness as mere 'spiritual malaise'.[81] He continues: 'In any case, psychoses are not "curable" even when a medical treatment is nowadays by and large possible. For the one who experiences depression, it casts a shadow over the entire world; he or she has descended into a dark hole and around them everything is black'.[82] Horn's analysis offers a much needed initial corrective to our attempts to understand Celan's later work, in that it reminds us both of the persistent presence of this illness during the last decade of Celan's life, and of its unglamorous and serious nature.[83]

My attempts to locate Celan's medical records for the final decade of his life have so far been in vain, and it is thought that the documents may have been destroyed. In the absence of both the appropriate documents and of the required medical expertise, I do not intend to discuss the possible state of Celan's mental health in the spring of 1966, or more generally during the final years of his life, and of its influence on his writing. However, I would like to contemplate briefly some of the more visible effects of this illness — and of its attempted treatment — on the composition of *Eingedunkelt*. Letters written during his hospitalization show that Celan was concerned that his subjection to anti-depressive (and probably anti-psychotic) medication was hindering his ability to concentrate, to read, and to memorize.[84] One of the reasons that *Eingedunkelt* has not received the critical attention common to the rest of Celan's work may well have to do with the uncertainty that surrounds this matter. Wiebke Amthor describes the *Eingedunkelt* materials as being unique in Celan's work, because they are marked by a 'partial verbal instability', evident in the numerous grammatical and orthographical errors, and in some cases corrections.[85] It is difficult to say with certainty whether these solecisms are evidence of the poet's dilapidated mental and linguistic capacities, or innocent slips of the poet's pen, or perhaps even an associative playing on words, instances of paronomasia.[86] Werner Hamacher cites the phonetic and positional proximity of 'das blutende Ohr' [the bleeding ear] to 'blühselige Botschaft' [bloom-blessed tidings] in the *Eingedunkelt* poem 'Having forsworn the light'[87] as a positive example of verbal unities undermining each other with their unique semantic potential, thereby bringing each of them into 'oscillation'.[88] In the genetic documents assembled under the poem entitled '<u>The empty middle</u>' [<u>Die leere Mitte</u>], the noun 'Schiffe' [ships] is crossed out and replaced by the roughly synonymous 'Boote' [boats]. This in turn is crossed out and replaced with 'Brote' [breads].[89] Although approximately homophonous with 'Boote', 'Brote' introduces a major semantic shift. In the poem '<u>The rope</u>' [<u>Das Seil</u>], the word 'Köpfe' [heads] seems well established — appearing in four consecutive drafts — before acquiring an additional consonant and becoming 'Knöpfe' [buttons] for two successive drafts.[90] In what perhaps constitutes a much clearer example of linguistic confusion, the drafts from '<u>The hot branding iron here</u>' [<u>Das am Gluteisen hier</u>] show how in one version 'lobsingend' [praise-singing] becomes 'lobsinkend' [praise-sinking], and 'gesteuert' [steered] is spelled phonetically but incorrectly 'gestäuert'.[91] These examples suggest that, in *Eingedunkelt*, what Lacoue-Labarthe calls 'the scant possibility of poetry' is threatened even more than usual by the struggle to leave a series of coherent marks.[92]

Celan's as yet unpublished diaries also show signs of the difficulty he had in correctly articulating himself during this period of hospitalization. In a reference to his reading of the German translation of Wolfe's *Of Time and the River*, he writes: 'Continued reading in Th. Wolfe, Of Town and River [Von Stadt u. Strom]'.[93] Or again: 'Discovery that ~~I~~ my memory, when it comes to ~~re rember~~ remembering,

~~rebels~~ sometimes leaves me in the lurch, so that from sentence to sentence I do not know which topic ~~I here or there~~ I am dealing with'.⁹⁴ Such an unambiguous statement — in content and form — of the confusion Celan experiences clearly renders the distinction habitually made by genetic criticism between intentional authorial variants and unintentional textual errors much less certain than is usually the case, casting doubt on the applicability of any notion of intentionality. Celan's illness should not be understood as a biographical backdrop to many of the poems written in the 1960s, nor as potentially corrupting information external to the texts, but simply as part of the reality carried within the language of the sous-oeuvre, part of the reality that the sous-oeuvre makes available to us. The oeuvre has little time for such uncertainty, as Amthor makes clear. It is only when considered in the context of the sous-oeuvre, and of a poetics that remains unfinished, that such fragile articulation might be accommodated and read.

The neologism 'eingedunkelt' can be translated literally as 'indarkened', but other English language translators and commentators have provided various alternatives. Fairley translates 'eingedunkelt' as 'benighted', thereby recalling Milton's *Animadversions*: 'O if we freeze at noon after their earthly thaw, let us fear lest the sun for ever hide himself, and turn his orient steps from our ingrateful horizon, justly condemn'd to be eternally benighted'.⁹⁵ Pierre Joris writes that the *Eingedunkelt* poems point toward an 'en-darkening' and suggests the title 'Tenebrae'd'.⁹⁶ Gillespie opts for 'Darkened In', maintaining the sense of the German, but not preserving its precarious status as neologism or as a compound verbal unit.⁹⁷ Emmerich sees the title as a sign of the continuity of the cycle with Celan's established oeuvre, and in particular with its constant reflection on the repercussions of the Holocaust.⁹⁸ Rolf Michaelis traces the meaning of the past participle to the infinitive 'eindunkeln', which describes the way day transitions to night, the irresistible process of daily indarkening.⁹⁹ When translated to the individual myth of the poet, however, indarkening loses the joyful certainty of resurrection and threatens to become singular and irreversible: 'Is this word, that can barely be found in any German dictionary, not an indicator of the poet working his way into darkness, into silence, into death?'¹⁰⁰ Fairley says that *Eingedunkelt* 'asks to be read as literally as possible; it describes an actual darkness'.¹⁰¹

The 'actual darkness' described by the title of the cycle unambiguously inscribes the unfinished cycle within a tradition of poetry written in the darkness of depression or psychosis. Erich Trummler described Hölderlin's mental illness as 'Umnachtung',¹⁰² which — although usually translated as 'derangement' — might more accurately be understood as night [Nacht] that gathers around [um] the subject. Christoph Theodor Schwab expressed something similar when giving Hölderlin's eulogy in 1843: 'for already night has beleaguered his spirit'.¹⁰³ For both Schwab and Trummler, the night is something external that invades, occupies, and disturbs the poet's mind. In contrast, Celan's neologism seems to describe a slipping into night, more reminiscent perhaps of Max Jacob's psychological instability: 'Every day it gets a little darker: and now it's like a slipping or sliding [glissade]. Allowing oneself to slip to death. After, it carries on like that, but you no longer realize it. Just a vague

Fig. I.4. Gisèle Celan-Lestrange, 'Enténébré / Eingedunkelt', 1966, etching, private collection. © Eric Celan, Paris.

sense of apprehension like a tunnel and then the accident'.[104] Jacob wrote these lines in relative isolation at the monastery of Saint-Benoît-sur-Loire. In contrast to the walled-in, introspective imaginary of *Eingedunkelt*, the poems in Jacob's collection *Infernal Visions* are populated with external scenes: trains, tailors, dining out, an urban landscape in which men adopt animal forms. Celan's cycle pursues the opposite dynamic. The prefix 'ein-' in 'eingedunkelt' simultaneously narrows and intensifies the abstract notion of 'dunkeln' or darkening. In the past participle form, the title evokes a dark and narrow strait, an uncompromising passage through which the subject's mind has already slipped.

There remains one important dimension to the word 'eingedunkelt' that helps to explain why Celan adopted it to describe his writings from the spring of 1966. Friedrich Kluge's etymological dictionary — which Celan possessed and used extensively throughout his working life — traces the etymology of 'dunkeln' [to darken] to words, which express dampness, humidity, and closeness, most accessible to us through the English adjective 'dank'.[105] 'Eingedunkelt' evokes not only the darkness of depression and psychosis, but also its unhealthy and unpleasant dampness. The theme of dampness occurs with increasing frequency in Celan's later work. Henri Meschonnic notes how Celan's 'language is mixed with water',[106] which is the very 'matter of time',[107] and that this is how a bond is created between 'writing, the body, and death'.[108] I suggest that the dampness of 'eingedunkelt', however, pertains specifically to the effects of a treatment to which the poet was subjected during his hospitalization, known as insulin shock therapy. Insulin shock therapy had been developed by the psychiatrist and neurophysiologist Manfred Sakel in the late 1920s to treat cases of schizophrenia and other related mental illnesses.[109] The injection of excess insulin was designed to induce hypoglycemia in the patient, causing nervousness, weakness, and sweating. If injected in sufficiently large doses, the insulin would cause the patient to fall into a coma. It was thought that by artificially inducing a comatose state, any psychological disturbances would be erased from the patient's mind, creating a mental *tabula rasa*. Once the patient had regained consciousness, he or she would engage in appropriate social activities to re-learn how to think and interact 'correctly'.[110] Activities might include games of cards, board games, or even volleyball.

Between 2 May and 8 June 1966 — that is, immediately after the composition of the *Eingedunkelt* poems — Celan was subjected to a milder version of this treatment.[111] He describes the effects of this treatment in a letter to Gisèle:

> My treatment, this morning, went normally — at around half past ten, after drowsiness and sweating and, this time, without the accompaniment of 'divagations' — I quote the report by the nurse, Mr. Mann (like Thomas) — , I was re-sugared and up. For my neighbor it took longer and was, once again, quite painful to witness. They give him the 'comatose shock' [le choc comateux] whereas I get the 'humid shock' [le choc humide]. (I am learning, you see.) They re-sugared him by intravenous injection to bring him back from 'paradise'. *[In English:]* (Sorry for this cruel language).[112]

Beyond the general connotations of depression and psychosis, therefore, the neologism 'eingedunkelt' is meant specifically, if hermetically, to reference the excessive sweating and resulting sensation of dampness caused by the injection of excess insulin during the spring of 1966.[113] On 2 May, the day the insulin therapy began and in anticipation of the humid shock he was about to undergo, Celan composed the following poem, the final composition of the unfinished *Eingedunkelt* cycle:

> Lindenblättrige Ohnmacht, der
> Hinaufgestürzten
> klirrender
> Psalm.[114]
>
> [Linden-leafed unconsciousness,
> clattering psalm
> of the fall
> upward.]

Throughout his hospitalization, Celan sent Gisèle newly composed poems in lieu of conventional correspondence. This poem was also sent to Gisèle with the following note:

> Quatre lignes, le soir, voici-les [sic], aux feuilles
> de tilleul faisant évanouissement, le gardant.

> Le tout, pour les précipités vers le haut,
> est un psaume, dans un bruit de métal.
>
> Il faut avoir le courage d'accepter des poèmes si courts.[115]
>
> [Four lines, this evening, here they are, to the linden
> leaves bringing fainting, keeping it.
> All of it, for those who fell upward,
> is a psalm, amidst a noise of metal.
>
> You have to have the courage to accept such short poems.]

Writing in *Die Zeit*, Rolf Michaelis aligned this poem with the defining narrative of the *Nibelungenlied*'s Siegfried, who bathed in the blood of the dragon he had killed, thereby attaining invincibility. This was compromised only where a linden leaf had fallen on his back, preventing contact with the dragon's blood. Siegfried was subsequently killed when a spear pierced this spot. It is this narrative that encourages Michaelis to suggest: 'Doesn't Celan, bearing in mind the Germanic hero Siegfried, dare through this poem to entertain the insane notion of combining fall with rise?'[116] I believe this to be unlikely, if only because the legend of Siegfried's death was adopted as a central narrative in the rise of German nationalism and subsequently National Socialism, the signing of the Armistice in 1918 being considered an analogous stab in the back.[117] 'Lindenblättrig' [linden-leafed] is much more likely to reflect the linden trees that still grow within the walled enclosure of the psychiatric hospital of Sainte Anne, and which would have been in bloom when the poem was composed. The notion of falling upward echoes Hölderlin's description of the challenge facing the great poet: 'The point at which sobriety leaves you is the point where your enthusiasm begins. The great poet never abandons himself, he may elevate himself as far above himself as he wishes. One can *fall* into the height, as well as into the depth'. Hölderlin explains that the poet must strive to achieve poetic expression between the height and the depth.[119] It is his dubious prerogative to warn against the madness that poetry can lead to if this balance is not achieved.[118] It is the same balance that Celan projects for himself here. This final poem therefore seems to announce the 'linden-leafed unconsciousness' to come, a document of resignation to medical treatment, but also of hope in an improbable, insulin-induced fall upward.

Unfinished Poetics

Paul Celan's Unfinished Poetics comprises four chapters. The opening chapter, 'Learning to Read in the Pre-Text', seeks to inaugurate a new mode of poetic reading, modeled on the reading not of the authorized and published oeuvre, but of those parts of the sous-oeuvre that — although inscribed by the poet — were never intended for public consumption. We now live at a time when genetic documents relating to the major works of many of the more prominent modernist authors are available for consultation, in print or in electronic format, be it Hans Walter Gabler's synoptic editions of Joyce's *Ulysses* or Jean-Yves Tadié's publication of extensive drafts relating to Proust's *In Search of Lost Time*. In the case of Celan, the published pre-text now greatly exceeds in volume the poems and prose pieces authorized for publication by the poet. What we understand by Celan's published oeuvre is very different to the published work that was left by the poet. Despite this new textual reality — and the facility with which readers can, if they so choose, access the pre-text — there has been no consistent effort to induct readers in the essentially unfinished domain of the pre-text.

Genetic documents relating to literary works are now normally subjected to one of two critical approaches, both of which are teleological, and both of which are reserved for specialists. Those who participate in traditional hermeneutics will read and seek to interpret the most complete version of a given text, drawing on alternative or previous versions only where this enhances a reading of the definitive text. Textual and genetic criticism similarly privileges the final text, whether real or imagined, as the horizon to its organizational logic, and arranges the pre-text accordingly. It becomes apparent when faced with a wealth of edited, transcribed, and published genetic documents — such as those that now constitute *Eingedunkelt* — that other more creative, less systematic, a-teleological approaches to interpretation are required, if readers in search of new constellations of meaning are to be able to exploit the pre-text. Any such attempt will necessarily run up against deep-rooted opposition. Today's culture still clings to the completed, authorized, and published text. It continues to be troubled by situations which appear indifferent to, or which appear to endanger, the notion of an embodied and mentally coherent reading or writing subject. Although the three following chapters move away from the pre-text, and from the specific questions raised by textual and genetic criticism, this opening chapter creates the conditions necessary for the subsequent exploration of the sous-oeuvre. It opens up Celan's oeuvre to the uncertainties of the sous-oeuvre, it dislocates critical conventions and expectations, and it motivates and supports the broader examination of marginal texts and themes.

Celan did not like his work to be compared to that of the nineteenth-century French poet Stéphane Mallarmé, despite the fact that both produced poems that were often difficult to read and understand. It might therefore be something of a surprise to discover that in March 1966 — during the composition of *Eingedunkelt* — Celan read and heavily annotated a newly published paperback edition of Mallarmé's poems, prefaced by Jean-Paul Sartre. There are only two other documented moments at which Celan encounters Mallarmé, namely his translation of the rondel 'Si tu veux..'. in the late 1950s, and a mysterious moment in the 1960 Büchner prize speech, 'The Meridian', where Celan asks if it is not time to 'think Mallarmé to the end?' In chapter two, 'Engaging Mallarmé', each of these loosely connected and uncharacteristic encounters with the French poet is examined for the way it transforms Celan's conception of the tasks and possibilities of poetry. Central among these alternative poetics — some of which are sketched out in *Eingedunkelt* — is the genesis of an embryonic poetics centered on the promises and possibilities of suicide, in which the composition of each poem constitutes a rehearsal for the final and greatest poem, the poet's self-destruction.

In his 1953 article 'Cultural Criticism in Society', Theodor Adorno states that to write poetry after Auschwitz is barbaric.[120] The phrase is often taken in isolation and out of its original context, and it seems that Celan may also have taken it at face value. It has been suggested that it should instead be seen as an attempt to 'intensify the dialectical tension between culture and barbarism', and that 'poetry' stands for any cultural reflection on the Holocaust.[121] It is this attempt to remember and warn against reiterations of the Holocaust that runs the risk of becoming complicit in the process of destruction. As Adorno puts it later in *Negative Dialectics*: 'All post-Auschwitz culture, including its critique, is garbage'.[122] In chapter three, 'Poetry after Frankfurt', the role of literature is re-examined in the wake of what might be called an aftershock of the Holocaust: the Federal Republic of Germany's first major legal attempt to bring to justice those responsible for committing crimes at Auschwitz-Birkenau between 1941 and 1945. The trial — known as the Frankfurt Auschwitz Trial — began in 1963 and reached its conclusion in August 1965. In October, Peter Weiss staged *The Investigation*, a theatrical interpretation of the trial, which provoked debate across Europe and the United States. No attempt has been made to examine Celan's response to the trial or to the play, despite the fact that it structures many of the poems composed in the mid 1960s. In this chapter, I uncover Celan's hermetic response to the trial and the play in three poems and several aphorisms. Where both the legal and theatrical events seek in their respective ways to draw the Holocaust to a close, Celan's poems and aphorisms demonstrate not only the continuing complicity of the trial and the play in the Holocaust, but his conviction that the only appropriate form of justice is to be found in the act of reading poetry.

Celan's interaction with the visual arts has been repeatedly examined, notably by Eric Kligerman, who remarks that Celan maintained a much closer relation to the visual arts than to music.[123] Besides his early introduction to Edgar Jené's sketches and his translation of the screenplay to Alain Resnais's 1955 documentary *Nuit et brouillard* [Night and Fog], Celan wrote a handful of ekphrastic poems including 'UNTER EIN BILD' [Under a picture],[124] 'BLITZGESCHRECKT' [Frightened by Lightning],[125] and 'BEI BRANCUSI, ZU ZWEIT' [At Brancusi's, à deux].[126] From 1952 he was married to the graphic artist and engraver Gisèle Celan-Lestrange, and in an interview with Hugo Huppert in 1966 said that engraving [Graveurkunst] had the most profound influence on his poetics.[127] This fourth and final chapter, 'Rembrandt, Mandel'shtam, and the Limits of Ekphrasis', re-examines Celan's relation to the visual artist whose work was perhaps most important to him, namely Rembrandt van Rijn. Attempts to understand Celan's engagement with Rembrandt have so far been restricted to the only published poem in which he mentions Rembrandt by name. Here, I demonstrate how Celan's engagement with Rembrandt should be understood not through the restrictive trope of ekphrasis, as is commonly presumed, but through the work of the Russian Jewish poet Osip Mandel'shtam, who also wrote a small number of poems in honor of Rembrandt. This unexpected instance of triangulation allows us to perceive how Celan's engagement with Rembrandt is motivated not by the painter's powers of representation, but by his manipulation of the material qualities of oil paint and canvas. It is this material reality that Celan identifies and seeks to recreate in his poems.

Paul Celan's Unfinished Poetics aims to discover and develop modes of reading and interpretation that go beyond those formed in the encounter with completed, authorized, and published texts. It invites the reader of Celan — and of modern literature in general — to step outside of canonical frames of reference and interpretation, and to experience a poetics that is constantly in the process of being formed. It argues for a broader understanding of poetry that is not restricted to the unicity of the individual poem, but which subsists — in unexpected and unconventional ways — in those parts of a poet's textual production most often considered preparatory, superfluous, or otherwise redundant. It aims to provide a model for disturbing critical conventions that discourage readers from experiencing the ways in which literature exceeds what criticism can say about it. Poetry is perhaps never more itself than in those moments when it is unfinished, unexpected, discarded, and overlooked. It is these unfashionable and understudied regions of Celan's oeuvre that this book seeks — imperfectly and partially — to illuminate.

Notes to the Introduction

1. 'Oder es kommt / der türkische Flieder gegangen / und erfragt sich / mehr als nur Duft' (Paul Celan, *Eingedunkelt. Historisch-kritische Ausgabe*, ed. by Rolf Bücher and Andreas Lohr, assisted by Hans Kruschwitz and Thomas Schneider, vol. 12 of *Werke. Historisch-kritische Ausgabe. I. Abteilung: Lyrik und Prosa* (Frankfurt a.M.: Suhrkamp, 2006), p. 195). See Figs. I.1 and I.2. Unless otherwise indicated, all translations are my own.
2. George Steiner, *On Difficulty and Other Essays* (Oxford: Oxford University Press, 1978), p. 45.
3. George Steiner, 'A Terrible Exactness', *Times Literary Supplement* (11 June 1976), 709–10 (710).
4. The German Academy for Language and Literature was founded on 28 August 1949 to mark the bicentenary of Goethe's birth. It has awarded the annual Georg Büchner prize for literature written in German since 1951.
5. Hans Mayer, *Umerzogene Literatur* (Berlin: Siedler, 1988), p. 225.
6. Leonard Olschner, 'Dark Origins', *Times Literary Supplement* (13 October 2000), 9 (9).
7. Steiner, 'A Terrible Exactness', p. 710.
8. Michel de Certeau, *The Mystic Fable*, trans. by Michael B. Smith (Chicago: University of Chicago Press, 1992), p. 17.
9. J. M. Coetzee, 'In the Midst of Losses', *The New York Review of Books*, 48.11 (5 July 2001), available at <http://www.nybooks.com/issues/2001/07/05/>, [accessed 5 August 2015].
10. The relation of 'oeuvre' and 'sous-oeuvre' should not be confused with that of 'littérature' and 'sous-littérature'. Where 'sous-littérature' defines texts that are 'pure vehicles of ideology', 'littérature' removes itself from the ideology, distorting it, or causing it to malfunction (Thomas Aron, *Littérature et littérarité: un essai de mise au point* (Paris: Belles-Lettres, 1984), p. 83). Henri Meschonnic uses 'sous-littérature' to describe a body of literature produced through translation, when the 'ideology' of the target language distorts the language of the original language (Henri Meschonnic, *Pour la poétique II. Épistémologie de l'Écriture — Poétique de la traduction* (Paris: Gallimard, 1973), p. 411). In an alternative iteration — somewhat closer to the notion of sous-oeuvre — Alain Mercier uses 'sous-littérature' to describe anti-dogmatic, uneducated, and unrefined literature in seventeenth-century France (Alain Mercier, *La Littérature facétieuse sous Louis XIII. 1610–1643. Une bibliographie critique* (Geneva: Droz, 1991), p. 5).
11. Pierre Larousse, *Grand dictionnaire universel du XIXe siècle, français, historique, géographique, mythologique, bibliographique, littéraire, artistique, scientifique, etc.*, 17 vols (Paris: Administration du Grand dictionnaire universel, 1866–1890), XIV, p. 948.
12. Geoffrey Hartman, *Saving the Text. Literature/Derrida/Philosophy* (Baltimore: The Johns Hopkins University Press, 1981), p. xxi.
13. Celan initially entitled the cycle of poems now known as *Eingedunkelt* 'Das Nach-Fadensonnen-

Poem' [The After-Fathomsuns-Poem]. Chronologically, its composition occurs after the final poem of *Fadensonnen*'s first cycle, and before the first poem of its second cycle.
14. On the Internet, 'Eingedunkelt' is today almost uniquely synonymous not with Celan's unfinished cycle, but with the song cycle written for alto solo voice by Aribert Reimann, which sets nine of the eleven poems published in 1968 to music. See Aribert Reimann, *Eingedunkelt für Alt-Solo* (Mainz: Schott, 1995). For Celan's interaction with Reimann see Axel Englund, *Still Songs: Music In and Around the Poetry of Paul Celan* (Farnham: Ashgate, 2012), pp. 91–92.
15. Doctors treating Celan are said to have described him as having suffered a 'bouffée délirante' or 'delusional rush' (Bertrand Badiou, 'D'une main — et d'une autre main —. Préface', in Paul Celan and René Char, *Correspondance: 1954–1968. Avec des lettres de Gisèle Celan-Lestrange, Jean Delay, Marie-Madeleine Delay et Pierre Deniker. Suivie de la Correspondance René Char–Gisèle Celan–Lestrange, 1969–1977*, ed. by Bertrand Badiou (Paris: Gallimard, 2015), pp. 9–31 (p. 29)). The term 'bouffée délirante' is specific to French nosology, and describes an acute, transient, nonaffective, and nonschizophrenic psychotic disorder (Henri Chabrol, 'Chronic Hallucinatory Psychosis, *Bouffée Délirante*, and the Classification of Psychosis in French Psychiatry', *Current Psychiatry Reports*, 5.3 (2003), 187–91 (187)).
16. The attack occurred on the night of 24 November. Gisèle fled with Eric to the home of Jacques and Jacqueline Lalande. The following day, Celan left Paris for London, returning on 26 November. On 28 November, he was interned in the psychiatric hospital at Garches, Hauts-de-Seine. On 5 December he was transferred to a private psychiatric clinic at Suresnes in the western suburbs of Paris. It was from here that Celan was moved to Sainte Anne in the 14th *arrondissement* in Paris on 7 February 1966 and where he remained until his release on 11 June (Paul Celan and Gisèle Celan-Lestrange, *Correspondance (1951–1970)*, ed. by Bertrand Badiou and Eric Celan, 2 vols (Paris: Seuil, 2001), II, pp. 558–59).
17. A rare contemporary reflection of the events leading to Celan's incarceration is found in Emil Cioran's diary entry for 5 January 1966, where he writes: 'I learned yesterday evening, at a dinner, that P. Celan has just been interned in a mental asylum, after he attempted to slit his wife's throat'. He adds: 'He had a great charm, this impossible man, and, although difficult and complicated in company, one would forgive him everything, as soon as one had forgotten the unwarranted and ludicrous grievances he held against everybody' (E. M. Cioran, *Cahiers 1957–1972*, foreword by Simone Boué (Paris: Gallimard, 1997), p. 326).
18. Celan's association with Suhrkamp officially began on 21 December 1966, when he signed two contracts, one for a projected edition of his complete works, and another for the collection *Atemwende* [*Breath-Turn*]. These contracts effectively brought an end to his association with the Fischer Verlag (Celan and Celan-Lestrange, *Correspondance*, II, p. 563).
19. Samuel Beckett et al., *Aus aufgegebenen Werken* (Frankfurt a.M.: Suhrkamp, 1968).
20. Ibid., p. 194.
21. Paul Celan, *Eingedunkelt: und Gedichte aus dem Umkreis von Eingedunkelt*, ed. by Bertrand Badiou and Jean-Claude Rambach (Frankfurt a.M.: Suhrkamp, 1991). Celan's archives were officially purchased by the German Schiller Society at Marbach a. N. The contract was signed by Gisèle Celan-Lestrange and Eric Celan on 16 November 1989.
22. Harald Hartung, 'Späte Flaschenpost. Gedichte aus dem Nachlass Paul Celans', *Frankfurter Allgemeine Zeitung* 233 (8 October 1991), L15.
23. Rolf Michaelis, 'Der beschriftete Ankerstein', *Die Zeit* (11 October 1991), L9.
24. Wolfgang Emmerich, 'Review of Paul Celan, *Eingedunkelt: und Gedichte aus dem Umkreis von Eingedunkelt*', *Der Buchtip*, Radio Bremen, 7 December 1992.
25. Ibid.
26. Hartung, 'Späte Flaschenpost', L15.
27. Certeau, *The Mystic Fable*, p. 9.
28. Charlie Louth, review of Paul Celan, *Selected Poems and Prose of Paul Celan*, trans. by John Felstiner (2000) and Paul Celan, *Fathomsuns / Fadensonnen and Benighted / Eingedunkelt*, trans. by Ian Fairley (2001), *Translation and Literature*, 11.1 (2002), 123–35 (128).
29. Olschner, 'Dark Origins', 9.
30. Paul Celan, *Gesammelte Werke in sieben Bänden*, 7 vols (Frankfurt a.M.: Suhrkamp, 2000), III, p. 200.

31. Ibid., III, p. 189.
32. Ibid.
33. Philippe Lacoue-Labarthe, *La Poésie comme expérience* (Paris: Bourgois, 1986), p. 69.
34. Hans-Georg Gadamer, *Gesammelte Werke*, 10 vols (Tübingen: Mohr Siebeck, 1999), IX, p. 447.
35. Peter Szondi, 'Lecture de *Strette*. Essai sur la poésie de Paul Celan', in *Poésies et poétiques de la modernité. Traduction française de textes de Peter Szondi sur Mallarmé, Paul Celan, Walter Benjamin, Bertolt Brecht*, ed. by Mayotte Bollack (Lille: Presses universitaires de Lille, 1981), pp. 165–99 (p. 168).
36. Celan, *Gesammelte Werke in sieben Bänden*, III, p. 186.
37. Gadamer, *Gesammelte Werke*, IX, p. 446.
38. Steiner, 'A Terrible Exactness', p. 710.
39. Steiner, *On Difficulty and Other Essays*, p. 46.
40. Alexander von Bormann, 'Notgesang der Gedanken. Nachgelassene Gedichte von Paul Celan', Sender Freies Berlin, November 1991.
41. Rolf Ulrich Kunze, 'Nachlassverwaltung', *Stadtblatt Osnabrück* (March 1992), n. p.
42. Sven Sagé, 'Celans Gedichte: Zauberstab', *Treffpunkt* (23 November 1991), n. p.
43. Andreas Härter, 'Präzision der Dunkelheit: Gedichte von Paul Celan aus dem Nachlass', *Evangelische Kommentare. Monatsschrift zum Zeitgeschehen in Kirche und Gesellschaft*, 25.6 (1992), 371–72 (371).
44. John Felstiner, *Paul Celan: Poet, Survivor, Jew* (New Haven: Yale University Press, 1995), p. 231.
45. Ibid., pp. 230–31.
46. Paul Éluard, *Choix de poèmes 1914–1941* (Paris: Gallimard, 1942).
47. 'Wer dem Gedicht nicht die Widerstandskraft des Unmittelbaren mitgibt, hat kein Gedicht geschrieben' (Paul Celan, *Mikrolithen sinds, Steinchen: Die Prosa aus dem Nachlass. Kritische Ausgabe*, ed. by Barbara Wiedemann and Bertrand Badiou (Frankfurt a.M.: Suhrkamp, 2005), p. 53). The note is dated 2 January 1966, and occurs on page 142 of Éluard's *Choix de poèmes*.
48. André Gide and Paul Valéry, *Correspondance, 1890–1942*, ed. by Peter Fawcett (Paris: Gallimard, 2009), pp. 133–34.
49. Martin Heidegger, *Gesamtausgabe*, 102 vols (Frankfurt a.M.: Klostermann, 1975–2014), V, p. 17.
50. Ibid., V, p. 53.
51. Celan, *Eingedunkelt*, p. 218.
52. Ibid., p. 167.
53. Thomas Wolfe, *Von Zeit und Strom. Eine Legende von Hunger des Menschen in der Jugend*, trans. by Hans Schiebelhuth, 2 vols (Berlin: Rowohlt, 1936). Preserved at the German Literature Archive, Marbach a. N.
54. Celan, *Eingedenkelt*, pp. 212–17.
55. James Joyce, *Ulysses*, trans. by Georg Goyert, 2 vols (Basel: Rhein-Verlag, 1928). In a diary entry dating from this time, Celan writes: 'Tried to read Joyce, Ulysses: but the / eyes are, despite the [illegible letter] are, on account of the small / characters, they [?] not not participating'. Unpublished diary entry for Monday, 21 March 1966. Preserved at the German Literature Archive, Marbach a. N., Manuscript Department, Tagebuch 18 (20 March 1966–22 April 1966), D 90.1.3305, F 2395.
56. Celan, *Eingedunkelt*, p. 91.
57. Homer, *Die Odyssee*, trans. by Wolfgang Schadewaldt (Hamburg: Rohwohlt, 1958).
58. Jacques Derrida, *Schibboleth pour Paul Celan* (Paris: Galilée, 1986), p. 61.
59. Gadamer, *Gesammelte Werke*, IX, p. 445.
60. An exception to this can be found in Pierre Joris's exhaustive translation of the genetic documents relating to 'The Meridian' into English (Paul Celan, *The Meridian. Final Version — Drafts — Materials*, ed. by Bernhard Böschenstein and Heino Schmull, assisted by Michael Schwarzkopf and Christiane Wittkop, trans. by Pierre Joris (Stanford: Stanford University Press, 2011)).
61. For a translation of twenty-three *Eingedunkelt* poems into Norwegian, see Paul Celan, 'Eingedunkelt', trans. by Espen Stueland, *Vagant* [Bilag], 1 (1996), 3–8. The eleven *Eingedunkelt* poems published in 1968 have also been translated into Catalan (Paul Celan, 'Eingedunkelt: Enfosquit', trans. by Jordi Ibáñez Fanés, *Reduccions, revista de poesia*, 65–66 (1996), 32–53). For Ming Meng's translation of certain of Celan's poems into Mandarin, including several *Eingedunkelt*

poems, see <http://www.douban.com/group/topic/6470140/>, [accessed 16 February 2017].
62. Paul Celan, *Corona. Selected Poems of Paul Celan*, trans. by Susan H. Gillespie (Barrytown: Station Hill, 2013).
63. Paul Celan, *Fathomsuns / Fadensonnen and Benighted / Eingedunkelt*, trans. by Ian Fairley (Riverdale-on-Hudson: Sheep Meadow Press, 2001).
64. Paul Celan, *Die Gedichte. Kommentierte Gesamtausgabe in einem Band*, ed. by Barbara Wiedemann (Frankfurt a.M.: Suhrkamp, 2005), p. 267.
65. Celan, *Fathomsuns and Benighted*, p. 271.
66. Celan, *Corona*, p. 165.
67. For an alternative translation of this poem, see Felstiner, *Paul Celan: Poet, Survivor, Jew*, pp. 230–31. Wayne Clifford also translates this poem in *The Exile's Papers: Part Two: The Face as its Thousand Ships* (Erin: Porcupine's Quill, 2009), p. 92.
68. Homer, *Die Odyssee*, p. 40. Although Celan's copy of the book — preserved at the German Literature Archive, Marbach a. N. — contains a large number of handwritten annotations, this passage is not annotated. Celan underlines 'Opferruf' on p. 60. See Fig. I.3.
69. Schadewaldt was most likely familiar with Albin Lesky's 1943 article on the etymological origins of θάλασσα (Albin Lesky, 'ΘΑΛΑΣΣΑ', *Hermes*, 78.3 (1943), 258–69).
70. Gadamer, *Gesammelte Werke*, IX, p. 444.
71. Ibid., IX, pp. 444–45.
72. Samuel Beckett, *Texts for Nothing*, trans. by Samuel Beckett (London: Calder & Boyars, 1974), p. 16.
73. Michel Foucault, *Language, Counter-Memory, Practice. Selected Essays and Interviews*, ed. by Donald F. Bouchard, trans. by Donald F. Bouchard and Sherry Simon (Ithaca: Cornell University Press, 1977), p. 116.
74. Hartung, 'Späte Flaschenpost', L15.
75. Badiou, 'D'une main — et d'une autre main —', *Correspondance*, pp. 30–31.
76. Cioran, *Cahiers 1957–1972*, p. 475. For details of this attack, see Paul Celan and Gisèle Celan-Lestrange, *Correspondencia (1951–1970). Con una selección de cartas de Paul Celan a su hijo Eric*, ed. by Bertrand Badiou and Eric Celan, preface by Francisco Jarauta, trans. by Mauro Armiño and Jaime Siles (Madrid: Siruela, 2008), p. 978. On 20 January 1969, Michel Leiris wrote the following regarding this event: 'Recently over lunch with [Denise Naville], we spoke about Paul Celan, German poet whom I admire, and with whom I had, quite by chance, on a bus, quite a long conversation, during which we got on very well indeed, and this around eight days before he would try to commit suicide by stabbing himself in the heart' (Michel Leiris, *Journal 1922–1989* (Paris: Gallimard, 1992), p. 630).
77. A parallel can be drawn between Celan's 1966 hospitalization (during which *Eingedunkelt* is composed) and that of 1968–1969. During this latter hospitalization, Celan writes thirty-four poems and explicitly says that they should never be published (Paul Celan, *Die Gedichte aus dem Nachlass*, ed. by Bertrand Badiou, Jean-Claude Rambach, and Barbara Wiedemann, with notes by Barbara Wiedemann and Bertrand Badiou (Frankfurt a.M.: Suhrkamp, 1997), pp. 253–86).
78. Felstiner, *Paul Celan: Poet, Survivor, Jew*, p. 231.
79. Ibid., p. 229.
80. Peter Horn, *Die Garne der Fischer der Irrsee: Zur Lyrik von Paul Celan* (Oberhausen: Athena, 2011).
81. Ibid., p. 12.
82. Ibid., pp. 12–13.
83. Compare to André Breton's comment on Antonin Artaud, who was also treated at Sainte Anne in the late 1930s: 'I do not have to account in his stead for what he has experienced nor for what he has suffered. I do not wish to cast the blame on any particular individual, least of all on a man who is known to some of us and who, by all accounts, has been very understanding and has shown great compassion toward Artaud. The clinical methods about which our friend may have cause to complain must be ascribed to an institution that we will never cease to denounce as a barbaric anachronism, the very existence of which — with its potential for concentration camps and torture — is in itself a decisive indictment against so-called civilization as we know it today' (André Breton, 'A Tribute to Antonin Artaud' in André Breton, *Free Rein (La Clé des champs)*,

trans. by Michel Parmentier and Jacqueline D'Amboise (Lincoln: University of Nebraska Press, 1996), pp. 77–79 (p. 78)).
84. Celan and Celan-Lestrange, *Correspondance*, I, pp. 353–54.
85. Wiebke Amthor, '11. Nachlass', in *Celan-Handbuch: Leben, Werk, Wirkung*, ed. by Markus May, Peter Gossens, and Jürgen Lehmann (Stuttgart: Metzler, 2008), pp. 132–40 (p. 138).
86. When revising *Finnegans Wake*, James Joyce often changed individual letters in words. For instance, '"manyvoiced" becomes "marryvoising"' (Finn Fordham, 'Introduction', in James Joyce, *Finnegans Wake*, ed. by Robbert-Jan Henkes, Erik Bindervoet, and Finn Fordham (Oxford: Oxford University Press, 2012), pp. vii–xxxiv (p. xxv).
87. Celan, *Eingedunkelt*, p. 59.
88. Werner Hamacher, 'The Second of Inversion. Movements of a Figure through Celan's Poetry', trans. by Peter Fenves, in *Word Traces: Readings of Paul Celan*, ed. by Aris Fioretos (Baltimore: The Johns Hopkins University Press, 1994), pp. 219–63 (pp. 233–34).
89. Celan, *Eingedunkelt*, p. 228.
90. Ibid., pp. 220–24. 'Knöpfe' reverts to 'Köpfe' in the subsequent and final versions.
91. Ibid., p. 235.
92. Lacoue-Labarthe, *La Poésie comme expérience*, p. 37.
93. Unpublished diary entry for Monday, 21 March 1966. Preserved at the German Literature Archive, Marbach a. N., Manuscript Department, Tagebuch 18 (20 March 1966–22 April 1966), D 90.1.3305, F 2395.
94. Unpublished diary entry for Friday, 25 March 1966 (Ibid.).
95. John Milton, *The Works of John Milton, Historical, Political, and Miscellaneous* (London: Millar, 1753), p. 96. See also Ian Fairley, 'In that Dark Durance: Paul Celan's *Eingedunkelt*', in Paul Celan, *Fathomsuns / Fadensonnen and Benighted / Eingedunkelt*, trans. by Ian Fairley (Riverdale-on-Hudson: Sheep Meadow Press, 2001), pp. 251–53 (p. 252).
96. Paul Celan, *Breathturn into Timestead. The Collected Later Poetry*, trans. by Pierre Joris (New York: Farrar, Strauss, and Giroux, 2014), pp. 19 and 231.
97. Celan, *Corona*, pp. 151–75.
98. Emmerich, 'Review of Paul Celan, *Eingedunkelt*'.
99. Michaelis, 'Der beschriftete Ankerstein', L9.
100. Ibid.
101. Fairley, 'In that Dark Durance', p. 252.
102. Erich Trummler (ed.), *Der kranke Hölderlin: Urkunden und Dichtungen aus der Zeit seiner Umnachtung* (Munich: Recht, 1921).
103. Christoph Theodor Schwab, 'Aus dem Berichte von Christoph Theodor Schwab', in *Der kranke Hölderlin: Urkunden und Dichtungen aus der Zeit seiner Umnachtung*, ed. Erich Trummler (Munich: Recht, 1921), pp. 107–18 (p. 107).
104. Max Jacob, *Visions infernales* (Paris: Nouvelle Revue Française, 1924), p. 60.
105. Friedrich Kluge, *Etymologisches Wörterbuch der Deutschen Sprache*, ed. by Walther Mitzka, assisted by Alfred Schirmer, 18th ed. (Berlin: De Gruyter, 1960), p. 147. Szondi describes Celan as 'an avid reader of dictionaries — who filled a small notebook with all the words in Jean Paul whose meaning is no longer clear today' (Peter Szondi, *Celan Studies*, trans. by Susan Bernofsky with Harvey Mendelsohn (Stanford: Stanford University Press, 2003), p. 43).
106. Henri Meschonnic, 'On appelle cela traduire Celan', *Cahiers du chemin*, 14 (1972), 115–49 (124).
107. Ibid., 125.
108. Ibid., 124. Pöggeler recounts how during Celan's meeting with Heidegger in the Black Forest in July 1967, a planned walk on the Horbacher Moor had to be cancelled because the path was waterlogged (Otto Pöggeler, *Spur des Worts: Zur Lyrik Paul Celans* (Freiburg: Alber, 1986), p. 152). In the poem 'Todtnauberg' — subsequently sent to Heidegger — this is visible in the lines: 'die halb- / beschrittenen Knüppel- / pfade im Hochmoor, / / Feuchtes, / viel' [the half- / trodden log- / paths on the high moor, / / humid, / much] (Celan, *Die Gedichte*, p. 282).
109. Sakel was a Jew born in Nadvirna, a town that lies under the Carpathian Mountains and about 100 km from Celan's native Czernowitz. He emigrated to the United States in 1936, and died in New York in 1957.

110. Frédéric Masseix, 'L'insulinothérapie', in *Soin, Étude et Recherche en Psychiatrie*, available at <http://www.serpsy.org/piste_recherche/choc/masseix_ choc.html>, [accessed 8 January 2015].
111. Celan and Celan-Lestrange, *Correspondance*, II, p. 561.
112. Ibid., I, p. 462.
113. Celan returns to the neologism 'eingedunkelt' during August 1967, when he composes a prose poem that begins with the word (Celan, *Mikrolithen*, p. 84). Despite the word's appearance here, the surrealist imagery appears to align the prose passage less with the preoccupations of the *Eingedunkelt* cycle than with Celan's early Romanian poems, or with the collection of aphorisms and parables in prose gathered under the heading 'Gegenlicht' [Counterlight] (Celan, *Gesammelte Werke in sieben Bänden*, III, pp. 163–65) and first published in 1949 in the Zürich journal *Die Tat* (Hamacher, 'The Second of Inversion', p. 224). For a brief commentary of the prose poem see Celan, *Mikrolithen*, p. 482.
114. Celan, *Eingedunkelt*, p. 295.
115. Celan and Celan-Lestrange, *Correspondance*, I, p. 451.
116. Michaelis, 'Der beschriftete Ankerstein', L9.
117. *Eingedunkelt* features a knife blow, but this more likely reflects Celan's attempted stabbing of Gisèle: '<u>With the rotating</u> / clump of sight you collide, / by ice-fire shine [bei Eisfeuerschein], / / Glimpsed, glimpsed! — stuck through [Durchstossen]' (Celan, *Eingedunkelt*, p. 188).
118. Friedrich Hölderlin, *Sämtliche Werke: Grosse Stuttgarter Ausgabe*, ed. by Friedrich Beissner, 8 vols (Stuttgart: Cotta, 1946–1985), IV, p. 243.
119. Heidegger adopts Hölderlin's expression to express the more general projection of language and man's being: 'Language speaks. If we let ourselves fall into the abyss denoted by this sentence, we do not go tumbling into emptiness. We fall upward, to a height. The height of this fall opens up a depth. Together, they measure out a site in which we would like to become at home, so as to find the dwelling place for the essence of man' (Martin Heidegger, *Poetry, Language, Thought*, trans. by Albert Hofstadter (New York: Harper & Row, 1975), pp. 191–92 (translation modified)).
120. Theodor W. Adorno, *Prisms*, trans. by Samuel and Shierry Weber (Cambridge: MIT Press, 1981), p. 34.
121. Alex Thomson, *Adorno: A Guide for the Perplexed* (London: Continuum, 2006), pp. 123–24.
122. Theodor W. Adorno, *Negative Dialectics*, trans. by E. B. Ashton (New York: Seabury, 1973), p. 367.
123. Eric Kligerman, *Sites of the Uncanny. Paul Celan, Specularity and the Visual Arts* (Berlin: De Gruyter, 2007), p. 152.
124. Celan, *Die Gedichte*, p. 94. Reflects on Vincent Van Gogh's 'Wheatfield with Crows' (1890, Van Gogh Museum, Amsterdam).
125. Ibid., p. 284. Incorporates references to Théodore Géricault's 'A Horse Frightened by Lightning' (c. 1813–1814, National Gallery, London).
126. Ibid., p. 280.
127. Kligerman, *Sites of the Uncanny*, p. 152.

CHAPTER 1

❖

Learning to Read in the Pre-Text

The Valley of Campan, p. 51, footnote:
> ... 'as in the houses of Jews (in memory of Jerusalem in ruins), something must always be left <u>unfinished</u>'.
> for <u>remembering</u> in the poem — remembering as absence — [1]

Toward a New Literature

One of the greatest challenges for anyone concerned with the reading and study of modern literature today is perhaps the presence of an unprecedented volume of published genetic documents, increasingly available to readers of literature in print, online, or in other digital format. By genetic documents, I understand all those textual traces that precede a realized or projected literary work of art, or what Paul Valéry called 'the interior process which the work brings to term', the work's 'pre-history' which remains 'mysterious and irreducible to clear and distinct notions'.[2] If, as Almuth Grésillon explains, the object of genetic criticism 'is made up of written documents, usually manuscripts',[3] then the phenomenon that this chapter aims to focus on can be considered a derivative of genetic criticism, namely the transcription and publication of manuscript traces, the somewhat paradoxical publication of the pre-text as text.

Initially, the focus of textual critics (those responsible for identifying, editing, transcribing, and publishing the documents relating to the process of textual composition), was on the publication of documents relating to the masterpieces of the modern era, from Friedrich Beissner's controversial decipherment of Hölderlin's hymns and fragments,[4] to Jean-Yves Tadié's inclusion of *Jean Santeuil* and other earlier versions of Proust's *In Search of Lost Time* in his Pléiade edition,[5] to the publication of synoptic versions of Joyce's *Ulysses* alongside the text originally published in 1922 by Hans Walter Gabler.[6] More recently, however, genetic documents relating to even the most marginal and seemingly inconsequential of unfinished works have been made available to the public in their entirety. This is the case for Paul Celan's unfinished *Eingedunkelt* cycle, for which an exhaustive genetic edition was published in 2006.[7]

Plans to reproduce drafts relating to Celan's published work were first formulated in the months following his death. In December 1970, Peter Szondi wrote to Jean

Bollack with evident excitement to announce that Beda Allemann had persuaded Siegfried Unseld at Suhrkamp to publish an edition of Celan's work 'with variants'.[8] Allemann in fact had more ambitious plans. That same year he had founded the 'Bonner Arbeitsstelle für die Celan-Ausgabe', a research team whose aim was to publish exhaustive transcriptions of the genetic documents relating to all poems, prose, translations, both published and unpublished, and other notes and annotations inscribed in books that Celan had read. In these historical-critical editions — so called because they are inscribed in a tradition of 'analyzing the transmission [of the text] historically'[9] rather than the final authorial intention — texts are reproduced using a system of codes and symbols to describe the topography of the manuscript or typescript page. For instance, a word or line that has been crossed out in the manuscript document will, in the historical-critical edition, appear un-scored but within square brackets, to distinguish it from properly un-scored text. Reproducing the precise visual disposition of the text as it appears on the page is less important than an accurate and definitive description of the text's appearance. Facsimiles of manuscript and typescript documents tend not to be included in these editions.

The historical-critical edition of Celan's works was intended to provide a precise account of all the textual traces that precede the publication of a given work. Conscious that some of these documents might be of interest to a wider readership, Suhrkamp soon conceived an alternative edition of Celan's genetic documents — published between 1996 and 2004 — this time under the direction of Jürgen Wertheimer. The purpose of the so-called 'Tübingen Celan Edition' [Tübinger Celan-Ausgabe] was to publish a smaller selection of transcriptions from the genetic documents relating only to the collections of poems that Celan had either published or prepared for publication, as well as the preparatory documents relating to the Büchner Prize speech, 'The Meridian'.[10] In contrast to the exhaustiveness aimed for by Allemann's historical-critical edition, the Tübingen edition was intended to provide a more accessible overview of a given work's textual process toward completion. In order to highlight what the editors call the 'compositional dynamic' of the textual process, usually only four separate stages of a given work's composition are presented, spread over the two pages of the open book. This means that the reader can perceive the movement toward completion with a single glance. Where the historical-critical edition uses a system of symbols and codes to convey the layout of text on the manuscript or typescript page, the Tübingen edition reproduces the topographical aspect of the document diplomatically, that is to say, it imitates the layout of the manuscript or typescript in print. The Tübingen edition also includes facsimile reproductions of a small selection of manuscript and typescript documents, allowing the reader glimpses into the material reality of the archive itself.

Despite attempts to attract a readership toward the realm of unfinished textual traces, it remains unclear how willing or able contemporary readers of literature are to engage with and create meaning within the pre-text. Although in the modern era, certain revolutionary works, such as Mallarmé's 'Un coup de dés' ['A Throw of the Dice'] (1897) and Joyce's *Finnegans Wake* (1939) have fundamentally challenged our understanding of the spatial and temporal potential of the text, it cannot really be said that they have succeeded in encouraging readers to address their preference for completed, authorized, and published literary works, presented according to established typographical and publishing conventions. Spatially, for example, a poetic text is identified by the presence of lines of verse, stanzas, individual poems, cycles of poems, and collections of verse. Temporally, the definitive text is usually considered to be that text's most significant manifestation, and as almost always succeeding in time the composition of less significant drafts, variants, and other notes. When Umberto Eco described the openness of the modern literary work to infinite readings, he may well have had a work such as Mallarmé's in mind: 'Thus, even an art that upholds the values of vitality, action, movement, brute matter, and chance rests on the dialectics between the work itself and the 'openness' of the 'readings' it invites'.[11] But Eco resolutely subscribes to the dominant convention of reading completed, as opposed to unfinished, texts: 'A work of art can be open only insofar as it remains a work; beyond a certain boundary, it becomes mere noise'.[12]

The desire to read completed texts even in the unstable realm of the pre-text is perhaps no more manifest than in the way that Hölderlin's late drafts and fragments were presented to the reading public in the years following the Second World War. Friedrich Beissner, editor of the Stuttgart edition of Hölderlin's complete works, sought to provide definitive versions of poems when it was difficult if not impossible to identify anything as unambiguous as a completed text. Manuscripts dating from 1800 to 1806 — during which time Hölderlin is thought to have become mad — show several often greatly differing versions of the same text written one on top of the other, creating an almost undecipherable textual palimpsest. As Richard Sieburth describes the manuscripts dating from this period:

> Textual strata of different dates lie superimposed upon each other, at times barely legible, fault lines suddenly interrupt a phrase; rich lodes of image tail off into margins often crowded with outcroppings of revision. Given their verbal imbrication, definitive readings of these manuscripts become virtually impossible: the editor finds himself not simply reproducing but instead constituting — and thereby inventing — the text at hand.[13]

It was only with the publication of the so-called Frankfurt Edition under the editorship of D. E. Sattler — published from 1975 through 2008 — that the constitution of definitive texts through the creative intervention of the editor was replaced by a presentational structure that allowed for the representation of the difficulties, uncertainties, and ambiguities of the pre-text. Sattler's edition invites the reader into the generation of text, not only providing a photographic reproduction of the manuscript, but also its diplomatic transcription, as in the Tübingen editions of Celan's works. There follows what Sieburth calls a 'phase analysis',[14] in which the temporal sequence of each stage of composition is identified through the use of different typefaces. At the end of this 'phase analysis', a provisional final version of the text is presented.

The over two hundred manuscript and typescript documents discovered in a single envelope in Celan's office after his death in 1970, entitled *Eingedunkelt*, do not present the same degree of illegibility as Hölderlin's palimpsestic hymns. Where the manuscripts so vividly described by Sieburth are products of over-writing and multiple conclusions, the documents gathered under *Eingedunkelt* offer for the most part instances of under-writing and incompletion. It is as a collection of essentially unfinished texts, rather than of multiple texts inscribed on the same manuscript, that it challenges the conventional reader's preference for completed, authorized, and published literary texts. In this chapter, I explore how the contemporary reader of literature can learn to become aware of and even listen to the 'noise' that Eco locates beyond the boundary of the completed text, and thereby to experience the openness of all text, not just the text of the finished work. I ask how we as readers of literature can become more sensitive to the literary potential of the mass of genetic documents now available in print. It may be that our ways of understanding reading and literature will have to change to better engage with this now accessible excess of text, language, and meaning, of that which has almost always been edited out — 'eliminated', as Bernard Cerquiglini says — 'not only from the readable but from the thinkable'.[15] How prepared are we for the encounter with literary works that now seem more than ever 'dauntingly uncontained'?[16] Specifically, I am interested in learning to hear how the pre-text itself asks to be read, not according to the external logic of the completed text, but in its own, strange, subversive, noisy, and often dangerous ways. My aim is to bring something of the 'philologist's attentiveness to language' that Barbara Johnson suggests might be enough to open up 'irresolvable difficulties, *resistances* to meaning, or other, unexpected meanings' within the pre-text as text.[17]

If these questions need to be asked, it is because the pre-text has not been published with the reader of literature in mind. On a practical level, the publication of the pre-text ensures that as time passes and the material state of original and manuscript documents deteriorates, reproductions of the archive will continue to exist in print and digital format. The publication of the pre-text ensures that the compositional processes that brought the definitive works we can buy and read in bookstores or online are preserved for posterity and made publically available in the present. But the preservation of the pre-text may in fact stem precisely from the desire to not read the pre-text, from the view that the pre-text is not to be read. Derrida perceives the urge to preserve the archive as a response to the reader's destructive relation to the archive: 'there is in the relation to the archive a desire, a movement to erase, to destroy even that which we can preserve. If this destruction of the archive were not possible [...] then neither would we have the desire to keep [garder]. If I want to keep, it is because I know that I can want to not keep, or that others can want to not keep'.[18] The desire to keep the archive might therefore be said to stem from a desire to not read the archive. If the archive were to lend itself to reading, there would be no reason to entertain the notion of either its preservation or destruction. The publication of the pre-text is a result of its illegibility. It is published because it is not meant to be read, or rather, it is published to be not read.

The notion that the pre-text can be made public on the condition that it is not read is confirmed by the attitude of many critics, who prefer to relegate the pre-text to the shadows of the definitive text. Henri Meschonnic[19] and Laurent Jenny both attempt to put the pre-text in its place, when they point out that without the 'consecration of the text that it precedes', there would be little reason to consider the pre-text in the first place.[20] The pre-text is an after-thought. But as Jenny goes on to note, the establishment of the pre-text is nevertheless a dangerous event, as it has the effect of undermining the unity and the significance of the very textual entity that gave it significance in the first place.[21] Grésillon agrees when she notes that the publication of the pre-text has undermined 'the sacrosanct *auctoritas* of the text'.[22] The definitive work, long privileged with the exclusive attention of readers because of a convention whose origins have long been forgotten, is exposed to the possibility that it might be 'just another state among others'.[23]

As it is published and made accessible to readers, the pre-text will prove increasingly unavoidable if not irresistible. It is in the nature of the pre-text to be voluminous, a voluminosity created through its extravagant way of playing sameness and difference off each other through repetition. The material reality is that genetic texts now constitute a huge part of many major modern authors' published textual production. As Pierre-Marc de Biasi notes, Flaubert's oeuvre — which includes no more than six or seven great works — 'rests, like the visible part of an iceberg, on a floating platform of manuscripts more than ten times its visible height'.[24] Beyond its vast physical presence, the pre-text can also be a domain of unusual pleasure. In the case of well-known works — besides a sense of bewilderment at the additional volume of supposedly inferior text — a reader might well experience the delight of what Cerquiglini calls the 'aesthetic of return with pleasure in variance'.[25] I ask if the published pre-text should continue to serve primarily as a tool for enhancing the experience of reading definitive works of literature. Alternatively, could the pre-text be read alongside the definitive work, as an extension of its text in time or what Louis Hay, one of the founders of modern genetic criticism, calls the text's 'third dimension'?[26] Or should we now approach the pre-text in preference to the definitive work, as offering a new type not only of textuality but of literature, for which we have yet to develop a hermeneutic sensitivity and appreciation? It may be that our reluctance to engage with the pre-text on its own terms stems from a legitimate fear of the transformations it might bring about not only in the domain of literature, but in the way the human mind operates.

Shortly after the turn of the millennium, Jean-Michel Rabaté heralded our entry into 'the context of an expanding archive',[27] claiming that the published presence of genetic documents had already forced the reader of literature to confront a new type of materiality and temporality. '*Finnegans Wake*', says Rabaté, 'is a text which aims at giving birth to a new reader, a reader who has to approach the difficult and opaque language less with glosses and annotations than through the material evidence of the notebooks, drafts, corrected proofs'.[28] The ideal reader of Joyce's later work would be what Rabaté calls a 'genreader', 'one who 'will become a 'genetic' reader [...] both engendered by the text and engendering the text'.[29] Other instances of this movement toward the exploration of the pre-text as text that can be read include Arno Schmidt's *Zettel's Traum*[30], 'a deliberately proliferous, unresolved structure'[31] that appears to present a working typescript, including deletions, additions, and handwritten amendments. Francis Ponge includes the process of production as part of the finished literary text in his *La fabrique du 'Pré'*.[32] When Ponge publishes the transcription of unpublished outlines, sketches, and rough drafts dating from between 1922 and 1964 in *Writing Practices, or, Perpetual Incompletion*, he describes them as marking the birth of 'a new literary genre'.[33] As Gérard Genette argued in a short but forceful apology for the manuscript in *Le Monde*, 'the excess of the pre-text' and 'the absence of *ne varietur*' do not invalidate its quality as readable literature: 'as a simple reader, the analysis of manuscripts, where it is possible, can only enhance our "ability to read and enjoy texts"'.[34]

Others are less certain that the publication of the pre-text has any relevance for a contemporary reader of literature. Jenny observed in 1996 that despite believing that the publication of the pre-text would herald 'a new age of criticism',[35] it instead turned readers away from reading. Genetic criticism, he says, 'had the effect of shoring up new interpretations, but of inventing a link with the text that suspends the hermeneutic relationship. It does not have as its primary objective the reading of texts but rather the discovery of their origin'.[36] Michel Contat, editor of Jean-Paul Sartre's complete works, saw the pre-text as remaining a specialist domain, and suggested that the work of textual and genetic critics was not so much a necessity, as both gratuitous and evidence of a very high degree of civilization. He suggests that genetic criticism offers 'a relation to the book which permits work on the text and the pre-text without any obvious benefit to society, a little like in a Talmudic community'.[37] Hans Walter Gabler — introducing the German tradition of textual editing to an English reading audience — warns that these products are not so much meant to be read as used: 'By its historicist allegiance, the German scholarly edition endeavors to do justice to the text so conceived. It is aimed less at the reader than at the user of the edition'.[38] More recently, Sally Bushell — author of an important critical study of genetic criticism in the Anglo-American tradition which focuses on the 'textual process' in Wordsworth, Tennyson, and Dickinson — describes the pre-text as a 'rich domain of... manuscript drafts' that readers still do not naturally know 'how to journey through'.[39] 'There is a need', she opines, 'for a genetic criticism to clearly define the hermeneutics of reading the *avant-texte*, and I am not sure that this has yet been undertaken'.[40]

Although there is not yet sufficient evidence to confirm Rabaté's claim that we are a community of 'genreaders', the alternative notion that the pre-text should be reserved for specialists is somewhat disappointing, and fails to account for the appeal that the growing volume of published genetic documents could have for a reader of literature. The reality, however, is that the reading public has so far shown little interest in an increasingly accessible pre-text. Geert Lernout cites the example of the Gallica project, established by the 'Bibliothèque Nationale' to electronically reproduce and make available on the web facsimiles of canonical books and their manuscripts. The genetic dossier relating to Émile Zola's *Le Rêve* is, he says, 'of all the thematic dossiers available on Gallica [...] the one that has been least popular with browsers'.[41] If on the off-chance a reader does show interest in the pre-text, the strangeness of its unfinished domain, its messy and repetitive nature, its slight variations or variance — not to mention its moments of uncanny familiarity — will most likely discourage readers from seeking anything other than easily discernable teleological trends toward the final text that they know and recognize. The publication of the pre-text appears to have simultaneously elevated and relegated its status as readable text. Much like the holy of holies or the host in the tabernacle, the significance of the published pre-text to the reading of literature is usually acknowledged, but its real presence is reserved for and appreciated by the select few — the textual high priests — and then only in ceremony or in the extremes of hermeneutic pursuit.

One could be forgiven for imagining that by opening up the closed stability of the modern text, the reader would be released into a new domain of literary possibility, in which textual traces could be read without regard for the completed text. The pre-text would thereby offer a textual domain in which to enjoy unlimited hermeneutics or — to displace and re-motivate a climbing term — to free-read, to read without ropes or to 'solo', with all the risks that this entails. But this has not been the case. The opening up and theoretical charting of this textual domain continues to take its bearings from the 'completed version, ready for the press, authenticated and authorized'.[42] Even the most persuasive critics writing on the pre-text and the creative process — including Bushell, who is sensitive to its hermeneutic potential — invite us to perceive what they call the 'movement of writing' or the 'textual process' of the pretext toward its final form as definitive text. When Biasi argues for an approach to the pre-text 'that would allow us to support the structural study of the text with a *poiesis* of the *avant-texte*',[43] he also sees the new dimension brought to writing as being that of process. His idea is 'to widen the concept of writing by opening up access to writing's temporal dimension'.[44] The problem with both of these approaches is that by perceiving the process of composition in time, the logic of the *telos* — of the completed work, whether realized or projected — continues to exercise its organizing power over the domain of the pre-text. Despite its revolutionary potential, if not intent, genetic criticism has not yet managed to shake itself free of the *telos*.

Daniel Ferrer and Michael Groden explain that the continued fixation of genetic criticism with the *telos* has to do with its curiously hybrid theoretical origins. On the one hand, it 'grows out of a structuralist and post-structuralist notion of "text" as an infinite play of signs'.[45] On the other hand, it 'accepts a teleological model of textuality and constantly confronts the question of authorship. Like old-fashioned philology or textual criticism, it examines tangible documents such as writers' notes, drafts, and proof corrections, but its real object is something much more abstract — not the existing documents but the movement of writing that must be inferred from them'.[46] This chapter seeks to challenge both the conviction that a global 'movement of writing' should be inferred from genetic documents relating to a given work, and the notion that the pre-text has an end, as its prefix seems to indicate. In privileging the notion of a 'movement of writing', genetic criticism deprives itself of the freedoms won for it by structuralism and post-structuralism. Once textual editors have succeeded in identifying, ordering, editing, transcribing, and publishing genetic documents, it is often felt that the most important part of the work has been done. This chapter is intended to remind readers that such textual scholarship is at most the completion of a preparatory stage, the publication of an archive that has so far been the exclusive resort of the aristocrats of reading: vacationing scholars, university teachers, and archivists. The products of textual scholarship should be the prelude to further interpretation and exploration of the pre-text. It should be accessible to all readers of literature. It has the potential to radically transform the ways we read and create meaning.

The purpose of this opening chapter will therefore be to establish whether it is possible to exploit the pre-text in more creative and less teleological ways than has been the case so far. Taking Paul Celan's *Eingedunkelt* as a case-study, I engage with unfinished poems from an unfinished cycle as they are now available to the reading public, namely as a convolute of ordered, transcribed, edited, and published genetic documents. *Eingedunkelt* presents a unique perspective on the nature and potentialities of the pre-text, and the expectations a reader might bring to it, primarily because it refuses to a significant degree to present final or near final versions of individual texts. It lends itself to any investigation seeking to avoid the movement of writing toward the final text, and to instead let the pre-text speak for itself, in what might well be unusual, unpredictable, or unrecognizable ways.

The unusual pre-textual domain of *Eingedunkelt* could usefully be compared to that of Flaubert's workbooks, as edited and presented by Pierre-Marc de Biasi. Biasi warns his readers that the 'carnets' are not to be read as one would read a novel, or even a personal diary: 'This edition is a gamble. And the gamble is that this book potentially reveals a new form of reading'.[47] For Biasi, this new way of reading is one that allows the reader to see the creation of the writer's thought as manifested in traces of text. I am less interested in reconstituting the writer's thought process, than in inviting the reader to feel at liberty to read within the pre-text, without concern for processes of thought or composition. Just as Biasi's edition is neither 'a work by Flaubert nor a work on Flaubert, but a sort of interface where the writing of the author, his thought and his projects, their possible interpretation [...] circulate simultaneously',[48] so too I would like us to detach the historical-critical edition of *Eingedunkelt* from Celan's authorship. I aim instead to promote the pre-text as a domain in which the authority of the author and the limits of the work of art count less than the potential for a reader to transform what it means to read and to create meaning among traces of text.

In the case of *Eingedunkelt*, two schools of thought complicate any attempts to explore the pre-text for its poetic potential. The first relates to conventional genetic criticism, the second to Paul Celan's conception of the poem.

Textual critics and geneticists are often overtly hostile to the idea of subjecting genetic documents to literary interpretation. As Bushell notes: 'hermeneutic practice is rarely undertaken on the text-critical side of studies of process, where critical concern is usually with the relative status of texts rather than with their interpretation'.⁴⁹ In her study of the genesis of Flaubert's *Madame Bovary* and *A Simple Heart*, Raymonde Debray-Genette — one of the pioneers of the theorization of the pre-text and of genetic criticism as a practice — distances her study from the risks associated with interpretation. Instead she privileges the structural and analytical objectivity that she believes to be necessary for the proper exploitation of genetic texts: 'we can only situate ourselves [...] in relation to the inscribed trace, in the degree to which it has been preserved; we can only attempt to analyze and structure the totality of preserved signifiers, avoiding hermeneutics as far as possible'.⁵⁰ More recently in his work on Flaubert, Eric Le Calvez is even more insistent on the permanent incompatibility of literary interpretation with the complexities and uncertainties of the genetic process: 'In fact, the perspective that closely follows the process of writing necessarily destroys the aims of hermeneutics [...] There are too many meanderings, too many reversals, too many problems of causality, of finality, and above all of arbitrariness in the process of creation for us to interpret with certainty, and above all with objectivity and modesty'.⁵¹

In both cases, the logic of the *telos* — of the completed text, whether realized or not — is imposed on the way that the task of genetic criticism is conceived. Any purpose other than one which helps us better understand either the movement toward the final text or the final text itself is said to be lacking in objectivity, certainty, analytic precision, and even in modesty. Le Calvez's appeal for modesty in the way genetic texts are interpreted betrays a curious uncertainty and even fear on the part of genetic and textual critics. It is a little like the loving anxiety felt by the parents of adolescent children who are on the point of becoming aware of their independence and power, an awareness of the ways in which genetic documents might lend themselves to investigations that do not respect the patriarchal *telos* of the final text. Genetic criticism has developed a set of social norms and acceptable practices, according to which a healthy interest in textual processes should be married to the stability of the final text. It is just this marriage that this chapter seeks to question and undermine, in the hope of revealing new modes of reading.

Second, and more specifically with regard to *Eingedunkelt*, Paul Celan himself excludes the genesis of the text from the poetic in what we might call Celan's denial of origins. In notes made in 1959 and 1960 when preparing what will become his Büchner Prize acceptance speech, 'The Meridian', Celan exclaims: '!!To speak nowhere about the creation of the poem [von der Entstehung des Gedichts]; but always only about the created poem [vom entstandenen Gedicht]!!'⁵² There is here no acknowledgment of the 'labouring' that must ultimately remain invisible but that W. B. Yeats admits to in 'Adam's Curse': 'A line will take us hours maybe; / Yet if it does not seem a moment's thought, / Our stitching and unstitching has been naught'.⁵³ Neither is there the serendipity of a Baudelaire sniffing out rhymes and tripping over words as if they were paving stones, as in the verse poem 'Le soleil'.⁵⁴ Where Baudelaire and Yeats find pleasure and reassurance respectively, Celan ostensibly refuses to mythologize the textual process within the definitive poem.

For Celan the poem is always already poem and never preparation for the poem. It has always already been. It pre-exists us and exercises authority over us: 'we do not know where the poem, which <u>precedes</u> us, is pointing us'.[55] The poet's task, as Celan perceives it, can be formulated in terms of Heidegger's notion of 'authentic' existence, in which the individual responds to language as a preexistent totality: 'Man acts as though he were the shaper and master of language, while in fact language remains the master of man'.[56] The poet is therefore not an author who invents, but one who, like a troubadour (from Old Provençal 'trobar' meaning 'to find'), encounters, retrieves, and arranges for the present the text that has always pre-existed the poet. The poem is therefore not a product whose production can be traced to constituent parts or creative processes.[57] Elsewhere, Celan writes: 'Poems are not producible [herstellbar]; they have the liveliness of mortal souls [die Lebendigkeit sterblicher Seelenwesen]'.[58] This means that Celan's poetics is not only the prerogative of the completed, authorized, and published poem. The poem also has the mystical distinction of resembling human existence.

There are two main reasons why Celan's apparent rejection of the genetic process in thinking about the poem is perplexing. First, there is strong evidence to suggest that Celan was always aware that the genetic documents relating to his published poems — and even the annotations inscribed in books — might someday be subject to scrutiny. As Bucheli notes, 'that Celan meticulously recorded every step of his work, that he often used different writing utensils to make subsequent corrections (occasionally with the corresponding date) in order to keep the different layers of the editing process visible, is proof of the significance he ascribed to the creative process'.[59] Celan's concern with ordering and certifying his own writings can be traced to the trauma experienced from 1953 onward, when he was first accused of plagiarism by Claire Goll, wife of the Franco-German poet Yvan Goll. Although Celan was probably aware that these documents and annotations might later be read by archivists and critics, it is less likely that he envisaged such documents to be of interest to the reading and interpreting public.

The second reason that Celan's refusal to consider the ontological potential of the pre-text is somewhat problematic is that his completed and published poems are characterized by fragmentariness — broken syntax, absent verbs, fragmented words, dislocated lines — and what we might call the plastic manipulation of the page's whiteness. As Celan notes in the months preceding his Büchner Prize speech, taking cognizance of his poem's paradoxical state of completed incompletion: 'The poem, [...] writes Valéry, is language in a state of becoming; that is, language in statu nascendi, language becoming free'.[60] The poem for Celan is stalled in genesis, unable to grow further, but also unable to shrink, a birth suspended in the very moment of dying: 'There is a "poem in the poem": it is in every word-thread [Wortfaser], in every interval'.[61] The poem culminates in its 'morae and colons',[62] in both its shortest and least meaningful syllables, and in the interruptions brought about by punctuation.[63] The poem is most itself in these fragments of pure sound and pure silence that precede meaning. It is this essential fragmentation — this inherent state of genesis — that guarantees poetry's mortality and humanity, both the point at which the poem begins to speak, and the point at which the poem refuses to speak further, where its text appears and where its text disappears. And when Celan notes:

'The poem today — it is a breath-turn, crest-times [Kammzeiten][64] and soul-turn, that's how you recognize it — be aware of it',[65] he identifies that which makes the poem poetic, the point (or perhaps better the fold) where the poem moves from speech to silence, and from silence to speech, the crest at which the poem's soul and breath is turned and folded in on itself, to create small pockets — small tombs, Mallarmé might say — of meaning and memory.

Given the central importance of the fragmented and unfinished to Celan's notion of the poem, Celan's denial of the poetic potential of the genetic process, and the published presence of Celan's pre-text, I aim here to incorporate the ways we read genetic texts into the ways we think about poetry and the poetic. I ask if the unfinished and unauthorized parts of *Eingedunkelt* — as well as those of Celan's more established collections of poems — can be the spur to the development of new reading practices. In their 2006 edition of *Eingedunkelt*, Rolf Bücher and Andreas Lohr proceed by presenting the genetic process of each of the thirty-five poems separately and consecutively, beginning in each case with a final text where a final text existed, or a composite text where this was not the case. Each draft is then presented in chronological order, to the extent to which this can be ascertained, starting with the earliest and progressing to the latest known version. In contrast to the presentational method of the Tübingen Celan Edition, there are no facsimiles, and the text is not reproduced diplomatically, but using a system of symbols and signs. I do not argue that these texts should be presented differently, or that the editorial choices made by Bücher and Lohr could be improved. Nor am I proposing to undo the meticulous work of textual critics, who, when arranging the traces that make up the pre-text, seek wherever possible to ascertain the chronological order of composition. Nor am I suggesting that the transcription of manuscript traces into print typeface, whether diplomatically or otherwise, does not provide us with a legitimate object for study and interpretation.[66] I am instead calling for us to turn the intended orientation of this instance of textual editing to other — hermeneutic — ends, without intervening in the way the edition is arranged. The approach of textual scholarship, while effective as a basic principle for the editorial presentation of pre-textual materials, cannot be followed as a model for reading in the pre-text. As readers of literature in the pre-text, we need to discover ways of identifying and revivifying the natural resistance of unfinished text to the teleological and chronological perspectives developed by textual criticism.

The pre-text is a textual domain that has been opened up to us through the labors of textual criticism, but for which genetic criticism has not yet provided the tools necessary for readers to usefully and profitably exploit it. I therefore propose to examine the genetic materials relating to a single poem, 'The Rope' [Das Seil], as presented in Bücher and Lohr's historical-critical edition. I explore three ways in which readers might begin to re-imagine the potential of the pre-text once the major preferences and prejudices of textual and genetic criticism have been suspended. This enables us to begin to sketch out the contours of a poetics of the pre-text. In the next section of this chapter, I examine what might normally be considered the temporal and spatial edges of the pre-text closest to the finished work, by reading two definitive versions of the same poem. I show how the legal and literary device conventionally used to bring the pre-text to a close can instead be used to loosen the chronological and teleological perspectives of genetic criticism, opening the pre-text up to free-reading techniques. In the subsequent section, I challenge the tendency of genetic criticism to model its epistemological structures on organicist metaphors, and specifically those relating to 'genesis'. By examining four consecutive fragments of the pre-text, I show how such metaphors stifle the pre-text's unusual ways of creating meaning. In the final segment, I examine an extreme edge of the pre-text that is rarely fully acknowledged by genetic criticism, namely the non-verbal annotations inscribed in published works by an author as reader, which Edgar Allan Poe described — somewhat tongue in cheek — as 'a very idle practice'.[67] The ultimate purpose of this chapter is to sensitize the reader of literature to the unsettling and un-decidable ambiguities of a new literature of the pre-text.

Definitive Versions

For authors writing in German, the completion of a text, and therefore of a given textual or genetic process, is commonly signaled by the author's inscription of the words 'endgültige Fassung' [definitive version], a phrase that is roughly synonymous with the French 'bon à tirer' or 'ready for press'. As Ferrer and Groden put it: 'the institution of the "bon à tirer" has a great importance for genetic criticism, for it marks historically the simultaneous birth of the modern text and its counterpart, the pre-text, the authorial working manuscript. It establishes a disjunction between the private sphere of creation and the public sphere of the printed text'.[68] The inscription of 'definitive version' is an established literary convention, but it is one that is weaker and less stable than an author might wish and a reader presume. In both the French and German iterations of genetic criticism much has been done over the past forty years to make any such authorial pronouncement on the status of a given fragment of the pre-text of minimal importance. Even in the more author-centric Anglo-American tradition of textual editing, the notion of authorial intention has been found to be less significant than previously thought, as demonstrated by Jerome McGann, who stresses the social ways that a text continues to be composed after the author has relinquished the text and passed it for press.[69]

For a reader who refuses to 'use' the pre-text, as Gabler invites and expects them to,[70] and who instead seeks to read it, the inscription of 'definitive version' remains a significant feature in the pre-textual landscape. The words themselves offer what would appear to be a relatively safe place to start reading. Rhetorically, the substantive 'Fassung' [version] — even without the qualifying adjective 'endgültig' [definitive] — is reassuring in its intimations of composure and self-control, of fixed and immutable dimensions. 'Fassung' can variously describe the metal setting that holds a precious stone, or a pool of water captured from a flowing stream, or a load fastened to a dray-cart with rope, or a vat [Fass] that holds a measure of good wine, or a concept [die Fassung eines Gedankens] which is mentally taken up and comprehended. The 'Fassung' is that which — albeit catachrestically — grasps, captures, contains, and secures. The definitive version represents a moment where part of the pre-text elects to project itself beyond the rest of the pre-text by appealing for its own inscription and multiplication as a completed text. From the perspective of a reader of the pre-text, it is therefore less a sign of authorial intention than a political act on the part of the text. It seeks to establish the authority and primacy of one fragment of text through the disenfranchisement of all other traces of text. It is a manifestation of the 'monarchical strain' that Peter Szondi ascribes to every work of art.[71] Simply by its existence, the work of art 'would like to destroy all other works of art'.[72] It proclaims what Raymond Carney calls the 'critical fiction' of completion, where text that is inherently unstable and continuous claims for itself stability, stasis, and distinction.[73]

In the historical-critical edition of *Eingedunkelt*, the documents relating to the poem called 'The Rope' amount to twelve separate drafts. The drafts are ordered chronologically — to the extent that this can be ascertained — and numbered H^{1o} to H^{1c}, with H^{1o} being the earliest, and H^{1c} the latest version.[74] The twelve drafts include three texts that are marked 'definitive version', namely versions H^5, H^3, and H^{1b}. Of these three definitive versions, two were sent by Celan to Gisèle, the first on 6 April 1966, with a list of the poem's vocabulary translated into French, and the second on 17 April. As these two definitive versions of the poem are the only texts from the twelve to have been released into 'social transmission'[75] — albeit in the most limited sense possible — it is on these two manifestations of the definitive text that I want us to focus our readerly attention. By emphasizing the equal degree to which the two texts reproduced below were completed and made public, the chronological and teleological frame of the historical-critical edition can be suspended. The 'collation' of the two texts below should not be understood in the derivative sense of the term as the comparison of two texts in an attempt to find an ideal, Platonic text, as the term is used in the Anglo-American tradition of textual editing. Instead, 'collation' should be understood in its etymological sense, as describing two parts of the pre-text that have been brought together and laid side by side, from the Latin 'collatus', past participle of 'conferre' [to bring together]. To facilitate reading and interpretation, I have translated the codes and symbols used in their transcription by Bücher and Lohr, to obtain texts that go some way to visually resembling the disposition of the text in the original manuscripts. A literal translation into English follows:

I
                                  auch mit deinen Händen

Das Seil, zwischen zwei hoch-
wohlgeborene K̶n̶Köpfe gespannt, oben,
        auch mit deinen Händen
langt, nach dem Ewigen Draußen,

das Seil
soll singen — es singt,
                                ‖   Endg. Fassung
Ein Ton r̶e̶i̶ß̶t̶   ‖
reißt an den Siegeln,   6.4.1966
die du befremdet erbrichst.[76]

———

II

Das Seil, zwischen zwei
Köpfe gespannt, hoch oben,
langt, auch mit deinen Händen,
nach dem Ewigen Draußen,

das Seil
soll jetzt singen — es singt.

Ein Ton   Endg. Fassung
reißt an den Siegeln,   17.4.1966
die du erbrichst.[77]

I
                                  also with your hands

The rope, taut between two high-
wellborn h̶a̶heads, above,
        also with your hands
reaches, after the Eternal Outside,

the rope
should sing — it sings,
                                ‖   Fin. Version
A tone t̶e̶a̶r̶s̶   ‖
tears at the seals,   6.4.1966
that you estranged break open.

———

II

> <u>The rope</u>, taut between
> two heads, high above,
> reaches, also with your hands,
> for the Eternal Outside,
>
> the rope
> should now sing — it sings.
>
> A tone   Fin. Version
> tears at the seals,   17.4.1966
> that you break open.

To obtain a better preliminary understanding of the relationship between the two poems reproduced above, and in a broader effort to understand the nature and dynamics of the pre-text, I begin by applying the distinction Michel Foucault makes between 'similitude' and 'resemblance'. 'Resemblance' implies the presence of a primary reference or a model that prescribes and classifies copies on the basis of an imperfect mimetic relation of a poem to a previously composed poem. 'Resemblance' moves in two antithetical or diametrically opposed directions, and in doing so reinforces the linear structure of the series of resemblance. This is what Daniel Ferrer refers to as the 'double orientation of textual genesis',[78] motivated simultaneously by a 'logic of anticipation' and a 'logic of retroaction'.[79] As Foucault puts it: 'Resemblance predicates itself upon a model it must return to and reveal'.[80]

In the case of conventional genetic criticism, the model to which each resembling version returns to and reveals is not only the earliest datable trace, but also the final text — as ideal notion or realized event — toward which a set of genetic documents might be said to move. In his introduction to the exhaustive transcription of Flaubert's manuscripts relating to *A Simple Heart*, for example, Giovanni Bonaccorso sees it as the main task of the textual critic to reconstitute the chronology of composition through the exploitation of all existing manuscript traces: 'In our opinion, faulty chronology can only lead to faulty reasoning, and risks invalidating long and patient [archival] work. [...] we need, wherever possible, to offer the reader [of these genetic texts] the chance to follow the itinerary undertaken by the author during the process of creation'.[81] This approach has the benefit of reinforcing the notion of the independent work of art, of which each genetic text is an identifiable although imperfect iteration of the work itself.

'Similitude', on the other hand, occurs where there is no initial, paternal point of reference: 'the similar develops in series that have neither beginning nor end, that can be followed in one direction as easily as in another, that obey no hierarchy, but propagate themselves from small differences among small differences. [...] Similitude circulates the simulacrum as an indefinite and reversible relation of the similar to the similar'.[82] In contrast to the linearity of the series occasioned by 'resemblance', similitude creates a network of events, much like a cluster of stars bound in loose federation by their own gravitational force. The notion of similitude allows us to perceive each fragment of text as inhabiting its own realm of time and space, offering a unique set of conditions for the creation of meaning.

The inscription of 'definitive version' by two similar fragments of text invites the reader of the pre-text to consider these fragments according to the principle of similitude. The similitude that governs each fragment also extends to the notion of authority, in that each fragment, by its very presence, as Szondi says, seeks to confirm the other fragment's illegitimacy through its own legitimacy. It is an irresolvable relationship that finds a parallel in Certeau's definition of the 'schism', in which two incompatible schools of thought or persuasion continue to exist alongside each other, with neither one being able to impose on the other the law of its reason or of its force.[83] This means that even in the objective relationship of similitude that governs the ways the fragments relate to each other, each fragment seeks to impose the principle of resemblance, and with it the notion of hierarchy. The claim of each fragment to definitiveness therefore complicates any model of similitude, by labeling all other fragments heretical.

In the case of Paul Celan's work, the relationship of destructive similitude is further complicated. As mentioned above, Celan maintains that the definitive version of the work of art possesses 'the liveliness of mortal souls'. How does such 'liveliness' operate as text? Szondi indicates that it is a liveliness that seeks to annihilate all other traces of text. This conviction is echoed by the conventions of editing and publishing, which present the text without preparatory traces. Is this a liveliness that overcomes separation, reverses dissemination and restores continuity between fragments? Or does the poem as mortal being — as possessor of a soul — seek to preserve its discontinuity and separation? Is there, simultaneous to each text's respective claim to exclusive legitimacy — already implied in the establishment of their respective isolation, and confirmed through the counter-inscription of 'definitive version' — also the possibility that each text requires the other text to exist? Does each text already live and breathe within the other? Is the mutual destruction they threaten actually countered by the existence of a common body and a common soul? These are some of the preliminary questions that arise when we go behind or under the established and public oeuvre and into the 'sous-oeuvre' to consider the ways in which fragments of text in Celan's pre-text function both internally and in relation to other fragments of text.

In what follows, I approach these two fragments of the pre-text from four distinct perspectives. Each perspective reveals a way in which meaning can be pursued in the pre-text, which is lost or repressed by the conventional editing techniques and the presentational apparatus of textual scholarship and genetic criticism. Reading within the pre-text will therefore be understood not as reading traces of a work (whether projected or realized) that has not been finished, but as exploring some of the elementary structures of that which is ontologically unfinished. That said, even within the essentially unfinished realm of the pre-text, the presence of individual fragments suggests that distinctions can and should be made between its parts, that limits can be drawn, and that fragments can achieve some sort of preliminary completion. To better understand the way that completion operates within the incomplete, we begin by asking how the juxtaposition of two similar and different fragments of text — fragments that are both exclusive and co-existent — can present simultaneously both discontinuous and continuous qualities.

In *Philosophical Investigations*, Ludwig Wittgenstein explains that when he sees a face, he is able to see beyond the separateness of one face to another face by noticing their apparent similarity: 'I look at a face [Ich betrachte ein Gesicht], at once I notice its similarity with another face. I *see* that it has not changed, and yet I see it differently'.[84] Where there was an essential dislocation and juxtaposition, there is now, simultaneously, the independence of dislocation ('I *see* that it has not changed') and the intimacy of contiguity ('and yet I see it differently'.) This is what Wittgenstein calls 'noticing an aspect'.[85] As he goes on to explain, not everyone will notice the aspect as he does. Some are aspect-blind. They will look at one face and will notice its likeness to another, but will not see the face or text altering before their eyes. They will not see the movement from dislocation to contiguity, from one fragment to another fragment, from one soul to another soul. Each face and text — as happens with versions in genetic criticism — will remain an independent fragment with greater or lesser similitude to other fragments, which can then be ordered according to a perceived process of development.

In the case of these juxtaposed fragments, I suggest that the attentive reader of the pre-text is invited to perceive the aspect and to thereby make a connection between the two texts that would otherwise go unnoticed. The texts appear to achieve this through the image of the rope [Seil]. In the second text reproduced above, the rope is strung between two heads, and in the first it is tied between two honorable, or literally two 'high-well-born' [hochwohlgeboren] heads.[86] In both cases, the rope reaches for the Eternal Outside. The 'Seil' [rope] that reaches, stretches itself beyond its usual phonetic and orthographic form to become — for those who can see and even hear the aspect — a 'Seele' [soul]. The rope that reaches for the Eternal Outside therefore becomes a soul or perhaps a rope-soul. The rope thereby establishes a certain tenuous continuity, a thin line of shared humanity between two otherwise disembodied heads. It is a line that both separates and connects, and that offers the possibility of passing from one to the other, but only for those readers who have a head for heights and who can walk the wire. The individuality of each fragment is maintained. The bodies of the two texts — their times, their spaces, their contexts — are unique and separate. As Stanley Cavell writes of human bodies, so we might say of these textual fragments: 'The truth here is that we *are* separate, but not necessarily *separated* (*by* something); that we are, each of us, bodies, ie., embodied; each is this one and not that, each here and not there, each now and not then'.[87] At the same time, it is this separation that each of these texts denies, both through the figure of the rope that reaches for the Eternal Outside, and through its acoustic and scriptural materiality, which invites us to perceive the slippage from 'Seil' to 'Seele'. In each fragment the reaching rope offers the fragment the possibility of overcoming its separation, just as in Benjamin Fondane's poem 'Ulysses': 'visitors sometimes enter wearing diving suits / and bear in mind the rope that ties them / to the outside world'.[88]

Here, though, the stakes are not so much bathylimnetic as meteorological. The rope provides a thin, swaying passage through the sky — with echoes perhaps of Spinoza's fluctuating soul[89] — for those who are willing, in the words of Nietzsche's

Zarathustra, to make a living out of living dangerously.[90] The rope overcomes the essential dislocation between human bodies, between souls, and between fragments, all the while reminding us of the impossibility of ever denying these radical dislocations. The texts instead resemble two plateaus that 'communicate with one another across microfissures, as in a brain'.[91] The logic that motivates each fragment is not only common to both fragments, but requires the presence of a similar if not identical logic in the other fragment to exist, just as a tight-rope is only taut and ready for performance if tied securely at two ends. The acoustic, scriptural, and semiotic slippage between 'Seil' [rope] and 'Seele' [soul], means that the fragments ask us not to read them as versions H^5 and H^{1b}, two discrete and non-consecutive entities in a linear series based on resemblance. Instead, we are invited to perceive them as juxtaposed with sufficient proximity for a rope to be cast — or even a body and a soul to be forged — between them. It is just this sort of creative relationship between fragments, in which the completion or independence of the fragment is fractured and becomes open to the possibility of contamination with other similar fragments of text, that genetic criticism, seeking to illustrate the process of composition on the basis of resemblance rather than similitude, chooses not to preserve or acknowledge.

Although the example of the aspect indicates that the reader of the pre-text should be prepared to read between fragments of the pre-text, reading within a single text will also demand a new and heightened sensitivity, in particular to the new ways in which syntax is forced to operate. The German Romantic Jean Paul once claimed that every poet had to either straddle or jump between two ropes in the pursuit of poetry: the poetic slack wire [poetisches Schlappseil] and the philosophical tight wire [philosophisches Straffseil].[92] In the second fragment reproduced above, it is initially unclear whether the rope referred to at the beginning of the second stanza constitutes a repetition of the rope referenced in the second word of the fragment, or if in fact it represents two separate ropes taut between two heads.

> <u>Das Seil</u>, zwischen zwei
> Köpfe gespannt, hoch oben,
> langt, auch mit deinen Händen,
> nach dem Ewigen Draußen,
>
> das Seil
> soll jetzt singen — es singt.
>
> [<u>The rope</u>, taut between
> two heads, high above,
> reaches, also with your hands,
> for the Eternal Outside,
>
> the rope
> should now sing — it sings.]

The juxtaposition of two semantically and syntactically adequate phrases would usually call for the establishment of two autonomous phrases through the insertion of a period in the place of the comma that ends the first stanza. The comma that divides the two autonomous phrases, whilst hinting at the respective adequacy of each phrase, maintains the sentence's authority and continuity through the line of silence and whiteness that intervenes between the first and second stanzas. The comma — one of the few elements common to all versions of the poem — deprives the first phrase of the closure and stability a period might offer, and the second phrase of the syntactic freedom it requires to start anew. And yet each phrase continues to express itself adequately, apparently regardless of the doubt introduced by their juxtaposition in the same sentence. It is, to offer a cartoon analogy, as if on both sides of an abyss, a rope has been tied at its end and suspended high in the air. Each of the two ropes is taut in the belief that its other end is tied securely on the other side. Neither rope is aware that it is the end of the other rope, not its own, that has been secured.[93]

The two stanzas therefore straddle a dimensional fault-line. They inhabit a moment of unreality, of impossible suspension above the abyss of meaninglessness. At this point, some readers will notice the aspect of the rope. They will see the rope as changed but still the same, and will perceive the shift from one phrase to the next, from the rope that longs for the Eternal Outside to the rope that sings. It is these readers who are able to cross from one side to the other, from one rope to the other, without falling. The reader who is aspect-blind — the realist, the literalist, the tight-rope walker who sees each rope as separate and each fragment as discontinuous — will, half way across, discover the end of the rope and its fixation in nothing but thin air, and fall to their death on the ground below.

This is, more or less, what happens to Nietzsche's rope-dancer in the town of 'Bunte Kuh' in *Thus Spake Zarathustra*. Zarathustra commiserates with the dying rope-dancer and celebrates his dogged commitment to the absolute autonomy of the single rope, saying that as a reward he will bury him with his own two hands. He in fact ends up carrying the rope-dancer's dead body over his shoulder, apparently reluctant to abandon a newfound and rare spiritual colleague. Only when the body begins to decompose does he feel compelled to fulfill his pledge. This inability or unwillingness to see ropes and souls in their continuity is what Cavell describes as 'a kind of illiteracy; a lack of education'.[94] It is the illiteracy that refuses to read beyond the norms of syntax, but it is also the illiteracy that refuses to read beyond the confines of the single fragment of verse, and beyond the self-contained soul of each definitive version. The vision required by a reader to pass from one phrase to the next in this second fragment is no different in essence from the vision required to pass from one fragment to another. The difference is one only of intensity. We might even say that each of these fragments is not by definition separate, but constitutes a privileged moment of textual intensity, randomly occurring and unpredictable coagulations of signs and sense, like tubers that grow underground.

In the first fragment reproduced above, incompletion manifests itself in a different but still potentially productive way. The mode of operation of the first fragment requires its reader to follow its logic closely, even into those moments where the conventional means of creating meaning are apparently in jeopardy. The first fragment's apparent similarity to the second fragment is in part attenuated by the absence of a period at the end of the second stanza and the presence in its place of a comma:

> das Seil
> soll singen — es singt,
>
> Ein Ton ~~reißt~~
> reißt an den Siegeln,
> die du befremdet erbrichst.
>
> [the rope
> should sing — it sings,
>
> A tone ~~tears~~
> tears at the seals,
> that you estranged break open.]

With this comma, the first poem insists on the continuation of the phrase through the end of the second stanza, across the empty line that follows, through to the third stanza and the poem's only period. The insistence of this claim to syntactic continuity is, though, challenged by the presence of a capital 'E' in 'Ein Ton' [a tone], which disregards the authority of the comma and seeks to establish a new phrase. This discrepancy would usually be thought of as a simple mistake. A reader would normally be encouraged to consider other more coherent versions. But as readers or explorers of the pre-text, we need to slow down and ask if the apparent infelicity might be read in other ways. Does the syntactically nonsensical comma point not, in fact, to the breakdown of syntactic norms, nor to the error of the poet, but to the poem as it reaches beyond itself for what it calls the 'Eternal Outside'? Is this the point at which the poem reaches for that which exists outside of verbal expression?

I suggest that the comma in '— it sings, / /' betrays the presence of a phrase that continues and concludes in the whiteness that surrounds the text. We are at this point asked to read what is present in the text but not visible to the eye. The whiteness that follows the comma is not the whiteness familiar to us through established and recognized poetic forms and publishing conventions. It is a whiteness that asks to be read not only as the negative that allows darkness of text to distinguish itself, but as white text which cannot be seen, but whose presence is indicated by the introductory comma. The role of the comma in understanding this part of the text is not unlike the role it plays in Louis Marin's reading of Paul Klee's painting 'Ad Marginem', a painting that Marin insists 'will remain, in this place of writing, invisible'.[95] Here, Marin evokes the 'black comma, like the sound hole of a violin, inscribed on the figure of a horn or a trunk, an incongruous sound hole',[96] to demonstrate how the painting uses its margins — both the edges of the painting itself and of the medium — to 'interrogate the relations of convertibility between saying and seeing'.[97] But where Marin's marginal comma interrupts the logic of painting to touch the logic of language, in Celan's text, the predominant logic of inscribed language becomes, also on its margins, a logic of seeing, or rather of not seeing.

Despite his refusal to consider the poem's genesis, an approach which attempts to read the whiteness in the text is encouraged by Celan, who repeatedly calls for the reader of poetry to take cognizance of that which has been written but which cannot be read: 'One should finally learn to read this breath, this entity of breath into the poem [...] it comes on <u>breath-ways</u>, the poem, it is pneumatically <u>there</u>: for everyone'.[98] This is the moment in the text when the poem begins to assert its autonomy and independence, not only from the author and the reader, but from inscribed and audible language itself. And so in the pre-text of Celan's oeuvre, we arrive at a conception of literature that is very close to that exemplified by the impersonal poetics of Stéphane Mallarmé. In his late critical poem *Crisis of Verse*, Mallarmé describes the words in a poem as creating meaning independently of any reader or writer. They instead 'light each other up through reciprocal reflections like a virtual swooping of fire across precious stones'[99] generating meaning through the clash of their inequalities. The analogy Mallarmé uses to describe their independent creation of meaning by words among themselves is, in the original French, 'comme une virtuelle traînée de feux'.[100] 'Traînée' is the trail of a comet across the night sky, translated by Barbara Johnson as a 'swooping'. But in the textual and typographical sense, 'une traînée' describes an ellipsis, a series of dots that visually mark the irruption of silence into written speech.[101] I suggest that this secondary sense of 'traînée' might help us to understand Celan's syntactically incoherent comma. The comma is here not only that which signals the transition of visible script to invisible script. It is also that which marks the point at which the poem begins to create meaning in ways that lie beyond the reader's ability to recognize and to read inscribed text. In other words, the text continues to compose itself indefinitely, and independently of its author, in its departure from visible inscription.

In this fourth and final reading of these two definitive versions, I focus on the final stanza of the second fragment. I suggest that we can identify here an attempt to achieve definitiveness, not through the conventional projection of definitiveness through the inscription of 'definitive version', but through the semantic and syntactic tensions of the fragment itself. It is my contention that in the following fragment — itself taken from the second fragment reproduced above — the text attempts to distinguish itself from all other text by obliterating all other text:

> Ein Ton
> reißt an den Siegeln,
> die du erbrichst.
>
> [A tone
> tears at the seals,
> that you break open.]

If this fragment is to render the stanzas that precede it unnecessary — in much the same way that the definitive text seeks to establish the superfluous nature of all other text — then it needs to show that it both contains and surpasses everything that has previously been inscribed. Given the brevity of this enigmatic formulation, we might consider it a sort of riddle. Timothy Bahti reminds us that the riddle is 'intimately involved with the whole process of reducing language to visible form',[102] and is not coincidentally a cognate of reading. To what extent does this riddle succeed in reducing the excess of the pre-text?

Curiously, in the final stanza it is possible to identify traces of the very words that make up the stanzas that precede it. For instance, if we lend our ear to the historical sound-box offered by the etymology of the word 'tone', we can discern a deep echo of the rope that is taut between two heads earlier on in the poem. This is because 'tone' in English and 'Ton' in German come from the Greek τείνω [teínō] meaning to tense, stretch, or extend, and which in German would be 'spannen'.[103] The establishment of an indefinite, un-modulated, and dehumanized tautness in the word 'tone' constitutes the ultimate attempt of the poem to achieve irrevocable definition, to speak with clarity and without ambiguity, and to obliterate the unnecessary traces of all that has come before, not only in the second poem itself and in the first poem, but in all other traces of its genetic process, perhaps even all textual traces.

'A tone' is the point at which the poem seeks to utter pure meaning. 'A tone' inhabits the eternal and immanent present of its acoustic and textual trace.[104] It refuses to strive for an Eternal Outside, and instead strives to internalize all that has gone before: the definitive poem and its illegitimate pretender, all traces of the genetic process, all language, perhaps, to achieve the immanence of an Eternal Inside. The tone in this final stanza is that which would abolish lyric, as it presents a similar tension to the proverbial poet's lyre string, or the singer's tensed vocal cords, or even the tight-rope walker's high-wire, primed for performance. But it refuses to give individual form to each of these manifestations. 'A tone' is the point at which the text in-darkens, the point at which language and light tighten. It is a rehearsal through language of the 'tzimtzum', where song contracts, where both the divine and the human are denied, and where poetry becomes redundant.[105]

It is important, though, not to remain at the level of individual verbal units, but to set each examined unit in its syntactic context. The 'tone' operates through the verb 'reißt an' meaning to tear or rip at: 'A tone / tears at the seals' [an den Siegeln]. At this point, we might be tempted to pursue the various ways in which the meaning of 'seals' or 'Siegeln' might be modulated. Are these seals to be understood as inscribed objects with which to create a seal, or as the seals themselves, imprinted into some material, be it wax, wood, stone, or even flesh? The reader's task is in fact much simpler, as all he or she is required to do is remember what has just been read. The words 'an den Siegeln' or 'at the seals' constitute both visually and acoustically the re-inscription and contraction of four words that appear earlier in the fragment: namely 'Seil' [rope], 'soll singen' [should sing], and 'singt' [sings]. 'A tone tears at the seals' therefore describes the fragment's attempt to tear at its own textual body. If we then recall that the verb 'reissen' [to tear] has etymological roots in the Old High German 'rizan', meaning 'to rip' but also 'to write', as well as being a cognate of the English 'write',[106] then the internal operations of the fragment become even more interesting. The fragment not only tears at the seals like a beast or a man with no need for language. It writes upon its own seals, much as Hölderlin wrote upon his own poems, creating poetic palimpsests. In attempting to obliterate all text that has preceded it, the fragment inscribes upon its own inscribing body. It writes on its own writing in a sort of textual auto-da-fé.

The attempt of this fragment to write all other text into oblivion has intriguing implications for any reader of the pre-text. On one level, the fragment is able to re-write and contain, and thereby reproduce, the textual process that has preceded it, so that the textual process is not something that occurs prior to this fragment in stages that can be ordered chronologically by textual critics. The genesis of this fragment is constantly occurring within the fragment, as it writes on the parts of the poem that precede it, both destroying and reaffirming them. The textual process is not something that can be displayed in its entirety in sequence, because it is also constantly occurring within the fragment itself. This is why Daniel Ferrer is not entirely right to say that 'if the study of manuscripts is necessary, it is indeed because the final text *does not contain* the whole of its genesis'.[107] The process or movement of writing — fetish of genetic and textual criticism — does not make itself entirely available to chronological classification and categorization. It is also intricately bound up in the way meaning is created.

Each of these four brief readings of the pre-text demonstrates a way of reading where a reader might not normally feel the desire or sense the opportunity to create meaning. In the first case, Wittgenstein's concept of the aspect allows us to begin to explore different ways in which two non-consecutive, distinct phases of the textual process can be brought together and read not as parts of a process toward a final text, but as two points in a new textual structure. The second example illustrates how a reader of the pre-text must be sensitive to the need for a new syntax of unfinished traces, which will be able to create units of meaning where conventional syntax, developed for completed texts, breaks down. The third reading alerts us to the constant presence of text that is present but not visible to the reading eye, text that any new syntax of the pre-text must take into account. And the fourth example demonstrates how the pre-text re-writes itself, not according to the sequential, teleological, and chronological organizations developed by conventional textual and genetic criticism, but poetically, that is to say, in a way in which the process of writing is caught up in the process of meaning, to create zones of differing semantic and textual intensity.

The second person singular referenced by each of these fragments is perhaps nothing less than the projection of the future reader of the pre-text, Rabaté's 'genreader': 'A tone / tears at the seals, / that you break open'. You are the emancipated reader of the pre-text, able to break open the seals imposed by conventional textual and genetic criticism. But this line also contains a warning. In the list of French words that Celan sent to help his Francophone wife understand the German, 'erbrechen' is translated as 'ouvrir par la force, arracher' [to open up by force, to tear open] and this is how it has been translated here.[108] But 'erbrechen' as a transitive verb can also mean 'to vomit'. 'Ein Ton / reißt an den Siegeln, / die du erbrichst' could therefore also read: 'A tone / tears at the seals / that you throw up'.[109] This is a reminder that a 'genreader', a reader of the pre-text, should expect to feel overwhelmed by this excess of text and meaning suddenly at their disposal.

Genetic Fallacies

Almuth Grésillon notes that it has become common practice, when describing the pre-text and its functions, to evoke two main types of metaphors: one that borrows from organicism and the other from constructivism.[110] Of these two types of metaphors it is those relating to the organicist conception that are, as Ferrer notes, 'difficult for genetic studies to get rid of'.[111] 'Even those who believe in an essential discontinuity between the genesis and the work as it is transfigured by its completion', he says, would doubtless hesitate to assert 'that the butterfly does not depend on the caterpillar'.[112]

Foremost among the organicist metaphors is 'genesis' and its variants. Its success stems from its benevolent familiarity. It bears the promise of mammalian fertility, the irreversible sequence of mysterious conception, obscure gestation, revelatory birth, and the joy of life. It conveys the sense of an almost irresistible unfolding of an organic being. And it assumes the messy, unusual, and often violent operations of the pre-text into the largely positive cultural, social, and religious connotations of genesis, the founding myth that establishes Judeo-Christian culture. The psalms, for instance, sing of the enticing notion that our bodily existence is not the happy and arbitrary coincidence of necessary particles, but has been pre-ordained with the creation of the universe: 'For thou hast possessed my reins: thou hast covered me in my mother's womb. [...] My substance was not hid from thee, when I was made in secret, and curiously wrought in the lowest parts of the earth. Thine eyes did see my substance, yet being unperfect; and in thy book all my members were written, which in continuance were fashioned, when as yet there was none of them'.[113]

It is this same sense of 'continuance' — of a book in which all its 'members' are written before they come into being — that has inflected the operations of genetic criticism. These attractive metaphors not only make the unattractive pre-text seem less threatening. They also encourage us to perceive, to the best of our ability, the equidistant turns of each version, and the global 'movement of writing' toward its realization as definitive text, as if it had always been 'written in the book'. It is by applying familiar metaphors (in all senses of the term) to the uncanny and undesirable realm of the pre-text that genetic criticism is able to deploy familiar epistemological structures within an otherwise unfamiliar and unattractive domain.[114] This is not to say that there has not been some resistance to this terminology. Jean Bellemin-Noël jokingly refers to genetic criticism's 'genito-obstetric vocabulary'.[115] Although drawing to a significant degree on the findings of French 'critique génétique', Anglo-American textual and literary criticism largely avoids the term 'genesis'. Bushell, for instance, describes the process of composition as a 'textual process' or as a 'process of the text'. And yet 'process' also relies on the epistemological ground won for it by the notion of 'genesis', and could be considered an organicist metaphor in disguise. The notion of 'genesis' has succeeded in homogenizing the pre-text, bestowing upon it an external pattern and purpose, and showing how the pre-text moves from exploratory traces through a sequence of drafts to culminate in the finished work. The notion of 'genesis' has prevented the pre-text from speaking for itself.

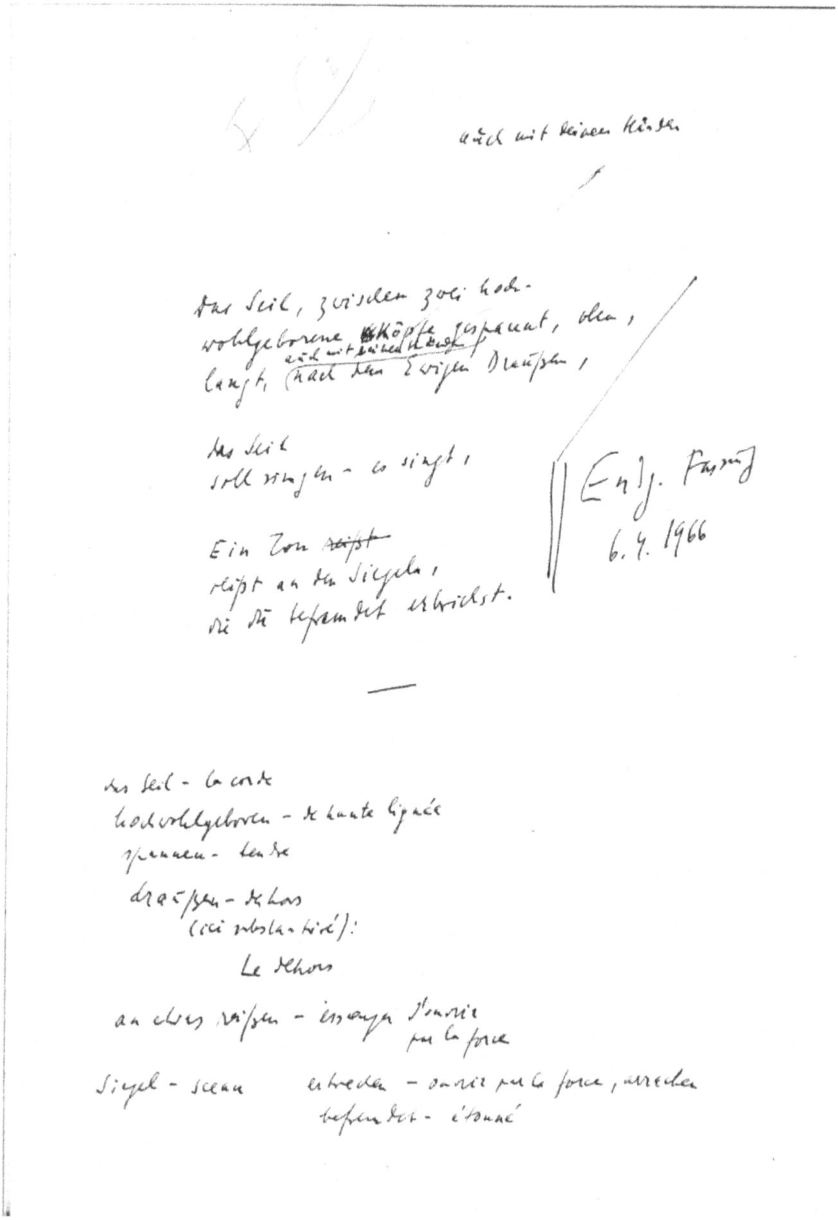

FIG. 1.1. 'Das Seil', definitive version, with list of vocabulary translated into French. Blue ink. Ms (Briefwechsel PC-GCL) / 6.4.1966. © Deutsches Literaturarchiv, Marbach a. N.

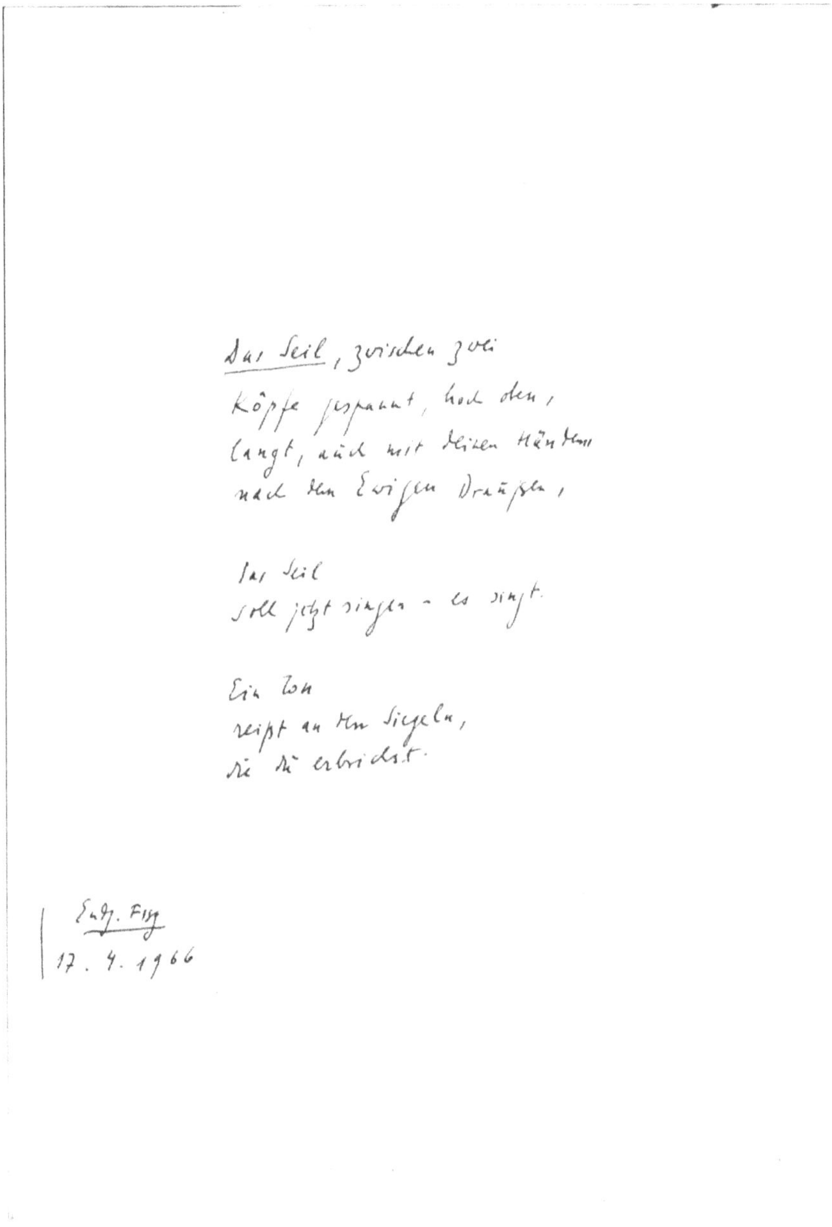

Das Seil, zwischen zwei
Köpfe gespannt, hoch oben,
langt, auch mit deinen Händen
nach dem Ewigen Draußen,

Das Seil
soll jetzt singen – es singt.

Ein Ton
reißt an den Siegeln,
die es erbricht.

Endg. Fsg.
17. 4. 1966

FIG. 1.2. 'Das Seil', definitive version. Blue ink. Ms (Briefwechsel PC-GCL) / 17.4.1966.
© Deutsches Literaturarchiv, Marbach a. N.

Although the larger purpose of this chapter is to find ways of reading in the pre-text as it is presented to us by the labors of genetic and textual criticism, the more immediate aim of this section is to show how the pre-text invites its readers to question the organicist structure of its presentation. Recognizing the largely uncontested influence of positive genetic metaphors and perceiving the opportunity to conceive of the pre-text in alternative ways will have significant implications for readers of the pre-text. Instead of reading each version in the context of a larger process or genesis toward the idea of a completed text, the reader can learn to become more sensitive to movements within the pre-text that are not global and monolithic, as genesis implies, but local and unpredictable. One of the things we should draw from *Eingedunkelt* in general and from 'The Rope' in particular is a newfound appreciation for the inconsistencies, the messiness, the violence, the confusion, and the repetitions of the pre-text.

H¹⁰

<u>Seiltänzerzorn</u>   / der Zorn des düpierten Seiltänzers

Erhebungen am Tatort

                              unbußfertig

hinausfeuern
das basiliskenhafte an seinem Blick

    durch verwerfliche Kunstgriffe vom ~~Hochseil~~ auf den Boden
gezwungen   Hochseil

Han Suyin

Seiltänzer-Zorn, ~~am Tatort~~

Vom Seiltänzer und seinem Zorn

\ Vom Seiltänzer und seinem Zorn,
/ das Seil, zwischen zwei Köpfen gespannt,
langt nach dem ewigen Draußen,

der ~~die~~ Spieldosen~~, hal~~

     das Seil, zwischen ~~die~~ zwei Köpfen benannt,
     langt nach dem ~~bestä ewigen~~
              beständigen Draußen

Spieluhren kommen[119]

Here I examine four fragments of the pre-text of 'The Rope'. In the chronological terminology preferred by genetic criticism they constitute versions H^{10} to H^6 (H^7 is not reproduced), and precede the two definitive versions discussed in the previous section. At a first glance, it is difficult to understand how such texts could ever be termed 'genetic'. They are better described by a term used by Carol Jacobs in the context of Benjamin's advocacy of literality in translation, namely 'teratogenesis' — a monstrous manifestation of words, in which the conventional structures of grammar and syntax have been partially dismantled.[116] Given the appearance of these textual cuts, scabs, scarrings, and stumps — of language tangled up in 'the mishaps of transmission'[117] — it is perhaps fitting to note that Celan considered giving the unfinished cycle we now know as *Eingedunkelt* the title 'Narbenwahre' or 'Scar-True'.[118]

H^{10}

<u>Rope-dancer-anger</u> / the anger of the duped rope-dancer

Investigations at the scene of the crime

         unrepentant

to fire out
the basilisk nature of his stare

  through reprehensible tricks from the ~~highwire~~ onto the ground

forced   highwire

Han Suyin

 Rope-dancer-anger, ~~at the scene of the crime~~

Of the rope-dancer and his anger

Of the rope-dancer and his anger,
the rope, made taut between two heads,
reaches for the eternal Outside,

of the ~~the~~ music box, ~~rin~~

 the rope, named between ~~the~~ two heads,
 reaches for the ~~const~~ eternal
   constant Outside

music boxes come

H⁹

~~Vom Seil~~

~~Vom Seiltänzer und seinem Zorn~~

~~das Seil, zwischen zwei hoch-~~
~~wohlgeborenen Köpfen gespannt,~~
~~langt nach~~

Das Seil, zwischen zwei hoch-   oben,
    wohlgeborene Köpfe gespannt, ~~droben, hoch oben,~~ ᵒᵇᵉⁿ,
langt ⁿᵃᶜʰ dem ewigen Draußen,

~~das Seil.~~ Es muß
    ~~muß~~ (singen — es singt ~~mit~~
    mit

Die¹²⁰

H⁸

~~Ein Tänzer,~~

Das Seil, zwischen zwei hoch-
wohlgeboren~~en~~ Köpfe gespannt, oben,
langt nach dem ewigen Draußen,

das Seil

muß singen — es singt
mit.

Das Scheppern der

Schel<u>len</u>-Attrappe — vorläufig
    reichts ~~es~~ aus.¹²¹

H⁹

~~Of the rope~~

Of the ~~rope-dancer and~~ his anger

the rope, between two high-
born heads taut,
reaches for

The rope, between two high-   above,
   well-born heads taut, ~~up there high above~~
reaches ̲f̲o̲r̲ the eternal Outside, ~~above,~~

~~the rope,~~ It must
   ~~must~~ (sing — it sings ~~with~~
   with

The

H⁸

~~A dancer,~~

The rope, made tight between two high-
born heads, above,
reaches for the eternal Outside,

the rope

must sing — it sings
along.

The clanging of the

ma<u>ke-beli</u>eve bells — temporarily
   suffices ~~it~~.

H⁶

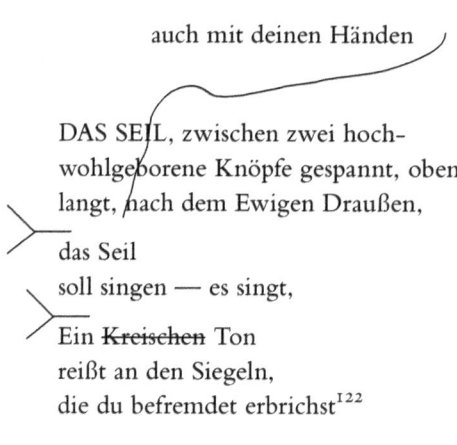

                  auch mit deinen Händen

DAS SEIL, zwischen zwei hoch-
wohlgeborene Knöpfe gespannt, oben,
langt, nach dem Ewigen Draußen,
das Seil
soll singen — es singt,
Ein K̶r̶e̶i̶s̶c̶h̶e̶n̶ Ton
reißt an den Siegeln,
die du befremdet erbrichst[122]

H⁶

                  also with your hands

THE ROPE, between two high-
well-born buttons taut, above,
reaches, for the Eternal Outside,
the rope
should sing — it sings,
A s̶c̶r̶e̶e̶c̶h̶i̶n̶g̶ tone
tears at the seals,
that you estranged break open

    These traces of language and meaning — the result of what Valéry calls the writer's 'severe labor'[123] — are the textual condition that *Eingedunkelt* mostly inhabits, as it is in fragments of texts such as these — ordered, transcribed, and printed — that it is available to us today. To learn to read profitably in the pre-text, we need to explore ways of thinking about these texts that allow for the text's presence as text rather than as stages in a global textual process toward a definitive text. This does not mean that there will be no movements among these texts that might be described as processual or even genetic, but it does mean that we should allow for smaller, more incoherent, less unified movements. To enhance and structure this investigation, I draw on a short story by Franz Kafka called 'In the Penal Colony', which although ostensibly about judicial processes, also overlaps in a number of unexpected ways with our discussion of textual genetic processes, and can help guide alternative approaches to reading in the pre-text.

    The most striking element of the coincidence of 'In the Penal Colony' and genetic criticism occurs in the very first line of the story: '"It is a peculiar apparatus", the

Officer said to the Traveler, casting an admiring sort of gaze at the apparatus, with which he was, however, quite familiar'.[124] Although here the apparatus describes the machine that puts men to death, it also echoes the technical term subsequently used in German textual editing to describe the editorial structure through which transcribed manuscripts are presented and published. In Kafka's story the apparatus is made up of three parts called the 'bed' [das Bett], the 'inscriber' [der Zeichner], and the 'harrow' [die Egge],[125] combining the libidinal, the graphic, and the agricultural respectively. The apparatus is designed to inscribe the sentence on the prisoner's body. So instead of being tried and prosecuted, the condemned man — in this case a soldier accused of disobeying and insulting a superior — is simply fastened into the apparatus, and the commandment he has broken is inscribed onto his body.[126]

For a given sentence to be inscribed on the condemned man's body, a manuscript is carefully inserted into the inscriber, much as a paper roll is inserted into a pianola. The manuscripts, or 'hand-drawn designs', are all the work of the former Commandant of the penal colony, now deceased. They are preserved in a leather portfolio by the Officer, who handles them with the militant care of an archivist, not allowing others anywhere near them, and washing his own hands before touching them. When the Traveler is shown one of the manuscripts, all he can see is a Pollockian pattern of crisscrossing lines that cover the paper so thickly 'that one could only see the white spaces with difficulty'.[127] When invited to 'read' the manuscript by the Officer, he is unable to: '"It is very elaborate", he explains. "Yes", the Officer laughingly concedes, "it's certainly no calligraphy for school children. You have to read in it for a long time"' [Man muss lange darin lesen].[128] The manuscript does not lend itself to conventional and superficial modes of reading, but this is not only because of its illegible handwritten script. The sentence inscribed in the manuscript is meant to be read and understood only by the prisoner upon whose body the sentence is inscribed. So when the Officer explains that one must 'read in' the manuscript for a long time, he is at some level referring to the fact that it is a text that is understood through inscription, not through the surficial act of reading.

The process made possible by Kafka's apparatus is therefore one that has been established in advance, and which does not depend on the case of the individual suspect. All suspects are subjected to the same process. All are condemned to death. And all have their distinct sentence inscribed in the same way upon their body, until such point that they 'understand' their crime and punishment.[129] In other words, the structure of the judicial process in the penal colony is the same, regardless of which manuscript is inserted into the apparatus. In this it is not unlike the structure of the genetic process as prescribed by genetic criticism. When reading in the pre-text, the reader is not meant to understand the script immediately through the eyes. He is meant to see it as part of a long and painful compositional process, which will climax in the moment of revelation, when a movement of writing is identified. It comes to an end when the final version emerges from the apparatus, much as the body of the condemned man is ejected from the apparatus and into the pit below after the prescribed twelve hours of inscription.

Once the Traveler has been inducted in the intricacies of the apparatus and the judicial procedure, the Prisoner is placed in the machine and the Officer turns it on. The Traveler initially watches the procedure with indifference, then growing interest and disgust, and in this his attitude toward the apparatus might be said to resemble that of a reader faced with the apparatus of the pre-text for the first time. The parallel between the Traveler and a reader of the pre-text becomes stronger when we consider that the Traveler is referred to not by name but by his activity. When Certeau describes the reader, he describes someone who, like the Traveler, is always on the move: 'Far from being writers — founders of their own place, heirs of the peasants of earlier ages now working the soil of language, diggers of wells and builders of houses — readers are travellers; they move across lands belonging to someone else, like nomads poaching their way across fields they did not write, despoiling the wealth of Egypt to enjoy it themselves'.[130] This not only means that the reader is a traveler, and that the Traveler is in some sense a reader. It also means that the island upon which the Traveler finds himself is a text that can be read and understood, although it is an unimportant and marginal one. As a penal colony, it is a domain to which undesirable elements of society are removed, just as the pre-text is constituted of similarly undesirable traces of text. The island is as far removed from the economic, cultural, political, and social operations of the homeland, as the pre-text is from the operations of the definitive text.

The parallel structures of pre-text and penal colony go beyond the general analogies made so far when we consider the four variants of 'The Rope' reproduced above. Before turning the apparatus on, the Officer warns that because of an excessively worn cog in the inscriber, the apparatus screeches so much that one cannot makes oneself understood.[131] When it becomes evident to the Officer that the Traveler does not approve of the process, he orders the Prisoner to be removed, and takes the place of the Prisoner in the apparatus himself. It is only once the machine is running with the Officer inside that the screeching cog falls silent, although the absence of this sound is at first not noticed by the Traveler: 'The Traveler had already been staring at [the apparatus] for a while, before he remembered that a wheel in the engraver was supposed to screech [daß ein Rad im Zeichner hätte kreischen sollen]; but everything was quiet, not the slightest whirr [das geringste Surren] could be heard'.[132]

Curiously, the word Kafka uses to describe the screeching of the wheel [gekreischt, kreischen] also occurs on one occasion in the genetic materials of Celan's 'The Rope':

> Ein ~~Kreischen~~ Ton
> reißt an den Siegeln,
> die du befremdet erbrichst.[133]
>
> A ~~screech~~ tone
> tears at the seals,
> which you estranged break open.

In the context of what the officer describes as the correct operation of the machine, the screech is an annoying imperfection, but it does not prevent the intended

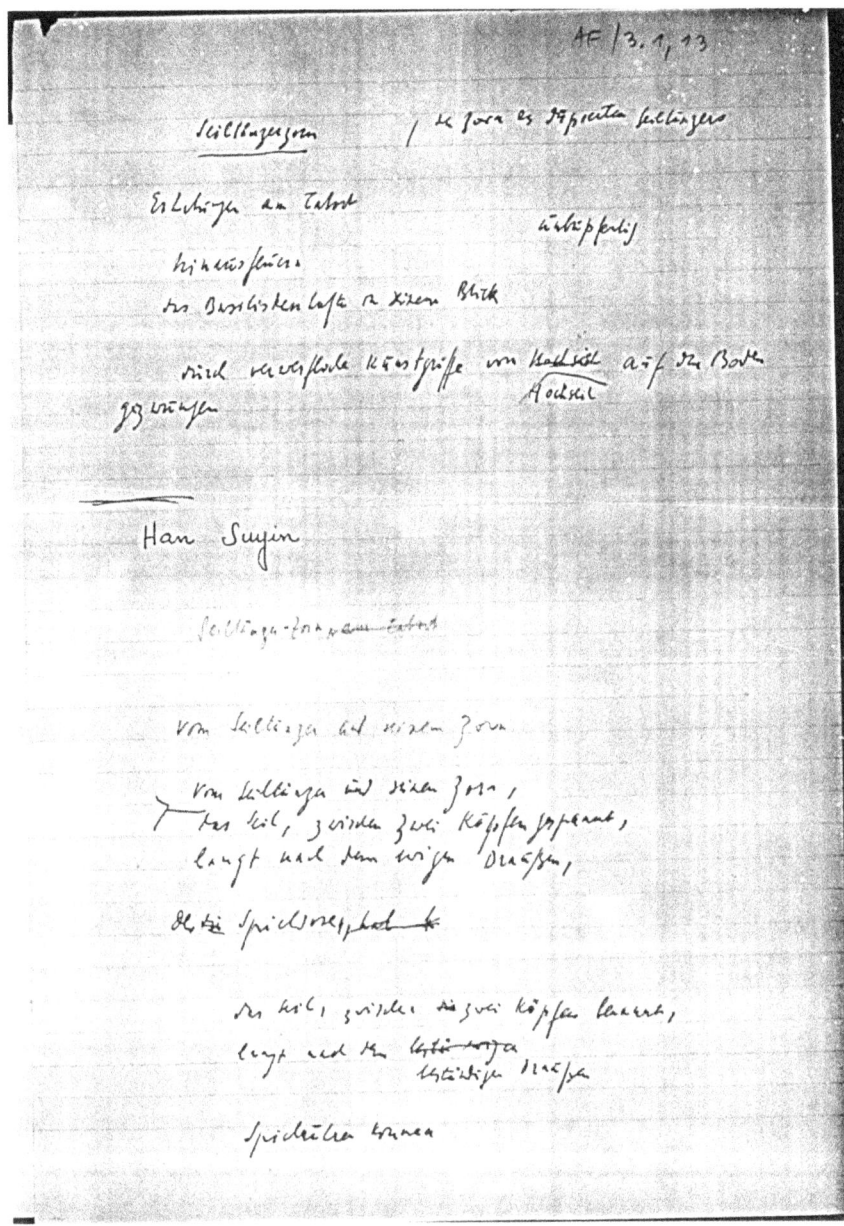

Fig. 1.3. 'Seiltänzerzorn', draft from 'Das Seil'. Black ink, blue ink, and pencil on loose sheet of paper. Ms (Af / 3.1, 13). © Deutsches Literaturarchiv, Marbach a. N.

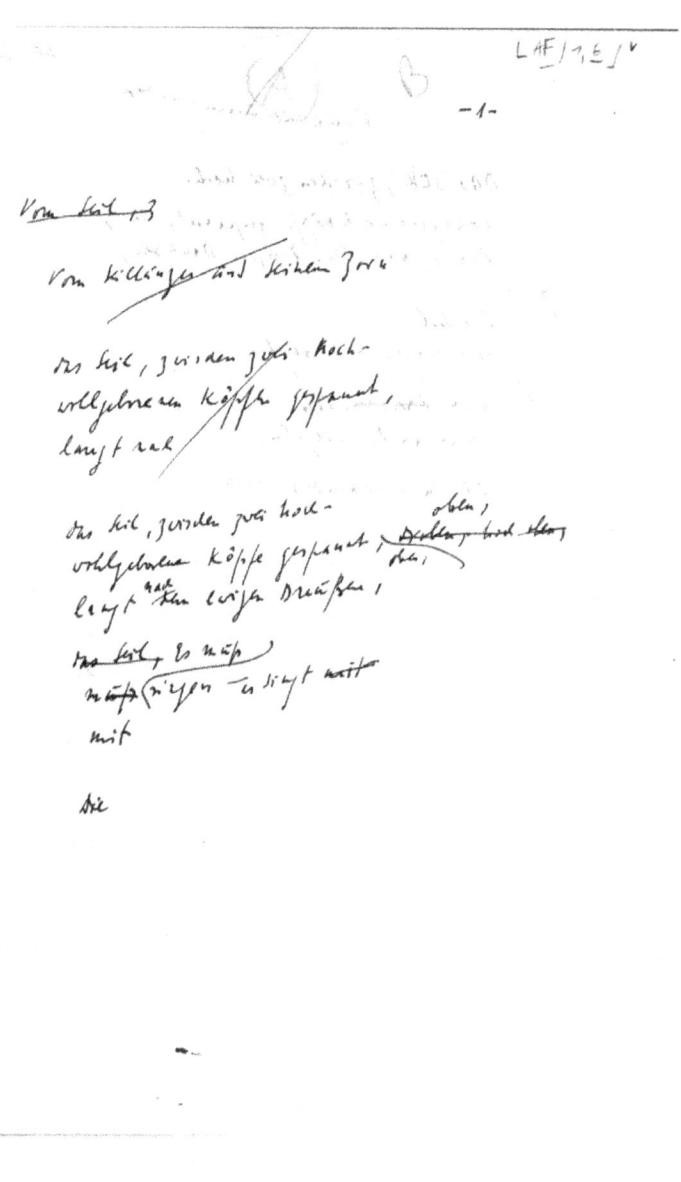

Fig. 1.4. 'Das Seil', draft. Blue ink. Ms (Af / 1,6 / v). © Deutsches Literaturarchiv, Marbach a. N.

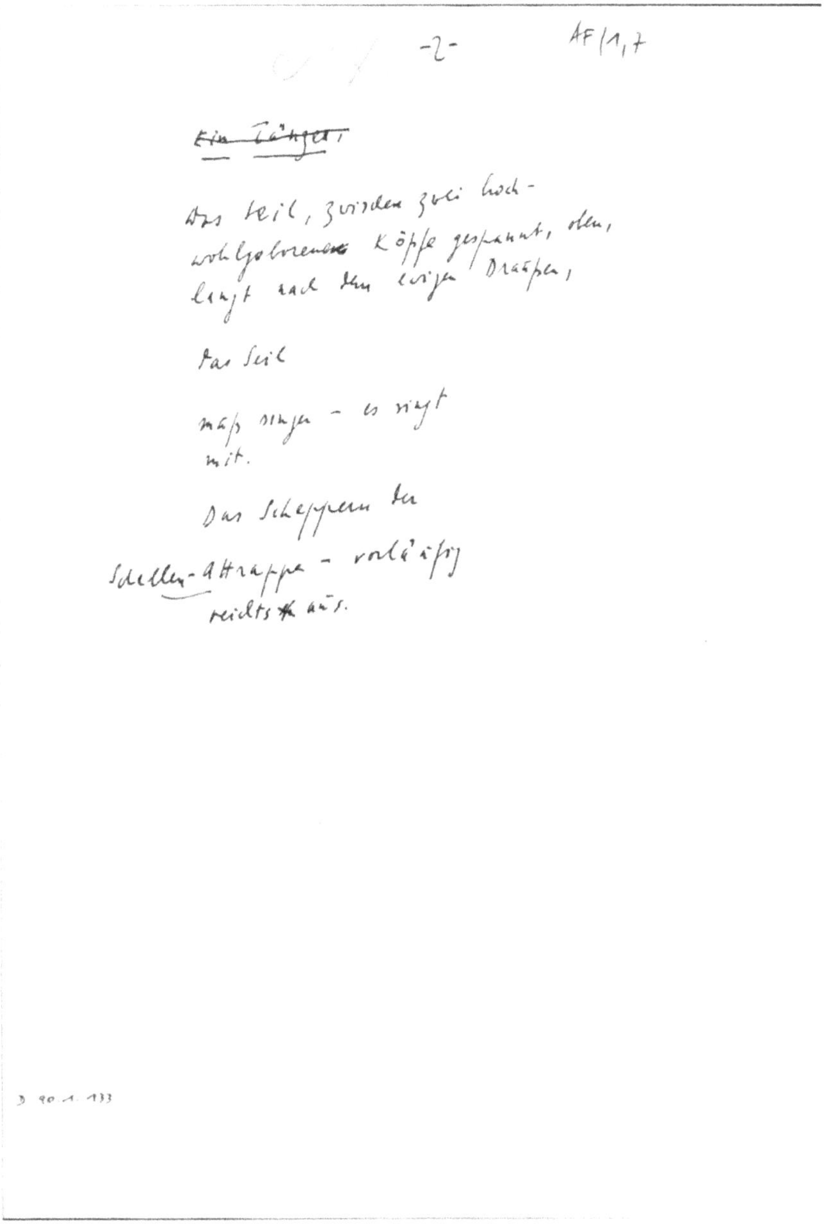

FIG. 1.5. 'Ein Tänzer', draft from 'Das Seil'. Blue ink. Ms (Af / 1,7). © Deutsches Literaturarchiv, Marbach a. N.

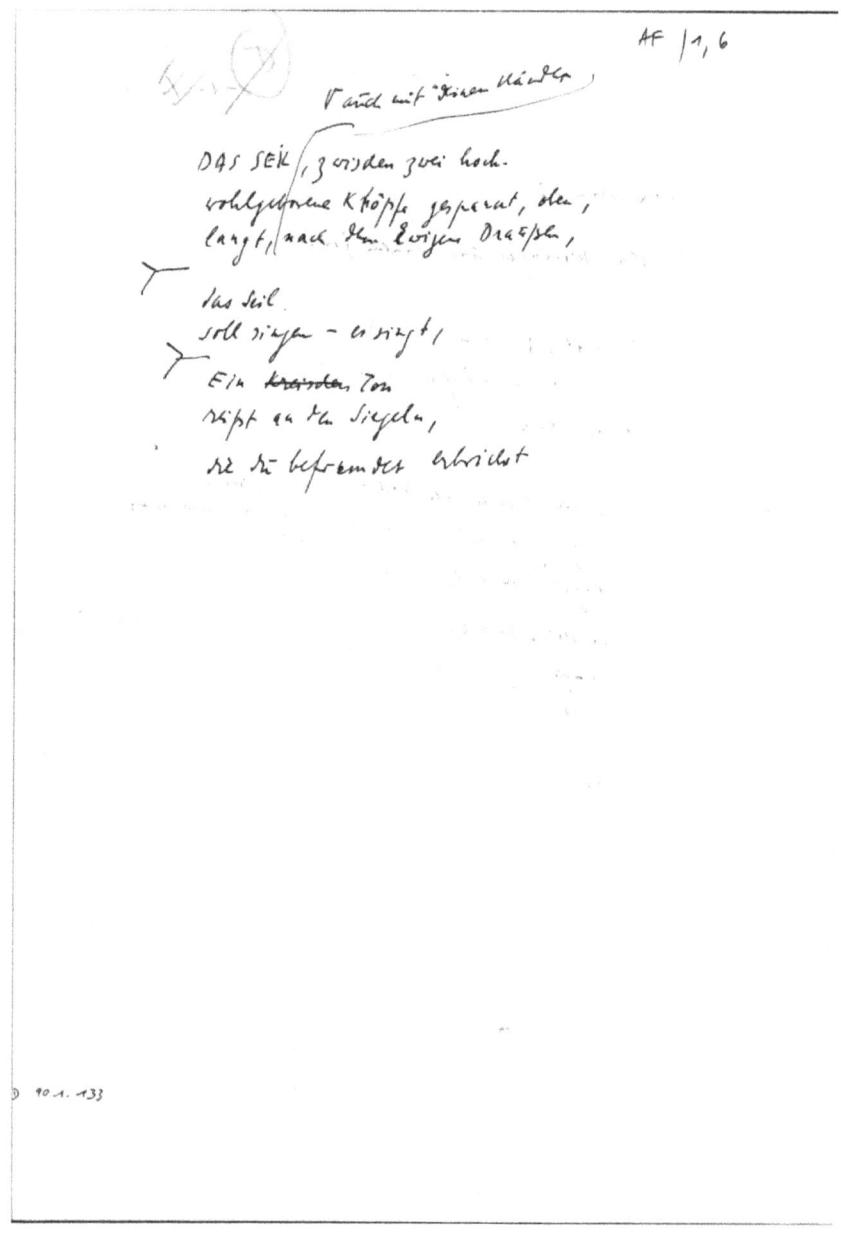

FIG. 1.6. 'Ein Kreischen', draft from 'Das Seil'. Blue ink. Ms (Af / 1,6 r) / D. 90.1.133. © Deutsches Literaturarchiv, Marbach a. N.

twelve-hour process from being realized. Its absence, however, coincides with the machine's disintegration and the Officer's death. If the screech is the function of some material resistance within the apparatus, we can hazard that in genetic criticism, the screech that guarantees the proper functioning of the genetic apparatus is one caused by the presence of the *telos*, of the future end point of the process, which allows the process to continue toward its realization. The screeches in Kafka's machine and in Celan's draft remind us that in a process that proceeds in time, the organizing principle of the *telos* not only operates prospectively, indicating what should occur in the future. It also operates retrospectively. The projection toward the *telos* is also necessarily a retrojection back from the *telos* to the present. The machine requires these contradictory resistances to function 'correctly', just as the apparatus of genetic criticism requires the resisting force of the *telos*. The presence of the screech, in both Kafka's apparatus and Celan's writing machine, therefore assures the correct functioning of the process, Kafka's toward the sentencing and death of the condemned man, and Celan's toward the inscribing and birth of the definitive text.

In the functioning of Kafka's apparatus, there appears to be a causal link between the removal of the Prisoner and the absence of resistance in the machine. The introduction of the Officer coincides with the absence of the screech, the perfect operation of the machine, and its total destruction. A similar replacement is evident in Celan's four drafts. Despite the repeated insertion of the rope-dancer [Seiltänzer] and his rope-dancer-anger [Seiltänzerzorn] in H^{10}, both are crossed out in H^9 ('Of the rope-dancer and his anger'). When the figure of the rope-dancer reappears in H^8 he no longer dances on a rope, but is a simple, earthbound dancer [Ein Tänzer], who is immediately crossed out ('A dancer'). In version H^6, both the rope-dancer and the dancer are absent. The dancer has been definitively removed from the apparatus.

We might speculate that just as the Prisoner is replaced by the Officer, so too, in Celan's texts, the dancer is replaced by one who usually assures the proper operation of the writing machine, namely the author himself. When Roland Barthes and the Structuralists define and describe the death of the author, they do so from the perspective not of unfinished texts, but completed texts. As Barthes puts it: 'the voice loses its origin, the author enters his own death, writing begins'.[134] The death of the author is simple, like opening a hotel room door, entering, and letting it close behind you. What Kafka's story reminds us when set alongside the pre-text is that the death of the author is never as clean, as unified, or as unambiguous as Barthes implies. The notion of genesis, and the practice of genetic and textual criticism in general, reserve space for authorial intention to express itself, as the text traces the movement of writing toward its intended form in the definitive text. The author is not only alive in the pre-text, but in the process of creating, if not procreating. But what a re-examination of the pre-text in the light of Kafka's writing machine demonstrates, is that the death of the author is not a *telos* that exists at some close point in the future. There will be moments when the author, much like the Officer in the story, is forced to clamber into his own writing machine and die unceremoniously. And he must realize this action not once over the course of the 'genesis' of the work of art, but at every moment that he or she leaves a deposit of ink, lead, or graphite on the page.

The pre-text therefore represents an infinite series of suicidal entries into the machine, multiple abdications of authority. The term 'genetic' process is not only a misleading way of describing what might better be described as a thanatic process, but this thanatic process is constantly being re-played in each trace of text. The so-called genetic or textual process, the genesis, or the process of composition, is not a single unified movement of creativity. It might more accurately be seen as a process of disintegration and auto-destruction. The authority of the author that has been found to be unsustainable in the definitive text is equally unsustainable in the pre-text. Although genetic criticism aims to protect the intention of the author until such point that the text is able to exist by itself, authority and intention are found to operate in much more sporadic and unpredictable ways throughout the pre-text. There is not one single genetic process. There are instead multiple and contradictory thanatic processes.

To read in the pre-text is, to quote François Roustang, to witness a horror: 'A reading that does not reach the point of horror cannot even begin to understand the text's source [...] The act of reading must itself pass through the deadly suffering in which the author originally found the strength to create. Nothing is closer to artistic creation than the moment of anguish from which the work's production must originate. The reader must endure this same anguish if he is to arrive at the work's real principle'.[135] The notions of horror, deadly suffering, and anguish perhaps provide more accurate metaphors with which to explore the pre-text, and which, at the very least, allow us to suspend the unrelenting genetic fallacy.

Allegories of Annotating

A text often referenced in discussions of the purpose and stakes of genetic criticism is Edgar Allan Poe's short story, 'The Purloined Letter' (1844). In their attempts to find the letter stolen from the queen by the minister, the Parisian police search every inch of the minister's apartment, without success. The armchair detective Dupin locates the letter by looking where letters are usually found, namely in the letter rack. Paul de Man reads the story as exemplary of the distinctions between the exactitude of philology and the truth of aesthetic intuition. Barbara Johnson repositions this critique of philological exactitude when she notes that the question is not one of the benefits of precision or imprecision, but how to 'break through preconceived notions of meaning in order to encounter unexpected otherness'.[136] When Almuth Grésillon reads the same story from the perspective of genetic criticism, she notes that the desired object is a manuscript letter. She focuses less on the philological acumen of the police, than on the uncanny talents of the minister who, like a genetic scholar, is both a 'poet and mathematician'.[137] His skill at concealing the letter in the open is equaled only by that of Dupin, whose ability to find the unconcealed letter makes the short story a 'perfect parable of the geneticist'.[138]

Grésillon's appeal to the notion of a 'perfect parable' not only gives expression to her evident excitement at seeing how Dupin's approach can be mapped, allegorically, onto the operations of the geneticist. It also, somewhat paradoxically, sees her revert to the norm of society's preference for completed texts when seeking to explain and promote the work of genetic criticism. The parable is perfect, that is, complete and fully satisfying, a sensation not often experienced in the unfinished, imperfect, and incomplete realm of the pre-text. In this final section, I consider parts of the pre-text that are so remote they tend not to be included in edited and published reproductions of the pre-text. These are annotations — both verbal and non-verbal — often inscribed in other published texts by the author as reader, and which are examples of what Debray-Genette calls 'exogenesis'.[139] They constitute an extremity of the pre-text that, in the context of 'The Purloined Letter', Dupin would have encountered only through the meticulous philological labor of the Parisian police.

I am interested in understanding how the act of reading is changed by the scriptural activity of previous readers. As readers in these extreme margins of the pre-text, we are not concerned with trying to re-create the historical process of the author reading. As Janice Radway pointed out in a lecture given in 1994, the process of reading is largely irrecoverable, being 'at once corporeal and ethereal, private and intersubjective'.[140] Any marginal traces left by a reader constitute at best fragments of an encounter with the text at a given moment in time, and cannot be used for historical reconstruction. I am also not interested in assembling a 'microhistory' to characterize Celan's personal reading habits, as it is likely that his particularities and idiosyncrasies — to the extent that they can be ascertained — will teach us little about reading in the pre-text in general. Instead, I suggest that something like a parable of annotation (although perhaps not a perfect one) can be identified in the interplay between a passage from a novel read by Celan and Celan's annotation of the passage.

An inspection of Celan's library at the German Literature Archive in Marbach am Neckar reveals that on 6 April 1966, the same day that Celan composed the first version of 'The Rope', he inscribed the date on the final page of a German translation of Joseph Conrad's *The Secret Agent*.[141] *The Secret Agent* is set in 1886 and was inspired by the late nineteenth-century rise of anarchism, and the ideologically motivated bomb attacks by proto-terrorists such as Auguste Vaillant — who tossed a home-made nail bomb into the lower house of the French Parliament in December 1893 — and Émile Henry's copycat attack on the Café Terminus the following February.[142] Two days later, Martial Bourdin died when chemical explosives he was carrying detonated outside the Royal Observatory in Greenwich Park. It is to events such as these that Mallarmé will refer in his lecture 'Music and Letters' when he travels to Oxford and Cambridge in early March of the same year and evokes 'the devices, whose explosion illuminates parliaments with a summary glow, but also cripple'.[143]

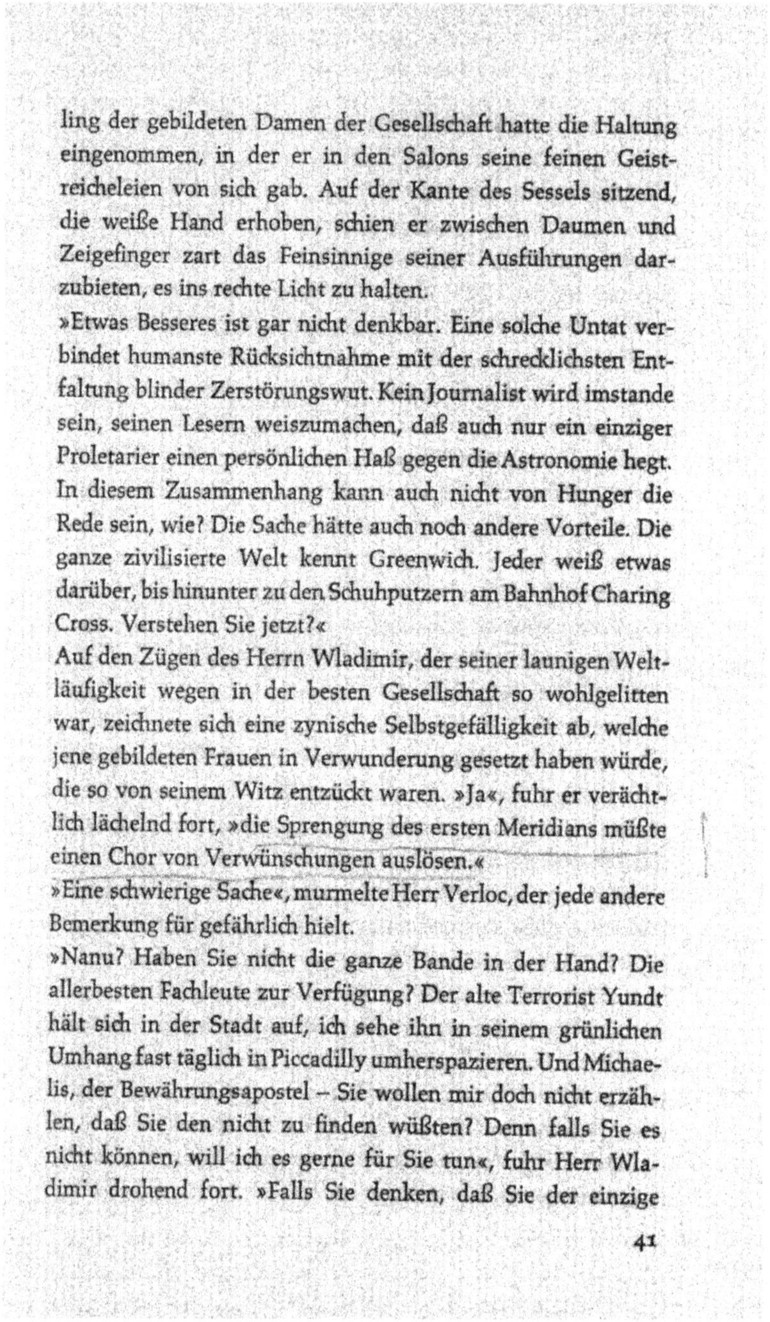

ling der gebildeten Damen der Gesellschaft hatte die Haltung eingenommen, in der er in den Salons seine feinen Geistreicheleien von sich gab. Auf der Kante des Sessels sitzend, die weiße Hand erhoben, schien er zwischen Daumen und Zeigefinger zart das Feinsinnige seiner Ausführungen darzubieten, es ins rechte Licht zu halten.

»Etwas Besseres ist gar nicht denkbar. Eine solche Untat verbindet humanste Rücksichtnahme mit der schrecklichsten Entfaltung blinder Zerstörungswut. Kein Journalist wird imstande sein, seinen Lesern weiszumachen, daß auch nur ein einziger Proletarier einen persönlichen Haß gegen die Astronomie hegt. In diesem Zusammenhang kann auch nicht von Hunger die Rede sein, wie? Die Sache hätte auch noch andere Vorteile. Die ganze zivilisierte Welt kennt Greenwich. Jeder weiß etwas darüber, bis hinunter zu den Schuhputzern am Bahnhof Charing Cross. Verstehen Sie jetzt?«

Auf den Zügen des Herrn Wladimir, der seiner launigen Weltläufigkeit wegen in der besten Gesellschaft so wohlgelitten war, zeichnete sich eine zynische Selbstgefälligkeit ab, welche jene gebildeten Frauen in Verwunderung gesetzt haben würde, die so von seinem Witz entzückt waren. »Ja«, fuhr er verächtlich lächelnd fort, »die Sprengung des ersten Meridians müßte einen Chor von Verwünschungen auslösen.«

»Eine schwierige Sache«, murmelte Herr Verloc, der jede andere Bemerkung für gefährlich hielt.

»Nanu? Haben Sie nicht die ganze Bande in der Hand? Die allerbesten Fachleute zur Verfügung? Der alte Terrorist Yundt hält sich in der Stadt auf, ich sehe ihn in seinem grünlichen Umhang fast täglich in Piccadilly umherspazieren. Und Michaelis, der Bewährungsapostel – Sie wollen mir doch nicht erzählen, daß Sie den nicht zu finden wüßten? Denn falls Sie es nicht können, will ich es gerne für Sie tun«, fuhr Herr Wladimir drohend fort. »Falls Sie denken, daß Sie der einzige

41

FIG. 1.7. '... die Sprengung des ersten Meridians...', Conrad, *Der Geheimagent*, p. 41. Pencil.
© Deutsches Literaturarchiv, Marbach a. N.

The main event in the novel is the premature explosion of a bomb by the perimeter wall of the Greenwich Observatory, which kills Stevie, a mentally retarded adolescent, given the task of planting the device by his brother-in-law, the anarchist and secret agent Adolf Verloc. Stevie's unintentional suicide bombing leaves only a large crack in the outer wall of the Observatory, but it is dubbed 'the blowing up of the first meridian'[144] by Mr. Vladimir, another anarchist. Given the title by which his October 1960 Büchner Prize speech is known, it is perhaps not surprising that, in his reading of the German translation, Celan underscores this line and inscribes a short vertical line in the margin.[145] The prime meridian, established at Greenwich in 1851, was an indication of the political might of the world's most powerful empire, able to chart the globe — spatially and temporally — through the definition of an imaginary line where east meets west. 'Go for the first meridian', Mr. Vladimir urges Verloc, 'You don't know the middle classes as well as I do. Their sensibilities are jaded. The first meridian. Nothing better, and nothing easier, I should think'.[146] The power structure of the textual realm has been organized in a similarly arbitrary way, such that an imaginary and omnipotent line has now long divided text from pre-text, authorized work from unauthorized text, and published from unpublished traces.

Chief Inspector Heat of the Special Crimes section — in charge of investigating the explosion — is not interested in the large crack in the Observatory wall, nor in the symbolic significance the bomb attack might have. He is instead concerned with seeing if the splattered remains of Stevie's crippled body that have been shoveled up and removed to the morgue can tell him anything about the identity of those responsible for the attack. Among the mix of Stevie's flesh, Greenwich gravel, and the 'strips and bits of bright tin'[147] of the homemade bomb on display, the Chief Inspector comes across a square piece of blue calico, stitched carefully on the underside of the lapel of the bomber's overcoat with an address written on it in purple marking ink. This label is a crucial piece of evidence. It identifies the pornographic shop from which the Verloc family earn their living, and over which they live, and so leads straight to the supposed perpetrators. Instead of revealing this key piece of evidence to the Assistant Commissioner, Chief Inspector Heat, keen to solve the case alone, initially conceals the existence of the label. He is forced to relinquish it in the course of a long conversation with his superior.

Celan reads and annotates the account of this conversation, lasting around thirty pages.[148] It is this passage that contains the textual germs of what will become 'The Rope'. In the course of the conversation, the Chief Inspector mentally pursues an elaborate allegory to describe the professional humiliation to which he is subjected, in which he imagines himself as a tightrope artist forced down from the high-wire of professional excellence by the Assistant Commissioner. Below are five extracts from Conrad's narrative. Celan marks three of the five occasions where the noun 'Seil' [rope] appears, on two occasions in the form of compound nouns 'high-rope' [Hochseil] (not present in the original English) and 'rope-dancer' [Seiltänzer]. He makes almost no other annotations in the passage:

> He felt at the moment like a tight-rope artist might feel if suddenly, in the

middle of the performance, the manager of the Music Hall were to rush out of the proper managerial seclusion and begin to shake the rope. [Er fühlte sich in diesem Augenblick wie ein Seiltänzer, der es erleben muß, daß während seines Auftrittes der Direktor aus der Zurückgezogenheit seines Büros herausstürzt, um am Seil zu rütteln].[149]

The indignation of a betrayed tight-rope performer was strong within him [In diesem brannte <u>der Zorn des düpierten Seiltänzers</u>]. In his pride of a trusted servant he was affected by the assurance that the rope was not shaken for the purpose of breaking his neck, as by an exhibition of impudence. As if anybody were afraid! Assistant Commissioners come and go, but a valuable Chief Inspector is not an ephemeral office phenomenon. He was not afraid of getting a broken neck. To have his performance spoiled was more than enough to account for the glow of honest indignation.[150]

As if in provoking answer to that thought, something like the ghost of an amiable smile passed on the lips of the Assistant Commissioner. His manner was easy and businesslike while he persisted in administering another shake to the tight rope [Lässig und kühl machte er sich daran, noch einmal <u>am Seil zu rütteln</u>]. "Let us come now to what you have discovered on the spot, Chief Inspector", he said.[151]

The Chief Inspector, who had made up his mind to jump off the rope, came to the ground with a gloomy frankness. [Der Hauptinspektor hatte sich entschlossen, endgültig das Seil zu verlassen und landete auf der Erde, wo er sich umdüstert, aber rückhaltlos vernehmen ließ].[152]

The Chief Inspector, driven down to the ground by unfair artifices, had elected to walk the path of unreserved openness [Der Hauptinspektor, durch verwerfliche Kunstgriffe <u>vom Hochseil</u> auf den Boden gezwungen, hatte beschlossen, den Pfad der Aufrichtigkeit zu betreten].[153]

Behind the initial allegory imagined by the Chief Inspector, who projects himself as a tight-rope artist disturbed in his high art of detection by the office-bound Music Hall manager (the Assistant Commissioner), another allegory — an allegory of the allegory — can be perceived, when we consider Celan's annotation of the text. When Derrida examines the relationship of annotations to the primary text, he perceives the relationship of authority between them as being a theologico-political one, much as was the case in the competing definitive versions earlier in this chapter. The 'absolute model of a text' requires the text to be 'absolutely performative, self-sufficient, self-interpretative, initial, and inaugural, and poetic in the strong sense of the word', a 'divine speech act or divine writing'.[154] Both the definitive text and the stock character of detective novels, the Chief Inspector, are institutions. As Heat puts it in his memorable and ungainly protest: 'but a valuable Chief Inspector is not an ephemeral office phenomenon'.[155] As institutions, they do not expect to have to justify their presence nor to explain the value that they bring. As Certeau explains, the social and technical functioning of contemporary culture hierarchizes the activities of reading and writing: 'To write is to produce text; to read is to receive it from someone else without putting one's own mark on it, without remaking it'.[156] The Chief Inspector's ideal of uninterrupted solo performance precisely echoes the desire of Conrad's work as definitive text. In both cases, the reader or spectator is expected to attend to the gravity and death-defying acrobatics of the performance, just as Elena Cornalba, whom Mallarmé sees dance in 1886 — from his 'proper seclusion' it should be noted — appears to be 'called into the air, to float there'.[157]

Here, though, just as the Chief Inspector is forced down from his allegorical self-projection by his superior shaking at the rope, so too the integrity of the text has been disturbed by Celan's act of annotation. The 'law' of the text necessarily means that, as Derrida puts it, 'all deceptions, transgressions, and subversions are possible'.[158] When Celan underscores parts of the text, the definitive nature of the text is questioned, and its immaterial eternal present is punctured by the historical present of having been read. An annotation is particularly threatening not only because it demonstrates the inadequacy of the text itself, which in some sense requires and calls for the annotation, but because the annotation allows itself a more protean mode of expression than the text can comprehend. Derrida speaks of a 'pragmatics of annotation',[159] because the annotation is not limited to the linguistic, rhetorical, or semantic norms of the text, but pragmatically adopts any mode of expression available to it. Anne Boleyn reportedly annotated Tyndale's *Obedience of a Christian Man* with her fingernail, leaving the imprint of her passage, but declining to leave a material trace or deposit upon the page. Brayman Hackel claims that this 'inkless marking' is evidence of her ambivalence toward the act of annotation.[160] Celan shares no such scruple, and inscribes his non-verbal annotations here in ink, but also elsewhere in pencil and on occasion with his fingernail. Virginia Woolf, in an essay that remained unpublished during her lifetime, objects to just this kind of permanent intervention in the work, when she writes: 'this anonymous commentator must scrawl his O, or his Pooh, or his Beautiful upon the unresisting sheet, as though the author received this mark upon his flesh'.[161] Although Woolf sees the annotation as a personal injury to the author himself, it is more appropriate to see the annotation as challenging the integrity of the text. Conrad describes the manager shaking the rope with characteristic irony as 'unfair artifices', which Danehl renders in German as 'reprehensible manipulations' [verwerfliche Kunstgriffe]. When Celan copies this passage into a notebook, he incorrectly transcribes 'verwerfliche' [reprehensible] as 'verzweifelte' [desperate].[162] Although we should probably not read too much into this error, it curiously sheds light not only on the anxiety experienced by the text whose integrity has been questioned, but on the desperation of the annotator, of the reader who interferes in the operation of the text, and of the manager who tugs at the rope.

I suggest that the act of shaking can be mapped onto the act of annotation in such way as to draw our attention to elements of annotation that would otherwise remain obscure but which are essential for any reader who wishes to explore this part of the pre-text. The verb used by Conrad's translator to translate 'shake' is 'rütteln'. 'Rütteln' also happens to be the verb used by Kafka's narrator to describe the Prisoner's delight as he shakes in the machine on learning of his imminent release.[163] Shaking is an integral movement of Kafka's writing machine, as the

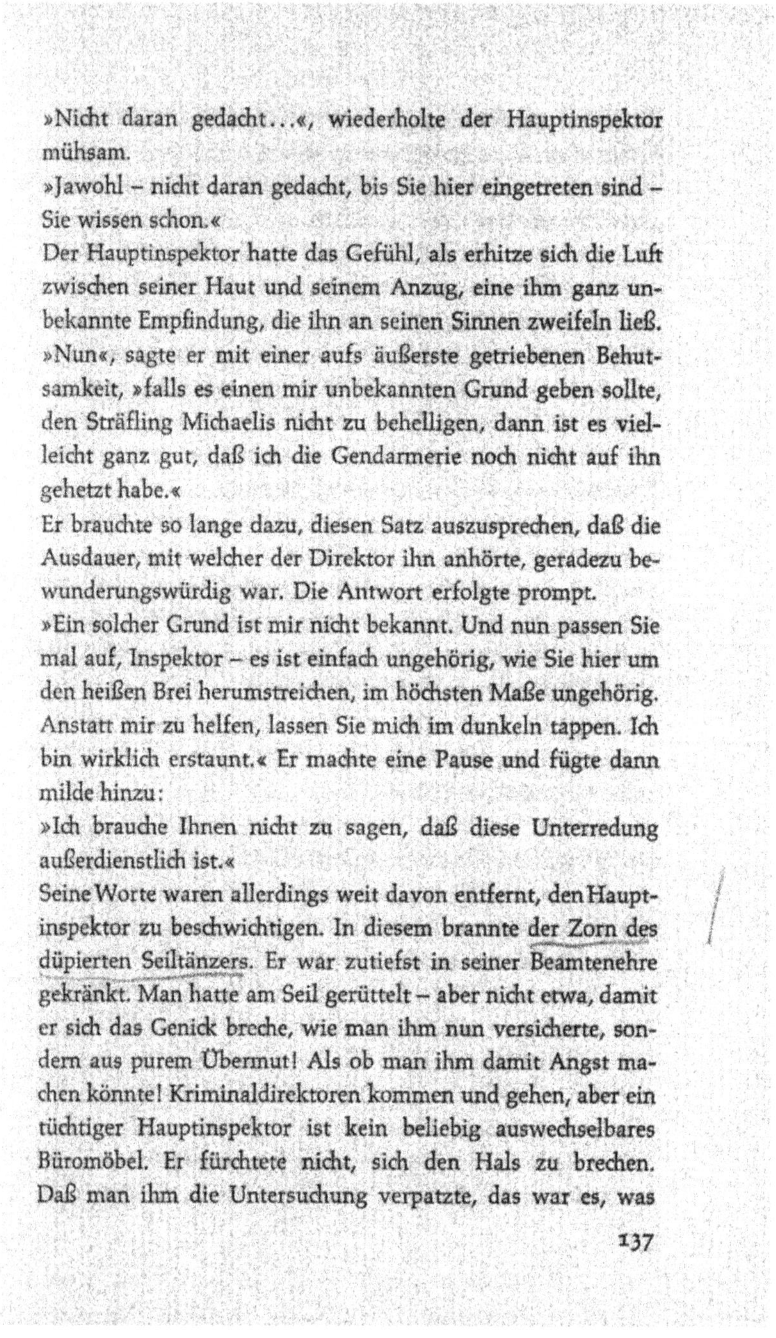

»Nicht daran gedacht...«, wiederholte der Hauptinspektor mühsam.
»Jawohl – nicht daran gedacht, bis Sie hier eingetreten sind – Sie wissen schon.«
Der Hauptinspektor hatte das Gefühl, als erhitze sich die Luft zwischen seiner Haut und seinem Anzug, eine ihm ganz unbekannte Empfindung, die ihn an seinen Sinnen zweifeln ließ.
»Nun«, sagte er mit einer aufs äußerste getriebenen Behutsamkeit, »falls es einen mir unbekannten Grund geben sollte, den Sträfling Michaelis nicht zu behelligen, dann ist es vielleicht ganz gut, daß ich die Gendarmerie noch nicht auf ihn gehetzt habe.«
Er brauchte so lange dazu, diesen Satz auszusprechen, daß die Ausdauer, mit welcher der Direktor ihn anhörte, geradezu bewunderungswürdig war. Die Antwort erfolgte prompt.
»Ein solcher Grund ist mir nicht bekannt. Und nun passen Sie mal auf, Inspektor – es ist einfach ungehörig, wie Sie hier um den heißen Brei herumstreichen, im höchsten Maße ungehörig. Anstatt mir zu helfen, lassen Sie mich im dunkeln tappen. Ich bin wirklich erstaunt.« Er machte eine Pause und fügte dann milde hinzu:
»Ich brauche Ihnen nicht zu sagen, daß diese Unterredung außerdienstlich ist.«
Seine Worte waren allerdings weit davon entfernt, den Hauptinspektor zu beschwichtigen. In diesem brannte der Zorn des düpierten Seiltänzers. Er war zutiefst in seiner Beamtenehre gekränkt. Man hatte am Seil gerüttelt – aber nicht etwa, damit er sich das Genick breche, wie man ihm nun versicherte, sondern aus purem Übermut! Als ob man ihm damit Angst machen könnte! Kriminaldirektoren kommen und gehen, aber ein tüchtiger Hauptinspektor ist kein beliebig auswechselbares Büromöbel. Er fürchtete nicht, sich den Hals zu brechen. Daß man ihm die Untersuchung verpatzte, das war es, was

137

Fig. 1.8. '... der Zorn des düpierten Seiltänzers', Conrad, *Der Geheimagent*, p. 137. Pencil. © Deutsches Literaturarchiv, Marbach a. N.

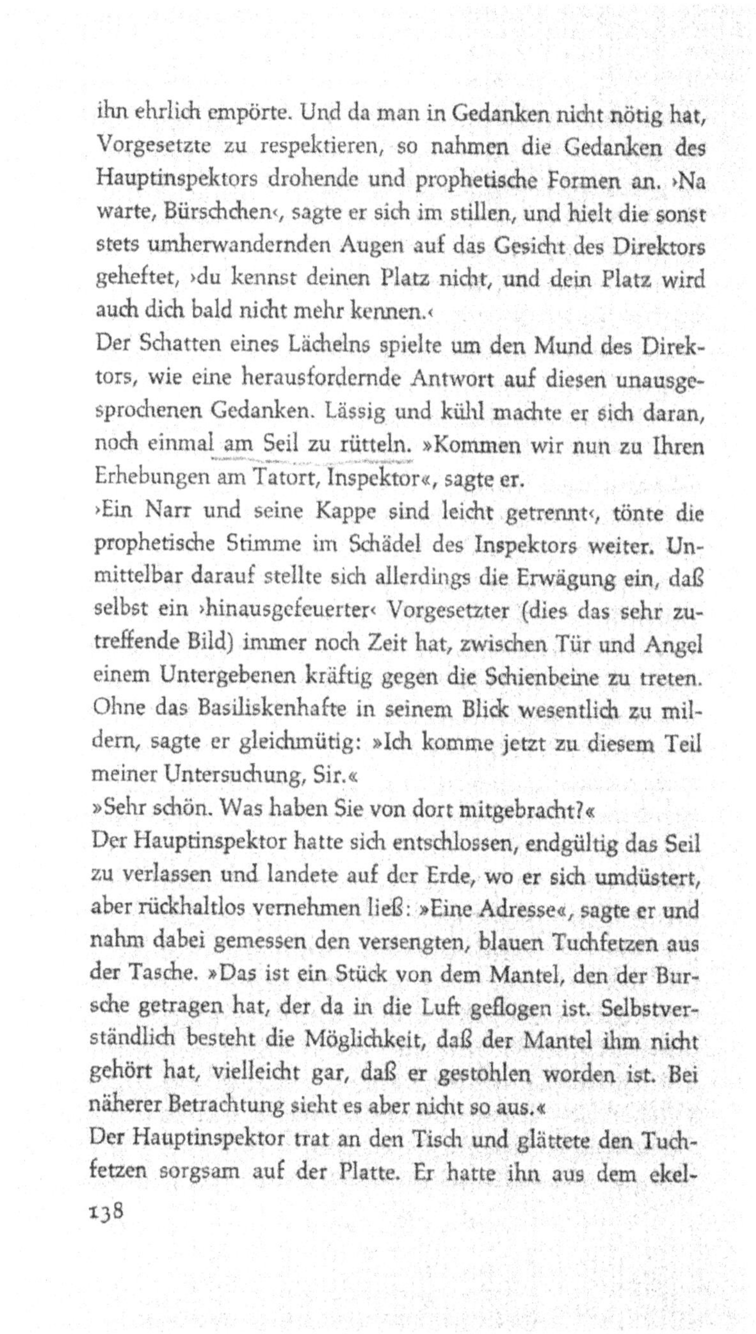

ihn ehrlich empörte. Und da man in Gedanken nicht nötig hat, Vorgesetzte zu respektieren, so nahmen die Gedanken des Hauptinspektors drohende und prophetische Formen an. ›Na warte, Bürschchen‹, sagte er sich im stillen, und hielt die sonst stets umherwandernden Augen auf das Gesicht des Direktors geheftet, ›du kennst deinen Platz nicht, und dein Platz wird auch dich bald nicht mehr kennen.‹
Der Schatten eines Lächelns spielte um den Mund des Direktors, wie eine herausfordernde Antwort auf diesen unausgesprochenen Gedanken. Lässig und kühl machte er sich daran, noch einmal am Seil zu rütteln. »Kommen wir nun zu Ihren Erhebungen am Tatort, Inspektor«, sagte er.
›Ein Narr und seine Kappe sind leicht getrennt‹, tönte die prophetische Stimme im Schädel des Inspektors weiter. Unmittelbar darauf stellte sich allerdings die Erwägung ein, daß selbst ein ›hinausgefeuerter‹ Vorgesetzter (dies das sehr zutreffende Bild) immer noch Zeit hat, zwischen Tür und Angel einem Untergebenen kräftig gegen die Schienbeine zu treten. Ohne das Basiliskenhafte in seinem Blick wesentlich zu mildern, sagte er gleichmütig: »Ich komme jetzt zu diesem Teil meiner Untersuchung, Sir.«
»Sehr schön. Was haben Sie von dort mitgebracht?«
Der Hauptinspektor hatte sich entschlossen, endgültig das Seil zu verlassen und landete auf der Erde, wo er sich umdüstert, aber rückhaltlos vernehmen ließ: »Eine Adresse«, sagte er und nahm dabei gemessen den versengten, blauen Tuchfetzen aus der Tasche. »Das ist ein Stück von dem Mantel, den der Bursche getragen hat, der da in die Luft geflogen ist. Selbstverständlich besteht die Möglichkeit, daß der Mantel ihm nicht gehört hat, vielleicht gar, daß er gestohlen worden ist. Bei näherer Betrachtung sieht es aber nicht so aus.«
Der Hauptinspektor trat an den Tisch und glättete den Tuchfetzen sorgsam auf der Platte. Er hatte ihn aus dem ekel-
138

FIG. 1.9. '... noch einmal am Seil zu rütteln', Conrad, *Der Geheimagent*, p. 138. Pencil. © Deutsches Literaturarchiv, Marbach a. N.

'bed' moves simultaneously up and down and from side to side in concert with the 'inscriber' and the 'harrow'.[104] Readers of manuscripts will be particularly aware that the inscribing hand not only moves to and fro across the page, but appears to shake as it writes. In his preface to Flaubert's workbooks, Biasi describes the author's handwriting as 'jerky, often difficult to decipher, sometimes "seismographic"'.[165] He even goes so far as to claim that 'in certain places one can unmistakably recognize the shaking of the carriage going over cobblestones'.[166]

That Celan's hand was shakier and less assured in its movements than usual when writing *Eingedunkelt* is clear from the relatively high number of letters and words that cannot be deciphered with certainty. Jenny suggests that we can follow these seismographic traces to 'return to that very shaking much as it was lived in the moment of a thought' and that such a trace can be redynamized 'so as to relive the event'.[167] In drawing attention to the shaking hand of the annotator, though, I am less interested in seeking to resurrect the physiological condition of the historical author at a given point in time, than in drawing the attention of anyone seeking to read annotations in their exploration of the pre-text to the inherent violence of this act. Although the Assistant Commissioner's shake at the rope may seem half-playful and mostly harmless, the etymological tenor of the verb 'rütteln' betrays its true character. It shares an Old High German root with 'reuten', 'roden' [both 'to grub up'] and 'Raub' ['robbery' or 'rape'], namely 'riuten < *riutjan', which is to make land arable by grubbing up trees and ripping out rootstocks.[168] The shake at the rope and the annotation both appear to be banal and unthreatening gestures, but they conceal a violence that uproots and deterritorializes.

A reader of annotations will also have to bear in mind that reading itself is a form of shaking, and that it is therefore imbricated in the act of writing, and vice versa. Although society has motives for maintaining reading and writing as discrete activities — as Certeau pointed out above — an examination of annotation reveals that writing and reading exist continuously alongside each other. This is made particularly evident when we note how shaking defines reading as well as writing. Certeau compares reading to undertaking an 'ephemeral dance' across textual space, 'an illicit, even secretive reinvention of the text — reading as resistance.'[169] He justifies this bold analogy by suggesting a gradual historical movement of reading. The movement of reading moves from the vagabondage of a body across space, to the swaying or shuckling of reading Jews, to 'the murmur of a vocal articulation' and 'the movement of a muscular manducation', to our current silent mode of reading, in which the movement of the body has withdrawn into the movement of the eyes, as they scan the page from side to side, and from top to bottom.[170]

The act of annotation should be understood in the context of this shift in reading toward the 'mobility of the eye'.[171] Annotation in the era of silent reading is the residue of the reading body that once moved in space or swayed, and of the reading mouth that once voiced the words it read. It is the trace of the 'cry of emotion' that Georges Bataille unexpectedly hears when he copies, and appropriates, a line of verse from René Char: 'I see that writing, beyond being a deliberate enterprise, and as such, down-to-earth, deprived of wings, can suddenly, discreetly, be broken and become nothing more than a cry of emotion'.[172] The modern reader does not read aloud, and Bataille's cry is not so much a sound as a textual trace that cannot be vocalized. It is with just this sort of trace that any reader of the pre-text will be familiar. More essentially than the average modern reader of literature, the reader of the pre-text is not only a silent reader, but one who has been condemned to silence. How could a reader ever hope to give voice to a 'screech'? The pre-text includes words that have been crossed out, insertions that defy linear reading in time, non-verbal signs for which there are no established vocalizations, and underlinings and other marks in other texts for which there are no vocal equivalents. This is not to say that verbalization will never be possible in the pre-text, but that — as readers used to reading institutional texts sanctioned for public consumption — this is still an element of the pre-text that resists our conventional understanding of what language and literature are, and what they do. It is through annotation that the traditional distinctions of reading and writing become indistinguishable from one another. To annotate a definitive text is to introduce it into the uncertain and ambiguous realm of the pre-text, to deterritorialize it, and to render foreign and strange what was for so long familiar and institutional.

Learning to Read in the Pre-Text

The pre-text has become an established feature of contemporary literary studies. Brought into being, developed, and justified through the combined labors of textual and genetic criticism, it constitutes a subsection of literature. It is a subsection not only in the sense that it is one part of the many parts that make up literature, but that it is considered an inferior part, a hinterland which subtends all of literature — a part of the sous-oeuvre. It is that upon which literature and the study of literature depend. But it is also that part of literature that is least known for its unique ways of creating meaning. The pre-text is most often perceived as a subsidiary of authorized, completed, and published literature, which can be exploited as and when the study of literature requires its alternative modes of expression. For instance, as a source of variants, it provides alternative formulations of a definitive part of the text, loosening the form of the definitive text, and allowing for readings that might otherwise not be possible. In the study of modern poetry — and particularly in the study of poetry as difficult and as laconic as Celan's frequently is — the opportunity to consult additional and related material can afford the small distance from the text required for the text to appear to breathe, and for reading to become possible.

By exploring three distinct features of the pre-textual landscape — the definitive version, the notion of genesis, and non-verbal marginalia — this chapter aims to establish some of the challenges that any poetics of the pre-text will have to negotiate, if the pre-text is to be read on its own terms and not according to modes of reading that have been developed in engagement with the completed text. The notions that have underpinned and structured the presentation of the pre-text — notions of consciousness, classification, progress, visibility, and readability — are unknown or imperfectly known in the pre-text. The reader of the pre-text will therefore initially be required to accept genetic and textual criticism's publication of the pre-text. But he or she should then feel free to interrupt and suspend this editorial program, which presents fragments of text so as to highlight the movement of writing toward the completed work. The reader of the pre-text can afford to be more creative and subversive in his or her approach to reading. He or she is not required to account for the coherence of the totality of fragments, but is free to realize small, independent acts of reading. It is these acts of free-reading — of soloing — that will best demonstrate the ways in which the pre-text remains a domain of excess and danger, of darkness, unpredictability, and un-readability.

Textual and genetic critics have been reluctant to acknowledge the potentially revolutionary impact that accessibility to the pre-text might have on reading. Bushell acknowledges that 'the relation of the reader to textual process is of a different order than that of the reader to the completed text',[173] but does not explain how this difference might be used to transform the ways we read literature more broadly. Jenny hints at a 'metamorphosis of reading', saying that the 'opening of the book' by genetic criticism 'does not leave reading untouched'.[174] But he perceives the possibilities for reading in the pre-text as severely restricted and restrained. It can exist only 'through partial syntheses and provisional punctuation', whereas reading is usually performed 'through the closure of signifying sequences'.[175] Instead of offering a text to be read, Jenny perceives the pre-text as offering a manifestation of the real and specifically of 'archival reality':[176] 'we are invited less to decipher documents than to participate in the experience of a genesis'.[177] Biasi, in his edition of Flaubert's notebooks, also perceives the pre-text as a locus of experience rather than reading, in which we are able to witness 'nothing more or less than the daily life of the '*homme-plume*' [man-as-pen].[178]

The cartoon-like association that the idea of the 'man-as-pen' evokes is not irrelevant, because both Jenny and Biasi appear to conceive of the pre-text as offering something akin to an historical ride in an intellectual theme park, in which the thought processes of a long dead literary giant — and nothing less than the 'secret of creation'[179] — can appear to be brought back to life. By privileging the fetish of the writer as thinking and inscribing man, a specter brought back from the dead through traces of text, they both overlook another more pressing instance of the 'real', the 'real' of the reader who now reads in the 'mess' of the pre-text. Instead of denying reading to the pre-text — by demonstrating how a conception of reading that has been forged through the social, cultural, and intellectual habit of reading completed texts is ill-suited to the pre-text — we need to learn how to read in the pre-text. This will mean thinking of reading as a mode of enquiry and investigation, rather than as a tool of consolidation and confirmation of what is already known. Learning to read in the pre-text is an invitation to re-examine what we do when we read, to read critically, and to thereby re-assess the judgments we make without thinking, and upon which we establish our perspectives and construct our opinions. The invitation to learn how to read in the pre-text is an invitation to radically rethink the purpose and potential of literature.

Notes to Chapter 1

1. Paul Celan, *Der Meridian. Endfassung — Vorstufen — Materialien*, ed. by Bernhard Böschenstein and Heino Schmull, assisted by Michael Schwarzkopf and Christiane Wittkop (Frankfurt a.M.: Suhrkamp, 1999), p. 103, §228.
2. Paul Valéry, *Oeuvres*, ed. by Jean Hytier, 2 vols (Paris: Gallimard, 1957–1960), II, p. 1146.
3. Almuth Grésillon, 'Slow: Work in Progress', *Word and Image*, 13.2 (1997), 106–23), 111.
4. Friedrich Hölderlin, *Sämtliche Werke: Grosse Stuttgarter Ausgabe*, ed. by Friedrich Beissner, 8 vols (Stuttgart: Cotta, 1946–1985).
5. Marcel Proust, *À la recherche du temps perdu*, ed. by Jean-Yves Tadié, 4 vols (Paris: Gallimard, 1987–1989).
6. James Joyce, *Ulysses: A Critical and Synoptic Edition*, ed. by Hans Walter Gabler, with Wolfhard Steppe and Claus Melchior, 3 vols (New York: Garland, 1984).
7. Paul Celan, *Eingedunkelt. Historisch-Kritische Ausgabe*, ed. by Rolf Bücher and Andreas Lohr, assisted by Hans Kruschwitz and Thomas Schneider, vol. 12 of *Werke. Historisch-kritische Ausgabe. I. Abteilung: Lyrik und Prosa* (Frankfurt a.M.: Suhrkamp, 2006).
8. Roman Bucheli, 'Work in progress. Zur Fortsetzung der historisch-kritischen Celan-Ausgabe', in *Neue Zürcher Zeitung* 235 (8/9 October 1994), 69.
9. Hans Walter Gabler, 'Introduction', in *Contemporary German Editorial Theory*, ed. by Hans Walter Gabler, George Bornstein, and Gillian Borland Pierce (Ann Arbor: University of Michigan Press, 1995), pp. 1–16 (p. 3).
10. There is no Tübingen edition of *Eingedunkelt* as it is not a completed and authorized cycle of poems.
11. Umberto Eco, *The Open Work*, trans. by Anna Cancogni (Cambridge: Harvard University Press, 1989), p. 100.
12. Ibid.
13. Richard Sieburth, 'Introduction', in Friedrich Hölderlin, *Hymns and Fragments*, trans. by Richard Sieburth (Princeton: Princeton University Press, 1984), pp. 3–43 (p. 34).
14. Ibid., p. 35.
15. Bernard Cerquiglini, *In Praise of the Variant. A Critical History of Philology*, trans. by Betsy Wing (Baltimore: The Johns Hopkins University Press, 1999), p. 45.
16. Kathryn Sutherland, 'Anglo-American editorial theory', in *The Cambridge Companion to Textual Scholarship*, ed. by Neil Fraistat and Julia Flanders (Cambridge: Cambridge University Press, 2013), pp. 42–60 (p. 55).
17. Barbara Johnson, 'Philology: What is at Stake?', in *On Philology*, ed. by Jan Ziolkowski (University Park: Pennsylvania State University Press, 1990), pp. 26–30 (p. 28).
18. Jacques Derrida, 'Archive et brouillon: table ronde du 17 juin 1995', in *Pourquoi la critique génétique? Méthodes, théories*, ed. by Michel Contat and Daniel Ferrer. Paris: CNRS EDITIONS, 1998), pp. 189–209 (p. 209).
19. Henri Meschonnic, 'L'Écriture de Satan', in Gustave Flaubert, *Bibliomanie et autres textes 1836–1839* (Paris: Jean-Cyrille Godefroy, 1982), pp. 5–11 (p. 6).
20. Laurent Jenny, 'Genetic Criticism and Its Myths', *Yale French Studies*, 89 (1996), 9–25 (10).
21. Ibid.
22. Grésillon, 'Slow: Work in Progress', 115.
23. Ibid.
24. Pierre-Marc de Biasi, 'Avant-propos', in Gustave Flaubert, *Carnets de travail*, ed. by Pierre-Marc de Biasi (Paris: Balland, 1988), pp. 7–14 (p. 8).
25. Cerquiglini, *In Praise of the Variant*, p. 36.
26. Louis Hay, '"Le texte n'existe pas". Réflexions sur la critique génétique', *Poétique*, 62 (1985), 146–58 (158).
27. Jean-Michel Rabaté, *James Joyce and the Politics of Egoism* (Cambridge: Cambridge University Press, 2001) p. 196.
28. Ibid.
29. Ibid.

30. Arno Schmidt, *Zettel's Traum: 1963–69* (Stuttgart: Stahlberg, 1970).
31. Grésillon, 'Slow: Work in Progress', 115.
32. Francis Ponge, *La fabrique du 'Pré'* (Geneva: Skira, 1971).
33. Francis Ponge, *Pratiques d'écriture, ou, L'inachèvement perpétuel* (Paris: Hermann, 1984), p. 7.
34. Gérard Genette, 'Ce que nous disent les manuscrits', *Le Monde* (17 November 1989), 31.
35. Jenny, 'Genetic Criticism and Its Myths', 11.
36. Ibid.
37. Quoted in Derrida, 'Archive et brouillon', p. 204.
38. Gabler, 'Introduction', p. 7. See also Grésillon, 'Slow: Work in Progress', 114.
39. Sally Bushell, *Text as Process: Creative Composition in Wordsworth, Tennyson, and Dickinson* (Charlottesville: University of Virginia Press, 2009), p. 8.
40. Ibid., p. 36.
41. Geert Lernout, 'Continental editing theory', in *The Cambridge Companion to Textual Scholarship*, ed. by Neil Fraistat and Julia Flanders (Cambridge: Cambridge University Press, 2013), pp. 61–78 (p. 73).
42. Cerquiglini, *In Praise of the Variant*, p. 34.
43. Pierre-Marc de Biasi, 'What is a Literary Draft? Towards a Functional Typology of Genetic Criticism', *Yale French Studies*, 89 (1996), 26–58 (54).
44. Ibid.
45. Daniel Ferrer and Michael Groden, 'Introduction: A Genesis of French Genetic Criticism', in *Genetic Criticism: Texts and Avant-textes*, ed. by Jed Deppman, Daniel Ferrer, and Michael Groden (Philadelphia: University of Pennsylvania Press, 2004), pp. 1–16 (p. 2).
46. Ibid.
47. Biasi, 'Avant-propos', p. 14.
48. Ibid.
49. Bushell, *Text as Process*, p. 7.
50. Raymonde Debray-Genette, *Métamorphoses du récit: autour de Flaubert* (Paris: Seuil, 1988), pp. 24–25.
51. Eric Le Calvez, *Genèses flaubertiennes* (Amsterdam: Rodopi, 2009), p. 14.
52. Celan, *Der Meridian. Endfassung — Vorstufen — Materialien*, p. 94, §165.
53. W. B. Yeats, *The Poems*, ed. by Richard J. Finneran (New York: Macmillan, 1989), p. 80.
54. Charles Baudelaire, *Oeuvres complètes*, ed. by Claude Pichois and Jean Ziegler, 2 vols (Paris: Gallimard, 1975–1976), I, p. 83.
55. Celan, *Der Meridian. Endfassung — Vorstufen — Materialien*, p. 121, §360.
56. Heidegger, *Poetry, Language, Thought*, p. 215.
57. A rejection of Gottfried Benn's claim that 'a poem is something that is "manufactured" and rarely "born"' (Gottfried Benn, *Probleme der Lyrik* (Wiesbaden: Limes, 1951), p. 6).
58. Celan, *Der Meridian. Endfassung — Vorstufen — Materialien*, p. 113, §302.
59. Bucheli, 'Work in progress', 69.
60. Celan, *Der Meridian. Endfassung — Vorstufen — Materialien*, p. 104, §239.
61. Ibid., p. 103, §227.
62. Ibid., p. 102, §218.
63. In prosody, a mora is 'a unit of metrical time equal to the duration of a short syllable', and in linguistics, 'the smallest or basic unit of duration of a speech sound'. The English 'mora' comes from the classical Latin 'mora' meaning 'delay', in both the legal context (delay in fulfilling a legal duty) and in grammar (a pause in speech or verse generally indicated by punctuation, a sustaining of the voice in the pronunciation of a syllable, cognate with Old Irish *maraim* — remain.) Here Celan is using the term 'mora' to indicate the unit of speech that — like silence — cannot be understood for itself and in itself, but without which there is no language.
64. 'Kammzeit' is literally 'crest-' or 'ridge-time', and describes the time taken to pronounce the 'Silbenkamm', which is the heaviest part of a syllable, for example 'ro' in the word 'Stroh' or 'tum' in the word 'Stumpf' (Carsten Høeg, 'Les syllabes longues par position en grec', *Acta Jutlandica: aarsskrift for universitetsundervisningen i Jylland*, 9.1 (1937), 183–96 (184)).
65. Celan, *Der Meridian. Endfassung — Vorstufen — Materialien*, p. 127, §394.

66. I do not share Cerquiglini's hostility to the 'fantasy of the facsimile' (Cerquiglini, *In Praise of the Variant*, p. 78).
67. Edgar Allan Poe, *The Complete Works of Edgar Allan Poe*, ed. by James A. Harrison, 17 vols (New York: Crowell, 1902), XVI, p. 1.
68. Daniel Ferrer and Michael Groden, 'Post-Genetic Joyce', *Romanic Review*, 86.3 (1995), 501–12 (509).
69. Jerome J. McGann, *A Critique of Modern Textual Criticism* (Chicago: University of Chicago Press, 1983).
70. Gabler, 'Introduction', p. 7.
71. Peter Szondi, *On Textual Understanding and Other Essays*, trans. by Harvey Mendelsohn (Minneapolis: University of Minnesota Press, 1986), p. 14.
72. Ibid. See also Adorno: 'Each [work of art], without the author necessarily having willed it, strives for the utmost, and none really tolerates its neighbor next to it' (Theodor W. Adorno, *Notes to Literature*, trans. by Shierry Weber Nicholsen, 2 vols (New York: Columbia University Press, 1991–1992), II, p. 76).
73. Raymond Carney, 'Making the Most of a Mess', *Georgia Review*, 35.3 (1981), 631–42 (634).
74. Celan, *Eingedunkelt*, p. 219.
75. D. C. Greetham, 'A history of textual scholarship', in *The Cambridge Companion to Textual Scholarship*, ed. Neil Fraistat and Julia Flanders (Cambridge: Cambridge University Press, 2013), pp. 16–41 (p. 19).
76. Celan, *Eingedunkelt*, p. 224.
77. Ibid., p. 218.
78. Daniel Ferrer, 'Clementis's Cap: Retroaction and Persistence in the Genetic Process', *Yale French Studies*, 89 (1996), 223–36 (223).
79. Ibid., 228.
80. Michel Foucault, *This Is Not a Pipe, with Illustrations and Letters by René Magritte*, trans. and ed. by James Harkness (Berkeley: University of California Press, 1983), p. 44.
81. Giovanni Bonaccorso, 'Problèmes de l'édition des manuscrits d'*Un coeur simple*', in Gustave Flaubert, *Un coeur simple, Corpus Flaubertianum*, ed. by Giovanni Bonaccorso and others (Paris: Société d'Édition 'Les Belles Lettres', 1983),) I, pp. xiii–xlviii (pp. xix–xx).
82. Foucault, *This Is Not a Pipe*, p. 44.
83. Certeau, *The Mystic Fable*, p. 19.
84. Ludwig Wittgenstein, *Philosophische Untersuchungen / Philosophical Investigations*, trans. by G. E. M. Anscombe (New York: Macmillan, 1964), p. 193.
85. Ibid.
86. 'Hochwohlgeboren' is a term used to address members of the lower aristocracy. Here, it is perhaps a reference to Gisèle, whose family — the Lestrange — was considered aristocratic. See also Poe's 'Marginalia': 'Nothing, to the true taste, is so offensive as mere hyperism. In Germany *wohlgeboren* [well born] is a loftier title than *edelgeboren* [noble born]' (Poe, *The Complete Works of Edgar Allan Poe*, XVI, p. 8).
87. Stanley Cavell, *The Claim of Reason: Wittgenstein, Skepticism, Morality, and Tragedy* (Oxford: Clarendon Press/Oxford University Press, 1979), p. 369.
88. Benjamin Fondane, *Le Mal des fantômes*, ed. by Patrice Beray and Michel Carassou, assisted by Monique Jutrin, foreword by Henri Meschonnic (Lagrasse: Verdier, 2006), p. 18.
89. Benedictus de Spinoza, *Éthique*, ed. by Bertrand Pautrat (Paris: Seuil, 1999), pp. 252–53.
90. Zarathustra says to the tight-rope artist who has fallen from the rope: 'you have made danger your calling, there is nothing to despise in this'. (Friedrich Nietzsche, *Also sprach Zarathustra. Ein Buch für Alle und Keinen. (1883–1885)*, part 6, vol. 1 of Friedrich Nietzsche, *Werke: Kritische Gesamtausgabe*, ed. by Giorgio Colli and Mazzino Montinari (Berlin: De Gruyter, 1968), p. 16).
91. Gilles Deleuze and Félix Guattari, *A Thousand Plateaus. Capitalism and Schizophrenia*, trans. by Brian Massumi (Minneapolis: University of Minnesota Press, 1987), p. 22.
92. Jean Paul, *Werke*, ed. by Norbert Miller, 6 vols (Munich: Carl Hanser, 1959–1963), V, p. 418.
93. Ryan identifies a similar open-ended structure in Celan's 'Faden' [thread], which does not bridge the divide between poet and world, but instead points beyond to the 'free' (Judith Ryan,

'Monologische Lyrik: Paul Celans Antwort auf Gottfried Benn', *Basis: Jahrbuch für deutsche Gegenwartsliteratur*, 2 (1971), 260–82 (269)).
94. Cavell, *The Claim of Reason*, p. 369.
95. Louis Marin, *On Representation*, trans. by Catherine Porter (Stanford: Stanford University Press, 2001), p. 341.
96. Ibid., p. 343.
97. Ibid., p. 344.
98. Celan, *Der Meridian. Endfassung — Vorstufen — Materialien*, p. 108, §262 and §263.
99. Stéphane Mallarmé, *Divagations*, trans. by Barbara Johnson (Cambridge: The Belknap Press of Harvard University Press, 2007), p. 208.
100. Stéphane Mallarmé, *Oeuvres complètes*, ed. by Bertrand Marchal, 2 vols (Paris: Gallimard, 1998–2003), II, p. 211.
101. Larousse, *Grand dictionnaire universel du XIXe siècle*, XV, p. 399.
102. Timothy Bahti, *Ends of the Lyric* (Baltimore: Johns Hopkins University Press, 1996), p. 5.
103. Kluge, *Etymologisches Wörterbuch*, p. 782.
104. Compare to the tone that concludes 'DRESS THE WORD-HOLLOWS' [KLEIDE DIE WORTHÖHLEN AUS]: 'and listen in to their second / and respectively second and second / tone' (Celan, *Die Gedichte*, p. 252). Hamacher proposes this poem as a guide to reading difficult texts (Hamacher, 'The Second of Inversion', p. 259).
105. 'Tzimtzum' describes the concentration or contraction of God necessary for the world to come into existence (Gershom Scholem, *Major Trends in Jewish Mysticism* (New York: Schocken, 1954), pp. 260–64).
106. Gerhard Wahrig, *Deutsches Wörterbuch*, ed. by Renate Wahrig-Burfeind (Gütersloh: Bertelsmann, 2001), p. 1041.
107. Ferrer, 'Clementis's Cap', 235.
108. See Fig. 1.1.
109. The semantic ambiguity inherent in 'erbrechen' also applies in the opening line of 'ALL YOUR SEALS BROKEN OPEN? NEVER', which is discussed in chapter three (Celan, *Die Gedichte*, p. 230).
110. Grésillon, 'Slow: Work in Progress', 108.
111. Ferrer, 'Clementis's Cap', 230.
112. Ibid., 224.
113. *The Holy Bible Containing the Old and New Testaments, Translated out of the Original Tongues and with the Former Translations Diligently Compared and Revised, King James Version 1611* (New York: American Bible Society, 1980), p. 564, Psalms 139. 13, 15–16.
114. On a related note, the organicist nomenclature of genetic criticism betrays the desire of its proponents to be seen as biologists of literature, re-booted philologists for the contemporary era, despite the fact that this has led to some fairly remarkable misnomers, not least among them the 'geneticist', whose ability to manipulate genetic structures in the interest of medical progress reflects gloriously, but somewhat incongruously, on the labors of textual and literary critics.
115. Jean Bellemin-Noël, 'L'infamilière curiosité', in *Leçons d'écriture, ce que disent les manuscrits*, ed. by Almuth Grésillon and Michaël Werner (Paris: Lettres Modernes, 1985), pp. 345–57 (p. 350).
116. Carol Jacobs, *Telling Time. Lévi-Strauss, Ford, Lessing, Benjamin, de Man, Wordsworth, Rilke* (Baltimore: The Johns Hopkins University Press, 1993), p. 136.
117. Sutherland, 'Anglo-American editorial theory', p. 57.
118. The 'Narbe' [scar] can also designate the 'stigma' of a flower, which is where the pollen grain germinates. The 'Narbe', along with the 'Griffel' ['pen' or 'stylus'] and the 'Fruchtknoten' ['ovary' but literally 'fruit-knot'] constitute a plant's female reproductive organs.
119. Celan, *Eingedunkelt*, p. 220.
120. Ibid., p. 221.
121. Ibid., pp. 221–22.
122. Ibid., p. 223.
123. Valéry, *Oeuvres*, II, p. 1147.
124. Franz Kafka, *Sämtliche Erzählungen*, ed. by Paul Raabe (Frankfurt a.M.: Fischer, 1970), p. 113.

125. Ibid., p. 115.
126. The verb Kafka uses to describe this fastening is 'fesseln' which shares a root with the German for 'version', namely 'Fassung', as already discussed (Kafka, *Sämtliche Erzählungen*, p. 113).
127. Ibid., p. 121.
128. Ibid.
129. Ibid. p. 122. Note that the administration of death shares its structure with the dodecasyllabic Alexandrine. Not only is the process meant to last twelve hours, but the moment of revelation occurs at the sixth hour, which coincides with the caesura in French prosody.
130. Michel de Certeau, 'Reading as Poaching', in *Readers and Reading*, ed. by Andrew Bennett (New York: Longman, 1995), pp. 150–63 (p. 159).
131. Kafka, *Sämtliche Erzählungen*, p. 115.
132. Ibid., p. 136.
133. Celan, *Eingedunkelt*, p. 223. See Fig. 1.6.
134. Roland Barthes, *Oeuvres complètes*, ed. by Éric Marty, 5 vols (Paris: Seuil, 2002), III, p. 40.
135. François Roustang, 'On Reading Again' in *The Limits of Theory*, ed. by Thomas M. Kavanagh (Stanford: Stanford University Press, 1989), pp. 121–38 (pp. 129 and 131).
136. Johnson, 'Philology: What is at Stake?', p. 29.
137. Grésillon, 'Slow: Work in Progress', 114.
138. Ibid.
139. Debray-Genette, *Métamorphoses du récit*, pp. 22–31.
140. Quoted in Heidi Brayman Hackel, *Reading Material in Early Modern England: Print, Gender, and Literacy* (Cambridge: Cambridge University Press, 2005), p. 140.
141. Joseph Conrad, *Der Geheimagent. Eine einfache Geschichte*, trans. by G. Danehl (Frankfurt a.M.: Fischer, 1963). On the same day, Celan also read and annotated parts of Lao Tse, *Tao-Tê-King. Das heilige Buch vom Weg und von der Tugend*, trans. by Günther Debon (Stuttgart: Philipp Reclam Jun., 1961).
142. See John M. Merriman, *The Dynamite Club. How a Bombing in fin-de-siècle Paris Ignited the Age of Modern Terror* (Boston: Houghton Mifflin Harcourt, 2009).
143. Mallarmé, *Oeuvres complètes*, II, p. 72. Mallarmé's friend, the art-critic Félix Fénéon, bombs the restaurant Foyot just a month later on 4 April, an attack which cost the poet Laurent Tailhade one of his eyes. During Fénéon's trial, Mallarmé made an official statement in support of his friend, which contributed to his acquittal (ibid., p. 686).
144. Joseph Conrad, *The Secret Agent. A Simple Tale* (Harmondsworth: Penguin, 1976), p. 37.
145. '... die Sprengung des ersten Meridians müßte einen Chor von Verwünschungen auslösen' [the explosion of the first meridian is bound to unleash a chorus of imprecations] (Conrad, *Der Geheimagent*, p. 41). The original reads: 'is bound to raise a howl of execration' (Conrad, *The Secret Agent*, p. 37).
146. Ibid., p. 39.
147. Ibid., p. 89.
148. Ibid., pp. 86–114. This corresponds to Conrad, *Der Geheimagent*, pp. 109–47.
149. Conrad, *The Secret Agent*, p. 100. Corresponds to Conrad, *Der Geheimagent*, p. 129.
150. Conrad, *The Secret Agent*, p. 107. Corresponds to Conrad, *Der Geheimagent*, p. 137.
151. Conrad, *The Secret Agent*, p. 107. Corresponds to Conrad, *Der Geheimagent*, p. 138.
152. Ibid. and ibid.
153. Conrad, *The Secret Agent*, p. 108. Corresponds to Conrad, *Der Geheimagent*, pp. 139–40.
154. Jacques Derrida, 'This Is Not an Oral Footnote', in *Annotation and Its Texts*, ed. by Stephen A. Barney (Oxford: Oxford University Press, 1991), pp. 192–205 (p. 193).
155. Conrad, *The Secret Agent*, p. 107.
156. Certeau, 'Reading as Poaching', p. 154.
157. Mallarmé, *Oeuvres complètes*, II, p. 170.
158. Derrida, 'This Is Not an Oral Footnote', p. 194.
159. Ibid.
160. Brayman Hackel, *Reading Material in Early Modern England*, p. 205.
161. Quoted in H. J. Jackson, *Marginalia: Readers Writing in Books* (New Haven: Yale University Press, 2001), p. 239.

162. Celan, *Eingedunkelt*, p. 78.
163. 'Whatever it was, he wanted, if he was allowed, to really be free and he began to shake himself [er begann sich zu rütteln], as much as the harrow would allow' (Kafka, *Sämtliche Erzählungen*, p. 132). The verb is also used to describe the Officer jolting the brass poles of the machine in anger when the Prisoner throws up: ' "All the Commandant's fault!" screamed the Officer and, beside himself with fury, shook at the brass rods in front of him [rüttelte besinnungslos vorn an den Messingstangen]' (ibid., p. 124).
164. Ibid., p. 116.
165. Pierre-Marc de Biasi, 'Préface', in Gustave Flaubert, *Carnets de travail*, ed. by Pierre-Marc de Biasi (Paris: Balland, 1988), pp. 15–119 (p. 49).
166. Ibid.
167. Jenny, 'Genetic Criticism and Its Myths', 22.
168. Wahrig, *Deutsches Wörterbuch*, p. 1071.
169. Certeau, 'Reading as Poaching', p. 150.
170. Ibid., p. 160.
171. Ibid., p. 161.
172. Georges Bataille, 'René Char et la force de la poésie', *Critique*, 53 (1951), 819–23 (820).
173. Bushell, *Text as Process*, p. 54.
174. Jenny, 'Genetic Criticism and Its Myths', 20.
175. Ibid.
176. Ibid., p. 23.
177. Ibid., p. 22.
178. Biasi, 'Avant-propos', p. 12.
179. Ibid.

CHAPTER 2

Engaging Mallarmé

> Yet our arc not for nothing
> Brings us back to our starting-place.[1]

Mallarmé the Fetish

Given Paul Celan's reputation for writing poems that are hard to understand, there has long been a tendency to compare his work to the hermetic verse and prose of the nineteenth-century French poet Stéphane Mallarmé (1842–1898). In 1958, speaking on the occasion of the award to Celan of the Literature Prize of the Free City of Bremen, Erhart Kästner sought to explain the poet's 'eschewal of intelligibility and of usual logic' as part of 'a long tradition that goes back to its founding with the great Mallarmé'.[2] The approximation of the Romanian-born postwar poet writing in German with the French symbolist poet is characteristic of many critical responses throughout the 1950s and 1960s. Writing in 1962, Hans Schwerte, a celebrated university professor and scholar of German literature (who had successfully hidden his past membership of the SS) saw in Celan 'the great art of Trakl and that of Yvan Goll' and behind all three poets 'the magical, interior vocabulary' of German Romanticism and the 'word-world of the so-called moderns', Baudelaire, Mallarmé, and above all Rimbaud.[3] In a more hostile critique from the same year, Peter Rühmkorf claimed that Celan's dominant metaphors (jug, well, urn, ashes, poppy, cup, mussel, shadow, black, poplar) were established symbols that had been introduced by Mallarmé, had become commonplace in German since Gottfried Benn and Georg Trakl, and had 'long lost their expressive potential from frequent overuse'.[4] Later, George Steiner would identify Celan as a poet who 'stands with Rimbaud and Mallarmé as one who has altered the scope of poetry, who has made possible but also more difficult [...] the articulation of certain states of feeling'.[5]

Others considered Celan's attitude toward his forebear in difficulty as more problematic. Henri Meschonnic saw Mallarmé as a 'necessary and deceptive literary reference' in the context of Celan's work.[6] Otto Pöggeler identifies numerous passing references to the 'maître' throughout Celan's work as signs of a sporadic and mostly antagonistic engagement with the French poet.[7] Notes left unpublished at his death in 1969 show that Theodor Adorno was sketching out a theory of poetic hermeticism with Mallarmé and Celan at opposite ends of the scale. If with Mallarmé, hermeticism was 'not free of the small-mindedness and desperate rapture of an art-religion that convinced itself that the world was created for the sake of a beautiful verse or a well-turned phrase',[8] then in Celan the experiential content of the hermetic was inverted: 'His poetry is permeated by the shame of art in the face of suffering that escapes both experience and sublimation. Celan's poems want to speak of the most extreme horror through silence. Their truth content itself becomes negative'.[9]

When considering Celan's relationship to Mallarmé, however, critics most often turn to the anecdote related by the Germanist Gerhart Baumann that dates from the final weeks of Celan's life. It concerns an article by one of Baumann's students, given to Celan to read, that compares Celan's poetry with that of Mallarmé at length.[10] Baumann describes how Celan angrily rejected the essay as 'a coarse, even malevolent misunderstanding' and insisted on not being compared to another poet.[11] This violent response is presented as typical of Celan's behavior in the final years of his life, during which he would break off long relationships over relatively small incidents. But Baumann also sets this response in the context of Celan's repeated expressions of antipathy toward Mallarmé, whom he apparently thought overrated. 'Mallarmé', Celan is reported to have said at one point, 'that too is a fetish!'[12] According to Baumann, Celan wanted the conditions and intentions of his poems to be understood as being altogether different from Mallarmé's:

> He did not destroy reality for the sake of the beauty of absolute form; he knew of no absolute symbolism, nor did he seek the pure self-consciousness of language; his word did not detach itself from that which happens, rather it bore witness to the act of passing through all that happens. His silence was not destruction, nor did it release any magic. Above all, he did not compose his poem impersonally; from the first draft onward, it was set up as a dialogue, as a "message in a bottle"'.[13]

Celan left little evidence of his understanding and assessment of Mallarmé, or of any eventual debt to the poet in the conception of his own poetic task. There are three documented moments where Celan is seen to engage with Mallarmé's work — each time in a significantly different way — none of which are mentioned by Baumann. In this second chapter, I look behind the screen of critical and anecdotal commonplaces, to reconsider possible reasons for Celan's restrained but repeated engagement with Mallarmé.

Thinking Mallarmé to the End

Celan makes his most prominent reference to Mallarmé during the Büchner Prize speech given in Darmstadt in October 1960. Subsequently published as 'The Meridian', this speech is regarded not only as a riposte to accusations of plagiarism, levied in various forums from 1953 onward by Claire Goll, and a polemic with Heidegger on the question of Being and poetry. It is also the work in which Celan most explicitly sketches the contours of that which generates and motivates his poetics. At one of the most enigmatic moments of the speech he asks whether we should not now 'think Mallarmé consistently through to the end'.[14]

To better understand this speculative evocation of Mallarmé, it is necessary to remind ourselves of the discussion on the relationship of 'poetry' or 'Dichtung' to 'art' or 'Kunst' in which it appears. This discussion acts much like a sound box in a violin, giving the momentary reference to Mallarmé a resonance and duration it would otherwise not have. To illustrate how art is distinct from poetry, Celan turns to Büchner's play *Danton's Death* (1835). Specifically, he turns to the character Camille Desmoulins who notes that Pygmalion's artistic creation, even when brought to life by Aphrodite, was irresistible but sterile: 'The Greeks knew what they were talking about when they said that Pygmalion's statue may well have come alive, but never gave birth to any children'.[15] It is this that Celan refers to when he states: 'Art, you will recall, is a puppet-like, iambic, five-footed and — mythology confirms this in the reference to Pygmalion and his creature — a childless being'.[16]

For Desmoulins and Celan, art is that part of existence that is barren and incapable of true generation or creation. Art is where the Self pursues organizations of matter that may be sculpted like Galatea, or move like the mechanical puppets in Büchner's other major play, *Leonce and Lena* (1836), but which has no breath of its own.[17] In the realm of poetry, art describes language that resolutely sticks to traditional laws of prosody, and that expresses itself only through pre-established modes of rhyme and meter, be they Schiller's 'five-footed iambs' — ridiculed here by Büchner — or other metrical feet. It is a necessarily sterile being because it is always self-motivating and self-generating. It is not difficult to identify Mallarmé's stubborn adherence to the rules of French prosody here. Even in 'A Throw of the Dice', the most disseminating and subversive of his texts, Mallarmé maintains that the rules of prosody remain: 'I am not transgressing this measure, only dispersing it'.[18] But in the context of Büchner's work, it is not to poetry but to speech-making that Celan turns, and specifically to the fluent verbosity of the revolutionaries Danton and Camille, whether it be on the soap box where they speak, or on the scaffold where they die 'almost iambically'.[19]

These manifestations of art are undercut by the simplicity and naivety of 'Dichtung' [poetry or literature], as represented in the play by the figure of Lucile, wife of Desmoulins. Lucile is the one for whom language, as Celan says, still possesses something personal, perceptible, and real. Lucile is one of the few for whom language includes 'breath, that is direction and fate'.[20] In the fourth and final act of the play, Danton and Camille prepare for their impending executions by expounding on a variety of poetic and philosophical topics. Their wives, on the contrary, approach death in silence. Danton's wife, Julie, imbibes a vial of poison while watching the night. Lucile loses her mind or, as Camille puts it, madness sits behind her eyes.[21] In the aftermath of what Celan calls Danton's and Camille's 'kunstreiche Worte', their 'art-rich words'[22] and beheading, the play ends with Lucile crying out 'Es lebe der König!' or 'Long live the King!' In the new reign of republican terror such words constitute a crime that precipitates her death by execution.

She utters these fatal words, Celan explains, not in recognition of the deposed *ancien régime*, nor in remembrance of a recently obliterated past, but rather in honor of the 'majesty of the absurd', of that which bears witness to the presence of the human, of the humane, and of humanity, in the very face of terror.[23] This 'Gegenwort' [counter-word] comes straight from the 'Gegenwart' [temporal present], the absurd present in which Lucile lives, breathes, and speaks. This simultaneously life-giving and life-taking utterance punctures the bubble of art. It is this gesture that Celan calls poetry. Poetry interrupts art and undercuts its claims to eternity. It does this by failing to properly hear what art is saying or, as Celan puts it, with reference to Lucile, it 'hears and listens and looks... and then doesn't know what all the talk was about'.[24] It listens, as Pöggeler puts it, 'kunstblind und politikfremd' [blind to art and a stranger to politics] but is touched by the 'breath, direction, and fate' of what has been said.[25] Poetry is embodied and realized in the human being who refuses to play according to the rules of the game, perhaps especially when the game is Mallarmé's supreme game of literature. Poetry, like Lucile, possesses all too human flaws and conceits. It is fickle and erratic, short sighted and temporary, ill-informed and delusional, terminal and mortal, perhaps suicidal.

As previous readers of the speech including Hans Mayer have proposed, Celan's initial intention was to define 'Dichtung' in relation to 'Kunst' in light of Gottfried Benn's *Problems of Lyric*.[26] In this speech, given at the University of Marburg in 1951, Benn claims that 'the monologic character' of the modern poem is 'beyond doubt'.[27] He distinguishes between the absolute, clear-sighted, monologic poem conscious of its status as construction that is 'Lyrik', and the naïve, expressionistic, sentimental poem that is 'Poesie' or 'Dichtung'. For Celan, though, poetry is not only essentially dialogical, a notion he develops throughout his poetic career, especially by engaging with Martin Buber.[28] Poetry is also — somewhat paradoxically — inextricably bound up with the idea of art, artifice, and artfulness, despite its essentially human and humane character.

The relation of 'Dichtung' and 'Kunst' or 'poetry' and 'art' is a complex relation that Celan finds most completely expressed in Büchner's character Lenz, from the unfinished prose piece of the same name (1836). For Lenz, the presence of the living, of life, and of breath is the one and only criterion in matters of art. To illustrate this, Celan withholds from speech to let Büchner speak in his place, who in turn speaks through the first person voice of his semi-fictional character, Lenz:[29]

> Yesterday, as I was walking up along the edge of the valley, I saw two girls sitting on a rock: one was letting her hair down, the other helping her; and the golden hair hung down, and a pale serious face, yet so young, and the black dress, and the other girl taking such pains. The Old German School's finest, most intimate pictures can scarcely give an idea of it. One might sometimes want to be a Medusa's head, so as to turn such a group into stone and call people over.[30]

The German 'Kunst' meaning 'art' comes directly from the Old and Middle High German 'kunst' meaning 'skill' or 'knowledge', and is related to the modern German 'können' — to be able to, or to know how to do something. 'Kunst' is therefore that which one 'can' do, that which one knows how to do. When walking in the mountains, Lenz comes face to face with the perfect image of two girls sitting on a stone and wishes he had the ability or the art to capture the moment for eternity, to freeze it in stone so that later passers-by might witness the same moment unchanged. Celan asks us to consider the irony of this moment: 'One would like to be the head of Medusa in order... to comprehend the artless as artless, by means of art!'[31]

There are two steps to the process of capturing the artless as artless through art, both of which Lenz is seen to execute. The first is to claim artistic impotence, an insufficiency of artfulness. This requires a removal of poetic desire out of the possibility and reality of the present indicative 'Man mag' [one wants] and into the contingency and hypothesis of the present conditional 'Man möchte' [one would like]. This implies that although one would like to transform the girls sitting on the stone into stone, it is beyond one's ability or art. Lenz is not really concerned with translating the scene before his eyes into stone as he claims, though, but into language. This is something he evidently achieves. We are those who are now called to the valley-side to see the two girls sitting on the stone, one helping the other to untie her hair, the long golden hair then hanging down, the serious pale young face, the black dress, the careful, studied attention of one girl to the other's needs. The claim of 'man möchte' to artistic impotence is a necessary fraud, a trick, a deception without which Lenz is unable to capture the naturalness of the scene.

The second step in the process of capturing the artless as artless through art is intimately bound up with the false claim of artistic impotence. It is the denial of one's Self. When Heidegger says of the impersonal pronoun 'man' [one, they], that when it is invoked, 'everyone is the other, and no one is himself', he is describing the impersonality of being [Dasein], the 'nobody' [Niemand] and 'being-among-one-another' to which alienated and inauthentic being surrenders itself.[32] When 'man' does something, no one does it, which means everyone does it. Art as understood by Celan shares many features with Heidegger's 'man'. For Heidegger, 'man' stands for theory, idle chatter, the generalities of public opinion. For Celan, though, art represents above all the denial of one's Self. It is this that he highlights in 'man möchte': 'It is of course not *one* would like [*man* möchte]: *I* would like [*ich* möchte]'.[33] I, Reinhold Lenz, but also I, Georg Büchner and I, Paul Celan, would like to be the head of Medusa. I would like to possess the art necessary to comprehend the artless as artless.

In order to achieve this translation of nature into text, it is necessary to appear to restrain one's own desire, to appear to forget one's Self, to appear to let others speak in one's place, and to let the sound of other voices ring out through one's own text. It is with what Celan calls one's 'self-forgotten I', the 'I' that is dissimulated behind the bland mask of 'man' [one], that 'I' can step out of the human and make its way into the un-homely sphere of the Other that is turned toward and facing the human. The deceptions of art — the denial of one's Self [Ich] and the denial of artistic ability [Kunst] — are as natural to us and as essential to us as the air we breathe. Even Ovid's solitary Pygmalion — disgusted by the whoring Propoetides — does not ask the gods to give him his 'ivory maiden' as a wife, but only 'one like the ivory maid'.[34] These denials of desire and oblique requests are the oldest 'uncanninesses' of human existence. They are the moments when we step outside of living, suspend our breath, and sacrifice ourselves, the moments in which we momentarily and artfully commit a sort of suicide.

It is these moments of artful remove and Self-denial through quotation, of false claims to artistic impotence and of the need to let other voices speak through one's own — moments in which we linger in the un-homely sphere just outside of the human — that we must recognize and reconnoiter if we are to understand the reference to Mallarmé that immediately follows this passage of the text:

> Is there not — I must now ask — in Georg Büchner, in the poet of creature, a perhaps only half audible, perhaps only half conscious (but for this reason no less radical — or precisely for this reason radical, in the real sense of the term) calling-into-question of art [radikale In-Frage-Stellung der Kunst], a calling-into-question from this direction? a calling-into-question that all contemporary poetry must return to, if it wants to keep on questioning? In other words, to leap ahead some: May we, as happens in many places now, proceed from art as from something that is given, and necessarily presumed, should we, to express it quite concretely, above all — let's say — think Mallarmé consistently to the end [sollen wir, um es ganz konkret auszudrücken, vor allem — sagen wir — Mallarmé konsequent zu Ende denken]?[35]

If, as Paul Celan claims in the final moments of his speech, the 'meridian' describes a circle ('I find something — like language — immaterial, but earthly, terrestrial, something circular..'),[36] and if, by the end of the text, he finds himself again at the point of departure ('Ladies and Gentlemen, I am at the end — I am back at the beginning'),[37] then this passage perhaps constitutes the moment at which the text is as far removed from its beginning and its end as it is possible to be. It is the extreme point of the meridian, or what in geometry is called the 'summit'. It is the moment at which the circle reaches its furthest limit and is about to curl back toward its source. It is the moment at which the text most clearly achieves the moment of 'Verweilen', of artful lingering and pause associated with 'Ich-Ferne' or 'I-remove'. It is, in the terms of Celan's speech, the moment at which 'Dichtung' most unambiguously assumes the form of 'Kunst'.

In a text replete with overt and covert intertextual, historical, contemporary and personal references, this constitutes one of the most perplexing moments, as it names the poet, but gives no indication as to which parts of Mallarmé's philosophy, morals, or aesthetics — the three elements that Gide says are fundamental to a literary oeuvre — we should consider.[38] Celan hides the nature of his engagement with Mallarmé from us, and from his Darmstadt audience, by withholding any specific textual or even biographical reference that might allow his audience to recognize something of Mallarmé beyond his name. He provides no opportunity to hear and puzzle over a fragment from Mallarmé's poetry, prose, or correspondence, as he does for both Nicolas Malebranche ('attention is the natural prayer of the soul'),[39] and Blaise Pascal ('do not reproach us for the lack of clarity as it is our profession').[40] Instead, the musician of silence is further reduced to silence.

Ute Harbusch notes that very few critics have examined this speculative invocation of Mallarmé with the required circumspection, and that the critical response to the question, whether we should think Mallarmé consistently to the end, instead of interrogating the question itself, has tended to provide an answer.[41] On the one hand, there are those who think that Celan does think Mallarmé to the end, whatever this might mean.[42] On the other, there are those, more numerous and more serious, who think that he does not.[43] As Petra Leutner notes, there is no consensus as to how this question, which Harbusch says has become a sort of shibboleth in Celan criticism,[44] should be understood.[45] What does it mean to think Mallarmé 'through to the end'?

Harbusch — perhaps sensitive to Mallarmé's claim to be 'profondément et scrupuleusement syntaxier' [profoundly and scrupulously a man of syntax][46] — hesitates over the three subsections of the phrase that precede the evocation of Mallarmé's name: 'to put it concretely, above all — let's say — think Mallarmé all the way to the end?' She asks in what ways the preceding qualifications modulate the reference to Mallarmé.[47] The rhetorical introduction of a concrete example, expressed 'concretely', that will illustrate what contemporary poetry should or ought to do, is immediately qualified by 'above all', which not only indicates the precise and specific nature of the comparison to come, but also indicates that the comparison will not elucidate all aspects of the issue at hand. This complex combination of qualifications is then further qualified by a colloquial 'let's say', which emphasizes not so much the specificity of the example as its arbitrary and *ad hoc* nature. The same could be said just as well through another example: 'The function that Mallarmé's name plays in the Büchner speech wavers between specificity and arbitrariness, between substantial necessity and casual illustration, a fact that we should bear in mind, when we ask about the importance that Celan might have ascribed to Mallarmé'.[48] It is not the only time Celan uses this particular rhetorical construction. In a letter to Gleb Struve — the Russian literary historian and editor of Mandel'shtam's works — Celan writes that Mandel'shtam was one of the few Russian poets who thought his time to the end: 'I know of hardly any other Russian poet of his generation, who was *in time* like he was, who thought with and from out of this time, who thought it to the end, in every one of its moments, in its objects and events, in the words that stepped up to objects and things and stood for them, simultaneously open and hermetic'.[49] Here, though, it is not Mallarmé who thinks his time to the end, but the audience and reader who are invited to think Mallarmé — as direct object — transitively 'to the end'.

If the notion of thinking Mallarmé to the end leads to a dead end, then we might resort to one tactic sometimes used to read the more impenetrable passages of Mallarmé's oeuvre. When language refuses to give up some part of the meaning it appears to contain, the attention of the reader is forced to shift from language's semantic function to its visual function. Mallarmé is always alert to the visual significance of language, particularly — although not exclusively — in his poems. He knows the value of different fonts, individual printed letters, punctuation marks, and those parts of the page than do not bear traces of text to the reader's efforts to create meaning. If we examine Celan's question as it appears on the page, we will see that it is followed by a single blank line. One possible way of interrogating this white space is to ask if this space was always blank, or if the definitive text has used the whiteness of the page to draw a veil over alternative verbal formulations. In the genetic edition of 'The Meridian', an alternative version of this part of the speech reads as follows:

> Or — I am leaping over certain things — , might we, as occurs everywhere nowadays, proceed from art as a given, should we, to express it quite concretely, think Mallarmé to the end — that is, think him ~~to death~~ maybe to death?[50]

Aware of this document, Harbusch asserts that thinking Mallarmé to the end should be understood not so much as a reference to Mallarmé's work, as to the man himself, and that to think Mallarmé to the end is, in existential terms, the same as to think him to death. Celan, she adds somewhat facetiously, might even have taken some pleasure in inviting his audience to think Mallarmé — of all poets — through to his physical death.[51]

If Mallarmé — whom Sartre describes as practicing 'the terrorism of politeness'[52] — were able to consider Celan's question, he would probably choose not to perceive the slight that Harbusch articulates. Instead, he would encourage us to consider how thinking him '~~to death~~ maybe to death' differs from thinking him 'to the end'. Anyone familiar with Mallarmé's work will likely see the second of these two formulations as a reference to his unfinished project to write the Book that would bring literature to a close. 'Everything', Mallarmé writes in 1895 — echoing his comments made to Jules Huret four years previously[53] — 'exists to end up in a book'.[54] On the night before he died of a coughing fit in the rooms he rented by the Seine at Valvins, Mallarmé wrote to his wife and daughter. He told them that if he were to suffer another attack and die, that they should destroy the 'pile of half-a-century's worth of notes' gathered behind an 'antique tapestry' in the apartment on the Rue de Rome.[55] To think Mallarmé to the end would require that these papers — 'the secret material of his great unfinished work',[56] the vast pre-text to the 'Livre' that will never come to be — be made accessible to readers. This has been the case since Jacques Scherer published the notes in 1957.[57]

In the context of Celan's speech, then, thinking Mallarmé's lifelong project consistently 'to the end' is to fully embrace the impersonality and remove of Lenz's 'man möchte'. It is to transform all human experience into language or symbol, to consciously adopt foreign voices, gestures, and actions. It is to eliminate those idiomatic traces of the individual's body and breath. In art, there is no space for inspiration, for hitherto unknown dimensions, for new poetic creations. It is in this sense that Michael Hamburger, Celan's friend, and one of his first (and finest) translators into English, sees it at the time. For Hamburger, the appeal to Mallarmé is 'a clue to [Celans's] artistic extremism, an extremism of diction and syntax', and that 'with Mallarmé Celan shares a strong aversion to the merely phenomenal and accidental, as opposed to the essential and archetypal'.[58]

By contrast, to think Mallarmé 'perhaps to death' or even '~~to death~~' is an invitation to conflate Mallarmé the man with Mallarmé the oeuvre, to break down the barriers between what is human and non-human, between poetry and art, between the personality and immediacy of 'ich mag' and the impersonality and remove of 'man möchte'. To think Mallarmé through to death complicates our understanding of that which constitutes literature, as such a movement cannot remain in the realm of the literary or artistic. It must encompass the poet as 'breath, that is direction and fate', the fragility and transience of human flesh, the precariousness of spirit, and the eternal presence of the poet's absence. It means that when we read literature, we will be obliged to think about that which is not usually perceived as inhering in literature. We will have to learn to hear what is said in the absence of language and to read what is not visible to the eye.

Whether we choose to pursue the meaning of that which remains written (thinking Mallarmé to the end) or whether we cling to that which is no longer written (thinking Mallarmé to death), Celan claims to be unable to go beyond the speculative formulation of this question: 'I have grasped ahead, grasped beyond — not far enough, I know — I return to Büchner's *Lenz*, that is to the — episodic — discussion that took place 'over table' and during which Lenz "was in good spirits"'.[59] I suggest that it is precisely through this rhetorical gesture of failure (thinking Mallarmé to the end is beyond me!) that Celan achieves the very extremity of art he claims he is unable to pursue. Here, in 'The Meridian', before our eyes and without our knowing, Celan indeed grasps and even goes beyond Mallarmé at the very moment where he claims to be unable to do so. It is in the white space that follows the invocation of Mallarmé's name or oeuvre (or both), and that precedes Celan's avowal of failure, that Celan thinks Mallarmé to the end, which is also a beginning.

The Mallarmé Celan succeeds in thinking to the end is not the Mallarmé of words. As he writes in his notes, the poem 'does not mean — or no longer means — , n'en déplaise à Mallarmé, in one of those phonetically, semantically, and syntactically over-differentiated language structures assembled from "words"'.[60] It is instead Mallarmé as poet and composer of silence. It is Mallarmé who, above all poets, takes delight in the absence of language, and who describes the silence of the page that marks the end of a line of verse as 'sole luxury after the rhymes'.[61] In the 1897 preface to 'A Throw of the Dice', Mallarmé offers to guide the reader's astonished eye not only over the scattered traces of language, but over the absence of language: 'The "blanks", in effect, assume importance, strike you before anything else'.[62] In a review of a Swinburne tragedy, published in 1876, he writes of silence as 'profound, divine, dwelling in the souls of readers'.[63] In grasping ahead and beyond into the white line that follows his unanswered and unanswerable question, Celan is in fact already incorporating Mallarmé's concept of whiteness — as that which constitutes the poem's intellectual infrastructure — into his own poetics: 'The poem's intellectual armature dissimulates itself and inhabits — takes place — in the space which isolates the stanzas, and among the white of the paper: significant silence that is no less beautiful to compose than verse'.[64] Armature should here be understood in its geological sense, as the crust that envelops organic fossils, and which is neither part of the fossil, nor of the rock.[65] The whiteness of Mallarmé's page is as essential to the poem as the crust in which fossils are couched. Celan appears to invite his readers — if not his audience — to perceive Mallarmé as contributing to the armature, to the 'significant silence' of his own poetic project.

It is after both his speculative, rhetorical question and the silence that follows it — marked in the text by a blank line — that Celan says: 'I have grasped ahead, grasped beyond — not far enough, I know [ich weiss]'. In trying to think Mallarmé to the end, Celan claims to have failed. And yet in his very admission of failure, we are also asked to detect something like proof of success. 'Ich weiss' means 'I know'. But 'weiss' might also — catachrestically — be read as the adjective 'white'. 'Ich weiss' would then give the juxtaposition of personal pronoun and adjective in 'I white'. This ungrammatical or fragmentary formulation would be a way of saying both that language understood only as that which is visible can lead us to assert a conclusive reading where in fact we are meant to read on; and that in order to read on we need to learn to read that which is not visible to the eye.

It would by no means be the only time that Celan plays on the semantic multiplicity of 'weiss'. In the poem 'KEINE SANDKUNST MEHR' [NO MORE SAND-ART] — one of the poems in which Pöggeler and others identify traces of an engagement with Mallarmé's 'A Throw of the Dice' — the ambiguities of 'weiss' again come decisively into play: 'Dein Gesang, was weiss er?'[66] or 'Your song, what does it know?' Here, the semantic instability of 'weiss' and 'er', invites us to read the comparative adjective 'weisser' or 'more white'. What is more white than your song, Mallarmé? What does your poetry know that we cannot unlock from its significant whiteness? This all too facile word play on 'weiss' is, in the context of this partial and marginal engagement with Mallarmé, perhaps Celan's own step toward poetry, where Lucile's was a short, sharp shout of 'Long Live the King!' and Lenz's those moments when it was disagreeable to him that he could not walk on his head.[67] It is, significantly, a step toward poetry expressed in the absence of language.

For Celan, that which surrounds the text, that which gives the text its life and meaning, is not only that which has been said, but also that which has not been said and that which has been said silently. It is not only that without the silence and whiteness that surrounds the printed text there is no text. It is that silence also speaks, albeit in ways unknown to conventional language. This silent mode of speech, this invisible mode of language is perhaps the most consistently overlooked element of any literary oeuvre, a major component of the sous-oeuvre. In the short prose piece 'Conversation in the Mountain' (1958), a fictional account of a meeting that was meant to have taken place at Sils Maria between Adorno and Celan, we read: 'and keeping silent is no keeping silent, no word is silenced and no sentence, it is just a pause, a word-gap, a blank space, you see all the syllables standing around it'.[68] Silence is not the absence of language — here the chatter of two Jews in the mountains — but speaks on its own terms and in its own way. It is this silence that we must learn to read and understand. The intertextual reference to Mallarmé's life and oeuvre is silent, but no less important for being so. Celan appeals to Mallarmé to teach us, readers of literature, to read not only that which we can see in print, but also that which we cannot see. He is asking us to see that which is at one and the same time wholly artful, because it dissembles itself, and wholly artless because it refuses to lend itself to symbolic expression in language.

Sartre and the Movement of Suicide

While hospitalized at Sainte Anne during the spring of 1966 — during which time he composes *Eingedunkelt* — Celan encounters and engages with Mallarmé in a very different way. Celan read relatively widely during this time, mostly work appearing in newly published editions by authors including Hans Henny Jahnn, Lao Tse, Joseph Joubert, Joseph Conrad, and Alfred Adler. The texts that were of particular importance in the composition of several *Eingedunkelt* poems appear to have been Hans Schiebelhuth's translation of Thomas Wolfe's autobiographical novel *Of Time and the River* (1936), James Joyce's *Ulysses* as translated by Georg Goyert (1928) (which Celan read at various other times), and Wolfgang Schadewaldt's magisterial prose translation of *The Odyssey* (1958). Most of these books, now preserved at the German Literature Archive at Marbach am Neckar, contain annotations, some of which Celan dated and which can be traced to this particular period of hospitalization.

Despite the fact that Celan was usually able to read literature in a number of foreign languages, including English, it is perhaps a preliminary indication of the state of his mental health at the time that almost all texts read were either in the original German or in German translation. One of the rare texts that Celan read in the original French was a newly published paperback edition of Mallarmé's poems, with a preface by Jean-Paul Sartre, entitled *Poésies*.[69] Celan had most likely seen the advertisement for the book as published in *Le Monde* on 12 March 1966.[70] Two days later, Celan wrote to Gisèle asking her to bring him 'the <u>Mallarmé</u> prefaced by <u>Sartre</u> in the new Gallimard series'.[71] The paperback book was in his possession by 17 March, the date he inscribed inside the front cover. The book contains a large number of annotations in blue and black ball-point pen, blue ink, and pencil, both throughout the poems and in Sartre's preface. In particular, the numerous references to suicide visibly provoke Celan's interest. Celan heavily marks the tercets in 'Le sonneur' ['The Bell-Ringer'] for example, in which the first person speaker reveals the futility of 'pulling the rope to sound the Ideal', and announces that 'one day, tired of having pulled in vain, / O Satan, I will take the stone away and hang myself'.[72] It is above all in the preface, though, that Celan leaves traces of his passage and intellectual engagement. Sartre presents Mallarmé not only as constantly preoccupied with the possibility of killing himself, but with this always imminent threat (or promise) of suicide as providing the structure and justification for Mallarmé's poetic activity.

An examination of Celan's archive reveals traces of a heightened interest in suicide as it manifests itself in works of both philosophy and literature. Between 1961 and 1963, in his translation class at the 'École normale supérieure', Celan set students preparing the *aggrégation* an extract from the first chapter of Balzac's *La Peau de chagrin* [*The Magic Skin*] (1831) for translation into German.[73] This passage includes the premonitory lines: 'There exists something both great and dreadful in suicide [...] Each suicide is a sublime poem of melancholy [...] a woman threw herself into the Seine from the *Pont des Arts*'.[74] In the final year of his life, Celan read Emil Cioran's essay 'Encounters with Suicide' and underscored fragments including the following: 'One only kills oneself if, in some respects, one has always been on the outside of everything. It is a matter of an originary in-appropriation of which one cannot be conscious. <u>He who is called to kill himself belongs only by accident to this world. Essentially, he is not of any world</u>'[75] and: 'To kill oneself is, in fact, to rival death, to demonstrate that one can go one better than it, to play a trick on it and <u>to redeem oneself in one's own eyes</u>, which is by no means a trivial matter'.[76]

The reading of Sartre's preface constitutes a distinctive and unusual moment both in Celan's engagement with Mallarmé, and with the question of suicide and its relation to literature. Where Cioran thought and wrote extensively about suicide in order to repeatedly defer his own, from *On the Heights of Despair* (1934) onward, suicide is not one of Sartre's central preoccupations. His engagement with the issue, here in the context of a discussion of Mallarmé's life and work, is perhaps less expected. Camus once wrote — inaccurately it turns out[77] — that Schopenhauer 'praised suicide before a well stocked table'.[78] A similar criticism might more accurately be leveled at Sartre for whom suicide, even as a philosophical concept, remains a mode of being rather than non-being, of living rather than dying. And yet it is through Sartre's examination of suicide in Mallarmé that Celan appears to perceive the possibility of forging a new type of poetics, in which the projected suicide of the poet plays an integral, constitutive, and confirming role in the creation, and subsequent interpretation, of individual poems.

Sartre's preface was not written specifically for the Gallimard edition of *Poésies*, but is a fragment of a larger, unrealized project to write an 'existential biography'[79] or 'psychobiography'[80] on Mallarmé, just as he had done for Baudelaire,[81] planned to do for Tintoretto, and would do for Jean Genet,[82] himself,[83] and Gustave Flaubert.[84] Although begun in late 1948, and partially published in an anthology edited by Raymond Queneau in 1953,[85] most of the materials relating to the project were destroyed when Sartre's apartment was bombed in January 1962 by the 'Organisation de l'armée secrète', a group of far-right paramilitaries opposed to Algerian independence.[86] Its composition between 1948 and 1952 occurs at a time when a number of seminal primary and secondary works had recently been released, including the first Pléiade edition of Mallarmé's complete works, edited by Henri Mondor and Gérard Jean-Aubry,[87] Mondor's two volume biography of Mallarmé,[88] and Maurice Blanchot's early writings on Mallarmé in *Faux pas* [*False Step*][89] and *La part du feu* [*The Work of Fire*].[90]

In the preface, a reprint of the 1953 edition, Sartre presents Mallarmé as an unlikely herald and hero of the twentieth century.[91] The son and grandson of civil servants, Mallarmé is destined to live out his life in government administration, but experiences a violent, although largely internal and silent, revolt against society, family, nature, and himself. His revolt is not that of an anarchist, as discussed in the previous chapter, but of a poet who wants to 'blow the world up' and whose violence is so entire, determined, and desperate that it transfigures itself into the 'calm idea of violence'.[92] There had been a time in the not-too-distant past when God underwrote all human enterprise, when poets were minor prophets, and God spoke through them. As there is no longer a God to guarantee poetic expression,

Mallarmé constructs his entire oeuvre upon a system that Sartre describes as 'a sort of analytic and vaguely Spinozist materialism'.[93] 'Nothing exists except matter, eternal murmur of being',[94] or as Mallarmé puts it in his 1895 speech 'Music and Letters': 'Nature takes place, we cannot add to it; cities, railroads, and other inventions change only the form of the material'.[95]

Given God's absence, man's appearance in matter is due only to the random operations of chance. His continued existence is a finite state of chance encounters, an absurd succession of random events that undermine all subsequent attempts to impose explicatory structures on existence, confirming what Graham Robb describes as the 'metaphysical futility of the organizing mind'.[96] The absolute subjection of man to the caprice of chance is the reason why man is 'an impossible dream'[97], a 'loser, a 'dead loss' among 'dead losses'.[98] And yet as a poet, Mallarmé wants to create an order of being superior to matter. It is the poet's task — his 'categorical imperative'[99] — to compensate as best he can for the absence of a divine being. Any such project is, by definition, bound to failure. It is despair at the impossibility of this situation that leads Mallarmé to formulate a new and 'pessimistic' metaphysics, based on the presupposition that man is irreversibly implicated in chance and matter. There are, though, two 'supernatural' acts available to man with which he can break out of this imprisonment in material determinism. One is crime, and the other is the supreme manifestation of crime, namely suicide.[100] The challenge for Mallarmé, and his lifelong goal, according to Sartre, is to create a poetics that effectively harnesses the supernatural potential of suicide.

It has become a commonplace throughout criticism on Mallarmé's work, and particularly since Blanchot's article 'Mallarmé's Silence',[101] to posit the unfinished 'Livre' or Book as the ideal but unrealized pinnacle of the poet's lifelong pursuit of beauty through literature. The paucity of evidence surrounding the Book facilitates the elaboration of a narrative that Mallarmé himself appears to have encouraged: 'It is now a fact', writes Blanchot, in response to Mondor's recently published biography, and somewhat prematurely, 'that we will only ever know very little about Mallarmé's work, and almost nothing about his conception of the great work that he was planning'.[102] Sartre's conceit is to replace this obsession with the Book, corroborated throughout the poet's correspondence, with a markedly different and less frequently attested obsession, namely suicide. Sartre would like his reader to believe that Mallarmé was constantly preoccupied with the possibility of ending his own life: 'Isn't it time to explode? In Tournon, in Besançon, in Avignon, Mallarmé very seriously envisaged suicide'.[103]

To support this stance, Sartre draws almost exclusively from *Igitur*, although, perhaps wary of being accused of working from too small a sample of Mallarmé's work, he at no point refers to the specific source. *Igitur* is a prose tale, written in Avignon during 1869 and 1870, and which both Blanchot and Sartre see as bringing to a close the crisis that had tormented the poet for the previous four years. Although incomplete, and difficult to read and understand in its detail, the tale appears to project a sort of Gothic allegory — in the style of Poe — of the existential crisis suffered by the poet in the second half of the 1860s, during which time Mallarmé was unable to write on account of his exposure to the absolute. 'It is a short story', Mallarmé writes to Henri Cazalis in November 1869, 'by means of which I hope to floor the old monster Impotence'.[104] As Bertrand Marchal explains, 'it's a question of reliving, through literature, which will have the effect of an exorcism, the crisis that Mallarmé believes he has overcome, but of which he must still remove the deep-seated germ'.[105]

In the tale, Igitur, the last member of his family line, is invited to fulfill an 'immemorial task' which will abolish chance. He leaves the room carrying a book and a candle, and descends into a crypt containing the tombs of his ancestors. Aware of the futility of his act, but faithful to his ancestral obligation, he accomplishes the act, which consists in either drinking 'the substance of Nothingness'[106] from a vial or in throwing the dice.[107] Crucially, though, in one draft it appears that Igitur is not required to either imbibe Nothingness or throw the dice: 'Igitur simply shakes the dice — movement, before going back to the ashes, atoms of his ancestors: the movement that is in him is absolved. One understands what his ambiguity means. / ? He closes the book — blows the candle out, — with his breath that contained chance: / and, crossing his arms, lies down on the ashes of his ancestors'.[108] Although Igitur is meant to either become at one with the void by consuming the absolute, or by throwing the dice and momentarily abolishing chance, it is enough for him to simulate the dice throw, and perhaps by extension the act of drinking from the vial, for his task to have been fulfilled.

This means that in what is clearly an allegory for the act of killing oneself, it is sufficient to act as if one were about to kill oneself. It is enough for the allegory to remain allegory. Engaging with the absolute, with the void, with Nothingness, through the fiction of a gesture is not only an acceptable alternative, it is in fact the only possible way of rendering his existence meaningful. When Sartre says that 'Mallarmé's Man, just like Pascal's, expresses himself in drama and not in essence',[109] he is also stating that for Mallarmé and Pascal, the only possible act is to pretend to act, to create fictions. Literature is nothing more or less than a fiction, which simulates and recreates the exposure to the absolute that Mallarmé claims to have experienced quite by chance during his crisis, and which he perceived as 'the intimate correlation of Poetry and the Universe'.[110]

Igitur is important not only because it uncovers the fiction — or what Mallarmé elsewhere calls 'The Glorious Lie'[111] — of all linguistic acts, and so offers a model for all poetic creation, or what Sartre calls his 'doctrine'.[112] It is also important in Mallarmé's personal history as it marks the moment at which he commits what Sartre calls a 'mock suicide',[113] much as Goethe was said to have survived his own existential crisis by describing the suicide of Werther in *The Sorrows of Young Werther*.[114] From this point on, Mallarmé lives a suspended death.[115] In Blanchot's terms, he becomes a figure for language itself, which 'is life that carries death and maintains itself in death'.[116] Although the text exists only as a series of drafts — and was dismissed as risible by Catulle Mendès, one of the few to have heard Mallarmé read from the text in person[117] — from this point onward, as Blanchot notes, Mallarmé will make almost no reference to the mental and physical troubles that had marked the years he spent in Tournon, Besançon, and Avignon, as a reluctant and less than capable teacher. *Igitur* both satisfies Mallarmé's need to eliminate himself, and confirms the importance of continuing to contemplate suicide on a daily basis.

Although *Igitur* provides a clear allegory that allows us to tie the act of pretending to throw the dice, to both the act of pretending to kill oneself, and to the act of literature, it is unclear just how this might be achieved in the individual poem. There are poems that include references, to varying degrees, to the paraphernalia and culture of suicide. Paul de Man draws attention to 'the future vial' that evokes 'the balmy Death' [la balsamique Mort] of suicide by poison 'for the weary poet that life withers'[118] in the verse poem 'Les fleurs', written three years before Igitur descends into the family crypt.[119] 'Le tombeau de Charles Baudelaire' concludes with a reference to the great poet's 'tutelary poison', which is 'Toujours à respirer si nous en périssons' [To always inhale even if we perish from it].[120] In the extended and unfinished manuscript on Mallarmé (first published in 1979) Sartre reads Mallarmé's anger toward his step-mother as being registered in the prose poem 'Poor Pale Child': 'They will make you bad, and one day you will commit a crime', writes Mallarmé to himself. This crime, says Sartre, in true hyperbolic fashion, is 'murder and martyrdom, assassination which, when it comes down to it, is suicide'.[121] One sonnet from the mid-1880s famously begins with the line: 'The beautiful suicide victoriously fled',[122] in which suicide is a metaphor for the setting of the sun. But none of these references are sufficient for the poems in which they appear to become what Sartre calls 'symbolic suicides'.[123] Suicide must be made 'effective'[124] in literature. To do this, the poem does not need to speak of suicide *per se*, but must realize a 'movement of suicide'. As Sartre writes, and Celan underlines: '<u>It is the very movement of suicide that must be reproduced in the poem</u>. Since Man cannot create, and since he has the ability to destroy, because he affirms himself in the same act which annihilates him, the poem will be a work of destruction'.[125]

In emphasizing the destructive work of poetic language — the '*negative* work'[126] of poetry — Sartre is clearly incorporating Blanchot's thinking, as expressed in 'The Myth of Mallarmé'.[127] But where Blanchot perceives the self-abolition of language as creating a new, 'more evasive reality'[128] that he will ultimately call 'music',[129] Sartre requires Mallarmé's poetry to prove the poet's engagement in and contestation with society. This is why he equates the 'movement of suicide' with the explosion of matter. In suicide, Sartre finds an emblem that brings the dissipated traces of destruction identified by Blanchot into the clarity of a single, uniterable event in time that is realized in and by the body of a unique individual. The notion of the 'movement of suicide' allows him to re-package and re-present Mallarmé's negative poetics in a mode that might in theory be applied to society itself. And so when Mallarmé says — a quarter of a century after writing *Igitur* — that 'I know of no other bomb, but a book',[130] despite the fact that this is said in opposition to violent resistance, Sartre eagerly takes Mallarmé out of context, and misquotes him, to say: 'the poem is the only bomb'.[131] The fact that most of the five hundred pages of manuscript that make up Sartre's projected book on Mallarmé will themselves be destroyed in a bomb attack takes the destructive and self-destructive power of literature to a level of realization in the real world not envisaged even by Sartre.

When it comes to explaining how this negative work operates in individual poems — including those that ostensibly have nothing to do with suicide — Sartre's exposition appears cursory, unsatisfactory, and strangely detached from the poems themselves. This is at least in part because the passage in which Sartre explains how he perceives the movement of suicide as operating in the poem is omitted in the 1966 publication in *Poésies*, just as it was when it was published in 1953.[132] It is here that Sartre outlines how 'the poem will be born from the poet's suicide'.[133] Suicide metaphorically describes the defining gesture of Mallarmé's negative poetics, namely impersonality, through which the poet allows his function as creator of meaning to be taken over by the poem itself, an idea that Sartre encounters in Blanchot's 'The Myth of Mallarmé'.

In the preface read by Celan, however, Sartre's relies principally on *Igitur* for textual corroboration of his thesis, and on a reading of a sonnet first published in 1885:

> 'Le vierge, le vivace et le bel aujourd'hui' ['The virgin, the vivacious and the beautiful today'] provides a perfect example of [Mallarmé's] <u>internal annulment of the poem</u>. 'Today' with its future is only an illusion, the present is reduced to the past, a swan which believed itself to act is only the memory of itself and hopelessly immobilizes itself "au songe froid de mépris" ["in a cold dream of scorn"]; an appearance of movement disappears, the infinite and undifferentiated surface of the ice remains. The explosion of colors and forms reveals to our senses a symbol which takes us back to the tragedy of man, and then the explosion dissolves into nothingness: this is the internal movement of <u>these extraordinary poems which are at one and the same time silent words and falsified objects</u>. Ultimately, in their very disappearance, they will have evoked the contours of some object "which tries and fails to escape" and their beauty itself will be like an *a priori* proof that *lack of being* is a *manner of being.*[134]

Although Sartre at no point engages in a sustained manner with the poems in which he claims to identify the internal movement of suicide, as Wellek notes,[135] he does identify its two principal dynamics. The first is the stiffening of the virgin and vivacious present into the past, the affirmative act of the swan's drunken wing as it freezes into the transparent glacier 'of flights that have not fled'. This is a shift from movement to stasis, from liquid to solid, from supple to rigid limb. It is a movement, to adopt Celan's terms, from the transience of life toward the eternal and infinite qualities of 'Kunst'. It is a movement that goes beyond the token denial of Self and the fake claim to impotence of Lenz's 'man möchte', and which passes to the most artful act man is capable of, his self-petrifaction in the supernatural act of suicide. The second dynamic of the 'movement of suicide' or the 'internal annulment of the poem' takes the form of an explosion which instantaneously dissolves into nothingness, an event in which the absent contours of the exploded and now vanished object are proof of its past existence, are proof that '*lack of being* is a *manner of being*'.

In Sartre's exposition of the movement of suicide, these two contradictory if not mutually exclusive dynamics of stiffening and explosion coexist. The first describes the physical stiffening of a body in *rigor mortis* in the minutes and hours following death. The second describes the metaphysical explosion of being as it breaks free from the fixity and limitations of human existence and re-enters the infinite and the eternal, haunting the material world with an absence of being. Not only are both constituent parts of the movement of suicide, but they should be understood as linked. They relate to each other in much the same way that the being-in-itself relates to the being-for-itself. Where the in-itself describes the being of objects without consciousness, such as a lifeless corpse, and is 'solid, self-identical, passive and inert',[136] the for-itself, which is 'fluid, non-self-identical, and dynamic',[137] depends upon the internal negation of the in-itself to come into being. The stiffening of matter precedes and occasions the explosion in spirit.

By emphasizing the central role of suicide in Mallarmé's thinking, Sartre does not provide a new interpretation of Mallarmé's work, so much as enhance and vulgarize the abstract and theoretical exposition of Mallarmé's negative poetics realized by Blanchot in *La part du feu*.[138] Beyond the allegorization of suicide in his unfinished *Igitur*, Mallarmé actually makes only limited appeals to suicide in his work and correspondence. Suicide is rejected alongside perspicacity as 'sterile' in his 1885 essay on Wagner.[139] In the prose piece in praise of Villiers de L'Isle-Adam — initially performed six times during a tour of Belgium in February 1890 — Mallarmé equates suicide with trickery: 'So much audacity — I believe truly, that there would be dupery, almost to the point of suicide'.[140] Five years later, in the prose piece 'Restricted Action', a young poet repeatedly confides to Mallarmé of his need to 'act', which Mallarmé understands is 'philosophically, to produce on many a movement that in return gives you the impression that you were its originator, so you exist: of which no one is sure beforehand'.[141] To 'act' is to eliminate oneself, to realize the only action capable of abolishing, and thereby confirming, one's being. Mallarmé maintains that this act should be realized only in the inscription of language, that it should remain a philosophical gesture: 'Your act is always applied to paper; for meditating, without traces, becomes evanescent, nor were you seeking to exalt an instinct in some vehement and lost gesture'.[142] Moments such as these, which indicate the mature Mallarmé's rejection of suicide in favor of literature, not only suggest that the poet has a deep understanding of suicide's true negativity. They also cast doubt on Sartre's provocative and unsubstantiated claims that barely a day passed without the poet being tempted to kill himself.

When Sartre attributes suicidal tendencies to Mallarmé, he conceives of suicide as 'philosophical' rather than 'plain', to adopt Camus terms.[143] He perceives of it less as a 'vehement and lost gesture' than as a variation of the many preciosities that characterize Mallarmé's life and work. This is why he goes to some lengths to create a caricature of the poet's biography. Mallarmé is portrayed as physically small, discreet in nature, and not all that interested in the opposite sex.[144] He suffers his metaphysical anguish 'completely' but 'modestly',[145] like a learned but sensitive nineteenth-century woman should. Yes, the world must be blown up, Sartre admits, but how might Mallarmé go about it 'without dirtying his hands in the process'?[146] Any doubt that we are meant to detect a trace of camp in Sartre's depiction of Mallarmé's affectations is dispelled when we read that 'a bomb is only a thing, after all, like a Second Empire armchair — just a little naughtier'.[147] Suicide, as Sartre sees it here, is little more than an exaggerated mannerism, a variation of the decadent movement away from the Real toward what is meant to be the Ideal, but which is nothing more than a denial or negation of the Real. By establishing suicide as mannerism, and thereby implicating it in a social rather than existential structure, in his larger book project Sartre will be able to use suicide as a vehicle to portray Mallarmé as implicated in the world and engaged in society.

The bold and largely unsubstantiated application of suicide to Mallarmé's life and poetry is facilitated by the fact that Sartre himself has a particular, abstract notion of suicide, which is less a mode of dying, than a mode of living, a 'being-toward-death' that is never intended to result in death.[148] In Sartre's examination of suicide as a possible act in *Being and Nothingness*,[149] some five years before he begins to write on Mallarmé, it is the 'self', in coordination with the 'self that I am not yet', which draws man to the abyss only to draw him away to continued life and safety:

> If *nothing* compels me to save my life, *nothing* prevents me from precipitating myself into the abyss. The decisive conduct will emanate from a self which I am not yet. Thus the self which I am depends on the self that I am not yet to the exact extent that the self which I am not yet does not depend on the self which I am. Vertigo appears as the apprehension of this dependence. I approach the precipice, and my scrutiny is searching for myself in the very depths. In terms of this moment, I play with my possibilities. My eyes, running over the abyss from top to bottom, imitate the possible fall and realize it symbolically; at the same time suicide, from the fact that it becomes a *possibility* possible for *me*, now causes to appear possible motives for adopting it (suicide would cause anguish to cease). Fortunately these motives in their turn, from the sole fact that they are motives of possibility, present themselves as ineffective, as non-determinant; they can no more produce the suicide than my horror of the fall can *determine* me to avoid it. It is this counter-anguish which generally puts an end to anguish by transmuting it into indecision. Indecision in its turn, calls for decision. I abruptly put myself at a distance from the edge of the precipice and resume my way.[150]

Three years after this passage appears in *Being and Nothingness*, Heidegger will argue that there is a need for poets and thinkers who can 'reach into the abyss', and that it should only be possible to turn away from the abyss once the abyssal has been 'experienced and endured'.[151] In contrast, Sartre's experience of the abyss is an ironic one, always safely at a remove. He does not so much experience and endure it mentally, as peer into it from the relative safety of the top of the precipice. His eyes run over the abyss from top to bottom, imitate the possible fall, and realize it symbolically. The figure which describes Sartre's encounter with the abyss, and which ensures that he will never make the leap into its depths, is a circle. Much like a magnetic motor, which revolves because of the rapidly alternating forces of attraction and repulsion, so too Sartre's agent is drawn to and repelled from death, creating a circle that remains self-enclosed, and that continues to rotate, both because and in spite of its reliance on the negative. When he says that '*rien*' or '*nothing*' compels him to save or lose his life, he is not only engaging in a rhetorical game. This 'nothing' is also, and perhaps more significantly, 'something', as 'rien', coming from the Latin 'res' [thing], confirms. The un-decidability of 'nothing' and 'something' engages in a perpetual circular motion, ceaselessly moving from nothing to nothing via something. This repetitive pattern is itself repeated in the following line, when the self moves to self via 'the self which I am not yet'.

The vertigo experienced in the apprehension of this circular dependence should be understood precisely as the mental sensation of whirling around in a circle, as indicated by its roots in the Latin 'vertĕre' [to turn]. The logic of vertigo applies also to the reasoning for and against suicide, as experienced on the edge of the philosophical abyss. The circular movement that leads Sartre to look deep into the abyss is the same circular movement that allows him to remove himself from the edge, and to postpone — this time and every subsequent time — his jump into the depths. As Alexandre Kojève explains, when discussing suicide in *The Phenomenology of Spirit*, Hegel has no interest in the radical Skeptic who would fulfill his human being by 'taking nihilism seriously' and killing himself, because 'by definition, he disappears by committing suicide, he ceases to be, and consequently, he ceases to be a human being, an agent of historical evolution. Only the Nihilist who *remains alive* is interesting'.[152] Similarly for Sartre, suicide is a valid and acceptable figure only if it remains figure, infinitely perpetuating its un-decidability, constantly postponing its realization. It is only of any value as long as it remains a fraud, a philosophical sleight of hand, designed to protect the subject from choosing death, even as it entertains death as a possibility that can be chosen.

Having expounded Mallarmé's poetics of suicide, Sartre will conclude his preface by claiming that Mallarmé was always conscious that his work was an enormous hoax:

> Mallarmé is something of a melancholy fraudster: he created and maintained, among his friends and disciples, the illusion of a great work, which would contain the entire world, he claimed to be preparing for it. But he always knew perfectly well that it was an impossibility. His life had just to appear subordinated to the absent object: the orphic explication of the Earth (which is nothing other than poetry itself).[153]

Sartre claims that Mallarmé made sure to relate to this unrealizable work in such a way that his own future death would assure the absence of this work for posterity. He knew that his passing would confirm the projected work as 'the highest ambition of the poet' and that its failure or incompletion would constitute nothing less that 'the tragic impossibility of Man'.[154] For thirty years, Sartre continues, Mallarmé played out the role of Igitur in front of everybody: 'In the complex system of this comedy, his poems had to be failures to be perfect. It was not enough for them to abolish language and the world, or even for them to annul themselves: they had to be futile sketches in view of an unknown and impossible work that death prevented him from beginning'.[155] Mallarmé lived his life as a performance artist might, not so much in a Gothic tragedy, as in an existential 'comedy'.[156] At some level of the revelation of this trickery, and the gullibility of the disciples who followed him so readily, we should also detect a somewhat prescient dig at one of

Mallarmé's contemporary disciples, namely Blanchot, whose utter certainty that the Book will always be absent will be shaken by the publication of the notes for the Book in 1957.

Mallarmé is not alone in exercising trickery over his followers, though, because Sartre also relies on an essential duplicity. We are led to believe throughout the preface that the suicide of the poet will complete these poems, much as Hans Urs von Balthasar argues that Christ's ministry can only be understood in the light of his subsequent death (and perhaps resurrection). If Sartre is to reconcile Mallarmé's great hoax with the poet's supposed preoccupation with suicide, then the poet must die an unforeseen death, a death in which chance asserts its irresistible power over man and his futile projects. Death must be 'random' and 'accidental', a 'terrible shipwreck'.[157] It is only in the light of an 'accidental death' that these 'symbolic suicides' will have fulfilled their intended role.[158]

For Sartre to be able to draw this conclusion, there needs to be an important narrative slippage from Mallarmé's supposedly life-long suicidal tendencies, to his unexpected death in September 1898 at the age of fifty-six. Sartre's reading of Mallarmé is built on both of these mutually exclusive possibilities, which perpetually engender and repel each other — one of which was not meant to happen but happened, and the other of which was meant to happen but did not. Rhetorically, the reader might be forgiven for missing this shift in emphasis. It is as part of the argument for Mallarmé's duplicity in regard to the Book that Sartre discreetly shifts the emphasis away from Mallarmé's daily preoccupation with suicide, to his awareness that only natural death would perpetuate the myth of the Book that 'was going to be very beautiful',[159] bringing not only all literature to a close, but the universe itself. Sartre both spells out Mallarmé's trickery, and hides behind its revelation, as he continues to argue for the centrality of suicide in poetry.

Sartre's psychological interpretation — although guilty of poetic license, autobiographical projection, misquotation, and hyperbole — successfully conveys the rare image of a Mallarmé tormented by very human uncertainties, passions, and delights. The notion that Mallarmé is driven by 'hate' and 'resentment'[160] or that he resisted suicide only for the sake of his daughter, Geneviève,[161] may be entirely fictitious, but it lends Mallarmé a dynamic of lived experience that is mostly absent in his highly stylized poems, as well as in Blanchot's essays from the 1940s. Any interpretation of Celan's annotation of Sartre's preface should be undertaken with caution. It should be noted, however, that although Celan consistently highlights or underlines references to Mallarmé's suicide, he does not make note of those moments when death is described as chance, accidental, or a terrible shipwreck, manifestations of unwilled death that are ultimately central to Sartre's argument. I suggest that whereas Mallarmé successfully fools his friends and disciples about the Book to come, Celan is also, at least momentarily, fooled by Sartre's thesis that suicide can effectively be applied to the act of writing poems.[162]

If our suspicion that Celan appropriates the poetics of suicide that Sartre elaborates and attributes to Mallarmé has any truth to it, then we might expect to see traces of what Sartre calls this 'doctrine' in the poem composed immediately after this reading. On 18 March 1966, the day following his reading and annotation of Sartre's preface and Mallarmé's poems, Celan completes a draft of a poem begun two days previously:

<u>Die Atemlosigkeiten des Denkens,</u>
auch auf den Gletscherwiesen,
ohne Beweis.

Über den Grossen Steinschild
stürzt ein Morgiger heim.
'Ihr Tiefgesenke
mit euren Trögen aus Lehm,
unterwegs'.

Rauhbrüchiges schabt
an Namen und Stimmen herum,
eine unverlierbare Nothand
brennt Sterniges ab.

Der durch nichts zu trübende Blick.

Einen Tod mehr als du
bin ich gestorben,
ja, einen mehr.[163]

[<u>The breathlessnesses of thinking</u>,
also on the glacier meadows,
without proof.

Over the Great Stone Shield
a one-of-tomorrow rushes home.
'You deep sumps
with your troughs of clay,
on the way'.

Rough and ruptured it scratches
names and voices around,
an emergency hand that cannot be lost
burns stariness down.

The glance that nothing troubles.

One more death than you
have I died,
yes, one more.][164]

The unusual plural form of the substantive 'Atemlosigkeit' [breathlessness, or shortness of breath] appears to be paralleled in *Poésies* by Mallarmé's similarly uncomfortable pluralization of 'crépuscule' [dusk] in the sonnet 'Renouveau' [Renewal]: '<u>Des crépuscules blancs tiédissent sous mon crâne</u> / Qu'un cercle de fer serre ainsi qu'un vieux tombeau' [White dusks become tepid in my brain / That a circle of iron clamps like an old tomb].[165] Both the circle of iron that tightens around the speaker's skull and the acoustic reinforcement of this tightening through the rapid repetition of /ɛʀ/ in 'cercle', 'fer', and 'serre', appear to inform Celan's 'breathlessnesses of thinking'.

The glacier meadows, in which these breathlessnesses of thinking are situated, appear to stem from one of the images frequently privileged by Mallarmé, namely the glacier. Although not included in Sartre's preface, in one of the letters that Mallarmé writes to Henri Cazalis from a hot and sticky Tournon in July 1866, the poet distracts himself from the 'torrid reality' of the 'glasshouse heat' by evoking images of the cold: 'for a month now, I have been among the purest glaciers of Aesthetics [...] Having discovered Nothingness, I have found the Beautiful'.[166] It is this absolute, where Poetry and the Universe meet, that Mallarmé is unable to capture. It remains, as Celan puts it, 'ohne Beweis' [without proof], until Mallarmé re-enacts the encounter through the discovery of fiction in *Igitur*. Celan may also have in mind 'Le pitre châtié' in which glacier water — properly called 'meltwater' — is mixed up in the clown's make-up, in a deliberately secular echo of the Christian cocktail of blood and water.[167] He will also have encountered the 'savage glacier' of which Hérodiade's father is unaware,[168] and 'the transparent glacier of flights that have not fled'[169] that Sartre evokes in his demonstration of the dual operations that combine in the internal annulment of the poem.[170]

Celan's use of the term 'Gletscherwiesen' [glacier meadows] displaces the Mallarmean glacier in both space and time, because it defines the meadows left behind once the glacier has receded back up the mountainside. 'Glacier meadows' typically contain large numbers of stones of various shapes and sizes that were at one point carried by the glacier, but which were deposited as the glacier melted. As we read in the geological handbook Celan frequently referred to when writing his poems, reading the surface of the earth in the wake of a glacier is very much like reading difficult literature. The challenges and rewards are comparable:

> It is therefore necessary to analyze stones as precisely as possible, as the entire history of the earth must be read from them. And in fact, they can inform the one, who understands their language, not only how and where they once came into being, whether they solidified from a molten mass on the earth's surface or within the earth's crust, whether they were amassed through wind or water, whether their current location was once a desert or a sea, but they also reveal their age.[171]

Although Celan refers to these glacial deposits in 'Rauhbrüchiges' [rough and ruptured], each of the five fragments of text that constitute the poem might with a little imagination be seen as something very much like the stones that are left behind once the Mallarmean glacier has retired to higher and cooler climes.

Here I focus on the final fragment, which is unusual both in the context of the poem, and more broadly in Celan's later poems, for its utter simplicity in syntax and vocabulary:

> Einen Tod mehr als du
> bin ich gestorben,
> ja, einen mehr.

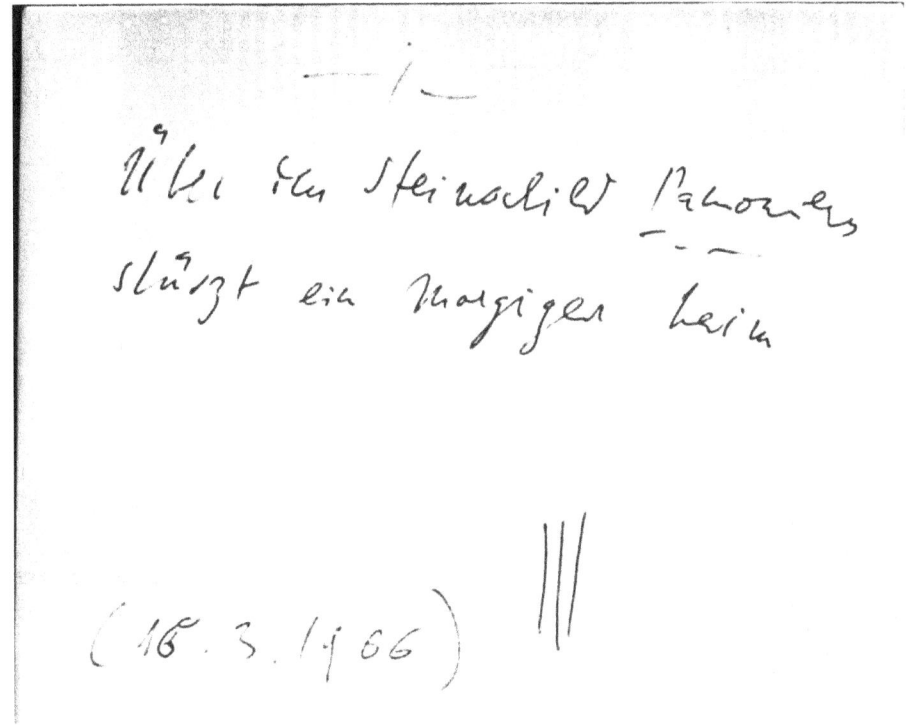

Fig. 2.1. 'Über den Steinschild Pannoniens / stürzt ein Morgiger heim', earliest draft of 'Die Atemlosigkeiten des Denkens'. Blue ballpoint pen and black ballpoint pen on front side of envelope. Ms (A 3.3; D 90.1.213) / 16.3.1966.
© Deutsches Literaturarchiv, Marbach a. N.

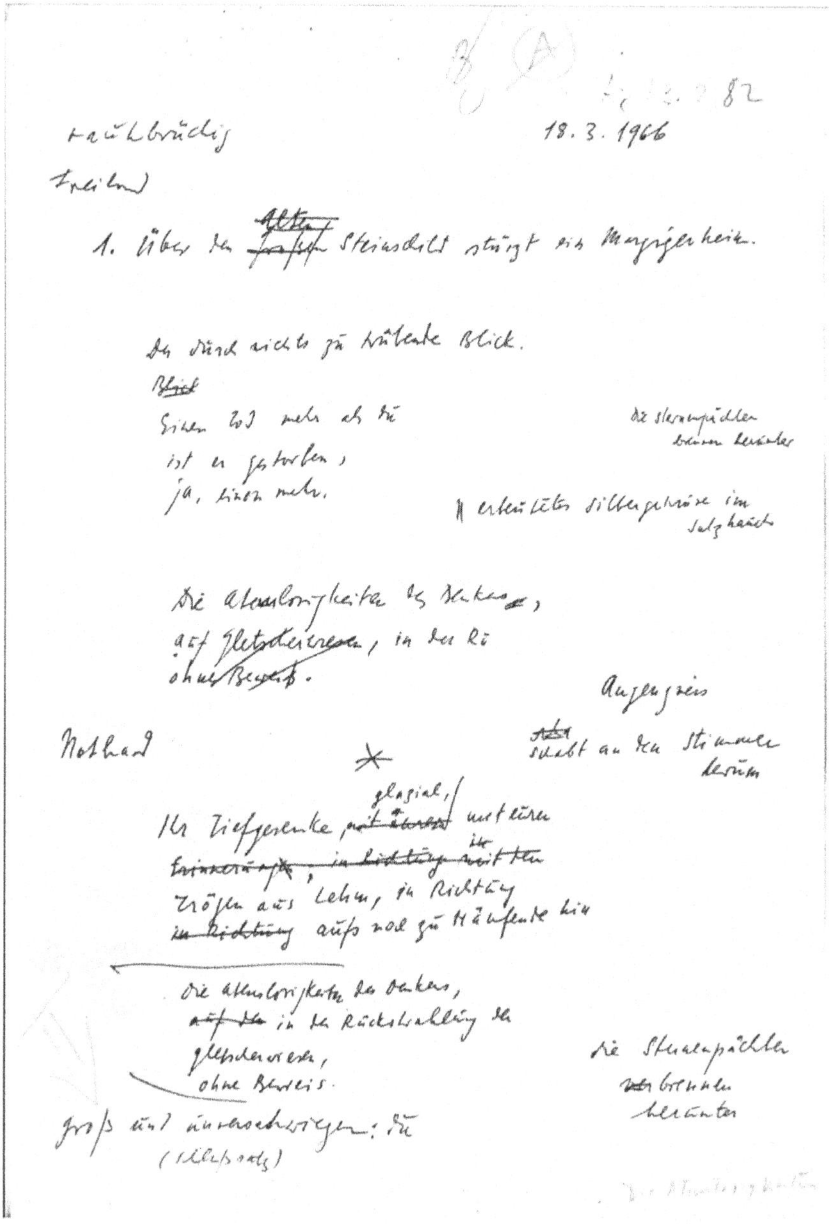

FIG. 2.2. 'Die Atemlosigkeiten des Denkens', manuscript draft.
Ts/Ds (AF 1, 41: Ag 1, 40) / D 90.1.132. © Deutsches Literaturarchiv, Marbach a. N.

[One more death than you
have I died,
yes, one more.]

The vaguely biblical repetition of verb and direct object — to die a death — appears to attribute agency to the speaker: the speaker dies a death, rather than dying intransitively, or simply being dead. It is from the perspective of this willed death, a death in which the dead is both agent and acted upon, that the poem addresses the unidentified second person. The notion of speaking from the perspective of death is not only a poetic conceit, as evidenced by Orpheus's passage through Hades, or the Master's passage to the Styx in Mallarmé's sonnet 'Ses purs ongles très haut...' ['Her pure nails very high...'].[172] It is also, since Plato's *Phaedo*, the hallmark of the philosopher. As the mature Deleuze puts it, some ten years before his own suicide by defenestration: 'For philosophers are beings who have passed through a death, who are born from it, and go toward another death, perhaps the same one'.[173] He then quotes the Québécoise writer Pauline Harvey, who says that although not a philosopher herself, she is fond of them, because 'they themselves believe that they are dead, that they have passed through death; and they also believe that, although dead, they continue to live, but in a shivering way, with tiredness and prudence [...] The philosopher has returned from the dead and goes back there'.[174]

The 'Morgiger' or 'tomorrow one' who rushes home across the continental stone shield bearing what appears to be a fictional citation, is a poet-philosopher, who returns to the world of the living. The image of returning from the dead is one we are familiar, and even comfortable, with. But Deleuze also says that the philosopher returns from the dead and 'goes back there', that is, goes back to death. It is as if the poet-philosopher not only returns from death but is always on the way back to death. The one of tomorrow rushes home across the stone shield to life, perhaps to an imaginary Bukowina.[175] But in the same movement he also rushes to the home that is death. When the final fragment tells us that its speaker has died one more death than us, we also hear the dead poet speaking from beyond the grave. Death is not only that from which the living poet speaks. It is also the once future, and now realized, death of the poet. It is a projective fiction that will at some near point in time, whether by the poet's hand as in the case of Celan, or by the hand of chance, as in the case of Mallarmé, be realized. As in Sartre's exposition of Mallarmé, the fiction of literature can only attain the status of truth once the poet has died. It is this conceit that this deceptively simple, closing fragment confirms.

Toward the end of April 1970, Celan was reported missing. On the desk at his home on the avenue Émile Zola in Paris — where since separating from Gisèle he lived alone — was Wilhelm Michel's biography of Hölderlin.[176] At the open page, a quotation from a letter written by the poet Clemens Brentano to Philipp Otto Runge, dated 21 January 1810, had been underlined by Celan: 'Never perhaps has such elevated grief been so gloriously uttered. <u>At times this genius becomes dark and immersed in the bitter spring of his heart</u>; mostly, however, his apocalyptic star shines, wonderfully touching bitterness, over the wide ocean of his sensibility'.[177]

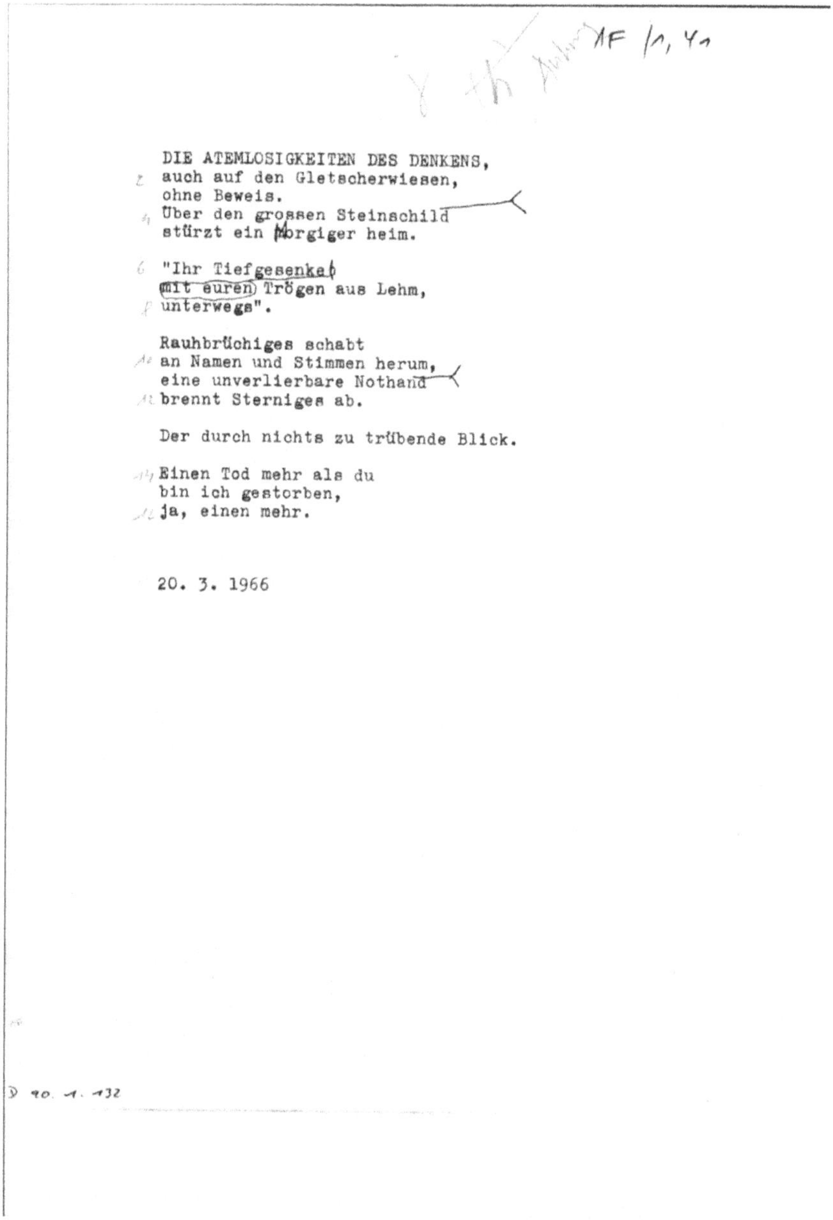

```
                              AF /1, 41

        DIE ATEMLOSIGKEITEN DES DENKENS,
   2  auch auf den Gletscherwiesen,
        ohne Beweis.
   4  Über den grossen Steinschild
        stürzt ein Morgiger heim.

   6  "Ihr Tiefgesenkes
        mit euren Trögen aus Lehm,
   8  unterwegs".

        Rauhbrüchiges schabt
  10  an Namen und Stimmen herum,
        eine unverlierbare Nothand
  12  brennt Sterniges ab.

        Der durch nichts zu trübende Blick.

  14  Einen Tod mehr als du
        bin ich gestorben,
  16  ja, einen mehr.


        20. 3. 1966
```

D 90.1.132

FIG. 2.3. 'Die Atemlosigkeiten des Denkens', typescript. Ts/Ds (AF 1, 41: Ag 1, 40) / D 90.1.132. © Deutsches Literaturarchiv, Marbach a. N.

This annotation is Celan's suicide note. On 1 May his corpse was found in the Seine at Courbevoie, several kilometers downstream from central Paris, from where it is generally thought he threw himself in.

Many friends and critics see an integral and explicatory relation between Celan's poetry and his suicide. In contrast to Sartre's Mallarmé, whose unfinished (and unfinishable) oeuvre required him to die unexpectedly — and for whom actual suicide would have undone the myth of the great Book to come — Celan's suicide appears to confirm the significance of what had increasingly become a difficult and repelling work. Writing in his journal a few days after the poet's body was discovered, Cioran said: ' — terrible night. Dreamt of Celan's *wise* decision. (Celan went all the way to the end, he exhausted all the potential ways of resisting destruction. In a certain sense, his existence has nothing fragmentary or failed about it: on the contrary, he fully realized himself. As a poet, he could not go any further; in his last poems he brushed up against *Wortspielerie* [word-play]. I know of no death either more pathetic or less sad'.[178] Primo Levi justified the obscurity of Celan's poetry as 'a pre-suicide, a not-wanting-to-be, a flight from the world, of which the intentional death was the crown'.[179] Yves Bonnefoy would also perceive Celan's suicide as confirmation and realization of his poetic work: 'I think that Celan chose to die as he did so that for at least once in his life [...] words and being might meet. [...] Just as Rimbaud ceased to write not out of spite or indifference but to continue to create meaning [...] so too Paul Celan died, continuing his poem, to finally discover what every poem desires: the union of the long phrase with a small part of being that it is not'.[180] Henri Michaux, commemorating Celan's death later that year, would aestheticize the act of suicide: 'Choose, he could still choose. The end wouldn't last too long. With the current, the effortless corpse'.[181] Erich Kahler learned of Celan's death on his own deathbed, and said that it proved that to 'be both a great German poet and a young Central European Jew growing up in the shadow of the concentration camps' was a burden too great for one man to bear.[182] Steiner identifies 'the resolution of death' in Celan's work from 1963 onward.[183] More recently, developing this trend to an extreme, Alexis Nouss argues that Celan's poetry is accessible only through his suicide, and that the poet's suicide has returned to death the 'aura' of meaning it lost in the camps.[184]

As a corollary of this popular consensus, it is assumed that Celan jumped to his death from the Mirabeau Bridge, which spans the River Seine between the fifteenth and sixteenth *arrondissements*. This is not only because the bridge was close to his apartment, but also because Celan referred to both the bridge and Guillaume Apollinaire's poem 'Le Pont Mirabeau' in his 1962 poem 'And With the Book From Tarussa'.[185] I think that it is important, however, to bear in mind how little this version of Celan's last moments in life can be corroborated, and how much it relies on fictional projections. Sartre's preface reminds us that although literature may appear to invite us to encounter non-literary or 'supernatural' acts — such as crime and suicide — in its domain, we will never actually find them there. This duplicity is just one of the hallmarks of literature, which, as Mallarmé knew, has always been the Great Lie, and a supreme fiction. Mallarmé's great fortune was to have projected a work greater than anything he, or any other man, could write, without equaling, and thereby destroying, the creation of the universe itself. Celan's misfortune is to have written a work that can now not be read without the event of his suicide imposing itself on the imaginary horizon of each poem. Not only is Celan's poetics commonly thought to culminate in the poet's suicide. Suicide also appears to provide a convenient tool with which to simplify the difficult task of explaining each part of this work in its singularity. Our awareness of Celan's suicide has come to inhibit the ways we read and interpret his poems. Perhaps the task of future readers of this work should be to read as though its poet continued to live.

Rondel, Rondel

Among the annotations Celan inscribed in the 1966 edition of Mallarmé's *Poésies*, there is a short diagonal dash next to the title of ten of the poems. This is usually an indication of his intention to translate the poem into German. Although there are a small number of fragmentary attempts at translating inscribed in the margins, none of the projected translations was completed.[186] Celan's only published translation of a poem by Mallarmé dates from the late 1950s, during which time he translated a number of nineteenth-century poems from the French, including Rimbaud's 'Le Bateau ivre', Baudelaire's 'La Mort des pauvres', and Nerval's 'El Desdichado'. As we have seen in the two preceding segments of this chapter, Celan's engagement with Mallarmé is infrequent and enigmatic, if not cagey. In the Meridian speech, he draws back from anything that might explain — to either his audience or subsequent readership — what the significance of this isolated and speculative reference to Mallarmé might be. His engagement with Mallarmé's poems at Sainte Anne is motivated and conditioned by Sartre's duplicitous exposition of how suicide might invest the act of reading and writing poems with new significance. The final part of this chapter examines Celan's engagement with Mallarmé through his translation of the poem that begins 'Si tu veux nous nous aimerons'.

'Si tu veux' was written to celebrate New Year's Day in 1889, possibly in collaboration with Méry Laurent, Mallarmé's mistress. She is thought to be the author of the poem's opening line and refrain.[187] The poem's ambiguous authorship and festive pretext might mean that it occupies the sous-oeuvre of Mallarmé's oeuvre. It is perhaps not the sort of poem that either Blanchot or Sartre, for instance, would deign to consider in their respective studies. But in contrast to studies of Celan's work, which have focused on the oeuvre at the expense of the sous-oeuvre, in recent years even the most marginal of texts inscribed by Mallarmé have been subject to critical examination. Mallarmé's circumstantial verse, of which this could justifiably be considered an example, is now considered an integral part of Mallarmé's poetic oeuvre. The same might be said of his translations of — and scholia on — English nursery rhymes, and of his writings on women's fashion. Mallarmé, the poet of nothingness and musician of silence, is now read as 'a writer very much concerned with the role of poetry as a response — perhaps our most valuable response — to the conundrum of living'.[188] Even poems as trivial and apparently inconsequential as 'Si tu veux' can now be read for the unique ways they give expression to Mallarmé's lifelong poetic project in the pursuit of beauty.

The reasons for which Celan chooses to translate this poem are, however, governed by other concerns. Here is the poem followed by a literal translation into English:

> Rondel II
>
> Si tu veux nous nous aimerons
> Avec tes lèvres sans le dire
> Cette rose ne l'interromps
> Qu'à verser un silence pire
>
> Jamais de chants ne lancent prompts
> Le scintillement du sourire
> Si tu veux nous nous aimerons
> Avec tes lèvres sans le dire
>
> Muet muet entre les ronds
> Sylphe dans la pourpre d'empire
> Un baiser flambant se déchire
> Jusqu'aux pointes des ailerons
> Si tu veux nous nous aimerons.[189]
>
> [Rondel II
>
> If you will we will love each other
> With your lips without saying it
> This rose do not interrupt
> Unless to pour a worse silence
>
> Never do songs project promptly
> The sparkling of the smile
> If you will we will love each other
> With your lips without saying it
>
> Mute mute between the rounds
> Sylph in Empire purple
> A flaming kiss rends itself
> To the points of its pinions
> If you will we will love each other.]

More than most poems by Mallarmé, this poem is remarkable for its circular structure. The rondel was originally a round dance, characterized not only by the circular movements described by the dancers, but also by the repetition of those movements and of the words that would have accompanied the dance.[190] The 'rond' of rondel can describe two distinct modes of circular movement. In the first of these, the movement of the 'rond' is more intensely re-created when a stone is tied to a string and swung around one's head, not unlike the culminating gesture of Maldoror in Lautréamont's *The Songs of Maldoror*, when he swings the body of a boy tied to a rope from atop the column in the Place Vendôme: 'The swing whistles through space, the body of Mervyn follows it everywhere, always kept away from the center by centrifugal force, always keeping a mobile and equidistant position in an aerial circumference independent of matter'.[191] Here, the centrifugal force exerted on the stone is kept in check by the consistently greater centripetal force, which tends toward the fixed center of the hand that holds the string. Maldoror lets go of the lasso to propel his victim's body across Paris and into the roof of the Pantheon where, the narrator claims, his remains can still be seen.[192] In the case of both the dancers and of the stone, however, the rotatory movement is maintained to create an orbit balanced between opposing forces.[193]

The second movement described by the 'rond' is that of capillary waves that move outward from a central motivating point. These can be found in the concentric ripples made on the surface of water, when someone throws a stone into a stream or spits into a lake, what Joyce describes as 'concentric circles of waterrings'.[194] It is this figure that Nerval employs to describe one of the more comprehensible forms taken by his insane visions during his first major breakdown in 1841: 'Immense circles traced their way through infinity, like the rings touched off in water by a falling body'.[195] It is perhaps this image that Mallarmé has in mind when he writes in a draft of *Igitur*: 'and I see myself as resembling the tranquil wave of a narcotic, whose vibratory circles coming and going create an infinite limit that cannot reach the calm of the center'.[196] But the 'rond' as incessant movement outward need not be restricted to the surface of a liquid. On at least two occasions, Mallarmé perceives this movement as taking place in the air. See, for example, the opening stanza of this 1895 sonnet, in which each round is abolished by the round that follows:

> Toute l'âme résumée
> Quand lente nous expirons
> Dans plusieurs ronds de fumée
> Abolis en autres ronds.[197]

In his critical poem, 'Restricted Action', he seems to evoke the leisurely conceit that consists in blowing smoke-rings to describe an ideal form of poetic expression: 'but first, doesn't it make sense to express oneself spatially? like a cigar tracing circumvolutory patterns, whose vagueness, at the very least, is outlined against the harsh, electric light of day?'[198] Regardless of the medium through which these alternative rounds manifest themselves, and in addition to the tight circle of the stone on a string, the 'ronds' of the rondel also describe ceaseless movement outward, circumlocutory games of dissipation and transience. When reading Mallarmé's rondel, it is necessary to remain aware of the contradictory dynamics of the 'rond' upon which it is formed.

A rondel typically consists of thirteen octosyllables arranged in two quatrains followed by a quintet. The first two lines of the first quatrain, and the last two lines of the second quatrain are identical. The last line of the poem then repeats the first.[199] Mallarmé's rondel initially appears to subscribe to the balance of centripetal and centrifugal forces of traditional form, with thirteen perfect octosyllables and rhymes on 'rond' and 'ire'. As such, the poem demonstrates the persistence of prosody, or what Mallarmé calls the 'strange mystery' that 'sprung forth in incubatory times'.[200] For Mallarmé, the rules of prosody are by no means arbitrary, but come into being with the birth of the universe, and even now precisely echo the rhythm of the world's conception, incubation, and continuing presence. The reader is invited to glimpse here a part of the universe's pattern, of its disposition in miniature, and of its exemplary order. As Mallarmé claimed in 1895 when contemplating the rise of 'vers libre', it is this order and stability that will always remain, despite the new personal prosodies that an individual might spontaneously contribute, 'partaking of his or her breath':[201] 'Similarity between poetry and ancient proportions; some kind of regularity will last because the poetic act consists of suddenly seeing that an idea can be broken up into a certain number of motifs that are equal in value, and to group them; they rhyme; as an external seal, the final words relate to their common measure'.[202]

For Mallarmé, then, the poetic act consists of two parts. First, the act of suddenly seeing an idea break into a number of equal motifs, and second, the act of grouping these motifs in rhymed and measured lines and stanzas, of translating them into verse. The rhymes that bind these lines of verse are an external seal, a stamp, echoing those rhythmically made by round dancers on the medieval dance-floor. Rhymes guarantee the common measure and ancestry of dance and poetry. Mallarmé maintains that the similitude between lines, the ancient proportions of verse will remain because they are proof of the poetic act, the hallmark of consummation and fidelity, visual and acoustic progeny that attest to the successful marriage of word and idea. It is this organization of language, which 'philosophically makes up for the deficiency of languages' which are 'imperfect insofar as they are many'.[203] The rhymes and measures of verse reverse language's dissipation and dissemination, and thereby approximate — in admittedly modest and imperfect ways — the primordial language, the word that according to Saint John's gospel, was at the beginning, that was with God, and that was God.

Besides the external seals of rhyme, the old proportions of stanzas, and the regularity of syllables that characterize the vast majority of Mallarmé's verse poems, it is the principle of repetition that above all defines the rondel, both as a dance and as a text. Mallarmé does not limit repetition to the reiteration of the refrain 'Si tu veux nous nous aimerons', which occurs in lines one, eight, and thirteen, and 'Avec tes lèvres sans le dire', which occurs in lines two and seven. He develops the rondel's ancient principle of repetition to repeat individual words within the poem. 'Muet' [mute] is repeated at the beginning of the quintet, and 'nous' [we / us] in the opening, middle, and final lines. The repetition of 'nous' in 'nous nous aimerons' [we will love each other] is particularly striking, not only because it occurs in the first and last lines (naturally prominent positions in verse), or because it occupies the metric and rhythmic heart of the poem, namely the two central syllables in the poem's central octosyllable. In a poem of only sixty-eight verbal units, the repetition of the same monosyllable on six occasions begins to constitute a threat to the principle of differentiation, and with it the very notion of linguistic (let alone poetic) expression.

It should be countered, of course, that the repetition of 'nous' is by no means a willful expression of meaninglessness, of pure sound that would deny meaning.

Indeed, without an explicit object, the very sense of the verb 'aimer' is largely empty. 'Nous aimerons' as a non-reflexive verb expresses the intention to love, but it does not define the object toward which that abstract dynamic is directed and with which the subject can meet and realize its plan to love. The repetition of 'nous' is therefore not only necessary for the correct grammatical construction of the verb 'aimer' in its reflexive form. It also ensures that the semantic force of the verb is not contradicted. The repetition of 'nous', as direct object of the verb 'aimer', inflects the abstract (you might say 'aimless') dynamic of loving, and turns it back toward the verb's subject, which is now also its direct object. The reflexive verbal construction 'nous nous aimerons' — to pursue the geometric analogies already privileged by the rondel — might therefore be said to exert a centripetal, curving force on the tangential, straight force of loving, allowing us — catachrestically — to tie the 'nous' to the 'nous', to literally 'noue' [tie] the 'nous' [we] to the 'nous' [us]. As Mallarmé says elsewhere: 'Every soul is a melody that needs to be re-tied [qu'il s'agit de renouer]'.[204]

The proposed unity of the first and second person singular pronouns in a collective first person pronoun is fraught with uncertainty in the poem, as it depends for its realization on the assent of an anonymous You [tu]. 'Tu' is also the past participle of the verb 'taire' [to be silent]. This means that the realization of the first person plural pronoun is entirely reliant on the whim of the second person non-speaker. 'Si tu veux nous nous aimerons' not only reads 'if you want we will love each other'. It also suggests that if the You wants, 'We will become Us'. The 'nous' will become 'nous'. The 'nous' will both transform itself and remain the same. The conclusion of the poem with a line identical to its initial proposition prevents the reader from knowing whether the union desired by the first person speaker with the silent second person is ever achieved, or whether the notion of their union in a first person plural pronoun will always remains hypothetical and future. This uncertainty perpetually defers the desired union and ensures that the rondel will continue to turn between 'nous' and 'nous', between desire and lack. It is the same movement that we see in the rotary motion of the libido, whose aim is never to reach its object, but to repeatedly circle around it.[205] In the absence of punctuation, it is the cycle of desire that groups together these individual lines of verse, thereby contributing, in a small way, to the return of the originary, supreme, and mythical Language.

The various repetitions of 'nous' can be understood as expressions of the same principle of repetition that motivates the poem's refrain and the rotary movement described by the dancers. The question remains, though, whether the same principle of repetition is in operation in 'Muet muet', which occurs in the opening line of the quintet. Unlike the repetition of 'nous', which is required by conventional rules of language for the correct formation of the verb 'aimer' in its reflexive form, the repetition of 'muet' is harder to explain. It is initially unclear whether this repetition is meant to have any meaning, or whether it constitutes, as Robb puts it, a 'reploiement noir',[206] 'a black folding in', a tucking together of the wings whose tips appear in the penultimate line, and which are perhaps attributable to the sylph. The notion that the repetition is essentially meaningless, and that it should be read for its acoustic and visual qualities, creating a sort of black hole, is on one level appealing. And yet it is precisely here — where no meaning appears to avail itself — that we should persevere to find meaning. When faced with the notion of blindness, Heidegger argues that 'for a man to be blind, he must in his essence be one who sees. A piece of wood can never go blind. When a man does become blind, the question is always whether the blindness comes from lack and loss, or whether it comes from superabundance and excess'.[207] Similarly, the mute must also in essence be one who speaks. The question is whether his muteness stems from speaking too little or too much, and what implications this might have for the structure of the poem and for the poem's eventual translation.

The irruption into the rondel of one who does not speak should not disturb the dancers' perpetual pursuit of unification with the other, because, much like the mute, dancers do not express themselves through speech, but through the silent movement of their bodies. The mute mute — the mute whose muteness is folded in on itself and who is doubly silent — would therefore be unable to 'interrupt the rose', something the poem explicitly prohibits. The only gesture available to a mute mute, drawing on the logic of the poem, would be to kiss the You (who is also 'tu' or 'silenced') with his lips, but without speaking [avec tes lèvres sans le dire]. The identification of the mute with the non-speaking lips of the refrain, and by extension with the flaming kiss in line eleven, might be corroborated by the form of the word 'muet'. This is because 'muet' acoustically mimics — although it may not strictly speaking stem from — the Greek 'μύειν' [múein], which means to close the lips or the eyes. It is from this verb that the word 'mystery' comes, because the initiate into the secret rites of religious mystery must also keep their lips sealed.[208] The mute who is mute because he speaks too little would, it seems, be an unproblematic addition to the mysterious rites of these silent and circling dancers, and by extension to the particular constellation of repetitions that constitute the rondel.

And yet the mute also protests too much. For 'muet' to require repetition, there must be something that 'muet' alone cannot express. The appearance of the word by itself is not only metrically and rhythmically insufficient. It is inadequate in expressing the notion of muteness. It is in insisting on this muteness, in confirming his inability to speak, that the mute repeats the only word he knows. Paradoxically, this means that all of a sudden, from the depths of doubled-down muteness, the mute in fact begins not only to speak, but to speak in excess of sound and meaning. It is a form of speech that would not be possible outside of written expression. In the realms of un-inscribed language, such as dance and song, from which the rondel comes, it is not possible to mimic muteness and to distinguish it from simply being mute. In the inscribed time and space of the poem, however, the mute speaks mutely by repeating its muteness. Its muteness remains, but now it is a muteness that exists not because it speaks too little, but because it speaks too much.

In one of his articles on ballet, Mallarmé maintains that mime and dance possess distinct forms of silence that should never be confused: 'the mime and the dance, suddenly hostile to each other if one forces them together'.²⁰⁹ The dancer, whom Mallarmé chooses to perceive as being illiterate, expresses herself in silent steps (if we discount the inelegant thud of her wooden-toed ballet shoes on the stage boards, a manifestation of material reality that Mallarmé acknowledges).²¹⁰ The mimic, on the other hand, speaks through the silence of bodily gestures, through which he imitates and exaggerates the gestures of others. The silence of the mute constitutes a third category of silence. The mute mimics muteness and becomes a mute mute. In the logic of the poem, the mute who imitates muteness introduces a form of silence that is beyond the comprehension of the rondel as both dance and poem. It is an instance of silence not as the absence of sound, but as undifferentiated sound that can therefore not be heard. It is an absence that is not so much absence as absolute presence, a presence that is so total it cannot be discerned.

Unlike the steps of the dance, therefore, which are followed by each of the dancers and which structure the poem, the silence of 'muet muet' constitutes a threat to the ability of the poem to continue in its playful and never-ending rotations around speech and silence, desire and lack. There is the risk that a reader, upon encountering the fold of muteness, might confuse it with one of a number of other words with which it shares phonemes, thereby losing track of its muteness and ascribing loud and colorful associations where we were only meant to read 'mute'. We might, to use a hunting term, default,²¹¹ lose the trail of the mute prey and disperse, distracted by more attractive homophones. Because 'un muet' is also a type of rattlesnake, a creature identified (at least in English) by the unusual sound it makes. If we distort the pronunciation of 'muet' by shifting from an open to a closed 'e', we end up with the verb 'muer', which can mean to change or to molt. It also describes the sloughing of a snake's skin, the breaking of an adolescent's voice, and the irruption of a deer from a wood. It is paradoxically here, where the poem folds muteness upon muteness, that the mute's silence begins to stumble into homophony, near-homophony, polyphony, and perhaps even cacophony. It is here, in the repetition of 'muet', that the imitation of the universe's harmony — and perhaps even its reparation — begins to falter, and that the poem and the dance begin to fall apart.

The inscription of the rondel's frivolous and popular form therefore puts an end to both its frivolity and its general accessibility. It is also the inscription of the rondel that makes possible, and even necessary, its future self-destruction. It is for this reason that a reader will, with sufficient attention, begin to recognize signs of dissemination and dissipation at work within the poem. The principle of repetition no longer appears to describe the clean, perpetually self-generating circles of the rondel as illustrated by the orbit of a stone tied to a string. Instead it points to the penetration and dispersal of 'ronds' in ripples of water or smoke rings, to the breakdown of the hitherto unified body of individual dancers and lines of verse, to dissipation in all senses of the word. In 'entre les ronds' — between the rounds, or, enters the rounds — we can see and hear an imperfect repetition of 'l'interromps' [interrupts it]. The Latin 'inter' is bastardized as French 'entre', and 'romps' is recast as 'ronds', which recreates its sound but defaces both its sense and scriptural appearance. Besides the insertion of 'les' between 'entre' and 'ronds', which further disrupts the search for the pure and self-sustaining circle of sense, white space infiltrates the line, dispersing the letters, again disturbing its imperative to not interrupt. It is as though an explosion has blown the letters apart, and the reader has been privileged with a snapshot of the blast. The snapshot captures the moment before the letters have been blown too far apart for us to perceive their origins in lines of verse.

The silent music of the rondel has been interrupted. Muteness has been uttered. The closed circles that pursued love and silence have been broken and opened up to our eyes and ears. The closed lips have been prized apart. The scintillating smile has probably been wiped away. This poem, which initially appeared flirtatious and insincere, in fact has important things to say about poetry. Poetry is not satisfied with the bland proposition to engage in casual love ('If you will we will love each other'). Nor is it obedient to the tame imperative not to interrupt ('This rose do not interrupt it'). It is instead explosive ('A flaming kiss rends itself / To the points of its pinions'). It enters where it is not invited and breaks unexpectedly from the community of dancers. It breaks 'nous nous' apart. It splits 'muet' from 'muet'. Where initially this playful New Year's dance was measured and motivated by courteous rhymes on 'ronds' [/ʀɔ̃/], it now alternates between rupture ('rompt' and 'romps' [also pronounced /ʀɔ̃/]) and rage ('ire' [/iːʀ/]). Here, the letter 'r', which Mallarmé explicitly associates with the sound of rending, is the acoustic constant.[212]

Mallarmé's rondel initially projects itself as a perfect, self-contained, self-generating circle of sound and sense. It is when this projection is most perfectly realized, as in the pure repetition of 'muet muet', that the poem begins to disintegrate. As de Man says, 'poetic consciousness ends by annihilating form, as all pure consciousness destroys its object'.[213] The poem has become aware of its own mechanisms. It has taken cognizance of its impending destruction. It now knows that it requires external input to achieve the wholeness for which it formerly strove alone. It realizes that there will be a transformation, a transmutation, perhaps even a translation.

Although Mallarmé's poem appears to make space for the possibility of translation, a translation can take the poem in many different directions. There is no obligation on the part of the translator to respond to the poem's appeal for wholeness, and to repair or reverse the signs of its imminent disintegration. There is no reason to think that Celan, whose hostility to Mallarmé was made clear at the beginning of this chapter, and whose other encounters are marked by ambivalence, would feel obliged to respond directly to the poem's request. Here is Celan's translation of Mallarmé's poem, followed by a literal translation into English:

> RONDEL
>
> Willst du's, solls die Liebe sein,
> Du, dein Mund, wir sagens nicht,
> Schenkst der Rose Schweigen ein,
> Bittrer, so du's unterbrichst.

Lieder, willig, schicken kein
Lächeln, sprühen uns kein Licht,
Willst du's, solls die Liebe sein,
Du, dein Mund, wir sagens nicht.

Stumm-und-stumm, hier zwischenein,
Sylphe, purpurn, kaiserlich,
Flammt ein Kuss, schon teilt er sich,
Flügelspitzen flackern, fein,
Willst du's, solls die Liebe sein.[214]

[RONDEL

If you will it, it will be love,
You, your mouth, we don't say,
Pour silence to the rose,
More bitter, this is how you interrupt it.

Songs, willingly, send no
Smile, spray us with no light,
If you will it, it will be love,
You, your mouth, we don't say.

Dumb-and-dumb, here in-between,
Sylph, purple, imperial,
Flames a kiss, already splits itself,
Pinion-tips flicker, fine,
If you will it, it will be love.]

When in 1923 Walter Benjamin published his translations into German of Baudelaire's 'Parisian Scenes', he included a short preface called 'The Task of the Translator'. The preface offers a complicated if not confusing theorization of translation, in which, as Jacobs puts it, definitions are dislocated rather than established.[215] In attempting to discern the task of the translator as opposed to the task of the poet, Benjamin at one point claims, to quote Harry Zohn's paraphrase: 'Unlike a work of literature, translation does not find itself in the center of the language forest — but on the outside facing the wooded ridge; it calls into it without entering, aiming at that single spot where the echo is able to give, in its own language, the reverberation of the work in the alien one'.[216]

According to this analogy, the destructive reverberations detected rippling through Mallarmé's rondel may not be the product of internal operations alone. There is the possibility that the rondel was already reverberating with the sound of the translator's deliberate and measured cry from outside the poem's wooded enclosure. This means that on the edge of the language forest a translation of Mallarmé's rondel always already exists and interferes in the poem's ideal mechanisms. The poem and its translation not only exist simultaneously, but the translation subtends and informs the poem. The relationship of the poem to its translation might therefore be said to be mirrored in the relationship of the oeuvre to the sous-oeuvre. The translation does not derive from the poem. Instead, the translation already exists, overlooked, ignored, out of sight, manipulating the poem in invisible ways, until the translator reveals the full extent of its operations to the reader. It is only then that the translation becomes visible as part of the oeuvre of which it has up till then only been a hidden part.[217]

I believe that the purpose of Celan's translation is not to think Mallarmé's poem to the end — or to death — as Celan would suggest a couple of years later. Nor is it to reveal the translation as the afterlife of the poem, as Benjamin will suggest in his preface. Nor is it to develop a poetics of suicide. Instead, I argue that in this, the earliest documented encounter with Mallarmé's oeuvre, Celan attempts to reduce and reverse the mechanisms that motivate Mallarmé's poem. Instead of developing the oeuvre toward the extension, if not transcendence, of the oeuvre, Celan attempts, through translation, to reveal the sous-oeuvre contained and hidden in the oeuvre. He does not think the poem to its end so much as move it back toward a domain in which it is always unfinished, always beginning anew. I focus here on three of the most striking transformations realized in translation, although none is entirely distinct from the others. First, the problematization of speaking in the poem; second, the translation's resistance to repetition; and third, the reduction of the poem. These might subsequently be understood as fragments of a larger theory of translation.

The eternally unsatisfied pursuit of love in Mallarmé's poem relies on the distinct speaking roles attributed to each of the persons involved, but also on the undecidability of the first person plural pronoun 'nous'. As discussed above, if the silent second person singular accepts the first person speaker's proposition to love, then the exclusive 'nous' will become inclusive. The structure of the poem does not allow the reader to know if this happens or not. It revolves — potentially forever — around the reader's inability to distinguish 'nous' from 'nous'. In Celan's translation, such undecidable desire and loving is given short shrift. The circle of loving represented by 'nous nous' and repeated three times in Mallarmé's poem, is dismantled and depersonalized in Celan's translation. The first person lover and the second person beloved are absent from 'solls die Liebe sein' [let it be love]. The first person plural pronoun, so central to the French poem, is displaced to the second line of the German: 'wir sagens nicht' [we don't say]. Here, the first person plural pronoun is no longer implicated in the possibility of loving but in keeping silent.

The proposition to love has been displaced from the undecidable 'nous' and from the anonymous first person speaker, and is now allied with the second person singular: 'Willst du's, solls die Liebe sein, / Du, dein Mund...' [If you want, let it be love, / You, your mouth...]. Here, though, the integrity of the second person, his or her wholeness, appears to have been fragmented. The juxtaposition of 'you' and 'your mouth' suggests a dislocation between the speaker and his or her speech. When in Martin Luther's translation of the book of Exodus, God asks Moses to be his prophet, Moses initially demurs because of a similar dislocation of man and mouth: 'O my lord, I have time and again not been eloquent, also since the time, when you spoke with your servant; for I have a heavy speech and a heavy tongue'.[218] To which God replies: 'Who created the mouth for man? Or who made the dumb or deaf or seeing or blind? Haven't I done it, the Lord? So now go from here: I wish to be with your mouth and teach you what you should say'.[219] Moses has a heavy speech and a heavy tongue, so heavy that the words he uses to describe speech ('Sprache' [speech, language] and 'Zunge' [tongue]) are ignored by God in favor of 'Mund' [mouth]. God reminds Moses that He created a mouth for Moses, so that He could literally 'be with' Moses's mouth [mit deinem Munde sein], and teach Moses what to say with his mouth.[220] When Moses insists on his inability to speak, it is agreed that Moses's brother Aaron should speak for Moses (just as Zohn speaks to many of us in place of Benjamin, and Celan in place of Mallarmé), who will in turn speak for God. 'And he shall speak for you to the people; he shall be your mouth, and you shall be his God'.[221]

Something like this trinity of speakers and non-speakers — of God, prophet, and mouthpiece — is reproduced in 'Du, dein Mund, wir..'. [You, your mouth, we...]. In contrast to the biblical arrangement, however, which assures the transmission of God's message to His people, here the speaker of the poem enounces a pledge to keep silent: 'wir sagens nicht'. Harbusch claims that Celan's version sounds 'lighter', 'more song-like', and more oral than Mallarmé's original poem.[222] But it is important to be sensitive to the heaviness of Celan's speech. 'Du, dein Mund, wir sagens nicht' is a heavy mouthed, reluctant rendition of the smooth, unpunctuated, and overdetermined 'Avec tes lèvres sans le dire'. It inscribes Celan in a tradition of stuttering, stumbling, and otherwise impeded speakers from Moses to Hölderlin and beyond. This line of verse, alongside the passage from Exodus, is designed to remind us that fluency is not the guarantor of the most divine expression or of the most appropriate translation.

The purpose of this translated refrain may be more pressing than appreciated to this point in time. For those who would identify Mallarmé as a precursor of Celan — as many were wont to do at the time — the translation of this refrain can be read as a guide for future translators of Celan's work into French. In 1955, Celan came to meet the French poet André du Bouchet through the intermediary of René Char.[223] Du Bouchet would go on to undertake some of the most notable (but also most contested) translations of Celan's poems into French. Meschonnic, for instance, was scathing about them, describing one fragment as a Mallarméan parody: 'this is sous-du Bouchet, inferior to what he himself writes when he writes'.[224] Later, Lacoue-Labarthe will write: 'I think it necessary to remark that what we might call the 'Mallarmean' style of André du Bouchet's translations, their effete or precious quality, does not do justice to the lapidary hardness, the abruptness of language as handled by Celan. Or rather, the language that held him, ran through him'.[225] Although Lacoue-Labarthe makes no mention of Celan's sole translation of Mallarmé, it would not be surprising if this served as a structuring principle behind his criticism of du Bouchet. What seems certain, though, is that through this lone translation from Mallarmé, Celan attempts to guide (if not preemptively critique) future translations of his own work into French.

The second feature of Celan's translation I focus on here is its resistance to repetition. I shall approach this resistance through one of the most striking features of the translation, namely the prevalence of punctuation. As punctuation is all but absent in Mallarmé's poem, the reader is encouraged to conceive of each line as a distinct syntactic unit, introduced and concluded in the silent whiteness of the page. In the prose poem 'The Demon of Analogy', Mallarmé describes the blank space at the end of a line of verse in particular as procuring a 'painful pleasure'.[226] The pleasure lies not only in the opportunity to catch one's breath, but to create meaning out of a uniform number of syllables. The pain inheres, at least to some extent, in the knowledge that the line also asks to be read and understood in the broader, less defined context of the phrase, which most often exceeds the number of syllables in a line of verse. In the case of Mallarmé's rondel, however, there is more reason for pleasure than pain. For instance, in the absence of punctuation, the refrain in lines seven and eight appears to repeat and confirm its initial utterance in lines one and two. In the absence of punctuation, repetition is able to function as a major structuring principle in the poem.

Where Mallarmé's poem was articulated only by its concluding period, Celan's text is studded with three periods, and over two dozen commas. The deployment of punctuation not only interrupts the fluency of the French, it also renders the poem's principle of repetition less viable. Consider, for example, the translation of the refrain: 'Willst du's, solls die Liebe sein / Du, dein Mund, wir sagens nicht...' In the first instance, the syntax of the refrain is extended beyond the two lines of the original refrain. The second person singular pronoun, besides creating the first person in a trinity of persons ('You, your mouth, we...'), also constitutes the subject of the verb that opens the third line: 'Du [...] / Schenkst der Rose Schweigen ein...' [You [...] / Serve silence to the rose...]. The integrity of the refrain, made possible in the original poem by the absence of punctuation, is broken open in translation by its implication in the following line of verse. In the second iteration of the refrain, in the final two lines of the second stanza, the period prevents the refrain from repeating its first iteration. Repetition is denied at first by excess, and then by lack. It is as if the translator were stretching the poem to its alternative extremes, creating internal inconsistencies to destroy the poem's balanced, circular structure. And yet this disruption is an eventuality that the poem foresees, perhaps even stipulates: 'Cette rose ne l'interromps / Qu'à verser un silence pire' [Only interrupt this rose / To pour a worse silence]. Celan's translation not only responds to this invitation, by interrupting the silent structure of the poem through the application of punctuation. It also breaks the silence to comment on its own act: 'Bittrer, so du's unterbrichst' [More bitter, this is how you interrupt it].

The third feature of Celan's translation that I raise here is the reduction that it operates on the original poem. This can be seen at various moments and in a variety of forms, including the translation of the verb 'verser'. In French, 'verser' dances promiscuously with multiple possible meanings. These include pouring, spilling, spreading, modifying, turning, and perhaps even, catachrestically, and in imitation of the German 'dichten', to verse, to poeticize, to write poetry. More than any specific meaning, though, it captures the same circular motion that governs the ideal manifestation of Mallarmé's poem. It indicates the regular turns of the plough at the end of the furrow — which in Latin is a 'versus' — and by extension the repetition of rhymes at the end of each line of verse. 'Einschenken', which means 'to pour', or 'to serve', adopts only one of the French verb's possible meanings. But more than that, the verb's circular structure is compromised. This is because 'schenken' [to give, to give to drink] contains traces of the Indo-European root '*(s)keng-' meaning 'to be tilted, to be askew' and by extension 'to limp'.[227] This is an impediment not evident in 'verser'. If, in translation, the circling dancer in Mallarmé's rondel begins to limp, he or she will be forced to withdraw from the dance, again interrupting the ideal rhythm of never-ending rotations.

The problematization of speaking, the resistance to repetition, and the reduction of the poem all demonstrate how translation is never a repetition or a reproduction of the original. Celan's translation refuses to inscribe itself into the circular projections of Mallarmé's poem. Instead, translation destabilizes the original, throwing it out of orbit, to reveal something of the underlying tensions that the poem has successfully concealed. To translate is therefore not so much to reproduce in parallel, as suggested in Benjamin's image of the translator's cry from the edge of the wooded ridge. To translate is to take away from and to reduce the original to reveal things it already contained but of which it was not necessarily aware. To translate is to reveal the sous-oeuvre that has always inhabited the oeuvre, to reveal that which was subliminal and obscured.

To conclude, I consider the opening lines of the final stanza, in which the translation's reduction of the poem appears to be consolidated and confirmed: 'Lieder, willig, schicken uns kein / Lächeln, sprühen uns kein Licht…' [Songs, willing, send us no / Smile, spray us with no light]. The ability of poetry to either touch us ('uns ein Lächeln schicken') or elucidate for us ('uns Licht sprühen') is denied. The translation repeats its refusal to reproduce the delightful and aimless ambiguity of the French that it translates. In 'Jamais de chants ne lancent prompts / Le scintillement du sourire', 'prompts' can be read in two ways. First, it qualifies the plural noun 'chants' with which it agrees in gender and number. But it could also be read — acoustically if ungrammatically — as an adverb that describes the verb 'lancent' [throw].

The two negative statements of the German do not allow for any such playful ambiguity. And yet despite this, these lines undermine their own purpose, and the tendency of the translation as a whole. Because here, precisely where the poem denies the smile and light of poetry, a new rondel comes into being — unexpected and uninvited. In this new rondel, the capital 'L' of 'Lieder' [songs] is picked up by 'Lächeln' [smile], and 'Licht' [light], all three of which are circled by the organizing 'L' of the refrain — 'Liebe' [love]. Thus they create a rondel on L, a 'rond' on L, a 'rond L'. This new rondel — a creation of the translation — continues into the quintet, enriching its acoustic quality as it acquires the /f/ of 'Sylphe', 'Flammt', 'Flügelspitzen' and 'flackern', an alternative 'rond' that mirrors and multiplies the 'sylphe' and 'flambant' of the original poem.

The reduction of the poem — its movement toward silence and stasis — is somewhat forestalled by this squall of acoustic and visual repetitions. But what is it that motivates this subversive counter-rondel on 'L' in the first place? Does something other than chance subtend the alliteration of 'Lied' [song], 'Lächeln' [smile], 'Liebe' [love], and 'Licht' [light]? Does this new rondel also comment on the translation that has taken place? In a 1954 article, the linguist Hans Schwarz suggested that the acoustic echo of 'Lied' and 'Licht' in modern German was not accidental, and pointed instead to the existence of a shared etymological root, namely '*leu-'.[228] 'Lied' originally intends a 'song of praise', and by extension 'the granting of approval', an approval perhaps evident in Mallarmé's poem: 'if you wish, you may because I approve'. He or she who receives praise or approval, according to Schwarz, shines brightly in the eyes of onlookers, and is described in glowing terms. In this way they might glimmer and glisten like the sparkling of the smile, the blazing or flaming kiss, and the tips of wings that flicker or glint. Significantly, the light that Schwarz links to this glow of praise is a moist, living light, a light that could splatter us, which would contradict the translation's claim that 'Songs... spray us with no light'.

Not satisfied with finding a purely linguistic link between 'Lied' and 'Licht', Schwarz attempts to locate this relationship in a human activity or industry. He suggests that their common source lies in the practice of stripping bark from trees for its use in the tanning of hides. Once stripped of its dry and dark rind, the tree acquires a brilliant, yellow, fleshy whiteness. In English, this is commonly known as a 'blaze', a mark made on a tree, generally by chipping off a slice of bark, to indicate a path or boundary in a forest.[229] 'Stumm-und-stumm' [mute-and-mute] could profitably be misread as 'Stamm-und-Stamm' [trunk-and-trunk], thereby dislocating the stammerings of the translated mute into the gleaming whiteness of stripped tree trunks. It is among the tree-trunks that the glow of praise [Lied] might now dance smiling [Lächeln] through to the moist whiteness of light [Licht].

The creation of this counter-round is more than the moment at which the translation comes closest to recreating the spinning and self-sustaining 'ronds' of the original. It is also the moment at which we realize the nature of the profoundly different poetic approaches of Mallarmé and Celan. Mallarmé's repeated 'ronds' on 'nous nous' and 'muet muet' are integral elements of his playful fluency, motivated by homophony, and the resulting semantic, syntactic, and grammatical ambiguity. In contrast, the counter-rounds of Celan's translation are rooted in the concrete link of words to human activity, a direct indication not of alliteration and clever word games, but of man's interaction with the world around him in his attempts to survive the darkness and dampness in which he lives.

The moisture and light of the counter-rondel on 'L' cannot reverse the reduction the translation operates on the poem. This does, however, represent the moment at which the translation comes closest to recreating the spinning rounds of the original poem. It is, to use another of Benjamin's analogies, the point at which the tangent of the translation fleetingly and at a single point, touches the circle of the original.[230] And yet the tangent does not glance harmlessly off the circular form of the trunk as might be expected from the ideal, abstract geometry of Benjamin's image. Instead it penetrates the bark covering the trunk, interrupting its integrity, breaking through its skin, allowing us to begin to peel the skin away. This reveals the brilliant soft wet whiteness of the underlying translation, a whiteness that will soon dry, harden, and shrivel in the exposure to air, or simply in its newly visible existence. Unlike Shakespeare's sylph Ariel in *The Tempest*, who escapes from the cloven pine where he has been imprisoned thanks to Prospero's intervention, in translation Mallarmé's sylph remains identical and in place, occupying the opening word of the tenth line.

The translation is not, as Benjamin argues, the perpetuation of the original in an afterlife, but the uncovering of something that was already present in the original, something immanent to its life and vitality. There is no transcendence in translation. Instead, the search for an 'au-delà' among the circular 'ronds' and under the circular rind of the poem irreversibly deforms the original. It 'spoils' its trunk — to resurrect a defunct foresting term — leaving a gleaming scar, a glowing blaze that might act as a guide through the darkness of the forest.[231] As Peter Fenves says in his reading of another of Benjamin's essays, translation 'is the reduction'.[232] It is not mere coincidence that a syllable is stripped from each of Mallarmé's octosyllables to give heptasyllabic lines in Celan's German.

Celan's act of spoiling the rondel through translation, his stripping away of its poetic rind, makes me wonder whether at some level we are meant to hear an intimation of another, bastardized form of the rondel, in which its central consonants 'n' and 'd' are removed to give 'rouelle'. Although in contemporary French the noun 'rouelle' can be used to describe a number of flat objects that are circular in shape, such as a 'rouelle de Brie' or a 'rouelle de veau', historically it referred to the round ring of yellow felt or cotton that in 1269 — on the eve of the eighth crusade — Louis IX decreed all Jews should wear on both the chest and the back as an unambiguous means of identification.[233] This ruling followed the Fourth Council of the Lateran (1215), in which it was decided that Jews and Muslims living under Christian jurisdiction would be obliged to wear a defining mark or 'signum'.[234] The prescription of the badge was lifted in 1781 in the lands of the Austrian crown, after 1789 in France, and after 1798 in Rome, only to be reintroduced by the National Socialists in the form of a yellow cloth star from September 1941 onward.[235]

The 'rouelle' was ostensibly introduced to prevent Christians from inadvertently having relations with non-Christians.[236] This historical detail may be key to understanding why Celan would have been sensitive to this symbol of anti-Jewish discrimination at this point in time, and why Mallarmé's poem is selected for translation. Celan would have been aware from the editorial notes in the Pléiade edition of Mallarmé's complete works, which he owned, that Mallarmé initially wrote this rondel for his mistress, Méry Laurent, to celebrate New Year's Day in 1889. As Robb has detailed at length, Laurent was aware that the image of the rose was, among other things, a secret symbolic reference to herself.[237] Celan's translation dates from 27 and 29 December 1957, and so also marks the New Year. In addition to this, it appears that the poet may have translated the poem to celebrate — hermetically — his own extramarital affair. In October 1957, ten years after their first meeting and love affair, Celan resumed his relationship with the Austrian poet Ingeborg Bachmann.[238] It is through translating Mallarmé's poem and stripping the rondel of its fluent duplicities to reveal the broken 'rouelle' that it contains, that the Jew Celan ironically brands his illicit love affair with a Christian woman.

By repeatedly interrupting the fluency and playfulness of Mallarmé's rondel, and in defying the spatiality offered by Benjamin's model of the tree on the edge of the language forest, Celan can be seen to avoid the ironic gestures of both translation and criticism. The purpose of translation here is not, as de Man claims, 'to show in the original a mobility, an instability, which at first one did not notice'.[239] This mobility and instability was evident in the poem before its translation. Instead, the purpose of translation has been to reduce the mobility of the original, to peel away its canonicity, and perhaps even to reveal something of the anti-Semitism that has long been at the core of European Christian culture. Translation here is not a 'ripening' of the historical precedent or original.[240] Neither should we, as Benjamin suggests, seek to understand the original from the perspective of the translation. For there to be perspective there must also be distance, and here the appearance of the original has been stripped away to reveal the translation already concealed within it. The translation is already, and has perhaps always been, an inherent part of the original, just as the 'rouelle' has always, at various levels, been present in the rondel. In response to Celan's translation of one of Shakespeare's sonnets, Szondi says that he has 'replaced the traditional symbolist poem, which is concerned only with itself and which has itself as its subject-matter, with a poem that is no longer concerned with itself but that is itself'.[241] So, too, we might say that in translating Mallarmé's rondel, Celan has infiltrated the poem's ironic mechanisms, and sabotaged its self-conscious staging, to move the poem back toward the base fragments from which it originally came.

Circles

As we look back at the three moments that Celan engages with Mallarmé's work — in the late 1950s, 1960, and 1966 — a geometric figure emerges, which offers to condense and organize our reading of 'The Meridian', of Celan's reading of Mallarmé and Sartre, and of his translation of Mallarmé's rondel. It is a circle. In the Büchner prize speech, the unanswered question as to whether we should think Mallarmé consistently to the end marks the outermost point of the 'meridian' traced by Celan in front of his audience: 'I find something — like language — immaterial, but earthly, terrestrial, something circular...'.[242] Sartre's projection of suicide as that which motivates Mallarmé's poetics, and as the question he considers every day, depends on a concept of suicide that is circular in form. The self moves to self via 'the self which I am not yet', and draws back from the edge of the abyss. The only poem by Mallarmé that Celan chooses to translate — a rondel — is also built on a circle. The circle is a fiction, whose destructive nature is hidden by the eternal nature of its form. It is a fiction which, once set in motion, continues to motivate and to generate itself, much like the eternal repetition of the same in the task given to Sisyphus, who was condemned by the gods to ceaselessly roll a rock to the top of the mountain, from where it would roll back of its own accord.

In each of these three engagements with Mallarmé, Celan works to undo the circle, to interrupt its cycle, to fragment the figure. If the unanswered question of whether we should think Mallarmé consistently to the end is in fact answered — as we are invited to conclude — in the whiteness of the page, then the meridian has been punctured, dislocated, opened up to contamination, or to the possibility of other hemispheres. Similarly, Sartre's circle of suicide, as a figure that maintains the subject on this side of death, is broken open by Celan's own realization of suicide, an act that Sartre's model cannot begin to comprehend. It is an act that takes us beyond poetry, beyond literature, beyond anything anyone of us can say about Celan's poetics, except that any relation of literature to life escapes categorization, and is always left unfinished. Even in his much earlier translation of Mallarmé's rondel, the cracks and imperfections inherent in the original poem are amplified to such a degree that they overwhelm the characteristic circles of the poem itself, revealing the 'rouelle' in the rondel. What was a playful, flirtatious poem marking the illicit love between a married man and his demi-monde mistress becomes — through translation — not only a celebration of illicit love, but a broken commentary on the prevalence of postwar anti-Semitism. Translation removes the poem from its habitual orbit in the outer reaches of Mallarmé's lesser-known oeuvre and applies it to Celan's own extra-marital affair, which is itself circular in form, repeating the relationship begun ten years earlier. But more importantly, by revealing the 'rouelle' in one of Mallarmé's most carefree, playful, and inconsequential poems, Celan casts doubt on the innocence of a pre-Holocaust world, and on the integrity of its literature.

Celan's engagement with Mallarmé appears to be marginal and intermittent, an affair of the sous-oeuvre more than the oeuvre. And yet when each encounter is reconsidered on its own terms, it becomes evident how engaging with Mallarmé allows Celan to deal in economical but decisive gestures with some of the major concerns of his work: anti-Semitism, suicide, and poetics. Each present circular structures that Celan breaks open. This, in turn, begs the question of what should be done with the circle that this chapter traces through Celan's encounters with Mallarmé. How can any circular form be justified, when it is just this form that Celan dismantles and destroys? Perhaps it is time to think Mallarmé consistently through to the end.

Notes to Chapter 2

1. Friedrich Hölderlin, *Selected Poems and Fragments*, trans. by Michael Hamburger, ed. by Jeremy Adler (London: Penguin, 1998), p. 59.
2. Erhart Kästner, 'Wo Verschlüsselung ist, da ist Aufschluss. Aus Erhart Kästners Rede zur Verleihung des Bremer Literaturpreises an Paul Celan', *Frankfurter Allgemeine Zeitung* (31 January 1958), 10 (10).
3. Hans Schwerte, 'Die deutsche Lyrik nach 1945', *Der Deutschunterricht* 14.3 (1962), 47–59 (59). Schwerte's true identity was discovered in 1995 (*Paul Celan, die Goll-Affäre: Dokumente zu einer 'Infamie'*, ed. by Barbara Wiedemann (Frankfurt a.M.: Suhrkamp, 2000), p. 661). See also Ludwig Jäger, *Seitenwechsel. Der Fall Schneider/Schwerte und die Diskretion der Germanistik* (Munich: Fink, 1998) and Claus Leggewie, *Von Schneider zu Schwerte: das ungewöhnliche Leben eines Mannes, der aus der Geschichte lernen wollte* (Munich: Hanser, 1998).
4. Peter Rühmkorf, 'Das lyrische Weltbild der Nachkriegsdeutschen' in *Bestandsaufnahme. Eine deutsche Bilanz 1962. Sechsunddreissig Beiträge deutscher Wissenschaftler, Schriftsteller und Publizisten*, ed. by Hans Werner Richter (Munich: Desch, 1962), pp. 447–76 (pp. 464–65).
5. Steiner, 'A Terrible Exactness', 709.

6. Meschonnic, 'On appelle cela traduire Celan', 118.
7. Pöggeler, *Spur des Worts*, p. 121.
8. Theodor W. Adorno, *Aesthetic Theory*, ed. by Gretel Adorno and Rolf Tiedemann, trans. by Robert Hullot-Kentor (Minneapolis: University of Minnesota Press, 1997), p. 422.
9. Ibid., pp. 422–23.
10. See Gerhard Neumann, 'Die "absolute" Metapher. Ein Abgrenzungsversuch am Beispiel Stéphane Mallarmés und Paul Celans', *Poetica*, 3 (1970), 188–225.
11. Gerhart Baumann, *Erinnerungen an Paul Celan* (Frankfurt a.M.: Suhrkamp, 1986), p. 84.
12. Ibid., p. 85.
13. Gerhart Baumann, '"... durchgründet vom Nichts"', *Études germaniques*, 25.3 (1970) 276–90 (287).
14. Celan, *Der Meridian. Endfassung — Vorstufen — Materialien*, p. 5, §19.
15. Georg Büchner, *Sämtliche Werke und Briefe. Historisch-kritische Ausgabe mit Kommentar*, ed. by Werner R. Lehmann (Munich: Hanser, 1979), p. 37. This runs counter to Ovid's iteration of the myth, where Galatea gives birth to a son named Paphos (Ovid, *The Metamorphoses of Ovid*, trans. by Mary M. Innes (Harmondsworth: Penguin, 1955), p. 232). See also M. B. Benn, 'Anti-Pygmalion: An Apologia for Georg Büchner's Aesthetics', *The Modern Language Review*, 64.3 (1969), 597–604.
16. Paul Celan, *Selected Poems and Prose of Paul Celan*, trans. by John Felstiner (New York: W. W. Norton, 2000), p. 401.
17. Tiffany calls this — with reference to Baudelaire's essay 'Philosophy of Toys' (1853) and Kleist's 'On the Marionette Theater' (1810) — the 'unexpectedly broad horizon of the doll in modern poetics' (Daniel Tiffany, *Toy Medium: Materialism and Modern Lyric* (Berkeley: University of California Press, 2000), p. 72).
18. Mallarmé, *Oeuvres complètes*, I, p. 391.
19. Celan, *Der Meridian. Endfassung — Vorstufen — Materialien*, p. 3, §6c.
20. Ibid., p. 3, §5b.
21. Büchner, *Sämtliche Werke und Briefe*, p. 69.
22. Celan, *Der Meridian. Endfassung — Vorstufen — Materialien*, p. 3, §6b.
23. Ibid., p. 3, §8c.
24. Ibid., p. 3, §5b.
25. Pöggeler, *Spur des Worts*, p. 147.
26. Mayer, *Umerzogene Literatur*, p. 233.
27. Benn, *Probleme der Lyrik*, p. 44.
28. For an early examination of this relationship, see James K. Lyon, 'Paul Celan and Martin Buber: Poetry as Dialogue', *PMLA*, 86.1 (1971), 110–20. See also Maurice Friedman, 'Paul Celan and Martin Buber: The Poetics of Dialogue and 'The Eclipse of God'', *Religion & Literature*, 29.1 (1997), 43–62.
29. Büchner's Lenz is based on the poet Jakob Michael Reinhold Lenz (1751–1792). Lenz was a student of Immanuel Kant in Königsberg, later a friend of Goethe, and was found dead on a street in Moscow at the age of forty-one. For further details, see M. N. Rosanow, *Jakob M. R. Lenz, der Dichter der Sturm- und Drangperiode: sein Leben und seine Werke*, trans. by C. von Gütschow (Leipzig: Schulze, 1909), referred to in Celan, *Der Meridian. Endfassung — Vorstufen — Materialien*, p. 6, §24d.
30. Ibid., p. 5, §15.
31. Ibid., p. 5 §16a.
32. Martin Heidegger, *Gesamtausgabe*, II, pp. 170–71.
33. Celan, *Der Meridian. Endfassung — Vorstufen — Materialien*, p. 5, §16b.
34. Ovid, *The Metamorphoses of Ovid*, p. 232.
35. Celan, *Der Meridian. Endfassung — Vorstufen — Materialien*, p. 5, §19.
36. Ibid., p. 12, §50c.
37. Ibid., p. 10, §42a.
38. Gide and Valéry, *Correspondance*, pp. 178–79.
39. Celan, *Der Meridian. Endfassung — Vorstufen — Materialien*, p. 9, §35d.

40. Ibid., p. 7, §27.
41. Ute Harbusch, *Gegenübersetzungen. Paul Celans Übertragungen französischer Symbolisten* (Göttingen: Wallstein, 2005), p. 84.
42. Harbusch provides the following examples: Helmut Mader, 'Schweigsame Gedichte. "Atemwende" von Paul Celan', *Stuttgarter Zeitung* (11 October 1967), p. 35; Harald Weinrich, 'Kontraktionen: Paul Celans Lyrik und ihre Atemwende', *Neue Rundschau*, 79.1 (1968), 112–21 (117); Dietlind Meinecke, *Wort und Name bei Paul Celan: zur Widerruflichkeit des Gedichts* (Bad Homburg v. d. H.: Gehlen, 1970), pp. 245–46.; William H. Rey, *Poesie der Antipoesie: moderne deutsche Lyrik: Genesis, Theorie, Struktur* (Heidelberg: L. Stiehm, 1978), p. 194; Mayer, *Umerzogene Literatur*, p. 229; Frauke Bünde, 'Mallarmé und Paul Celan: Einfahrt in das Gedicht Hafen', *Lendemains*, 73 (1994), 54–63 (62).
43. Harbusch provides the following examples: Klaus Voswinckel, *Paul Celan: verweigerte Poetisierung der Welt: Versuch einer Deutung* (Heidelberg: Stiehm, 1974), p. 183; Gerhard Buhr, *Celans Poetik* (Göttingen: Vandenhoeck und Ruprecht, 1976), pp. 43 and 184; Marlies Janz, *Vom Engagement absoluter Poesie: Zur Lyrik und Ästhetik Paul Celans* (Frankfurt a.M.: Syndikat, 1976), p. 103; Ute Maria Oelmann, *Deutsche poetologische Lyrik nach 1945: Ingeborg Bachmann, Günter Eich, Paul Celan* (Stuttgart: Hans-Dieter Heinz, 1980), p. 255; Winfried Menninghaus, *Paul Celan: Magie der Form* (Frankfurt a.M.: Suhrkamp, 1980), p. 23; David Brierley, *"Der Meridian" — ein Versuch zur Poetik und Dichtung Paul Celans* (Frankfurt a.M.: Peter Lang, 1984), pp. 116–20; Pöggeler, *Spur des Worts*, p. 275; Dieter Breuer, 'Introduction', in *Deutsche Lyrik nach 1945*, ed. by Dieter Breuer (Frankfurt a.M.: Suhrkamp, 1988), pp. 7–9 (p. 8); Sieghild Bogumil, 'Zur Dialoggestalt von Paul Celans Dichtung, dargestellt am Gedicht "Stimmen" und seiner Spiegelung in "Landschaft" und "Wutpilger-Streifzüge"', *Celan-Jahrbuch*, 5 (1993), 23–52 (25); Lydia Koelle, *Paul Celans pneumatisches Judentum: Gott-Rede und menschliche Existenz nach der Shoah* (Mainz: Matthias-Grünewald, 1997), p. 126.
44. Harbusch, *Gegenübersetzungen*, p. 85.
45. Petra Leutner, *Wege durch die Zeichen-Zone. Stéphane Mallarmé und Paul Celan* (Stuttgart: Metzler, 1994), p. 156.
46. Mallarmé, *Oeuvres complètes*, II, p. 715.
47. Harbusch, *Gegenübersetzungen*, pp. 85–86.
48. Ibid., p. 86.
49. Quoted in Victor Terras and Karl S. Weimar, 'Mandelstam and Celan: A Postscript', *Germano-Slavica*, 2 (1976–1978), 353–70 (361). Letter dated 29 January 1959.
50. Celan, *Der Meridian. Endfassung — Vorstufen — Materialien*, p. 24, §19.
51. Harbusch, *Gegenübersetzungen*, p. 87.
52. Jean-Paul Sartre, 'Mallarmé 1842–1898', in *Les Écrivains célèbres*, ed. by Raymond Queneau, 3 vols (Paris: Mazenod, 1951–1953), III, pp. 148–51 (p. 148).
53. Mallarmé, *Oeuvres complètes*, II, p. 702.
54. Ibid., II, p. 224.
55. Valéry, *Oeuvres*, I, p. 623.
56. Ibid.
57. Stéphane Mallarmé and Jacques Scherer, *Le 'Livre' de Mallarmé: premières recherches sur des documents inédits*, preface by Henri Mondor (Paris: Gallimard, 1957). See also Mallarmé, *Oeuvres complètes*, I, pp. 945–1060.
58. Michael Hamburger, *The Truth of Poetry. Tensions in Modern Poetry from Baudelaire to the 1960's* (New York: Harcourt, Brace & World, 1970), p. 294.
59. Celan, *Der Meridian. Endfassung — Vorstufen — Materialien*, p. 5, §20a.
60. Ibid., p. 55, §17.
61. Mallarmé, *Oeuvres complètes*, II, p. 178.
62. Ibid., I, p. 391.
63. Ibid., II, p. 442.
64. Ibid., II, p. 659.
65. Émile Littré, *Dictionnaire de la langue française*, 4 vols (Paris: Hachette, 1881–1882), I, p. 194.
66. Celan, *Die Gedichte*, p. 184.

67. Celan, *Der Meridian. Endfassung — Vorstufen — Materialien*, p. 7, §25b.
68. Celan, *Gesammelte Werke in sieben Bänden*, III, p. 170.
69. Stéphane Mallarmé, *Poésies: Poésies, choix de vers de circonstance, poèmes d'enfance et de jeunesse*, preface by Jean-Paul Sartre (Paris: Gallimard, 1966).
70. *Le Monde* (12 March 1966), p. 15.
71. Celan and Celan-Lestrange, *Correspondance*, I, p. 385.
72. Mallarmé, *Poésies*, p. 36.
73. Celan and Celan-Lestrange, *Correspondance*, II, p. 326. On 22 May 1966, toward the end of his hospitalization at Sainte Anne, Celan asked Gisèle to bring him the following German translation of this work: Honoré de Balzac, *Das Chagrinleder*, trans. by Hedwig Lachmann (Leipzig: Insel, 1927).
74. H. de Balzac, *La Peau de Chagrin* (Paris: Garnier, 1967), p. 12.
75. E. M. Cioran, *Le mauvais démiurge* (Paris: Gallimard, 1969), p. 73.
76. Ibid., p. 75.
77. Paul S. Loeb, 'Suicide, Meaning, and Redemption', in *Nietzsche on Time and History*, ed. by Manuel Dries (Berlin: De Gruyter, 2008), pp. 163–90 (p. 167).
78. Albert Camus, *Essais*, introduction by R. Quilliot, ed. by R. Quilliot and L. Faucon (Paris: Gallimard/Calmann-Lévy, 1965), p. 102.
79. Rhiannon Goldthorpe, 'Mallarmé: Sartre's committed poet', in *Baudelaire, Mallarmé, Valéry. New essays in honour of Lloyd Austin*, ed. by Malcolm Bowie, Alison Fairlie, and Alison Finch (Cambridge: Cambridge University Press, 1982), pp. 222–41 (p. 224).
80. René Wellek, *History of Modern Criticism: 1750–1950*, 8 vols (New Haven: Yale University Press, 1955), VIII, p. 160.
81. Jean-Paul Sartre, *Baudelaire*, with a foreword by Michel Leiris (Paris: Gallimard, 1947).
82. Jean-Paul Sartre, *Saint Genet: comédien et martyr* (Paris: Gallimard, 1952).
83. Jean-Paul Sartre, *Les mots* (Paris: Gallimard, 1964).
84. Jean-Paul Sartre, *L'idiot de la famille: Gustave Flaubert de 1821–1837*, 3 vols (Paris: Gallimard, 1971).
85. Sartre, 'Mallarmé 1842–1898', in *Les Écrivains célèbres*, III, pp. 148–51.
86. Salvatore Grandone, *Lectures phénoménologiques de Mallarmé* (Paris: Harmattan, 2011), p. 23. The preface was republished as 'Mallarmé (1842–1898)', in Jean-Paul Sartre, *Situations, IX, mélanges* (Paris: Gallimard, 1972), pp. 191–201. Roughly a fifth of the project's five hundred pages was published as Jean-Paul Sartre, 'L'engagement de Mallarmé', *Obliques*, 18/19 (1979), 169–94. Sartre's complete writings on Mallarmé were published as Jean-Paul Sartre, *Mallarmé: la lucidité et sa face d'ombre*, ed. by Arlette Elkaïm-Sartre (Paris: Gallimard, 1986).
87. Stéphane Mallarmé, *Oeuvres complètes*, ed. by Henri Mondor and G. Jean-Aubry (Paris: Gallimard, 1945).
88. Henri Mondor, *Vie de Mallarmé*, 2 vols (Paris: Gallimard, 1941–1942).
89. Maurice Blanchot, *Faux pas* (Paris: Gallimard, 1943).
90. Maurice Blanchot, *La part du feu* (Paris: Gallimard, 1949). The first volume of Mallarmé's correspondence was published in 1959. Excerpts from this correspondence were previously available in Mondor and Jean-Aubry's edition of Mallarmé's complete works (1945), as well as in Mondor's two volume biography (1941–1942).
91. Sartre's preface provokes Blanchot into considering the possible role of suicide in the structure of Mallarmé's negative poetics in *L'espace littéraire* (1955), particularly in 'The Experience of *Igitur*'. Blanchot refuses to accept that suicide can ever be 'effective', as Sartre maintains, claiming instead that death cannot be an act, and that suicide is perhaps not even possible (Maurice Blanchot, *L'espace littéraire* (Paris: Gallimard, 1955), p. 42).
92. Jean-Paul Sartre, 'Mallarmé 1842–1898', in Stéphane Mallarmé, *Poésies: Poésies, choix de vers de circonstance, poèmes d'enfance et de jeunesse*, preface by Jean-Paul Sartre (Paris: Gallimard, 1966), pp. 5–15 (p. 5).
93. Ibid., p. 7.
94. Ibid.
95. Mallarmé, *Oeuvres complètes*, II, p. 67.

96. Graham Robb, *Unlocking Mallarmé* (New Haven: Yale University Press, 1996), p. 211.
97. Sartre, 'Mallarmé 1842–1898', p. 7.
98. Ibid., p. 8.
99. Ibid., p. 6.
100. Ibid., p. 9.
101. Blanchot, *Faux pas*, pp. 117–25.
102. Ibid., p. 121.
103. Sartre, 'Mallarmé 1842–1898', pp. 8–9.
104. Stéphane Mallarmé, *Correspondance*, ed. by Henri Mondor, with Jean-Pierre Richard, 11 vols (Paris: Gallimard, 1959–1985), I, p. 313.
105. Bertrand Marchal, 'Notices, notes et variantes', in Stéphane Mallarmé, *Oeuvres complètes*, ed. by Bertrand Marchal, 2 vols (Paris: Gallimard, 1998–2003), I, pp. 1135–1452 (p. 1346).
106. Mallarmé, *Oeuvres complètes*, I, pp. 475 and 480.
107. Ibid., I, p. 478.
108. Ibid., I, p. 477.
109. Sartre, 'Mallarmé 1842–1898', p. 8. Celan underlines this passage and copies Mallarmé's characterization of Hamlet in the margin: 'Seigneur latent qui ne peut devenir [Latent lord who cannot become]'.
110. Mallarmé, *Correspondance*, I, p. 259. Letter to Villiers de L'Isle-Adam, 24 September 1867.
111. Ibid., I, p. 208. Letter to Henri Cazalis, end of April, 1866. Orig. emphasis.
112. Sartre, 'Mallarmé 1842–1898', p. 10.
113. Ibid.
114. Ilinca Zarifopol-Johnston, *Searching for Cioran*, ed. by Kenneth R. Johnston (Bloomington: Indiana University Press, 2009), p. 78.
115. Sartre, 'Mallarmé 1842–1898', p. 14.
116. Blanchot, *La part du feu*, p. 324.
117. Catulle Mendès, *Rapport sur le mouvement poétique français de 1867 à 1900. Rapport à M. le ministre de l'instruction publique et des beaux-arts, précédé de réflexions sur la personnalité de l'esprit poétique de France, suivi d'un dictionnaire bibliographique et critique et d'une nomenclature chronologique de la plupart des poètes français du XIXe siècle* (Paris: Imprimerie Nationale, 1903), p. 137.
118. Mallarmé, *Oeuvres complètes*, I, p. 11.
119. Paul de Man, *The Post-Romantic Predicament* (Edinburgh: Edinburgh University Press, 2012), p. 49.
120. Mallarmé, *Oeuvres complètes*, I, p. 39.
121. Sartre, 'L'engagement de Mallarmé', p. 187.
122. Mallarmé, *Oeuvres complètes*, I, p. 37.
123. Sartre, 'Mallarmé 1842–1898', p. 13.
124. Ibid., pp. 10 and 11.
125. Ibid., p. 10.
126. Ibid.
127. Blanchot, *La part du feu*, pp. 35–48.
128. Ibid., p. 38.
129. Ibid., p. 41.
130. Mallarmé, *Oeuvres complètes*, II, p. 660.
131. Sartre, 'Mallarmé 1842–1898', p. 11.
132. The manuscript of the article submitted to Queneau in 1953 included this passage (corresponds to Sartre, *Mallarmé: la lucidité et sa face d'ombre*, pp. 157–63).
133. Ibid., p. 157.
134. Sartre, 'Mallarmé 1842–1898', pp. 11–12.
135. Wellek, *History of Modern Criticism*, VIII, p. 160.
136. Thomas Flynn, 'Jean-Paul Sartre', *Stanford Encyclopedia of Philosophy* (Fall 2013 Edition), Edward N. Zalta (ed.), available at <https://plato.stanford.edu/archives/fall2013/entries/sartre/>, [accessed 26 July 2017].
137. Ibid.

138. Contra Tarn, who evokes the 'richness' of Sartre on poetic suicide (Nathaniel Tarn, *The Embattled Lyric: Essays and Conversations in Poetics and Anthropology* (Stanford: Stanford University Press, 2007), pp. 71–72.
139. Mallarmé, *Oeuvres complètes*, II, p. 155.
140. Ibid., II, p. 23.
141. Ibid., II, p. 214.
142. Ibid., II, p. 215.
143. 'Je ne m'intéresse pas au suicide philosophique, mais au suicide tout court' (Camus, *Essais*, p. 135).
144. Sartre, 'Mallarmé 1842–1898', p. 14. A close reading of many of Mallarmé's poems would seem, on the contrary, to reveal an erotic obsession with the female body. See Daniel Sipe, 'Mallarmé et l'écriture du corps', *Nineteenth-Century French Studies*, 35.2 (2007), 367–83.
145. Sartre, 'Mallarmé 1842–1898', p. 14.
146. Ibid., p. 5.
147. Ibid.
148. The word 'suicide' itself indicates a shying away from the total contemplation of death. '–cide' comes from the Latin 'cidium' [killing]. Its monosyllabic form, echoed and confirmed in 'la mort' and 'der Tod', is embellished by the addition of two syllables in 'sui–' [of oneself]. It is the self that saves suicide from the complete devastation of death.
149. Jean-Paul Sartre, *L'être et le néant. Essai d'ontologie phénoménologique* (Paris: Gallimard, 1943).
150. Ibid., p. 32.
151. Heidegger, *Poetry, Language, Thought*, p. 92.
152. Alexandre Kojève, *Introduction to the Reading of Hegel. Lectures on the* Phenomenology of Spirit, assembled by Raymond Queneau, ed. by Allan Bloom, trans. by James H. Nichols (New York: Basic, 1969), p. 54.
153. Sartre, 'Mallarmé 1842–1898', p. 12.
154. Ibid., p. 13.
155. Ibid.
156. Ibid.
157. Ibid.
158. Ibid.
159. Ibid., p. 14.
160. Ibid., p. 6.
161. Ibid., p. 14.
162. See the following passages underlined by Celan: 'absence tightens things, penetrates them with its secret unity. It is the very movement of suicide that must be reproduced in the poem' (ibid., p. 10); 'poetry will be, as excellently formulated by Blanchot, 'this language whose entire power is to not be, whose entire glory is to evoke, in its own absence, the absence of everything" (ibid., p. 11); 'the moment of poetic plenitude must correspond to its annulment' (ibid., p. 11).
163. Celan, *Eingedunkelt* p. 142.
164. A stone shield is a large mass of basement rock 'having the form of a flat or gently convex peneplained platform and usually forming the nucleus of a continent' ('shield, n.', *OED Online*, March 2017, Oxford University Press, available at <http://www.oed.com/view/Entry/178068?rskey=Rcli6b&result=1&isAdvanced=false>, [accessed 14 March 2017]).
165. Mallarmé, *Poésies*, p. 32.
166. Mallarmé, *Correspondance*, I, p. 220.
167. Mallarmé, *Poésies*, p. 26.
168. Ibid., p. 48.
169. Ibid., p. 90.
170. For other appearances of the glacier see l. 24 of 'Cantique de Saint Jean' (ibid., p. 56) and l. 5 of 'M'introduire dans ton histoire' (ibid., p. 104).
171. *Brockhaus-Taschenbuch der Geologie. Die Entwicklungsgeschichte der Erde. Mit einem ABC der Geologie* (Leipzig: Brockhaus, 1955), p. 244.
172. Mallarmé, *Oeuvres complètes*, I, pp. 37 and 98.

173. Gilles Deleuze, *Cinéma 2. L'Image-temps* (Paris: Minuit, 1985), p. 201.
174. Ibid.
175. The earliest known trace of the poem, written on the front of an envelope the day before Celan's acquisition of *Poésies*, reads: 'Über den Steinschild Pannoniens / stürzt ein Morgiger heim' [Over Pannonia's stone-shield / a one of tomorrow rushes home] (Celan, *Eingedunkelt*, p. 144). Pannonia was a province of the Roman Empire located directly to the west of Celan's native Bukovina. See Fig. 2.1.
176. Wilhelm Michel, *Das Leben Friedrich Hölderlins* (Bremen: Schünemann, 1949).
177. Ibid., p. 516.
178. Cioran, *Cahiers 1957–1972*, p. 807.
179. Primo Levi, 'On Obscure Writing', in Primo Levi, *Other People's Trades* (New York: Summit, 1989), pp. 169–75 (p. 173).
180. Yves Bonnefoy, 'Paul Celan', in Yves Bonnefoy, *La Vérité de parole et autres essais* (Paris: Mercure de France, 1995), pp. 545–52 (pp. 545 and 547). Claire Goll asserted that Celan threw himself into the Seine for the same reason that Judas had hanged himself, namely for having betrayed his 'master', her husband Yvan Goll (Claire Goll, 'Ivan Golls Witwe: So war es', in *Die Goll-Affäre: Dokumente zu einer 'Infamie'*, ed. by Barbara Wiedemann (Frankfurt a.M.: Suhrkamp, 2000), pp. 684–91 (pp. 686–87).
181. Henri Michaux, 'Sur le chemin de la vie, Paul Celan...', *Études germaniques*, 25.3 (1970), 250 (250).
182. Quoted in Coetzee, 'In the Midst of Losses', n. p.
183. Steiner, 'A Terrible Exactness', 709. Harbusch draws away from the 'discrepancy' between the death of the poet through suicide, and notional or theoretical reconciliations of the poet's death with poetic creation (Harbusch, *Gegenübersetzungen*, p. 93). Horn considers the effect of the poet's mental illness on his final actions, recalling that a significant number of those who are depressive or manic-depressive attempt suicide (Horn, *Die Garne der Fischer der Irrsee*, pp. 253–54).
184. Alexis Nouss, *Paul Celan: Les lieux d'un déplacement* (Lormont: Le Bord de l'eau, 2010), pp. 372–73). Spire pursues a similar line of thought, calling the suicide of the poet 'the fruit of a displacement in time as in place, in language as in life' (Antoine Spire, 'Préface', in Alexis Nouss, *Paul Celan: Les lieux d'un déplacement* (Lormont: Le Bord de l'eau, 2010), pp. 7–17 (p. 7)).
185. Celan, *Die Gedichte*, p. 165. Felstiner claims he heard that Celan had attempted suicide from the Mirabeau Bridge in 1953, but is not able to corroborate this (Felstiner, *Paul Celan: Poet, Survivor, Jew*, p. 330).
186. Above the unfinished poem 'Hérodiade', Celan has written: 'Das nackte Gold / hebt sich weiss dir hinweg' [The naked gold / rises, white, away from you]. This is a free rendition of the third line of the poem: 'Des ors nus fustigeant l'escape cramoisi' [Naked golds thrashing crimson space] (Mallarmé, *Poésies*, p. 45). Alongside the lines 'Un inutile gisement / <u>Nuit, désespoir et pierrerie</u>' [A useless deposit / Night, despair, and precious stone] in 'Au seul souci de voyager' ['To the sole goal of sailing'], Celan translates the second line: 'Nacht, Verzweiflung, allerlei Gestein' [Night, desperation, all sorts of stone] (ibid., p. 99).
187. The poem's original title was 'Chanson, sur un vers composé par Méry' [Song, on a verse composed by Méry]. Celan translated the final version of the poem, as it is now commonly published, and as it appeared in a facsimile reproduction of the manuscript (Stéphane Mallarmé, 'Si tu veux nous nous aimerons', *La Plume* (15 March 1896), 173).
188. Roger Pearson, *Mallarmé and Circumstance: The Translation of Silence* (Oxford: Oxford University Press, 2004), p. 2.
189. Mallarmé, *Oeuvres complètes*, I, p. 57. See ibid., I, p. 134 for an alternative, earlier version of the same poem.
190. Scott describes how the rondel dance became a poetic form in the fourteenth century: 'the dance and music disappeared, as did the distinction between soloist and chorus, the forms became purely literary' (Clive Scott, *French Verse-Art. A Study* (Cambridge: Cambridge University Press, 1980), p. 165).
191. Lautréamont, *Les Chants de Maldoror et autres textes*, ed. by Jean-Luc Steinmetz (Paris: Librairie

Générale Française, 2001), pp. 347–48.
192. Ibid., p. 349.
193. Compare to Mallarmé's 'Billet', a sonnet — also in octosyllables — that 'simulates the whirlwind of a ballerina's pirouette' by performing 'a syntactic balancing act, having no main verb and being full of motion, like a circular dance going nowhere' (Roger Pearson, *Stéphane Mallarmé* (London: Reaktion, 2010), p. 147).
194. James Joyce, *Ulysses: The Corrected Text*, ed. by Hans Walter Gabler, Wolfhard Steppe and Claus Melchior, preface by Richard Ellmann (London: Bodley Head, 1986), p. 569.
195. Gérard de Nerval, *Selected Writings*, trans. by Richard Sieburth (London: Penguin, 1999), p. 270.
196. Mallarmé, *Oeuvres complètes*, I, p. 500.
197. Ibid., I, p. 59.
198. Ibid., II p. 216.
199. In the sixteenth century, the rondel (also known as the 'rondeau') could be composed of pictograms (Jean Céard and Jean-Claude Margolin, *Rébus de la renaissance. Des images qui parlent*, 2 vols (Paris: Maisonneuve et Larose, 1986), I, pp. 186–99).
200. Mallarmé, *Oeuvres complètes*, II, p. 208.
201. Ibid., II, p. 209.
202. Ibid.
203. Ibid., II, p. 208.
204. Ibid., II, pp. 207–08.
205. Slavoj Žižek, *Less than Nothing. Hegel and the Shadow of Dialectical Materialism* (London: Verso, 2012), p. 228.
206. Robb, *Unlocking Mallarmé*, p. 94.
207. Heidegger, *Gesamtausgabe*, VII, pp. 206–07.
208. 'mystery, n.1', *OED Online*, March 2017, Oxford University Press, available at <http://www.oed.com/view/Entry/124644?rskey=wpEl9n&result=1&isAdvanced=false>, [accessed 13 March 2017].
209. Mallarmé, *Oeuvres complètes*, II, p. 173.
210. Ibid., II, p. 172.
211. See Jean de la Varende, *Man d'Arc* (Paris: Grasset, 1939), p. 268.
212. Mallarmé, *Oeuvres complètes*, II, p. 1010.
213. Paul de Man, *Critical Writings 1954–1978*, ed. by Lindsay Waters (Minneapolis: University of Minnesota Press, 1989), p. 25.
214. Celan, *Gesammelte Werke in sieben Bänden*, IV, p. 817. First published in Paul Celan, 'Paul Celan: Vier Gedichte aus dem Französischen', in *Insel-Almanach auf das Jahr 1959* (Leipzig: Insel, 1958), pp. 31–33 (pp. 32–33).
215. Jacobs, *Telling Time*, p. 129.
216. Walter Benjamin, *Illuminations*, ed. by Hannah Arendt, trans. by Harry Zohn (New York: Schocken, 1968), p. 76.
217. For other readings of Mallarmé's poem and Celan's translation see John Felstiner, '"Here we go round the prickly pear" or "Your song, what does it know?" Celan vis-à-vis Mallarmé', in *Mallarmé in the Twentieth Century*, ed. by Robert Greer Cohn (Cranbury: Associated University Presses, 1998), pp. 203–11 and Harbusch, *Gegenübersetzungen*, pp. 93–106.
218. 'Ach Mein HERR, ich bin je und je nicht wohl beredt gewesen, auch nicht seit der Zeit, da du mit deinem Knecht geredet hast; denn ich habe eine schwere Sprache und eine schwere Zunge', Martin Luther, *Lutherbibel: Textfassung 1912* (Altenmünster: Jazzybee Verlag Jürgen Beck, 2016), p. 44, Exodus 4. 10.
219. Exodus 4. 11–12.
220. Luther, *Lutherbibel*, p. 44, Exodus 4. 12 and 15.
221. Exodus 4. 16.
222. Harbusch, *Gegenübersetzungen*, pp. 99–100. Harbusch draws a parallel between the use of male rhymes (instead of the alternating male and female rhymes in the French), the proliferation of monosyllabic verbal units, and shortened verses to the poems of Stefan George (ibid., p. 99).

223. Dirk Weissmann, 'Poésie, Judaïsme, Philosophie. Une histoire de la réception de Paul Celan en France: des débuts jusqu'à 1991' (doctoral thesis, University of Paris — III, 2003), available at <publikationen.ub.uni-frankfurt.de/oai/container/index/docId/12414>, [accessed 12 March 2016] p. 71.
224. Meschonnic, 'On appelle cela traduire Celan', 133. See also John E. Jackson, 'Traduire Celan: raisons d'un échec', *Colloquium Helveticum*, 3 (1986), 131–38 (137).
225. Philippe Lacoue-Labarthe, *Poetry as Experience*, trans. by Andrea Tarnowski (Stanford: Stanford University Press, 1999), p. 12.
226. Mallarmé, *Oeuvres complètes*, I, p. 417.
227. Kluge, *Etymologisches Wörterbuch*, p. 643.
228. Hans Schwarz, 'Lied und Licht', in *Festschrift für Jost Trier zu seinem 60. Geburtstag am 15. Dezember 1954*, ed. by Benno von Wiese and Karl Heinz-Borck (Meisenheim a. G.: Westkulturverlag Anton Hain, 1954), pp. 434–55.
229. 'blaze, n.2', *OED Online*, March 2017, Oxford University Press, available at <http://www.oed.com/view/Entry/20004?rskey=zOF7YF&result=2&isAdvanced=false>, [accessed 13 March 2017].
230. Benjamin, *Illuminations*, p. 80.
231. 'spoil, v.1, †b', *OED Online*, March 2017, Oxford University Press, available at <http://www.oed.com/view/Entry/187261?rskey=udi8ar&result=2&isAdvanced=false>, [accessed 13 March 2017].
232. Peter Fenves, 'The Genesis of Judgment: Spatiality, Analogy, and Metaphor in Benjamin's "On Language as Such and On Human Language"', in *Walter Benjamin: Theoretical Questions*, ed. by David S. Ferris (Stanford: Stanford University Press, 1996), pp. 75–93 (p. 90).
233. Danièle Sansy, 'Marquer la différence: l'imposition de la rouelle aux XIIIe et XIVe siècles', *Médiévales*, 41 (2001), 15–36 (15–16).
234. Ibid., p. 24. The circular shape of the 'signum' may have been a reference to the denarii or thirty pieces of silver paid to Judas. It could alternatively have represented the consecrated host (ibid., pp. 28–29).
235. Ruth Mellinkoff, *Outcasts: Signs of Otherness in Northern European Art of the Late Middle Ages*, 2 vols (Berkeley: University of California Press, 1993), I, p. 46.
236. Sansy, 'Marquer la différence', 23.
237. Robb, *Unlocking Mallarmé*, pp. 82–95. It is tempting to muse on the private messages contained in sonnets such as 'Éventail', in which the 'frigid roses' of the opening line melt, by the end of the second quatrain, 'En du rire de fleurir ivre' [into intoxicated laughter of blossoming] (Mallarmé, *Oeuvres complètes*, I, p. 68).
238. Celan and Celan-Lestrange, *Correspondance*, II, p. 507.
239. Paul de Man, *The Resistance to Theory* (Minneapolis: University of Minnesota Press, 1986), p. 82.
240. Ibid., p. 83.
241. Peter Szondi, *Schriften*, ed. by Wolfgang Fietkau, 2 vols (Frankfurt a.M.: Suhrkamp, 1978), II, p. 344.
242. Celan, *Der Meridian. Endfassung — Vorstufen — Materialien*, p. 12, §50c.

CHAPTER 3

Poetry After Frankfurt

... sì che dal fatto il dir non sia diverso.¹

Trial and Error

It has been said that the Holocaust functions as a cultural secret, a secret that — as Shoshana Felman and Dori Laub argue — 'we are still keeping from ourselves through various forms of communal or of personal denial, of cultural reticence or of cultural canonization'.² If the Holocaust is accessible to us today,³ it is accessible in what Felman calls the 'space of *slippage between law and art*'.⁴ Law, in the form of major trials, has attempted to draw limits around the atrocities and to bring closure to the trauma suffered by those who witnessed and survived the Holocaust. As a 'discipline of limits and of consciousness', law has been necessary 'to *totalize* the Holocaust and, through totalization, to start to apprehend its contours and its magnitude'.⁵ Art, on the other hand, as the 'language of infinity', has been required 'to mourn the losses and to face up to what in traumatic memory is not closed and cannot be closed'.⁶

It is principally as an exponent of Holocaust art, of the Holocaust as seen from a perspective of proximity and detail, and as a necessary antidote to the distant view of the law, that Celan's work is composed and understood. As George Steiner puts it, certain of Celan's poems 'circumscribe its intractable enormity in local detail because such inadequate circumscription is the mind's limit, its courtesy before the inhuman'.⁷ In this chapter, I examine Celan's engagement — through poetry — with legal attempts to atone for and come to terms with the Holocaust. Specifically, I consider Celan's response to the Federal Republic of Germany's legal efforts to bring those responsible for perpetrating crimes during the Holocaust to justice. No attempt has yet been made to establish the relation of Celan's poetic oeuvre to one of the most important Holocaust trials after the military tribunals that took place at Nuremberg, namely the Frankfurt Auschwitz Trial, which began in December 1963 and reached its conclusion on 19 August 1965.⁸

Although there is little explicit evidence either within or outside the poetic oeuvre that points to Celan's engagement with and meditation on the trial, it is in the nature of Celan's difficult idiom to conceal references to events, and to challenge the reader with the ethical task of reading and finding ways to understand that which initially appears to resist reading and understanding. An investigation such as the one undertaken in this chapter does not therefore require clear references to the trial as a pre-requisite to justify its initial approximation with Celan's oeuvre.

These references will become clearer as we proceed, and as unexplained fragments in both his published and unpublished work are elucidated. Familiarity with Celan's poetry has taught us that the understanding required to understand his poems is not that described by the violent act of grasping and taking up in one's hands of that which is evident. This is the sense of 'comprehension' which, in its Latin form 'comprehendere', also indicates the catching of fire and the seizing of criminals. To understand these poems, we turn to the etymological sense of 'understanding', which is to 'stand among' (as in the Latin 'inter' or the Sanskrit 'andar' [among, between]), or perhaps to 'stand before' as in the German 'verstehen'. It is sufficient for us to approach them, to stand among them, and to be in proximity to their unique act of witness. There is no need to comprehend or lay one's hands on them. This is not to say that understanding is never a violent action, but that any violence in understanding is difficult to perceive. Similarly, if the poem is violent, then it is violent in a way that is not immediately recognizable. Its violence will be bloodless and invisible.

The three poems discussed in this chapter date from the months that follow the completion of the Frankfurt trial. They do not constitute canonical touchstones of Celanian criticism and have rarely been subject to examination and interpretation. They might be said to constitute a part of the sous-oeuvre, samples of those later poems that appear to slip the grasp of comprehension and the gaze of critical attention. The purpose of reading these poems is not only to argue that Celan's engagement with the Frankfurt trial was in fact more extensive than has hitherto been thought, although it has remained concealed. I also argue that these poems are evidence of Celan's attempt to apply poetry to the questions of justice and retribution in the immediate wake of the most sustained and detailed description of the crimes committed at Auschwitz-Birkenau to that point in time. In short, this chapter examines the responsibilities of poetry not after Auschwitz, but after the Auschwitz trial at Frankfurt. This requires an examination not only of the trial, but also of the trial's representation on stage — just two months after the trial's conclusion — in Peter Weiss's play *The Investigation*.[9] Just as Felman cites the publication of Hannah Arendt's *Eichmann in Jerusalem* (1963) and Claude Lanzmann's film *Shoah* (1985) as works that 'added *a new idiom*' to the discourse on the Holocaust,[10] so too the Frankfurt trial, its immediate representation in the media, and its representation in Weiss's play, not only revealed the daily operations of Auschwitz-Birkenau in their detail, but radically transformed the way the Holocaust was perceived. The task of poetry after Frankfurt is therefore conditioned not only by the trial itself and its representation in the media, but by its representation as theater and literature.

Fritz Bauer, attorney general of the State of Hesse, architect of the trial, and later its presiding judge, believed that the Holocaust could not be adequately understood in legal terms as a sum of individual events.[11] Although the purpose of the trial was to try 'the layer of people who actually carried out Hitler's "Final Solution"',[12] Bauer wanted to avoid dividing the prosecution of those suspected of contributing to the Holocaust into discrete individual trials. Ultimately, twenty-two suspects were charged, out of a cumulative workforce that is now thought to have numbered from between six to eight thousand individuals. Defendants charged at Frankfurt could only be indicted under the German penal code in force at the time of the alleged crimes, which had been established with the founding of the German Empire in 1871. As Devin Pendas and others have explained, this code 'was oriented toward a radically different understanding of crime and human agency than that revealed in the Holocaust'.[13] This meant that those successfully prosecuted at Frankfurt were found guilty of breaking the laws of the National Socialist State in force at the time the events took place. As Sonja Boos puts it, 'the Auschwitz trial did not provide for charges against organized state-sanctioned murder'.[14] She thereby echoes Hannah Arendt's opinion that 'what the old penal code had utterly failed to take into account was nothing less than the everyday reality of Nazi Germany in general and of Auschwitz in particular'.[15] The legal concept of genocide [Völkermord], which could conceivably have described the crimes of some of the defendants, was introduced into the German penal code in 1954 and could only be applied to future infractions.[16]

The most serious charge of which a defendant could be found guilty was therefore murder. A defendant could only be found guilty of murder if it could be proven that he had been inspired by 'Mordlust' [murderous intent]. Carrying out the orders of the State, or of one's superiors — even if this consisted in gassing to death thousands of people at a time — could not be considered an infraction of the State's laws, and so did not expose perpetrators to the possibility of prosecution. Such an act would be considered 'Beihilfe' or 'aiding and abetting'. Of the original twenty-two defendants, twenty remained at the end of the trial.[17] Seven of these were convicted of murder, ten of accessory to murder, and three were acquitted. The sentences handed down ranged from three and a quarter years to life in prison. This latter punishment was extended to only six individuals, re-affirming what two years previously the German Jewish philosopher Ernst Bloch had bluntly described as 'scandalous acquittals and pet-punishments for Nazi butchers'.[18]

In the light of what is known about the Holocaust, and of its perpetration in the camps at Auschwitz-Birkenau in particular, it is difficult not to be surprised at the apparent leniency of the sentences, and to conclude that justice was not served at Frankfurt. Giorgio Agamben will explain this sense of injustice as resulting from a common confusion of ethical and juridical categories. We presume that the purpose of the law is to approximate, to the best of its function, justice and truth. Law, however, 'is solely directed toward judgment, independent of truth and justice. [...] The ultimate aim of law is the production of a *res judicata*, in which the sentence becomes the substitute for the true and the just, being held as true despite its falsity and injustice'.[19] In its decision to try those charged with crimes committed at Auschwitz under the penal code in place at the time of the alleged crimes, from the trial's very inception, the court at Frankfurt aimed to produce a judgment that would confirm the legal structure adopted for the trial.

The decision to return to the law in place at the time of the alleged crimes would therefore have far-reaching implications. Boos has suggested that it would have been possible and legitimate to try defendants according to a legal system reformed in the wake of the Holocaust, as happened at Nuremberg, which was designed to prosecute crimes that previous legal systems had not encountered.[20] The decision to return to the law of 1871, including the various amendments applied during the rule of the National Socialists, appears to have been motivated by a desire to preserve a clear distinction between past and present, through a clear distinction of their respective legal systems. By trying past crimes with a legal system of the past, any collective responsibility, or shortcomings in the legal system in place at the time, could be kept from contaminating both the current State and legal system, and the public consciousness.[21] In his 1989 lecture 'Force of Law', Jacques Derrida notes that above all things, the State fears '*founding* violence', that is 'violence that *founds*'.[22] The desire to preserve the current legal system from being used to prosecute the crimes of the Holocaust suggests that there was, at some level, a fear that the Holocaust contained crimes that — when revealed in their detail — could destroy the current law, and require a new law to take its place. By relegating the trial to a legal system that was no longer in force, any threat of declaring a new law could be averted.

And yet certain key elements of the old law were not retained. As if to repeat the same postwar turn to pacifist ideals that Walter Benjamin identifies in the aftermath of the First World War,[23] there was no possibility of sentencing a defendant to death under West German law. This is despite the fact, as Derrida explains, that for Kant, Hegel, and Benjamin, the legal system fully manifests itself only in the possibility of the death penalty: 'If the origin of the law is a violent positing, it manifests itself in the purest fashion when violence is absolute, that is to say when it touches on the right to life and to death'.[24] Or as Benjamin puts it: 'In the exercise of violence over life and death, more than in any other legal act, the law reaffirms itself'.[25] There is, therefore, in the conception of the form that the Frankfurt trial takes, not only a fear that the crimes revealed in the trial will contain a violence that might disrupt the current legal system, State, and society more broadly. There is also a fear of the necessary 'co-implication of violence and law', of the 'juridical essence of violence'.[26] If the foundation of a new State inaugurates a new law, and 'always does so in violence',[27] then the creation of a trial that removes the possibility of this revolutionary, State-founding violence, also removes the threat of violence that is required for the effective pursuit of justice.

To elucidate the nature of the violence inherent in justice, in the second part of 'Force of Law' Derrida turns to Benjamin's essay 'Critique of Violence' [Zur Kritik der Gewalt].[28] Here, Benjamin traces the founding violence of law to its arbitrary establishment in what Blaise Pascal — quoting Michel de Montaigne — calls the 'mystical foundation' of the law's authority.[29] The institution of law, and of justice through law, are achieved through the exercise of power or force. Benjamin calls this 'mythic' violence, as it stems from the Greek tradition of establishing and preserving the law. This is contrasted with 'divine' or — as Derrida glosses — 'Jewish' violence, which seeks to destroy the law and of which there are many examples throughout Scripture: 'If mythic violence is lawmaking, divine violence is law destroying: if the former sets boundaries, the latter boundlessly destroys them'.[30]

The word 'Gewalt' in the German title of Benjamin's essay should therefore be understood both in its conventional English sense as 'violence', and in its additional German sense as the legitimate authority of the State as socio-political body, the 'violence' or 'force' of administration.

If the law is established through the application of mythic violence, then how does the law relate to the violence on which it is meant to pass judgment, such as the violence of the Holocaust? Is the Holocaust an instance of mythic or divine violence? Was the Holocaust law-making or law-destroying? Is the violence of the Holocaust perpetuated, contained, or annulled by the violence of law? Does the violence of the Holocaust risk overwhelming the law called upon to judge its violence? Benjamin and Derrida do not agree on the nature of the relation of mythic and divine violence to an event as extreme as the Holocaust. Benjamin promotes divine violence as that which annihilates hypocritical law.[31] Derrida will counter that this notion is not only 'too messianico-Marxist or archeo-eschatological',[32] but that it comes too close to the sort of destruction subsequently achieved by the Holocaust. The notion of divine violence leaves open the temptation, Derrida says, 'to think the holocaust as an uninterpretable manifestation of divine violence insofar as this divine violence would be at the same time annihilating, expiatory and bloodless'.[33] Derrida's concern is based on the notion that the violence realized in the gas chambers and the cremation ovens might, from a distance, also appear to have been bloodless. Does this mean that the Holocaust should be perceived as an instance of divine rather than mythic violence? Was the Holocaust, Derrida goes so far as to ask, 'an expiation and an indecipherable signature of the just and violent anger of God'?[34]

Derrida claims to be terrified by this idea. However, he seems to overlook — deliberately or otherwise — the dark inventiveness of the Holocaust at this point. The violence of the Holocaust is not adequately described by the acts of gassing and burning alone. As Bernd Naumann writes in the immediate aftermath of the Frankfurt trial: 'murder in Auschwitz was committed in a variety of ways. Inmates were given injections of phenolic acid, beaten and tortured, arbitrarily and summarily executed, and made guinea-pigs in so-called medical experiments. Inhuman working conditions, unspeakably primitive sanitary conditions, inadequate diet, and the complete degradation of the individual all contributed their share: Debility, disease, and despair took the lives of tens of thousands'.[35] Despite the attempts of the Third Reich to undertake the Holocaust through the application of modern technologies, industrial processes, and logistics, its violence remained visible and shed blood in countless ways.

To properly understand the distinction between mythic and divine violence, and the violence of the Holocaust, it is not sufficient to evaluate whether or not the violence is visible. The act of making a visible or mythic act of violence less visible can itself amount to an act of visible or mythic violence. It is instead necessary to consider the relation of an act of violence to the law, conscious that mythic violence founds law whereas divine violence destroys it. The trial at Frankfurt demonstrates that the violence of the Holocaust was not a violence that destroyed the law. The

Holocaust describes a violence that adhered to, confirmed, and perpetuated the law of the State in place at the time. As the defendant Stefan Baretzki replied when asked about carrying out orders the purpose of which he claimed not to understand: 'They also told us that everything Hitler did was law'.³⁶ Even the *ad hoc* formation of a legal system particular to the concentration camps — in which people could be tried in a summary court, found guilty and put to death in a matter of minutes — although in strict terms a distortion and corruption of the law of the State, also indicates the law-creating, rather than law-destroying, faculty of the Holocaust's violence.

Although Derrida worries that adopting Benjamin's distinction between mythic and divine violence will make it necessary to perceive the Holocaust as an instance of divine, expiating violence, it is as mythic violence that the Holocaust is most to be feared, because it is then a violence that establishes law. At some level, the legal structure of the Frankfurt trial was designed to preserve the current legal system of West Germany, and by extension the West German State, and society at large, from continuity with and responsibility for the events of the National Socialist past. But this refusal to allow the Holocaust to contaminate the current legal, social, and political system also meant that the trial perpetuated not only the law and the State that made the Holocaust possible, and which the Holocaust in turn confirmed, but the Holocaust itself. Just as the State tolerates the workers' right to strike in Benjamin's example, so too the trial at Frankfurt both contained the violence of the Holocaust and allowed it to continue to express itself.

If the Frankfurt trial confirms and continues the Holocaust in its mythic violence, then what constitutes justice both for those responsible for having run the camps at Auschwitz-Birkenau and for those who suffered there, both directly and indirectly? Is law the only, or the most effective, means of securing justice? Derrida argues that justice requires law, despite the fact that even in the most successful legal trials, law and justice never coincide: 'Law is not justice. Law is the element of calculation, and it is just that there be law, but justice is incalculable, it demands that one calculate with the incalculable; and aporetic experiences are the experiences, as improbable as they are necessary, of justice'.³⁷ There can be no justice without the traversal of that which cannot be traversed. Justice is an experience of the impossible, and for the law to be just it would have to be able to acknowledge this paradox. But as Peter Schneck notes, 'paradox and aporia are anathema to any legal system, and the procedures and practices it considers to be appropriate or just'.³⁸ Law is designed to deny the paradoxical dimension of justice.³⁹

Although it may appear that Derrida is speaking of justice primarily from a theoretical and timeless perspective, the repetition of variations of 'calcul' [both 'calculation' and 'deposit'] suggests that he is speaking specifically from the perspective of one who lives after the Holocaust. By tracing the origin of the word to its etymological root in the Latin 'calx' [limestone], we encounter the limestone pebbles that, according to the mythology of etymology, were once used to undertake calculations. Derrida's insistence on the 'calx' of 'calcul', 'calculer', and 'incalculable' evokes the limestone quarried by concentration camp inmates at Buchenwald and, by extension, the calculated exploitation of slave labor in the brickyards at Sachsenhausen, the granite quarries at Mauthausen, and the sand and gravel pits at Auschwitz.[40] The repetition of 'calx' in this phrase symbolizes the accretions of injustice that inhere in the very words we use to express ourselves. When Derrida says that justice requires us to calculate with the incalculable, to count with what cannot be counted, the form of his phrase reminds us that traces of injustice will not disappear from the language and world in which we live. The Holocaust has left its heavy mark on us and on the language we use to communicate in more ways than we know. Although justice can never be objectified, weighed, and measured, within or outside of a court of law, it still invites us to measure that which can be measured. This is the meaning of the phrase: 'But incalculable justice commands calculation'.[41] It is not only that justice commands the impossible or the paradoxical, namely the calculation of the incalculable, but that in the language we use to communicate, the deposits or 'calculs' of injustice that we most often choose not to see, can still be identified and measured.

It is in the light of the Frankfurt trial, and of its difficult relation to justice, that a number of posthumously published aphorisms composed by Paul Celan at around the time the trial began can be read and understood. Specifically, these aphorisms convey both the poet's skepticism that legal means can be used to achieve justice, and the unusual conviction that reading poetry is the best means to realize justice. For instance: 'Whoever does not fight against evident evil, loses the protection of what cannot be seen'.[42] The poet's task, and the task of every human being, is to combat evil where it can be seen. In one of the rare moments that Celan mentions Auschwitz by name, another aphorism warns against any action that might obscure the suffering of the Holocaust: 'Whoever mystifies after Auschwitz, avoids the question of human suffering'.[43] An unpublished diary entry dating from the final months of the trial, written in a mixture of German and French, also registers Celan's skepticism that those responsible for running the camps were being brought to justice: 'on / a separate coffee table the open magazine / with the report on the Fft. Auschwitz Trial / (3000 — or so — murderers on the loose)'.[44] Celan's archive contains a number of cut out newspaper articles on the trial from the German press that echo precisely this concern.[45] An article torn from the pages of *Combat*, dated 20 August, the day following the trial's verdict, reads: 'It is clear that the punishments pronounced by the criminal court at Frankfurt are minimal'.[46] On the same day, in a letter to Gisèle, Celan writes: 'In the German and foreign newspapers, commentaries on the trial at Frankfurt. Nothing else could be expected. This will continue to feed those hypocrisies and lies for the next several light-months...'.[47]

The only poem by Celan to have been explicitly identified with the Frankfurt trial is 'A DRONING'. It was composed on 6 May 1965, the day that the hearing of evidence at Frankfurt came to a close:

> EIN DRÖHNEN: es ist
> die Wahrheit selbst
> unter die Menschen
> getreten,
> mitten ins

> Metapherngestöber.⁴⁸
>
> [A DRONING: truth
> itself has
> appeared
> among mankind,
> amidst a
> flurry of metaphors.]

Wiedemann suggests that when composing this poem, Celan had in mind or to hand a newspaper report that appeared in the *Frankfurter Allgemeine Zeitung* on 14 November 1964.⁴⁹ The anonymous author recounts how Alexander Princz — a former prisoner at Auschwitz-Birkenau responsible for driving containers of poison gas granules to the gas chamber in his horse-drawn trap — recalls seeing the camp guards operate the gas chambers: '[Wilhelm] Boger called an SS-man and was given a gas mask. Cartons were unloaded and Boger took out the containers that looked like tinned provisions. He opened them and passed them on. Other SS men threw them in through the open window, out of which a droning noise [ein Dröhnen] could be heard, as if many people were underground. The openings — the little windows — were then closed again, and I had to return immediately'.⁵⁰ The flurry of metaphors, synecdoche for the dislocation and displacement of truth through the language of law, not only obscures the droning of the muffled screams of asphyxiating human beings. It also mimics and perpetuates it, through the droning of meaningless legal chatter. The poem is an ironic celebration of the arrival of nothing less than 'truth' on earth by means of the German legal system. 'Truth itself' walks among mankind in much the way that 'the Word' was 'made flesh' and is purported to have 'dwelt among us'.⁵¹

An aphorism dating from nearly three months after this poem is composed appears to re-affirm Celan's take on the trial: 'The clarifiers, who cast light on everything — that is, what they declare to be 'everything' — that surrounds them, so as to better remain in the dark'.⁵² The droning that opens this short poem, and that signals Celan's engagement with the trial through the medium of poetry, not only describes the sounds of death at Auschwitz and of discourse at Frankfurt. It also signals the first note, the bass accompaniment or 'burden' of a song of lamentation, a modern threnody for the murdered, and also for those who were yet to die, in the Holocaust, which Celan felt had not yet come to an end.⁵³ After Frankfurt, the Holocaust becomes more not less insistent for Celan. The rhetorical staging of droning in the form of a poem therefore signals in a way that the private journal entry, newspaper report, or letter cannot the need to continue to respond to Auschwitz in the wake of its most extensive representation in language.

Die Ermittlung — The Investigation

To understand the repercussions of the trial, especially in the months following its conclusion in August 1965, it is necessary to look beyond the trial as an instance of law, and its near instantaneous representation in the media, and toward the representation of the trial as art. If, as Felman says, the purpose of law is to bring 'a conscious closure to the trauma of the Holocaust by drawing a boundary around a suffering that seems unending and unbearable',[54] then the purpose of art is to re-examine the wound, to bring closer what the law has distanced. Less than two months after the trial's conclusion, the German-born playwright Peter Weiss brought the trial to the theater. On 19 October 1965, *The Investigation: Oratorio in Eleven Cantos*, was first performed on sixteen stages in West and East Germany, as well as in London.[55] The play, popularly supposed to consist only of language recorded in the trial, was divided into eleven cantos, each further divided into three sub-sections. The text was set out on the page in short lines of usually no more than seven or eight words, and often just two or three. One reviewer of the play quoted anonymous sources from the world of theater who disparaged its form as 'weakly rhyming newspaper reports'.[56] It would prove to be one of the major cultural and theatrical events of the season in both East and West Germany. As the play was translated and performed on stages abroad in the months that followed, it provoked wide media coverage throughout Europe and the United States.[57]

Toward the end of October, Celan received a copy of Weiss's play from the Suhrkamp publishing house. Besides the date of acquisition inside the front cover — 27 October 1965 — there are no indications that the book was read. Celan probably never saw the play in person either, although it is possible he subsequently encountered one of the several radio or television recordings of the play, such as the version directed by Peter Schulze-Rohr and filmed by 'Norddeutscher Rundfunk' in 1966.[58] There are, however, a number of reviews and other articles cut out from German newspapers that betray Celan's interest in the play.[59] I suggest that it is in response to the play — which he may not see but about which he is able to read widely — that Celan composes a number of poems, of which three will be examined here. These poems respond to the trial and its representation in Weiss's play by proposing alternative, poetic forms of justice, modeled on a different form of violence to that deployed both in the Holocaust and in its legal treatment at Frankfurt.

An examination of Weiss's play is required to ascertain specifically its relation to the violence of the Holocaust and of the trial. If law is made and preserved through the use of violence as a means, and if all violence as a means is implicated in the nature of law,[60] then to what extent does this violence continue to operate in the trial's translation to the stage? As we cannot be sure that Celan read or saw the play, I propose to undertake a two-part approach to this question: first from the perspective of someone who has read or seen the play, and then from the perspective of someone who is familiar with certain elements of the play through newspaper reports, general discussion, and by having the script to hand.

It has often been noted that the proceedings of the courtroom and those of the stage share fundamental structural features. In her discussion of Adolf Eichmann's trial, for example, Susan Sontag highlights the ancient and reciprocal relations between the theater and the court of law.[61] Although from a strictly legal perspective — its juridical basis, the relevance of the evidence, the legitimacy of court procedures — Eichmann's trial was flawed, its purpose had never been purely legal. The Eichmann trial was an attempt 'to make comprehensible the incomprehensible' and to set down 'a great outcry of historical agony' for which there was no strictly legal justification.[62] The outcome of the Frankfurt trial was not as clear or as definitive as that of the Eichmann trial four years previously. It did not have the same impact on public opinion and on the public consciousness, nor can it be said to have made any significant progress toward resolving the great historical tragedy of the twentieth century, as Sontag claims the Eichmann trial did. But it went further than most Holocaust trials in adopting the trappings of the theater. To accommodate the interest of members of the public and the domestic and international press, the trial was moved from its initial location in Frankfurt City Hall — or what is called the 'Römer' — to a civic auditorium known as the Haus Gallus. Here, the judges were seated on the stage with velvet stage curtains behind them, whilst the proceedings took place before them in the auditorium.

In his directions for the play, Weiss actively seeks to resist the perceived affinities between the trial and the theater. He instructs his directors that no attempt should be made to 'reconstruct the courtroom before which the deliberations over the camp actually took place',[63] explaining, somewhat incongruously, that any such representation would be 'as impossible to the author as a representation of the camp on stage would be'.[64] Characters were required to refrain from acting out their part. The different experiences expressed in the play were to be expressed by 'at most, a change of voice or bearing'.[65] A report of Paul Verhoeven's production of the play in Munich noted that the actors playing the nine nameless witnesses, who are referred to only by number, read their lines from the black binders in their hands in hurried monotone.[66] The eighteen defendants, by contrast, not only express themselves freely, and often passionately, but are identified by name as they were in the trial.

Elements of naturalistic representation were therefore not absent from the play's production, but were denied to the nine witnesses, who constituted a small abstraction of the more than four hundred witnesses heard at Frankfurt. As was reported at the time, in the context of the robotic recitation of the witnesses, it was hard not to feel empathy for the more lifelike portrayals of the defendants. Such feelings would have been compounded by the fact that a contemporary member of the audience would recognize most if not all of the defendants from the recent coverage of their cases in the press. As the author Martin Walser observed, the cruelest among the defendants, such as Oswald Kaduk and Wilhelm Boger, 'have become stars'.[67] Weiss counters that the names of the defendants are meant to exist only 'as symbols of a system that implicated in its guilt many others who never appeared in court',[68] and appeals to his reader not to accuse the defendants once again through the medium of the play. By doing so he implicitly recognizes the juridical authority of the trial, and of its adequate resolution with regard to each of the defendants, within the limits of the law.

Given its partial resistance to conventional theatrical modes of representation, the play has often been seen as a leading example of documentary theater. Weiss would later describe this as theater 'which abstains from any kind of invention' and which 'adopts authentic material and re-presents it from the stage without either changing the content or editing the form'.[69] This is how the play was presented in press reports at the time.[70] West German law forbade the production of official transcripts of the trial proceedings, and although the testimonies were audiotaped, these were not released until the mid-1990s. This meant that Weiss — who attended a small part of the trial[71] — relied for most of his source material on Bernd Naumann's near-daily newspaper reports as published in the *Frankfurter Allgemeine Zeitung*.[72]

Weiss concedes in the remarks preceding the printed version of the play that 'only a concentrate of evidence can remain on the stage'.[73] He maintains, however, that 'this concentrate should contain nothing but facts as they were expressed during the court proceedings'.[74] The play therefore appears to claim a mediating and informational role, in that it reiterates the facts expressed in the courtroom in the theater. It is the stark exposition of factual details that strikes the first-time reader or spectator. As Oliver Clausen writes in an interview with Weiss published to coincide with Ulu Grosbard's direction of the play in New York: '"The Investigation" presents facts, facts, facts, to the point where still more facts become unbearable — yet they keep coming. These were the exact measurements of the gas ovens, this was the color of the poison, this is the sum (300,000 marks annually) which a former executive of a slave-labor factory even today receives as a pension from his grateful company'.[75] And yet there are numerous ways in which Weiss deliberately changes both the content and the form of the facts of discourse both witnessed in person by Weiss and recorded in text by Naumann, such that it becomes difficult for the play to lay claim to documentary objectivity at all.

I consider here two of the ways that the source texts — either Weiss's own notes or the newspaper reports of the trial as produced by Naumann — are manipulated by the playwright. One of the most striking features of the play is its use of relatively uncomplicated German, notwithstanding the use of Nazi jargon. During the trial, testimony was given in a total of nineteen languages and simultaneously translated into German. In Weiss's homogenous and economical German, the asperities of this multilingual forum, and the problems occasioned by the presence of so many languages, are erased. There is no indication of translation as having taken place, nor of people speaking languages other than German, nor of the repetition of evidence, of its distortion, of miscommunications and mistranslations, nor of things that are perhaps inexpressible in German.[76] Boos has argued recently that 'by eliminating the multilingual dimension of the trial, Weiss seems to suggest that the philosophical and ethical problem of witnessing [...] greatly transcends the (linguistic, communicative) problems commonly associated with the process of (literary) translation [...] At stake were arbitrary oppression and willful genocide, not linguistic fallacies and verbal misprision'.[77] Such statements are characteristic of Boos's examination of the play, in which Weiss's intentions are given the benefit of the doubt, and are cast as conforming to contemporary standards of Western political correctness. Boos overlooks the violence applied to the languages of testimony in their translation into German, and in the concealment that translation has taken place. The refusal to allow language to adopt opaque forms that resist immediate comprehension is an extension of the doctrine that perceives language solely for its representational function. It is a doctrine that assures maximal clarity through the homogenization of language. But it is also a doctrine that perpetuates National Socialism's characteristic brand of violence through representation, of the violence that seeks to eliminate difference, obscurity, and opacity.

The second striking feature of the play that I highlight here is its relative economy, a result of what might be called its violence of selection. Of the multiple forms of evidence used in the trial, Weiss retains only testimonial evidence in the play, that is, evidence that was pronounced orally by witnesses and defendants, and that was recorded as text. Weiss does not include testimonies by legal experts, historians, and uninvolved eyewitnesses. Neither is there any allusion to the mass of written, printed, or photographic material that was introduced as evidence, or to the court's extraordinary visit to the scene of the crimes at Auschwitz-Birkenau in December 1964. Giorgio Agamben identifies two words for 'witness' in Latin. 'Testis' originally derives from the proto-Indo-European root for 'the third person standing by', because in a trial or lawsuit, he is the third party who arbitrates between two rival parties.[78] 'Superstes' designates a person who has lived through or experienced an event in person, and who remains after the event to bear witness to its occurrence.[79] The material that Weiss includes in the play therefore comes almost exclusively from the 'superstes', from those who have lived through the event. A legal trial requires the third-person or 'testis' to judge according to the law and if not to produce justice, then to achieve the *res judicata*, the juridical product of a trial. The privileging of the 'superstes' over the 'testis' in the play removes the dynamic toward resolution, judgment, and punishment. For the 'superstes', it is not only that he does not have the authority to pass judgment, but that the categories that allow for the pursuit of juridical conclusions, if not justice, have collapsed.

The presentation of only testimonial evidence therefore seriously undermines any claim to represent the proceedings of the trial. In a legal trial, truth and justice can be approximated only through the interweaving of heterogeneous modes of discourse. The trial derives from and proceeds by what Felman and Laub call 'a crisis of evidence'.[80] This means that witness testimony is never made to stand by itself, but is always conditioned by other statements. As Judge Hans Hofmeyer said in his closing address, witness testimony is considered to be 'not among the best means of proof, particularly if the testimony of witnesses concerns events that took place more than twenty years ago and seen by them in a setting of unbelievable unhappiness and suffering'.[81] Although the play appears to depict court proceedings, its exclusive use of testimonial material means that it is necessarily directed toward a radically different end from the trial. Where the trial aims to secure objective truth and justice, to the degree that the legal system in place allows for this, a text that reproduces testimony forfeits the establishment of objective truth for a patchwork of subjective statements.[82]

The culture of the 'superstes' becomes most evident at those moments when it is difficult to distinguish those who perpetrated crimes from those who suffered them, and those who were onlookers. Emil Bednarek, one of the twenty-two defendants at Frankfurt — known in Weiss's play as Defendant 18 — was a prisoner who had become first capo or prisoner functionary and later block elder.[83] The testimonies of Witness 1 and Witness 2 include descriptions of their own acts that are sometimes indistinguishable from the criminal actions attributed to the defendants by the prosecution. The diary of Witness 2 — a camp doctor 'who issued the orders / at that time'[84] — includes entries such as: 'Went for a bicycle ride / in beautiful weather / Then / Present at 11 executions / 3 women who pleaded for their lives'.[85]

By restricting the material used to that provided by the witnesses and defendants, Weiss dissolves the distinctions between defendant and witness. All those involved in Weiss's version of the trial stand trial. Once the 'superstes' has given testimony, it is no longer important whether he or she is a defendant or witness. The 'superstes' is never innocent. Their narrative account is subject to judgment, not the judgment of the jury appointed specially for the Frankfurt trial, but the unaccountable and unpredictable judgment of every member of the audience and every reader of the play. The play's readers and spectators form a timeless community of 'testēs'. They function as an eternal third party to the proceedings of the 'superstitēs', always free to make their own judgments, but forever depriving the witnesses and defendants of the judgments that would allow them to obtain closure.

In a second evaluation of *The Investigation*, I privilege those elements that would more likely have been evident to someone who had not read or seen the play, but who possessed the script and read about the play in newspaper reports.

The subtitle describes the play as an oratorio in eleven cantos. An oratorio designates 'a large-scale, usually narrative musical work for orchestra and voices, typically on a sacred theme and performed with little or no costume, scenery, or action'.[86] Katja Garloff associates the collective laughter of the defendants as representing the chorus, 'while their individual, whining vindications correspond to the arias'.[87] Although some performances of *The Investigation* did include music between cantos, such as that composed by Luigi Nono,[88] the term 'oratorio' most accurately describes the play's lack of action, scenery, and costumes, rather than its relation to musical performance. 'Oratorio' is most often used to evoke highly aestheticized musical settings of Christ's passion, such as those realized in the seventeenth century by Heinrich Schütz (1585–1672) and in the eighteenth century by Johann Sebastian Bach (1685–1750). In common parlance, 'oratorio' is therefore most often implicated in the notion of suffering that has a purpose, such as Christ suffering death on the cross to purchase salvation for mankind. When applied to the trial of those responsible for imprisoning, torturing, and murdering hundreds of thousands of innocent civilians in the camps at Auschwitz-Birkenau, any appeal to the form of the 'oratorio' is problematic because it might be seen to impute a larger, redemptive purpose to mass suffering and death.

The sense of purpose that the form of the oratorio incongruously bestows on the Holocaust is reinforced by other conspicuous Medieval Christian references. The arrangement of the material into eleven cantos, each of which is further divided into three parts, making a total of thirty-three segments, deliberately echoes the number of cantos in each of the three parts of Dante's *Divine Comedy* (1320). This structural echo not only points to the remains of Weiss's unrealized project to create a modern adaptation of Dante's work — the material used in *The Investigation* was initially intended for his *Paradiso*, a section to be characterized by simple, short sentences, and an economical and factual use of language.[89] The structural resonance of Weiss's *Investigation* with Dante's *Divine Comedy* might also be seen to invite the viewer or reader to pursue contemporary, atheological equivalents to the theological implications of the circles of hell and purgatory, in which individuals suffer on account of the wrongs they committed during their life on earth.[90]

The original German title of the play, *Die Ermittlung*, also betrays something of the play's intended purpose. Although Peter Weiss finds most of the material for the oratorio in a newspaper reporter's written recordings of the courtroom proceedings, 'Ermittlung' [investigation] is a legal term used to refer to preliminary police investigations conducted to ascertain whether or not a crime has been committed and if there are grounds for an indictment and trial. With regard to the trial at Frankfurt and the prosecution of those suspected of having carried out crimes at Auschwitz-Birkenau, the 'investigation' took place during the five years that preceded the trial, and came to a close before the trial could begin in December 1963. This misnomer suggests that the principal subject matter of the play is not in fact the Frankfurt Auschwitz trial, and by extension the crimes of the Holocaust committed at Auschwitz-Birkenau in the first half of the 1940s. Instead it suggests that the play represents the investigative stage of a trial that has yet to come to court. The play is concerned with ascertaining whether a crime has been committed, and if there are grounds for a trial. This is to say that Weiss is less interested in investigating Germany's National Socialist past and its particular manifestation in the concentration camps, than in ascertaining whether there are grounds for trying contemporary West German society for its ongoing participation in capitalist culture.

The radical displacement of the play's focus away from the events of the Holocaust and toward a Marxist interpretation of the current socio-economic system of the West becomes clearer at moments when the play refers to companies — such as IG Farben — which benefited from the slave labor provided by the concentration camps, including Auschwitz, and which continued to amass substantial profits in the years following the war.[91] Robert Cohen cites the second part of the Canto of Lily Tofler, which is 'unrelenting in its exposure of the close cooperation between German industry and Auschwitz'[92] as the most explicit example of Weiss's critique of West German capitalism. At the time of its performance, the notion of public complicity in an ongoing crime was often amplified by the play's mise-en-scène. In his production of the play in Stockholm in February 1966, Ingmar Bergman had spotlights trained on the audience. As Sidra DeKoven Ezrahi explains, this was designed to implicate the contemporary spectator in a larger economic system 'that made Auschwitz possible'.[93]

Other elements of Weiss's manipulation of the material are less easy to identify. Although there are important interpretative decisions made in both selecting the material, and in modifying it, as mentioned above, Weiss also adds material of his own creation, without warning his reader or spectator that he is doing so. The author's political interpretation of the Holocaust is most explicitly expressed by Witness 3:

> Many of those who were destined
> to play the part of prisoners
> had grown up with the same ideas
> as those
> who found themselves in the role of guards
> They were all equally dedicated to the same nation
> And to the same growth in prosperity and profit
> and if they had not been appointed prisoners
> they could equally well have been guards
> We must drop the noble attitude
> that says the camp world is incomprehensible to us
> We all knew the society
> in which the regime originated
> that was capable of creating such camps
> The order that prevailed here
> was an order whose structure we were familiar with[94]

In a review of the play's performance in West Berlin, Walter Jens was critical of the fact that Witness 3 — who acts as a sort of interpreter to the proceedings — is not made to stand out from the other witnesses. There is no external indication that Witness 3 is giving voice to Weiss's own interpretation and is not repeating what was said in court. In interviews given at the time, Weiss explicitly confirms his intention to 'brand Capitalism', which he perceives as having 'benefited from the experiments of the gas chambers':[95] 'It is capitalism, indeed the whole Western way of life, that is on trial'.[96] According to this vision, the Holocaust, and National Socialism more generally, did not constitute an evil aberration specific to the German people at a particular point in time, but were the logical consequences of Western capitalism's pursuit of economic gain through the systematic exploitation of the weak.[97]

One of the symptoms of this focus — and which a prominent early commentator called a 'distressing enigma'[98] — is that there is no reference to the Jewish origins of the vast majority of those imprisoned and killed at Auschwitz-Birkenau. Nor is there any attempt to explain what Cohen calls 'the specific Germanness of the extermination of the Jews'.[99] As James E. Young points out, how can Weiss on the one hand claim that there are 'nothing but facts' in the content — if not the form — of the text itself, and neglect to mention that for every instance in which the original courtroom documents or journalistic articles referred to Jews, Weiss has replaced this with the term 'Verfolgten', a legal term defining 'those under persecution'.[100] The Jewish victims are defined not as Jews who become victims, but as a group defined exclusively as those 'persecuted' [die Verfolgten] by those who actively persecute them [die Verfolger]. The authorial violence that removes the religious or ethnic identity of the Jews — as well as their individual names — should be seen in the context of the National Socialist policy to eradicate all Jews. This policy was designed not only to destroy human lives by the millions but, as Derrida says, to enforce an order of representation that would abolish 'the possibility of giving, inscribing, calling, and recalling the name'.[101] It was a policy that ultimately sought to neutralize difference and to destroy singularity. It is this neutralization of difference and destruction of singularity that Weiss's concealment of the Jewish identity of the majority of victims might be seen to perpetuate.

To better understand the motive for this small but highly significant transformation in nomenclature, I turn to an interview given at the time of the play's performance, in which Weiss provides the following explanation for the absence of any reference to the Jews in his oratorio:

> The Nazis did kill six million Jews, yes, but they killed millions of others. The word 'Jew' is in fact never used in the play... I do not identify myself any more with the Jews than I do with the people of Vietnam or the blacks in South Africa. I simply identify myself with the oppressed of the world... *The Investigation* is about the extreme abuse of power that alienates people from their own actions. It happens to be a German power, but that again is unimportant. I see Auschwitz as a scientific experiment that could have been used by anyone to exterminate anyone. For that matter, given a different deal, the Jews could have been on the side of the Nazis. They too could have been the exterminators. *The Investigation* is a universal human problem.[102]

For Weiss, the Holocaust was less the result of decisions made by individuals according to their moral autonomy, than an inevitable result of historical logic. It is this attempt to abstract the Holocaust from its specific historical reality that is perhaps *The Investigation*'s most disturbing feature. As Ezrahi warns, 'the basic premise of a universal human tendency to respond uniformly to certain social stimuli can serve to dissipate the moral load that comes with particularity and historical accountability'.[103] The absence of any reference to the Jewish identity of the majority of the victims can be compared to the explicit reference to the twenty-five thousand Soviet prisoners of war who, in late 1941, were among the first to die at Auschwitz as a direct result of the Commissar Order [Kommissarbefehl]. Given Weiss's subsequent decision to join the Swedish Communist Party in 1968 and his pronouncements in the press at the time of the play's opening performances, it is hard not to perceive the selective identification of victims in the play as a function of the playwright's political persuasion and preference.

Regardless of the perspective Weiss may have had on the Holocaust and its legal treatment in contemporary Germany, his play can be seen to perpetuate just the kind of violence privileged by the Holocaust and, I would argue, the legal trials set up to try those responsible for the Holocaust. Derrida claims that 'Benjamin would perhaps have judged vain and without pertinence, in any case without a pertinence commensurable to the event, any juridical trial of Nazism and of its responsibilities'.[104] This is because any such trial would find it difficult if not impossible to avoid concepts — philosophical, moral, sociological, psychological, or psychoanalytic concepts, and especially juridical — that are not 'homogenous with the space in which Nazism developed'.[105] Weiss's play not only fails to break with the concepts central to National Socialism. In its drive toward homogenous representation — of testimony, of language, and of history — it continues to pursue the same eradication of difference, of singularity, and of uniterable existence.[106]

Bloodless and Bloody

In Celan's personal collection of the numerous newspaper cuttings from both the French and German language press that report on the trial at Frankfurt and on the performances of Peter Weiss's *Investigation*, only one article bears any trace of Celan's reading. In a short piece published in the *Frankfurter Allgemeine Zeitung* on 27 October 1965 — the date that Celan inscribed in his copy of the play — Peter Weiss writes to justify his heavy reliance on Bernd Naumann's reports of the trial in an attempt to avoid a legal suit for plagiarism. Besides the title, 'Peter Weiss Explains' — against which Celan has inscribed two oblique lines in blue ink — the only part of the article that bears traces of Celan's attention is the final sentence, where the following is underlined: 'I would like to thank Bernd Naumann, and to draw the attention of the reading public to this important contemporary document, in which the trial, which in my oratorio is given only concentrated form [als Konzentrat aufklingt], is described in the richness and complexity of the daily hearings'.[107]

Weiss's use of the word 'concentration' or 'Konzentrat' might, in any other context, be considered to be of little significance. Given the topic under discussion, however, and the fact that the trial of which Weiss has brought a 'concentrated' form to the stage was responsible for uncovering the criminal responsibility of individuals who operated the 'Konzentrationslager' or concentration camps at Auschwitz-Birkenau, it is improbable that the playwright could have used it without being aware of its implications. That Weiss's decision to use the word 'Konzentrat' is not coincidental would appear to be confirmed by his decision to use the same term in the remarks preceding the published play, in a line quoted above and repeated here: 'this concentrate [Konzentrat] is meant to contain nothing but facts, as they were expressed during the court proceedings'.[108]

Many English language critics have not picked up on this questionable echo. Both Ezrahi[109] and Young,[110] for example, repeat Swan and Grosbard's translation of 'Konzentrat' as 'condensation',[111] which — in unwarranted good faith — liberates the term of its concentrationary echoes. Although any attempt to interpret marginal traces should be undertaken with extreme caution, given the absence of any other signs of intervention in the body of the article, Celan's decision to underline this passage invites us to speculate as to its meaning and significance.[112] It is above all the wide range of alternative possibilities on the metaphorical axis of selection that would retain the same or a similar meaning that suggests that Weiss's choice is a deliberate and provocative one. At the very least, it challenges the notion that the Holocaust has — in some definitive way — branded the German language and irreversibly transformed the ways in which it can be deployed. This choice of word might therefore be said to challenge precisely the foundations of Celan's poetic oeuvre, conceived and inscribed in German despite its passage through 'the thousand darknesses of death-bringing speech'.[113]

I propose that in response to the play Celan composed one of his most impenetrable poems. 'ALL YOUR SEALS BROKEN OPEN? NEVER' was written on 23 November 1965, Celan's forty-fifth birthday. The previous day, he had been in Geneva to discuss the fragile state of his mental health with the Swiss literary critic and doctor, Jean Starobinski. The following day, he would attempt to stab Gisèle with a knife in their apartment at the Rue de Longchamp in Paris. It was this attack that brought about his enforced incarceration between November 1965 and June 1966, during which he composed the unfinished *Eingedunkelt* cycle:[114]

ALL DEINE SIEGEL ERBROCHEN? NIE.

Geh, verzedere auch
sie, die brief-
häutige, elf-
hufige Tücke:

dass die Welle, die honig-
ferne, die milch-
nahe, wenn
der Mut sie zur Klage bewegt,
die Klage zum Mut, wieder,

dass sie nicht auch
den Elektronen-Idioten
spiegle, der Datteln
verarbeitet für
menetekelnde
Affen.[115]

[ALL YOUR SEALS BROKEN OPEN? NEVER.

Go, con-cedar them
too, the letter-
skinned, eleven-
hooved perfidy:

that the wave, the honey-
far, the milk-
close, if
courage persuades it to lament,
and lamenting to courage, again,

that it does not also
reflect the electronic
idiot, who processes
dates for
menetekeling
apes.]

This poem has only rarely been subject to commentary and explication. Those who have endeavored to struggle for sense are often left feeling bitter and empty-handed. Ute Maria Oelmann, for example, writes: 'This poem is a nuisance. It knocks the reader's nose out of joint, above all the opening stanza in its incomprehensibility, and the final stanza in its un-lyrically aggressive vocabulary. [...] Even the title heading points to consistent enciphering'.[116] Perhaps more than any other text written by Paul Celan, this poem openly celebrates its hermeticism, rejecting any pretensions to comprehension that even experienced readers of difficult texts expect. As Friedrich Kluge reminds us, the adjective 'hermetic' refers to the legendary author of the *Hermetica*, Hermes Trismegistus, who is said to have discovered the art of closing glass tubes with a secret and airtight seal.[117] The poet seems here to effect and vaunt a very similar hermetic sealing. Its challenge to the reader is not unlike that voiced six years previously by the Yiddish poet and survivor of the ghetto at Vilna, Abraham Sutzkever: 'No matter how much the raven picks at my corpse, he won't be able to unseal my shimmering nucleus'.[118]

Given the presence of a number of unusual and incongruous terms, I examine the poem closely — in unfashionable detail — as if the poem were an unwilling witness in a trial. I aim to unseal something of the poem's 'shimmering nucleus' and to uncover a violent but concealed criticism of Weiss's play specifically, and the Frankfurt trial more generally.

*Go, con-cedar them
too,*

The juxtaposition of two imperatives — one monosyllabic and unambiguous, the other so hermetic as to prevent the reader from executing its command — simultaneously invites and repels the reader. Wiedemann suggests that the hypothetical verb 'verzedern' can be traced to the opening stanza of a folk song published in the *Jewish Songbook*, in which the cedar that 'slimly kisses the cloud' is situated in the Jewish Levant, where the 'rapid Jordan stream flows', 'where the ashes of my fathers rest', and where 'the blood of the Maccabees soaked the field'.[119] Ulrich Konietzny suggests that 'verzedern' indicates that something should be fashioned or worked like cedar wood [die Zeder], but also suggests it may refer to the 'common Israeli practice' of burning strongly scented cedar wood.[120] This refers to a purification ritual transmitted by God to Moses and Aaron, in which a red heifer without defect or blemish, and that has never been worked, is slaughtered and burnt with cedar wood, hyssop, and scarlet wool.[121] It is this process which is meant to purify 'the letter- / skinned, eleven- / hooved perfidy'.

In the book of Judges, we encounter a parable that may allow us to understand the violence of this strange neologism more precisely. The parable is spoken by Jotham to the people of Sichem. Jotham's brother, Abimelech, has just killed their father, Gideon, and seventy of their brothers. Despite his patricide and mass fratricide, the people of Sichem have chosen Abimelech as their king. In an attempt to show the people the risk they run by accepting such a leader, Jotham recounts the following parable. The trees set out to anoint a king to rule over them. The olive tree, the fig tree, and the vine all decline the honor. To elevation over all other trees, they each prefer their particular qualities, respectively fatness, sweetness, and the ability to cheer. The trees then turn to the bramble and ask it to be their king, and it replies, 'If in truth ye anoint me king over you, then come and put your trust in my shadow; and if not, let fire come out of the bramble, and devour the cedars of Lebanon'.[122] If Abimelech's ascendency is just and proper and the people of Sichem have done right to choose him as their king, Jotham explains, then they deserve to live in happiness. But if they are wrong to prefer Abimelech over Gideon, then they should be consumed by fire in the manner described.

Luther's translation of the last words spoken by the bramble reads: 'so gehe Feuer aus dem Dornbusch und verzehre die Zedern Libanons' [let fire come out of the bramble, and devour the cedars of Lebanon].[123] If this is read with Celan's poem in mind, we see and hear the poetic imperatives 'Geh' [go] and 'verzedere' [con-cedar] in this two-part biblical exhortation, with a notable transformation. Namely, 'verzehre die Zedern' [consume the cedars] has contracted into the hypothetical verb 'verzedern'. This presumably intends an intensification of this fragment of the verse into a purely verbal form to mean something like 'to destroy something in the way that divine fire devours the cedars of Lebanon' or, more abstractly, 'to incinerate with divine wrath' or, as I suggest, to 'con-cedar'.

The action called for by the poem's voice is not a benevolent process of purification, but a call to merciless destruction of someone who has committed a wrong, or of something that constitutes a wrong, namely 'this letter- / skinned, eleven- / hooved perfidy'. The violence of 'verzedere' is not an instance of Greek mythic violence 'which would install and preserve the law', but of 'divine (Jewish) violence, which would destroy the law',[124] an act that is, importantly, bloodless.[125] As such it desires the absolute destruction of an adversary, but refuses to destroy the adversary in a way that might both confirm a precedent, and set a new precedent, thereby re-establishing the old law anew. This would be to repeat the violence deployed in the Holocaust, in legal prosecutions of those responsible for committing crimes that contributed to the Holocaust, and in artistic representations of those legal prosecutions. Instead, 'verzedere' calls for a unique, singular, incomparable, uniterable act of total destruction. And yet it is also a destruction that must remain hidden. This explains Celan's relatively unusual decision to create a neologism to describe the act of destruction. As Benjamin explains, only mythic violence, the violence of representation, is recognizable: 'The expiatory power of violence is invisible to men'.[126] The meaning of any verb that would describe such violence must similarly be invisible.

> ... the letter-
> skinned,

The target of divine destruction is concealed behind the abstract and disseminating 'Tücke' [perfidy, deceit], a noun that occurs infrequently in Celan's published oeuvre.[127] Whereas 'perfidy' comes from the Latin 'perfidia' [faithlessness, falsehood, treachery] and perhaps from the phrase 'per fidem decipere' [to deceive by faith or trustingness], the German 'Tücke' comes from the Middle High German 'tuc', meaning a strike or a blow.[128] Although 'Tücke' deceives just as perfidy does, it does so through the application of physical violence.

The qualification of 'Tücke' by two compound adjectives — 'letter-skinned' and 'eleven-hooved' — invites us to establish more precisely its agent, object, direction, and magnitude. 'Häutig' [skinned] is phonetically indistinguishable from the adjective for 'today' [heutig], and 'der Brief' is a 'letter'. The compound adjective 'letter-skinned' [brief- / häutig] is conceivably a coded reference to the correspondence Celan received at the time of the poem's composition. One correspondent who might have provoked such a reaction — whether justified or not — is Paul Schallück, the German novelist and erstwhile president of the Germania Judaica.[129] Throughout their friendship, which began at the meeting of the Gruppe 47 at Niendorf in 1952, Schallück appears to have been an attentive friend, sensitive both to Celan's struggle with accusations of plagiarism and the effects of anti-Semitism more broadly. This attentiveness did not preclude a number of unexplained silences on the part of Celan. Schallück's letter is dated 21 November 1965, postmarked in Cologne on 22 November, and would have been waiting for Celan in Paris when he returned from Geneva.

The letter, the first contact between the two since Celan's visit to Cologne the previous autumn, is largely devoted to describing Schallück's past year, 'bedeviled' as he puts it, by the infection of a leg wound first suffered when, as a soldier in the Wehrmacht, he was shot by French resistance fighters on the Pont Neuf in Paris.[130] As Schallück explains, it was only this illness that prevented him from campaigning for the defeated Social Democratic Party in the 1965 West German federal election.[131] In spite of the 'deplorable' result, as far as German literature is concerned, Schallück sees reasons to be encouraged: 'But I am pleased that some of our authors have awoken from their reserve, and have opened their eyes. [...] Even in literature the years of blind alleys seem to be slowly coming to an end. Everywhere — and particularly in the theater — I see a struggle for new realities. This is something we have both discussed on several occasions. And I have always counseled patience. Gradually, I believe, patience will pay off'.[132] Given the convivial tone of the letter, and their continuing friendship, it seems unlikely that Celan would have taken offense at these comments on the current state of German literature per se. The most prominent strain of avant-garde theater in Germany in the mid-1960s was documentary theater, of which Peter Weiss's play was widely perceived to be its most important current manifestation. Schallück's reference to German theater's successful struggle for 'new realities' inevitably includes Weiss's *Investigation*, a 'perfidy' that Celan therefore qualifies as 'Brief-häutig' or 'letter-skinned'.

> ... *eleven-*
> *hooved perfidy*

Attempts to approximate 'perfidy' and Weiss's play are further strengthened by the second compound adjective that qualifies the noun: 'eleven- / hooved'. The oratorio is composed of eleven cantos — as its subtitle explicitly reminds us — and much has been made of the ways in which the structure of the play resembles Dante's *Divine Comedy*.[133] In an interview given in 1966, Weiss associates the number eleven with the natural form his research took as he gathered material for the oratorio: 'The enormous amount of material I gathered from the Frankfurt trial was concentrated into eleven big blocks of testimony, presented one after another. Each block was a closed complex. Some modern sculpture is neither abstract nor figurative, it's only a thing which stands there — a sense of this imbues the play'.[134] The evocation of blocks of material that 'stand there' contains an uncanny echo of Weiss's description of what remains of the gas chambers, seen during his visit to the site of the Auschwitz-Birkenau concentration camps in 1964: 'When you see the ruins from the gas chambers, they're just heavy blocks of concrete or iron or steel, with weeds already grown on them. You almost can't see them, but they're bits of our reality'.[135] The blocks of evidence gathered for the purpose of writing the play intentionally or not echo the heavy blocks of concrete, iron, or steel, that are the material remains of the gas chambers.

Given this curious meeting of eleven blocks of written material and the concrete blocks of the camp, it is perhaps not by chance that the part of the camp most often evoked in both the trial and *The Investigation* — and in which many of the most horrific crimes recounted took place — is Block Eleven, situated in the southwestern corner of the main camp. The execution wall or 'Black Wall' [schwarze Mauer] against which inmates were shot dead — and which provides the title for Weiss's seventh canto — ran between Block Eleven and the neighboring Block Ten. The eleven cantos of Weiss's oratorio most likely constitute a structural echo of the eleven blocks of material gathered by Weiss in the course of his research, as well as the material blocks that are all that remain of the gas chambers, which in turn are numerically echoed by the repeated references to Block Eleven. Celan's 'eleven-hooved perfidy', with its connotations of diabolical false witness, refers to the most visible of these references, namely the eleven cantos that constitute the play.[136]

> that the wave, the honey-
> far, the milk-
> close, if
> courage persuades it to lament,
> and lamenting to courage, again,

The divine destruction of the 'letter- / skinned' and 'eleven- / hooved perfidy' provisionally identified as Weiss's play, and urgently counseled by the poem, will, it is claimed, ensure that the 'wave' does not also reflect 'the electronic idiot' who 'processes dates for menetekeling apes'. Before this explanatory clause is completed, however, the nature of the wave is elaborated. The wave is both 'honey- / far' and 'milk- / close'. Although an earlier version of the poem has 'Jordanwelle' [Jordan wave],[137] this wave is almost certainly German, far from the land of honey promised in Exodus,[138] but close to the 'black milk of daybreak' of Celan's best known poem 'Deathfugue'.[139] The wave evokes the continuous ebb and flow of anti-Semitism and National Socialism in contemporary Germany, which may appear to recede at times, but which infallibly and rhythmically returns.[140] The wave's constant movement back and forth, but never away, is illustrated in the poem by the chiastic relationship of its motivating forces: 'if courage persuades it to lament, / and lamenting to courage again'. The initial instance of courage is that felt by those who have not been prosecuted for the crimes committed during the Holocaust, and who feel vindicated by both the results of the Frankfurt trial and the further publication of these events through Weiss's play. It can now be claimed with confidence that, if wrongs were committed, the trial has punished according to the rule of law, and the case has been closed. In short, it is time to move on, and any appeal to the contrary — such as that contained in each of Celan's poems — will no longer be tolerated. This chiasmus describes the indignation particular to the criminal who has wrongly been found innocent, and whose protestations of innocence continue to add to the crime that remains unpunished.

The chiastic structure of these two lines does not indicate a perfect and self-motivating circularity from courage to lament to courage. It instead demonstrates an irresistible escalation in which courage makes room for complaint, which in turn makes room for greater courage and greater complaint. As Max Horkheimer and Theodor Adorno formulate it in 'Elements of Anti-Semitism: Limits of Enlightenment', the obscure impulse that motivates anti-Semites in the first place, and that 'was always more congenial to them than reason takes them over completely'.[141] There is no rational justification for courage to give way to lament, and for lament in turn to give way to greater courage: 'Action becomes a purpose in itself, cloaking its own purposelessness'.[142] The wave of anti-Semitism and National Socialism may be rhythmic, repetitive, and controlled in its beginnings, but if courage persuades it to lament, it will once again grow to destructive proportions, realizing the totality with which it has 'always been profoundly connected'.[143]

> *that it does not also*
> *reflect the electronic*
> *idiot, who processes*

In light of the juxtaposition of the poem with Weiss's oratorio, the verb 'processes' [verarbeitet] in particular demands attention and explication. The notion of 'processing', especially in the impersonal form of the present participle, was an essential concept for the effective administration and running of camps such as those at Auschwitz-Birkenau. It permitted those who were responsible for administering the Holocaust to conceive of mass human extermination in administrative terms — as the 'processing' of material, rather than as the murder of human beings. For instance, in a document compiled by an official in Eichmann's department on 5 July 1942, it is noted that since December 1941 ninety-seven thousand people have been successfully 'processed' [verarbeitet] in three vans used as mobile gas chambers.[144]

The verb also appears in the eighth canto of Weiss's oratorio, in which one of the defendants recounts how inmates were selected to be put to death through lethal injection. Rather than describing the action of individual agents, he describes the administrative process that accompanied and made the execution possible:

Judge:	How were the selections performed
Defendant 9:	The camp physician looked at the prisoner
	and the record card with the diagnosis
	If he did not return the card
	to the prisoner physician
	but instead gave it to the clerk
	then it meant
	that the prisoner had been selected
	for injection
Judge:	What happened then
Defendant 9:	The cards were piled on the table
	and processed [und verarbeitet]
Judge:	What does processed mean
Defendant 9:	The clerk had
	to prepare a list from the record cards
	The list was passed onto the sanitary officers
	This is the list we used
	to conduct the patients away[145]

The description of how the 'separation' of those who were to continue living from those who were to be put to death begins with reference to 'the prisoner' [der Häftling] at whom the camp physician begins by looking. By the end of the description of the process, the prisoner has become one of a number of 'patients' [die Kranken] and is led off to death. In the interim, the human figure of the prisoner-patient is displaced by the material manifestation of the administrative procedure that will decide his or her fate. The gaze of the doctor shifts from the prisoner to the record card, which for the duration of the process will represent the human being whose information it contains. If the card is given to the clerk, then the 'prisoner' becomes a 'patient' and will be put to death.

Martin Walser notes how difficult it was to accept the ease with which the defendants at Frankfurt described atrocities that they had witnessed or perpetrated in simple workplace jargon [Dienstplan-Jargon].[146] Assassinations become separations; executioners — in a curious mélange of medical and military jargon — become sanitary officers; prisoners become record cards; and those condemned to death are named patients. 'And you can never tell for sure', Walser notes, 'if they use this jargon just because it almost totally conceals individual responsibility, or if they really don't have their own language to express their recollection of Auschwitz'.[147] At around the same time, in *Jargon of Authenticity*, and doubtless with the terminology used by the defendants at the Frankfurt trial in mind, Adorno will launch a devastating critique of the language used in existentialist philosophy in general, and by Heidegger in particular.[148] It is jargon, such as that used in this passage of Weiss's play, that causes 'the true object of the suffering [...] to disappear'.[149]

When Weiss repeats the terms recorded in newspaper reports by Naumann — including camp jargon — he does so without using visible punctuation. 'What does processed mean' [Was bedeutet verarbeitet], in the logic of the hearing from which it is a direct quotation, almost certainly adopts the intonation of a question. But in the re-contextualization of the oratorio, particularly in its written form, the fragment assumes a significantly different grammatical and rhetorical role. It is stripped of the dynamics natural to dialogue and becomes rhetorically under-determined. It would be too much to say that it becomes a simple unpunctuated statement of fact. This would be to bestow upon it more sense that it lays claim to. It is instead a phrase that is deprived of its natural syntactic rights, that is, etymologically, its right to arrange itself, or to be arranged, in such a way as to create meaning. It is, you might say, a musulman phrase, a phrase, which does not so much say, as not-say, and which does not propose a vision of things, but which has no vision, even as it casts its eyes around. It can be read in any order, and meaning remains limp, unmotivated, if not absent. 'Processed means what'. 'What means processed'. To be processed, as this phrasal fragment demonstrates, is to become faceless and disembodied, immune to human existence and justice. It is to become 'what' — an interrogative pronoun relieved of its interrogative faculty. Such is the effect of processing, of its administrative and pseudo-medical jargon, of its fluency and economy in understanding simple, deadly gestures, such as giving the record card to the clerk, instead of returning it (to whom it is not clear). Process marks the gestural presence of the State that orders and sanctions the acts committed at Auschwitz, that protects the psyche of those committing murder, that displaces murder into administrative procedures, and that even two decades later at Frankfurt would protect those charged with murder from prosecution.

The etymology of the word 'process' itself — which means 'trial' in its German form 'der Prozess' — reveals that the word has an appropriately deceptive and contradictory dynamic. As the Latin verb 'procedere' [to go forward, advance] it intimates progress, and thereby reveals the absurd incongruity of its application to the 'processing' of human beings at Auschwitz. If the verb is broken into its two constituent parts, we notice that the forward movement comes solely from the generic prefix 'pro'. The verbal portion of the verb 'process', namely 'cedere' [to yield, give up some right or property] indicates a giving way, a removal of self, a withdrawal. Where 'process' implies the presence of a final goal toward which the process proceeds, to 'cede' indicates a movement in which it is not the end point of the action that is important, so much as its beginning. To 'cede' is to relinquish in the present and for all time to come. He or she who cedes no longer exists, as far as the verb is concerned. They are no longer here, but elsewhere. They are no longer in life, but in what is not life, perhaps in death.

Much like Penelope weaving a burial shroud for Odysseus's father Laertes, 'process' weaves and unweaves itself, it commits the crime, and then makes as if to undo the crime. It is a particularly insidious instance of mythic violence, as it perpetrates violence and sheds blood, but then cleans up and gives to understand that no blood has been shed. Each layer of processing is an act of mythic violence, as it repeats and confirms the original act of law-instituting violence. It commits further violence in concealing the original instance of violence. It is a process in which it is no longer of importance whether each layer of representation was designed to conceal or reveal the specific nature of the event, as each fold in the process removes us from the hand of the criminal and the body of the victim, and leads us further into the linguistic hall of mirrors of multiple and irreversible representation.

dates

The direct object of the verb 'process' is 'date-fruits'. Oelmann notes that 'Datteln' [date-fruits] is acoustically similar to 'Daten' meaning temporal 'dates'.[150] This opens up the possibility of hearing in 'Datteln' the 'Daten' that are not dates in time but 'data' that an 'electronic idiot' might 'process'. If we inspect the historical fabric of the word 'Dattel' [date], rather than searching in its acoustic and visual vicinity, we see that the Greek 'δάκτυλος' [dáktulos] — from which the German for the fruit comes — means 'finger'.[151] These fingers, that are also dates, days, and data, are not the same as the living finger we see groping sutures and scars in Celan's seminal poem 'The Straightening': 'a finger / feels down and up, feels / around: / seems, palpable, here / it is split wide open, here / it grew together again — who / covered it up?'.[152] Neither do these fingers include Celan's finger which — looking to come full circle — searches hesitantly for the place of his birth and childhood toward the end of 'The Meridian': 'I am looking for all that on the map with a very imprecise, because unsteady, finger, on a map for children, I ought to point out'.[153] In a short pamphlet entitled *My Place* [*Meine Ortschaft*], which was distributed at the first performances of *The Investigation,* Weiss describes his visit to Auschwitz-Birkenau the previous December, a place for which he claims he was destined.[154] Informed by the research undertaken for the play, Weiss imaginatively recreates some of the crimes as he visits the parts of the camp where they occurred. In front of what remains of the standing cells he recalls: 'When [the corpses of inmates] were dragged out [of the standing cells], there were some, whose thighs bore teeth marks, whose fingers had been bitten off'.[155] The electronic idiot — whoever he may be, and who risks being reflected by the honey-far and milk-close wave if the poem's hermetic and violent commands are not followed — is one who processes not only dates but human fingers for apes to consume.

...for
menetekeling
apes.

We know from Celan's correspondence and poems from the early 1960s, that the ape or monkey [Affe] functions as shorthand and symbol for those whom Celan suspects of anti-Semitism. Intimately linked with this notion, and maybe motivating the symbolic connection in the first place, is the notion of anti-Semitism as imitation, already intimated in the cyclical image of the wave that recurs and grows. The anti-Semite, like the plagiarist, and the ape, mimics or apes, in German 'nachäffen'. In a letter to Alfred Margul-Sperber, dated March 1962, Celan writes: 'I can't publish anything more. You cannot imagine how the neo-Nazis are all over the place (those from Goebbel's 'Reich' and the 'others'). [...] These buggers are much better at aping [sind mimetisch begabter] than their predecessors'.[156] In a letter to Schallück dated June 1962, we again find Celan associating those who circulate anti-Semitic untruths with being highly talented in mimicry: 'But the lie prevails, you know it well, and, supremely gifted in mimicry [mimetisch hochbegabt] as it is, it commands both hill and vale'.[157] It is as if the decision to think and behave anti-Semitically could not be arrived at in any other way than through the imitation of other anti-Semites.

Since the Holocaust, mimesis and mimicry have often been considered key figures in theorizations of anti-Semitism. Although Daniel and Jonathan Boyarin argue for the importance of generational mimesis in the creation and continuation of Jewish identity,[158] and Horkheimer and Adorno perceive mimesis more generally as a foundational and natural process that capitalism seeks to control, mimesis or mimicry also characterizes anti-Semitic thought, and racism more broadly.[159] In his controversial *Réflexions sur la question juive*, Sartre identifies anti-Semitism as something that cannot be pursued alone but only in community, and specifically in a community based on a shared sense of the value of mediocrity: 'The phrase: 'I hate the Jews', is one expressed in company; by saying it, you become part of a tradition and a community'.[160] To be anti-Semitic is to adhere to a tradition and a community that coheres around the repetition of anti-Semitic discourse, creating what Vikki Bell calls a 'community network of anti-Semites'.[161] The Jew is only a pretext to the creation of this community founded on imitation, to the extent that, as Sartre puts it, 'if the Jew did not exist, the anti-Semite would invent him'.[162]

Besides being figures of mimicry and mimesis, the apes with which Celan concludes his poem also have literary forebears, such as those in Lev Shestov's essay entitled 'Darwin and the Bible': 'One part of mankind is really descended from the fallen Adam, feels in its blood the burn of its ancestor's sin, suffers pangs from it and aspires to the paradise lost, while the others really spring from the ape that is free of all sin; their consciences are at peace, nothing tortures them, and they do not dream of impossible things'.[163] Shestov's division of mankind into two sub-species defined not by race, nationality, or political persuasion, but by moral disposition, has consequences for any attempt to conceive of justice in either its theoretical or practical manifestation in the aftermath of the Holocaust. For the part of mankind conscious of its fallen state and defined by a desire to repair this inherent imperfection, the notion of justice as reparation for a wrong that is to be pursued — even if it can never entirely be achieved — is a natural and uncomplicated concept. Shestov aligns the other part of mankind with those who reject the history of Christian redemption, specifically Darwinians, although in Celan's appropriation of this dichotomy, the Darwinians are National Socialists and anti-Semites. For this part of mankind, man is little more than a skilled animal, a direct descendant of the ape. He is therefore free from any sense of right or wrong and wholly unconcerned with the task of repairing the world, of atoning for crime, and of pursuing justice.

Beyond Shestov's formulation, Celan's investment of the ape with anti-Semitic, or more specifically National Socialist, tendencies appears to be informed by the work of the Yiddish poet Jacob Glatstein (1896–1971). Surprisingly few if any substantive connections have been made between the poems of Glatstein and of Celan.[164] Although no documentary evidence to support their approximation has yet come to light, there are a number of textual echoes of Glatstein in Celan that are so precise as to suggest more than mere coincidence. Glatstein composed most of his oeuvre in New York, having abandoned his native Lublin in 1914 as a result of its increasingly threatening anti-Semitic culture. His poems predict the Holocaust, comment on it as it unfolds, and subsequently seek to establish lasting poetic memorials to the dead, not without considerable anger and violence. Glatstein often uses the figure of the primate to designate those guilty of anti-Semitism, recycling and revalorizing an established anti-Semitic trope in the process. In the aleph bet poem 'Lamentations for the Souls of Jewish Cities', first published in 1961, the concluding section headed with the letter 'yod' includes the lines:

> Don't convince yourself
> That this can be forgiven.
> Don't convince yourself
> That even the most beautiful reconstruction
> Can make us forget the evil.
> See how the face of the world
> Is already twisted and ape-like
> [...]
> Look carefully and see
> Whether the face of the world
> Has a single streak of soft Jewishness.
> Read the books and be astonished
> At how completely erased
> Are all the letters of compassion,
> All the letters of the Torah.[165]

Had Celan come across these poems, he would have been sufficiently versed in Yiddish — a language with which he was familiar from his childhood in Czernowitz — to identify the simian trope used to label anti-Semites. This is made particularly clear in a poem entitled 'Well Bred People':

> They have wonderful manners,
> Have compassion for elephants and flies.
> The sorrow of children in their cradles
> Affects them, the refined anti-Semites.
>
> They cry over Beethoven's quartets,
> Write down and remember proverbs,
> Help their fellow-man carry his burden,
> And love to caress women's hair.
>
> They're as skinny and shaky as a song,
> And get the urge to sing at sunsets,
> But should they see a Jew,
> They suddenly become wild apes.[166]

In his poem 'Mourners', Glatstein specifically prefigures Celan's poem by concluding with an image of apes who inscribe warnings of imminent destruction on the walls:

> We are a nation of mourners.
> Almost everything has happened to us already.
> The grimacing face on the crucifix,
> With all its black commands,

> No longer frightens us.
>
> Your own fear
> Now burns at your doorstep
> With punishments yet unborn.
> On the eve of onrushing destruction,
> The graffiti on the walls
> Are the fingerprints
> Of the insane wild ape.[167]

In Celan's poem, the graffiti inscribed on the walls on the eve of 'onrushing destruction' is referred to in the form of the word 'menetekel'. The 'menetekel' comes from the Aramaic section of the book of Daniel, which recounts how Belshazzar the king hosted a great feast for a thousand of his lords.[168] During this feast, the king orders for the vessels stolen from the Jewish Temple in Jerusalem to be brought out, and proceeds to drink from them, praising the pagan gods as he does so. The fingers of a man's hand then appear and write 'over against the candlestick upon the plaster of the wall of the king's palace'.[169] The text inscribed by the hand is visible only to Belshazzar, and to the captive Jewish prophet Daniel, who is able to read the writing and gives its interpretation. 'Mene mene tekel upharsin' [מנא מנא תקל ופרסין] means: 'God hath numbered thy kingdom, and finished it', 'Thou are weighed in the balances and are found wanting', and 'Thy kingdom is divided, and given to the Medes and Persians'.[170] Daniel is rewarded for his reading and interpretation and, later that night, Belshazzar is killed.

Historically the menetekel has been used to describe how a prevailing order of power that is perceived to be unjust or improper — a tyrannical regime or a religious heterodoxy — deservedly comes to a violent end. It is often used in hope rather than in expectation of such an end being realized. In Daniel, however, the menetekel pronounces the king's death sentence and is an instance of divine justice in action. In contrast to its biblical manifestation, the meneteking ascribed to the apes in Celan's poem cannot be the expression of divine judgment and punishment. It seems much more likely that it represents German justice as realized at Frankfurt, justice approximated through the deployment of mythic, law-affirming violence. In passing criminal judgment at the trial in Frankfurt, as well as in the ideological judgment of Weiss's oratorio, the meneteking apes mimic justice and literature. In the earliest — and least guarded — trace of the poem, written on a train between Montpellier and Avignon on 26 October 1965, the week following the first performance of Weiss's play, Celan writes 'the meneteking | arses' [die menetekelnde | Ärsche],[171] giving voice to the anger and violence that will later motivate the poem.

There remain several elements of the poem that I am not currently able to understand. The 'electronic idiot' who processes dates for the apes may recall Glatstein's rejection of the homogenous 'enlightenment' of the modern world in favor of a return to the more modest, individual, monadic enlightenment of Judaism: 'Good night, electricity arrogant world — / Back to my kerosene, my tallow-candle shadows, / Eternal October, tiny stars'.[172] The readings suggested here are provisional, partial, and particular to the perspective of the Frankfurt trial and Weiss's play. It remains possible to read the poem from other, equally if not more pressing angles. All of the poem's seals will never be broken open. It is a poem that more than many poems — even among those in Celan's difficult oeuvre — refuses or considerably restrains the communicative function of language. Celan's poem posits itself as active resistance to language's tendency toward that which is generally comprehensible. Through its resistance to communication, it is intended to confront the reader with the specific nature of the Holocaust, with the Holocaust not as the result of a general culture of crime, but of the Holocaust as sum of individual acts committed on Jewish individuals by German individuals. As Cynthia Ozick reminds us: 'the point *is* the specificity'. Just as 'every soul swallowed up by that martyrdom ought to be remembered for and in its specificity, with all its heritage and characteristics intact — the Jew for being a Jew, the Slav for being a Slav, the gypsy for being a gypsy',[173] so too when reading, each reading must retain the specificity of its unique encounter. The impenetrable seals of the poem are meant to transform the ways we read and seek to understand literary texts. The specificity of the poem resists 'comprehension', if we understand this etymologically as the single event of grasping an object in one's hands, to subsequently show the poem to others as having been comprehended. The poem instead solicits understanding as an individual, in which the reader approaches the poem and stands alongside it in an uniterable and incommunicable encounter. When speculating as to Walter Benjamin's possible response to learning of the Final Solution — had he lived long enough to do so — Derrida suggests that Benjamin would have ascribed the radicalization of evil to the 'fall' of human language into a mode that is purely communicative, representational, and informational.[174] By seeking to represent the Holocaust through language, both the trial at Frankfurt and Weiss's play not only fail to 'understand' the true nature of the Holocaust. They also add to and perpetuate the violence of the Holocaust.

The violence espoused by 'ALL YOUR SEALS' situates the poem outside of the law, in the absence of making, abiding by, and ruling by law. The poem critiques and criticizes the 'mythic, lawmaking violence' of Peter Weiss's play and of the trial, whose law-making it confirms and perpetuates, and of the Holocaust, which is in turn confirmed and perpetuated by the trial and the play. In 1921, at the end of 'Critique of Violence', Benjamin calls this mythic violence 'verwerflich' [pernicious].[175] He thereby pre-emptively comments on the mythic violence of the National Socialist State to come, and of its perpetuation — both intended and unintended — in the forms of the trial and the play. 'Verwerflich', as an intensification of the act of discarding or throwing away, indicates its ability to quash, to throw out of court, to overrule or to discard. Each manifestation of mythic violence discards or throws out cases, and more generally allows those who both knowingly and unknowingly participated in the Holocaust off the hook.

If mythic violence is 'verwerflich', then divine violence is 'called the prevailing' [die waltende heissen]. Derrida will dwell on the presence of Benjamin's first name in 'waltende', which stems from the Indo-European root meaning 'to be strong', something that Derrida does not mention.[176] It is just this sense of prevailing against the Holocaust and its aftermath that motivates the poem. As the opening line states, 'all your seals' will 'NEVER' be 'broken open'. These 'seals' multiply the divine 'seal' which is the mark of 'heilige Vollstreckung' or the holy enforcement or execution of law, and with which Benjamin concludes his essay: 'Divine violence, which is the sign and seal [Siegel] but never the means of sacred dispatch, may be called sovereign violence'.[177] Just as Benjamin's divine violence consists of an 'expiating moment that strikes without bloodshed',[178] so too Celan's poem situates itself in the absence of interpretation, which is not singular but repeated in every frustrated encounter with the text.

If the trial and its representation as a play both fail to adequately pursue justice, then it must fall to the poem to do so. For Derrida, justice 'happens' precisely where it can never happen, namely in the present, because justice always eludes the present. The poem declares its pursuit of justice from the moment it declares that its seals can 'NEVER' be broken open. As Charles Bambach puts it, 'the time of justice — if we can venture such a *topos* — is a 'now'-time on the order of Walter Benjamin's notion of *Jetztzeit*'.[179] The time of justice has little to do with the time required to gather evidence, to locate, arrest, and charge the defendants, the time of the trial itself, of arguments for the prosecution and for the defense, of witness testimonies and cross-examinations, of plaidoyers, deliberations, judgments, and sentencing. The one hundred and eighty-three days on which the court at Frankfurt convened to hear the Auschwitz trial are not a measure of justice. Neither are the three hours that German audiences were expected to sit in their seats to witness *The Investigation* in its entirety, although one reviewer described it as 'a relentless drumbeat that left theatergoers exhausted'.[180]

Justice, as Derrida puts it, 'does not wait', it does not need to wait, and in fact it cannot wait: 'A just decision is always required immediately, right away; as quickly as possible. It cannot provide itself with the infinite information and the unlimited knowledge of conditions, rules, or hypothetic imperatives that could justify it'.[181] To read Celan's poem is to enter into a non-time, a time outside of the past, present, and future, a time in which the 'NEVER' that concludes the title and first line momentarily becomes an 'ALWAYS', and where the unbreakable seals of the poem are open and legible. This is the instance of reading, 'the instant of decision' that is, as Kierkegaard says, 'a madness'.[182] Derrida assures us that 'this is particularly true of the instant of the just decision that must rend time and defy dialectics'.[183] If the mythic violence of the trial at Frankfurt, and of the Holocaust itself, was a 'lawmaking' violence, then Celan's poem invokes a divine violence that would destroy the law that made the trial and the Holocaust possible. If the poem provides a criticism of the mythic, Greco-Germanic violence of both the trial and the play, it also proposes an alternative concept of justice that is founded on a violence that is different: Jewish, poetic, and divine. This allows us to propose the reading and interpretation of poetry as a means of achieving justice, if only for the briefest of instants, in a moment of madness.

Belshazzar's Feast

In the first half of 'Force of Law', which precedes his interpretation of Benjamin's 'Critique of Violence', Derrida gives examples of some of the aporias that come about when 'law' is set against and distinguished from 'justice'. He says that for a decision to be just, it must 'not only follow a rule of law or a general law but must also assume it, approve it, confirm its value, by a reinstituting act of interpretation, as if, at the limit, the law did not exist previously — as if the judge himself invented it in each case'.[184] Similarly, the reader — to be 'juste' in his reading, to read 'justly' — cannot only read in conformity with the law of the poem as it stands before us. He or she must also read the poem as if they were re-inventing the poem, re-writing it, realizing the poem for the first time. For a reading to be 'just and responsible', it must 'preserve the law and also destroy or suspend it enough to have to reinvent it in each case'.[185] Each reading is 'other'. Each reading is, as Derrida puts it, 'different and requires an absolutely unique interpretation, which no existing, coded rule can or ought to guarantee absolutely'.[186] A reading should be both singular and iterative.

This concept of the just reading is, as Derrida notes, a theoretical projection and 'something that happens sometimes' and 'always in part'.[187] There is no human reading that can unseal what is divine in the text. Any reading of the poem will always go some way to contaminating the divine violence of the poem's creation with the mythic violence of reading and interpretation. Where the seals in the previous poem's opening line attempt to project a divine order of justice — seeking the absence of all law-making and of all meaning-making — any reading of the poem will introduce dimensions of violence not intended by the poem. This is the violence of interpretation brought by the reader in his or her reading of the poem. As Derrida puts it, the problem of justice, the attempt to affirm divine justice, 'will have been posed and violently resolved, that is to say buried, dissimulated, repressed'.[188]

Here, I propose that in the months following the Frankfurt trial and its representation on stages across Europe, Paul Celan undertakes to write poems which allow him to explore the role that poetry must assume not only in the wake of Auschwitz, but in the wake of its limited legal treatment at Frankfurt and elsewhere, and of its artistic representation in Weiss's play. To do this, I examine two poems composed during Celan's hospitalization at Sainte Anne in the spring of 1966, and which were both published in 1968, along with nine other poems, as *Eingedunkelt*.[189] I argue that the two poems constitute a continuation and development of the concerns of 'ALL YOUR SEALS' with the aftermath of the Frankfurt trial, but that they revisit, re-appropriate, and re-motivate the menetekel whose inscription was previously ascribed to contemporary anti-Semites. In this second engagement with the menetekel, Celan demonstrates intimate familiarity with the passage in the book of Daniel in which the menetekel appears. He also examines whether the menetekel may not in fact be an effective figure for poetry's own pursuit of divine justice. Only divine justice can abolish the limited structures of contemporary legal attempts to circumscribe the events of the Holocaust, can bring those guilty of crimes to justice, and can bear witness for those who were never able to bear witness for themselves.

As mentioned above, the neologism 'menetekelnd' [menetekeling] comes from the Aramaic riddle inscribed on a wall of the royal palace in Babylon. During a public feast, Belshazzar orders the golden and silver vessels stolen from the Temple in Jerusalem by his predecessor Nebuchadnezzar, to be brought out. As they drink from the stolen vessels, praising the gods of gold, silver, brass, iron, wood and stone, the fingers of a man's hand appear and write 'over against the candlestick upon the plaster of the wall'.[190] Belshazzar becomes aware of the hand in the process of writing, and is struck with fear. When he calls for his astrologers, Chaldeans, and soothsayers demanding that they read the writing and give its interpretation, they can neither read the writing nor interpret it. It is unclear from the original text, whether their inability to read the menetekel stems from their inability to decipher the script, or whether they are unable to see the script at all.[191] Those present at the feast — his princes, wives, and concubines — do not witness the menetekel either, although they see the physical and psychological effects of its inscription on the king. Belshazzar is the only person who experiences the inscription, as 'superstes', because although he does not recognize the script, or understand what it says, he recognizes it as a divine sentence. Daniel, who is not present to witness the inscription, is able to read and interpret the script. He is therefore not a 'superstes', able to see what Belshazzar sees, and give its interpretation in this way. He is instead a 'testis', one who has not seen, a third party, and witness to the communication that takes place between God and man.

The original Aramaic of this chapter in Daniel illustrates the logic of divine retribution through a series of lexical parallels, in which words of different if not antithetical meanings share a common consonantal root. For instance, the verb used to describe the vessels that Nebuchadnezzar has 'brought forth' from the Temple in Jerusalem [הנפק][192] shares a tri-consonantal root with the verb that describes the hand 'coming forth' [נפקו נפקה][193] to inscribe the writing on the wall. The crime of bringing the vessels out is punished by a gesture that imitates and replaces the initial gesture. The preposition used to locate Belshazzar's act of blasphemy, which takes place in public, 'before' [לקבל] the people,[194] is the same preposition used to situate the fingers of the hand that appear before or 'over against' the candlestick.[195] Again, the application of a parallel linguistic structure illustrates how the punishment responds precisely in kind to the crime committed. Similarly, the verb used by Belshazzar's wife to describe the skills 'found' in the prophet Daniel [השתכחת][196] is the same used by Daniel when he describes Belshazzar as having been weighed in the scales and 'having been found' wanting [השתכחת חסיר].[197] In each of these instances in the text, divine justice repeats and counters the human crime. This is the structure of divine retribution, most famously summed up in Leviticus as: 'fracture for fracture, eye for eye, tooth for tooth; as he has caused disfigurement of a man, so shall it be done to him'.[198]

Belshazzar's abuse of the sacred vessels provokes the realization of divine justice through the inscription of the menetekel. The menetekel is therefore a figure of

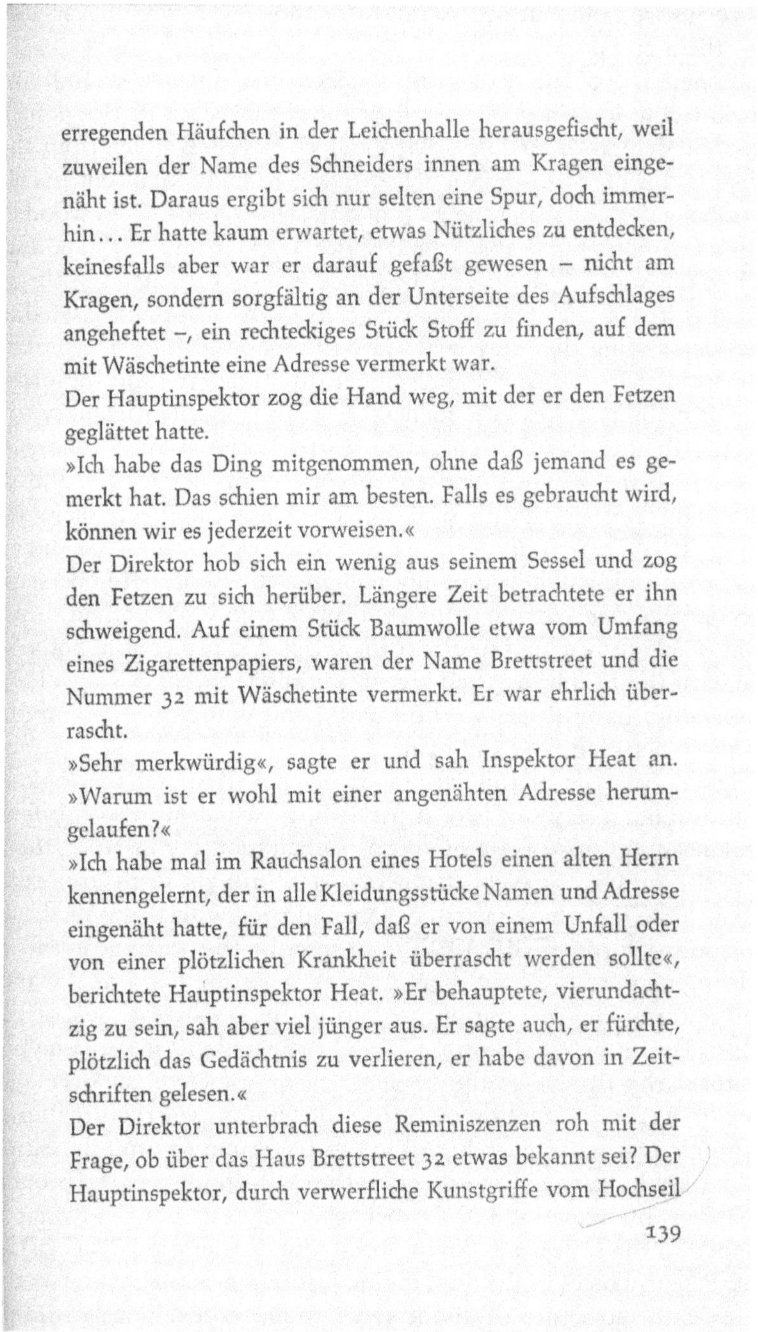

erregenden Häufchen in der Leichenhalle herausgefischt, weil zuweilen der Name des Schneiders innen am Kragen eingenäht ist. Daraus ergibt sich nur selten eine Spur, doch immerhin... Er hatte kaum erwartet, etwas Nützliches zu entdecken, keinesfalls aber war er darauf gefaßt gewesen – nicht am Kragen, sondern sorgfältig an der Unterseite des Aufschlages angeheftet –, ein rechteckiges Stück Stoff zu finden, auf dem mit Wäschetinte eine Adresse vermerkt war.
Der Hauptinspektor zog die Hand weg, mit der er den Fetzen geglättet hatte.
»Ich habe das Ding mitgenommen, ohne daß jemand es gemerkt hat. Das schien mir am besten. Falls es gebraucht wird, können wir es jederzeit vorweisen.«
Der Direktor hob sich ein wenig aus seinem Sessel und zog den Fetzen zu sich herüber. Längere Zeit betrachtete er ihn schweigend. Auf einem Stück Baumwolle etwa vom Umfang eines Zigarettenpapiers, waren der Name Brettstreet und die Nummer 32 mit Wäschetinte vermerkt. Er war ehrlich überrascht.
»Sehr merkwürdig«, sagte er und sah Inspektor Heat an. »Warum ist er wohl mit einer angenähten Adresse herumgelaufen?«
»Ich habe mal im Rauchsalon eines Hotels einen alten Herrn kennengelernt, der in alle Kleidungsstücke Namen und Adresse eingenäht hatte, für den Fall, daß er von einem Unfall oder von einer plötzlichen Krankheit überrascht werden sollte«, berichtete Hauptinspektor Heat. »Er behauptete, vierundachtzig zu sein, sah aber viel jünger aus. Er sagte auch, er fürchte, plötzlich das Gedächtnis zu verlieren, er habe davon in Zeitschriften gelesen.«
Der Direktor unterbrach diese Reminiszenzen roh mit der Frage, ob über das Haus Brettstreet 32 etwas bekannt sei? Der Hauptinspektor, durch verwerfliche Kunstgriffe vom Hochseil

139

Fig. 3.1. '...durch verwerfliche Kunstgriffe vom Hochseil...', Conrad, *Der Geheimagent*, p. 139. Pencil.
© Deutsches Literaturarchiv, Marbach a. N.

divine justice that not only surpasses all human justice in its realization, but that has the ability to respond to each crime in kind — that is, justly. It is a manifestation of justice that Daniel is able to interpret for us, as he has the ability, in Luther's words: 'Träume zu deuten, dunkle Sprüche zu erraten und verborgene Sachen zu offenbaren' [to interpret dreams, to uncover dark utterances, and to reveal hidden things].[199] In this he resembles a critic or poet after Auschwitz, whose task it is to decipher and interpret the dreams, dark utterances, and hidden things of modernity. Daniel's interpretation constitutes part of that punishment, in that it allows Belshazzar to take cognizance of the crime for which he is being punished. As Derrida says, 'it is unjust to judge someone who does not understand his rights, nor the language in which the law is inscribed or the judgment pronounced'.[200] Divine justice requires interpretation in order to be applied to human crimes. Belshazzar is killed later that night only once his crime and punishment have been explained to him.

In the two poems examined in this section, I suggest that Celan exploits the tale of Belshazzar's feast in order to create the conditions for a modern, post-Frankfurt menetekel. This poetic menetekel is intended to replace the all too human attempts to pursue and realize justice, at Frankfurt and elsewhere, for crimes committed in the Holocaust. The following poem was written and largely completed on 4 April 1966:

> VOM HOCHSEIL herab-
> gezwungen, ermisst du,
> was zu gewärtigen ist
> von soviel Gaben,
>
> Käsig-weisses Gesicht
> dessen, der über uns herfällt,
>
> Setz die Leuchtzeiger ein, die Leucht-
> ziffern,
>
> Sogleich, nach Menschenart,
> mischt sich das Dunkel hinzu,
> das du herauskennst
>
> aus all diesen
> unbussfertigen, unbotmässigen
> Spielen.[201]
>
> [FROM THE HIGH-WIRE forced
> down, you assess,
> what is to be expected
> from so many gifts,
>
> Pasty white face
> of the one, who falls upon us,
>
> Set the luminous hands, the luminous
> ciphers,
>
> Then suddenly, in the way of men,

> darkness infiltrates,
> which you distinguish
>
> in all of these
> unrepentant, unsubmissive
> games.]

The first three fragments of the poem can each be understood as a rewriting of a central element of the biblical account of Belshazzar's feast. Belshazzar pledges to give three gifts to the one who can read and interpret the script that he has seen inscribed on the wall: 'Whosoever shall read this writing, and show me the interpretation thereof, shall be clothed with scarlet, and have a chain of gold about his neck, and shall be the third ruler in the kingdom'.[202] Daniel responds by rejecting the gifts but agrees to read and interpret the writing on the wall: 'Let thy gifts be to thyself, and give thy rewards to another'.[203] Daniel explains Belshazzar's crime to him, which is to have abused the vessels of the Temple to praise gods 'which see not, nor hear, nor know' and to have omitted to glorify 'the God in whose hand thy breath is, and whose are all thy ways'.[204] Although Daniel announces the end of Belshazzar's reign, if not his life, the king commands that Daniel be given the gifts as promised. The giving of the gifts marks the last executive order of a blasphemous and oppressive regime condemned to destruction.

If we apply this narrative to the first fragment of the poem, the passive subject of the past participle 'herabgezwungen' [forced down] would not be the second person singular who is evoked in the second line, but an unnamed and absent subject, a subject who has been forced down from the poem itself, leaving the 'du' [you] to assess what to expect from all these gifts.[205] The identification of Daniel as recipient of Belshazzar's gifts appears to be strengthened by notes written less than a week before the composition of this poem, in which Celan evokes 'the three-times highly-gifted',[206] 'the untamed, / three times overwhelmed / with greeting and farewell',[207] and 'The untamed, three / times overshadowed with gifts'.[208] Once Belshazzar is figuratively forced down from the high-wire, Daniel asks himself what to make of these gifts with which he has been 'overwhelmed' and 'overshadowed', now that the order which bestowed them and gave them legitimacy has come to a violent end. The final act of Belshazzar as king is therefore to promote the Jewish prophet to a position of secular power that he will retain.

The second fragment appears to further support the relation of the poem to the biblical account of Belshazzar's feast. The source of the 'pasty' or 'cheesy' white face is Conrad's *Secret Agent*, in which the face of Verloc's overweight accomplice, Michaelis, is described as a 'käsiges Mondgesicht'[209] or 'pasty moon face' that 'drooped under the weight of melancholy assent'.[210] Although the line is not annotated by Celan, as many parts of the book are, Michaelis's pasty moon face enables us to attribute physical characteristics to an obese and incompetent criminal. A version of the poem immediately preceding the final version includes a telling insertion, which makes the connection with Belshazzar almost certain. In place of 'pasty white face' [Käsig-weisses Gesicht] we read 'pasty king-face' [Käsiges Königsgesicht].[211] This displaces the criminal's features from nineteenth-century

London to opposite the menetekel as it is inscribed on a wall in exilic Babylon. Although this telling qualification is removed in the final version, something of its power and significance continues to resound in the remainder of the fragment, as the face is attributed to 'him, who falls upon us', who attacks us. The aggressor of the collective first person is not simply criminal, as the source in Conrad's Michaelis indicates. His criminal authority is socially, politically, and legally sanctioned.

In Daniel, the pastiness of the king's face indicates the point at which Belshazzar recognizes the writing on the wall, the ultimate meaning of which he comprehends even though he cannot read or interpret the text himself. The removal of kingly qualification from the terror-stricken face allows the reader to perceive the faces of other, more contemporary oppressors of Jewish exiles, as they take cognizance of the divine retribution prepared for them. The poem invites its reader to insert any one of the twenty faces on trial in Frankfurt — made familiar to the public through their representation in newspapers and on television — and to imagine them experiencing the terror of knowing that they are now to pay the price for the crimes they have committed.

In Daniel, terror becomes a mode of knowing for the criminal, although we must be attentive to the texture of the Aramaic to recognize its true power. Belshazzar has one other physical reaction to seeing the writing on the wall, beyond the change in countenance that Celan includes here. In addition to this, his thoughts trouble him, 'so that the joints of his loins were loosed, and his knees smote one against another'.²¹² The Aramaic word for 'joint' is 'קטר'.²¹³ The three-letter root indicates a knot — such as a vertebra (which is a knot of bone) or a riddle (which is a knot in language). In another instance of the lexical parallel observed above, the word used to describe the king's joints is the same as that used to describe the 'hard sentences' [קטרין]²¹⁴ that Daniel is adept at resolving. Where Daniel is gifted with the unusual ability to interpret and understand difficult texts, Belshazzar comprehends the writing on the wall through the loosening of the knots of his body. The pasty white face of Celan's poem indicates that terror in the face of immediate divine justice is the only mode through which hardened criminals understand their crimes. Toward the end of Quentin Tarantino's film *Inglourious Basterds* (2009), leading Nazis in a cinema are attacked and massacred by two Jewish men, revisiting and repairing the injustice of the Holocaust through the hyperbolic fictions of Hollywood film. Although different in tone, I think we are invited to see something like this redeeming indulgence of fantasy at this point of the poem, in which criminals responsible for the Holocaust are made to understand their crimes, and suffer just retribution. The poem stages the realization of divine justice, and allows the reader to witness it, not simply as spectator but as 'testis', as the third party who ensures the realization of justice through the act of reading. It momentarily realizes what Bertrand Badiou identifies as the 'dream of action' that haunts all of Celan's poetic oeuvre.²¹⁵

The imperative that opens the third fragment calls for the poem to inscribe its menetekel, the sentence that will bring about the realization of divine justice. It is the nature of the menetekel, however, that it cannot be read by those for whom

FIG. 3.2. Rembrandt van Rijn, 'Belshazzar's Feast', 1635, oil on canvas, National Gallery, London, NG6350. Bought with a contribution from the National Art Collections Fund, 1964. © The National Gallery, London.

it is not intended. There has long been debate around the reasons for which the various wise men of Babylon were unable to interpret the writing on the wall when requested to do so by Belshazzar. In book three of *De termino vitae*, the Amsterdam rabbi and scholar Menasseh ben Israel (1604–1657) claimed that the wise men had been unable to read the text because it had been inscribed in five vertical columns from right to left, as depicted below, rather than in horizontal lines from right to left, as Aramaic and Hebrew are normally written and read:[216]

This is also how the menetekel appears in perhaps its most famous visual representation, namely the painting completed in 1635 by Rembrandt van Rijn, which Celan knew from his repeated visits to the National Gallery in London.[217] As Rembrandt and Menasseh knew each other — the former producing a set of four etchings for the latter's book, *Piedra gloriosa*, in 1655 — it is generally accepted that the painter consulted the rabbi on the subject of the Aramaic script.[218] An initial reading of the poem with the book of Daniel in mind encourages us to approximate the 'luminous hands, the luminous ciphers' and the menetekel as it appears in Rembrandt's painting. Here, the Aramaic letters appear to incandesce and are the sole depicted source of light. The candlestick 'over against' which the letters are said to appear has been displaced and subsumed into the glowing letters themselves.

In his translation of this line, Ian Fairley alters the function between the luminous hands and the luminous ciphers, superimposing one upon the other to create the familiar image of a clock face: 'Set the luminous hands on the luminous dial'.[219] 'Zeiger', here in the plural form, is anything that points including — besides the hands of the clock — the fingers of a human hand. 'Leuchtziffern' are literally luminous ciphers, digits, numerals, or figures, not a 'dial' as Fairley writes, which would be a 'Zifferblatt'. Where Fairley superimposes the luminous hands on the luminous digits, Celan juxtaposes them: 'Set the luminous hands, the luminous / ciphers'. Although we know that the imperative 'set' governs 'the luminous hands', it is less clear that it also governs 'the luminous / ciphers'. Given that the shared etymological root of 'Ziffer' ['digit' or 'number', cognate with French 'chiffre'] and 'cipher' comes from the Arabic 'صفر' [sifr] meaning 'empty' or 'void', it can be argued that the luminous ciphers relate more powerfully to the luminous white of the unfinished sentence and blank line that follows it.[220] This is to say that the luminous letters adopt a mode of presence that is invisible to the human eye. Contrary to Menasseh's interpretation, the biblical account suggests that the reason no one could assist Belshazzar in reading the writing was that he is the only one able to see it. Even Daniel, who reads the writing and gives its interpretation, does not see the writing, such is his ability to read and interpret what he has not seen. The imperative call to set the luminous pointer and ciphers is therefore a call to deploy the menetekel — figure of divine justice — within the poem. The menetekel is invisible for those to whom it is not addressed, just as here we are unable to see it. But the one for whom the menetekel is intended will know and recognize it when he sees it, and will turn pale in the face, his troubled thoughts and loose limbs interpreting and comprehending what previously he was unable to see and read.

The notion that the white space following this line contains invisible text — a divine menetekel that we cannot see and therefore not interpret, and of which the luminous ciphers are at most a reflection — is corroborated by the text that immediately follows the blank space. Rhetorically, 'Sogleich' [immediately, straight away] draws all that is by nature dissipative, disseminating, and invisible, into a single, visible, and legible moment in time and space. It both points to an immediately prior event that belongs to an order other than the order of language, and marks the re-establishment of human presence and measure. The 'darkness' that 'infiltrates' is therefore the darkness of inscribed language, the darkness that signals the limits of human expression, and that exists outside the glowing white script of the menetekel, as depicted by Rembrandt, and as seen by Belshazzar. But in contrast to the invisible presence of divine justice, the 'darkness' also represents the visible limits of human justice that can now be distinguished in the 'unrepentant' and 'unsubmissive' games of legal procedure at Frankfurt.

Another poem published as one of the eleven *Eingedunkelt* poems in 1968 also invokes the menetekel. Here, its purpose is to bring about justice not for the criminal but for the victim. The menetekel is made to function as a figure of the restorative part of retributive justice. The earliest trace of this poem is dated 3 April 1966, the day before the previous poem discussed was begun. Inscribed in capital letters, and functioning both as the poem's first line and title, the poem is written — and asks to be read — under the shadow of the adverb 'bedenkenlos'. 'Bedenkenlos' derives from the verb 'bedenken' meaning to consider or think upon, or literally to 'bethink'. If in Shakespeare's *Pericles, Prince of Tyre* Lysimachus can respond "'T is well bethought',[221] then 'bedenkenlos' can be rendered as 'un-bethought' or more simply 'unthinkingly'. It indicates the absence of reflexive, collective, or re-collective thought. In a recent translation of Isaiah 59, for instance — which confesses the nature and extent of man's sinfulness — 'bedenkenlos' describes the thoughtless chatter which ensures that 'judgment is turned away backward, and justice standeth afar off'.[222] Beyond this, however, the verb 'bedenken' is often used in conjunction with thinking about death. In the psalms, the singer asks God to teach us to 'think upon' [lehre uns bedenken] the fact that we all die.[223] To do something 'bedenkenlos', therefore, is not simply to do it without thinking, but specifically to do something without the thought of death. To return to Shestov's formulation as quoted above, to do something 'bedenkenlos' is to belong to that part of mankind that does not feel 'the burn of its ancestor's sin' in its blood, and to consider oneself free from all sin. It therefore evokes not only Belshazzar, who blasphemes without thought for his own mortality, but also the defendants at Frankfurt, who are not willing or able to associate the crimes they committed at Auschwitz-Birkenau with the thought of death:

BEDENKENLOS,
den Vernebelungen zuwider,
glüht sich der hängende Leuchter
nach unten, zu uns

Vielarmiger Brand,
sucht jetzt sein Eisen, hört,
woher, aus Menschenhautnähe,
ein Zischen,

findet,
verliert,

schroff
liest sich, minutenlang,
die schwere,
schimmernde
Weisung.[224]

[UNTHINKING,
against the obfuscations,
the hanging lamp glows
down here, to us

Many-armed fire,
now seeks its iron, hears,
from where, from the closeness of human skin,
a sizzing,

finds,
loses,

rough
spells out, over minutes,
the heavy,
glimmering
directive.]

As in the previous poem, this poem situates itself inside Belshazzar's besieged palace. The 'candlestick' 'over against' which the writing appears on the wall in the King James Version, is here a 'hanging lamp' which corresponds with the 'Leuchter' [lamp] in Luther's translation.[225] The menetekel is evident in the 'heavy, / glimmering / directive' that can be read for only a matter of minutes [minutenlang] in the final fragment. In an earlier version, the 'directive' is explicitly married with the luminosity of the pointer and ciphers of the previous poem: '(Die Weisung wird sein: / hier leuchte dich aus, / hier leuchte dich durch) [(The directive will come: / here light your way out, / here light your way through)]'.[226] But where in the previous poem it was also possible to identify Daniel and Belshazzar, here the poem moves away from the biblical account and makes more explicit the analogies between Belshazzar's feast and the Holocaust. Where in the biblical text, the same noun [היכלא] is used to refer to both the Temple in Jerusalem[227] and Belshazzar's palace,[228] here the Babylonian palace becomes confused not only with

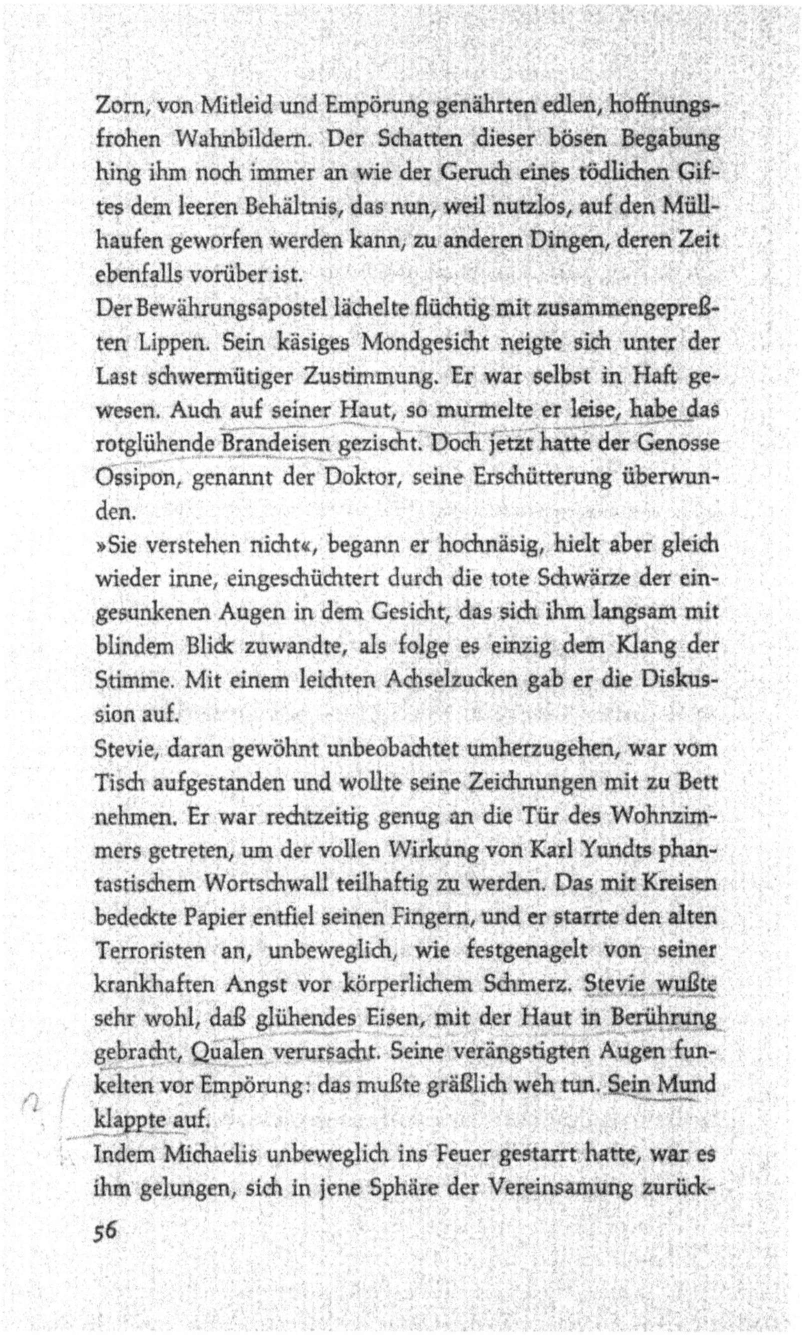

Zorn, von Mitleid und Empörung genährten edlen, hoffnungsfrohen Wahnbildern. Der Schatten dieser bösen Begabung hing ihm noch immer an wie der Geruch eines tödlichen Giftes dem leeren Behältnis, das nun, weil nutzlos, auf den Müllhaufen geworfen werden kann, zu anderen Dingen, deren Zeit ebenfalls vorüber ist.

Der Bewährungsapostel lächelte flüchtig mit zusammengepreßten Lippen. Sein käsiges Mondgesicht neigte sich unter der Last schwermütiger Zustimmung. Er war selbst in Haft gewesen. Auch auf seiner Haut, so murmelte er leise, habe das rotglühende Brandeisen gezischt. Doch jetzt hatte der Genosse Ossipon, genannt der Doktor, seine Erschütterung überwunden.

»Sie verstehen nicht«, begann er hochnäsig, hielt aber gleich wieder inne, eingeschüchtert durch die tote Schwärze der eingesunkenen Augen in dem Gesicht, das sich ihm langsam mit blindem Blick zuwandte, als folge es einzig dem Klang der Stimme. Mit einem leichten Achselzucken gab er die Diskussion auf.

Stevie, daran gewöhnt unbeobachtet umherzugehen, war vom Tisch aufgestanden und wollte seine Zeichnungen mit zu Bett nehmen. Er war rechtzeitig genug an die Tür des Wohnzimmers getreten, um der vollen Wirkung von Karl Yundts phantastischem Wortschwall teilhaftig zu werden. Das mit Kreisen bedeckte Papier entfiel seinen Fingern, und er starrte den alten Terroristen an, unbeweglich, wie festgenagelt von seiner krankhaften Angst vor körperlichem Schmerz. Stevie wußte sehr wohl, daß glühendes Eisen, mit der Haut in Berührung gebracht, Qualen verursacht. Seine verängstigten Augen funkelten vor Empörung: das mußte gräßlich weh tun. Sein Mund klappte auf.

Indem Michaelis unbeweglich ins Feuer gestarrt hatte, war es ihm gelungen, sich in jene Sphäre der Vereinsamung zurück-

56

FIG. 3.3. 'Auch auf seiner Haut [...] habe das rotglühende Brandeisen gezischt', Conrad, *Der Geheimagent*, p. 56. Pencil. © Deutsches Literaturarchiv, Marbach a. N.

the courtroom in Frankfurt, but also with the camps at Auschwitz-Birkenau.

Throughout the poems in *Eingedunkelt*, the first person plural pronoun 'uns' refers to people unified by the violence to which they are subjected. In the previous poem, the pasty face belongs to the one who 'falls upon' or attacks us. In 'WITH US' [MIT UNS], 'we' are 'the thrown about, the traveling, ~~often stolen from~~'.[229] Here, 'the hanging lamp glows / down here, to us'. The violence of the action becomes both more evident and more specific when we examine the use of the verb 'glühen' [glow] in the context of Luther's translation of the Old Testament. Of the eleven moments at which the verb 'glühen' is used, seven are used in conjunction with the fire of ovens.[230] The hanging lamp of Belshazzar's palace therefore burns in this poem with the heat and light of the crematoria in the camps, and without thought ('BEDENKENLOS') for those it incinerates.

The 'Vernebelungen' or 'obfuscations' against which the lamp glows in the poem also provide a conceptual passageway from Belshazzar's Babylon to Auschwitz-Birkenau. In Rembrandt's painting of Belshazzar's feast, the menetekel is surrounded by clouds of grey and black oil paint, from which the top part of the hand emerges to inscribe its message. The Aramaic letters glow against the dark clouds of paint. In German, 'Vernebelung' is an intensification of the noun 'Nebel' [mist, vapor, fog], and evokes clouds of smoke or gas, such as the hydrogen cyanide gas released through the vaporization of cyclone B crystals, as used in the gas chambers from 1942 onward.

Although the multiple arms that open the second fragment might in any other context call to mind the Hindu deity Ganesha, here they can more pertinently be associated with the hanging lamp of the first fragment. A 'menorah' for instance — such as those stolen from the Temple — has eight arms around a central stem. The flames usually associated with the menorah, which etymologically privilege the way they shine, are here displaced in favor of 'fire' [Brand], which in its English and German forms goes back to the notion of burning and branding. This transformation indicates not only an historical abuse of the menorah, comparable to Belshazzar's misuse of the stolen sacred vessels and the National Socialist's appropriation of Jewish property. As part of this theft, the candelabrum acquires the features of those actions that are required to ensure its appropriation, namely the death of their rightful owners. Here the many arms of the menorah are set alight like the limbs of victims burned in the crematoria.

It is in this context of fragmented but deliberate references to both Belshazzar's palace and the horrors of the camps that the manifestation of the menetekel should be understood. It occurs at a moment in the text when common grammatical and typographical conventions are suspended. The capital 'V' that opens the second fragment suggests that a new sentence has begun, although the absence of punctuation at the end of the first fragment precludes any definitive assessment. As a substantive in the nominative case, the 'many-armed fire' is probably the agent of the verb 'seeks' in the line that follows, although the introduction of a supplementary comma between the agent and verb makes this less certain. The grammatical and syntactic structure of this part of the poem makes it appear unfinished, even though many of these idiosyncrasies are retained in successive versions. The incoherences of the text as inscribed text do not persist, however, when the text is read aloud and heard, as the absence of a period at the end of the fourth line and the presence of a comma at the end of the fifth do not radically transform how the text sounds. It is therefore not as mistakes or signs of incompletion that we should understand these inconsistencies of punctuation, but as a call to hear rather than to look, to listen rather than to read.

The appeal to acoustic rather than visual faculties is confirmed in the second fragment: 'Many-armed fire, / now seeks its iron, hears, / from where, from the closeness of human skin, / a sizzing [Zischen]'. The word 'Zischen' is used on one other occasion in Celan's published work, in the early poem 'Song of Foreign Brothers', probably dating from 1941.[231] Here — in contrast to its Rimbaldian if not Rabelaisian application there — the verb appears to originate from three texts that Celan read at the time of the poem's composition.

First, in Schadewaldt's translation of *The Odyssey*, the verb 'zischen' [sizz] is used to describe the sound that Polyphemus's eye makes when it is stabbed with a burning olive stake by Ulysses: 'And like a man, a blacksmith plunges a large axe or a hatchet [oder ein Schlichtbeil] into cold water, to cool the powerfully hissing thing [das gewaltig zischende] off — so that it once again has the strength of iron — : in this way did his eye hiss [so zischte sein Auge] around the olive wood stake'.[232]

Second, in a passage from Conrad's *Secret Agent*, which Celan read and annotated on 6 April, the verb appears again, this time in the form of a past participle: '[Michaelis] had been a prisoner himself. His own skin had sizzled under the red-hot brand, he murmured softly' [Auch auf seiner Haut, so murmelte er leise, habe das rotglühende Brandeisen gezischt]. The theme of the branding iron is further developed a few lines later: 'Stevie knew very well that hot iron applied to one's skin hurt very much' [Stevie wusste sehr wohl, dass glühendes Eisen, mit der Haut in Berührung gebracht, Qualen verursacht].[233]

Finally, on 1 April, *Le Monde* published a review of the first performance of Weiss's *Investigation* in France.[234] The review includes a quotation from a translation into French of Weiss's autobiographical novel *Vanishing Point*, in which he describes his experience as a German Jewish painter during the Second World War.[235] Reflecting on the revelation of the concentration and death camps through the media in 1945, Weiss writes: 'For a long time, I felt guilty for not being among those who bore, branded into their flesh, the identification number of their abjection [inscrit au feu dans leur chair leur matricule d'abjection], for having escaped, and for only ever being nothing more than a spectator. I had grown up to be annihilated, and I hadn't been. I ought to have perished, to have sacrificed myself; since I had never been imprisoned, assassinated, or killed on the field of battle, I had at the very least to feel guilty'.[236]

The blinding of Polyphemus and the branding of Michaelis contrast with the absence of any mark on the skin of Peter Weiss, who refers to the branding of prisoners at Auschwitz-Birkenau with an identification number.[237] Weiss's use of the term 'branded into their flesh' [inscrit au feu dans leur chair] — a translation into

French of the German 'ins Fleisch eingebrannt'[238] — is not an accurate description of the way numbers were inscribed on the skin of prisoners at Auschwitz-Birkenau. As Weiss himself describes in *My Place* and *The Investigation*, the numbers were either inscribed directly onto the rib cage with ink,[239] or ink was rubbed into the skin after being pierced with a needle.[240] In the temporary constellation created by the reading of these three texts, however, Celan is able to conceive of the inscription onto human flesh in terms of the application of a red-hot iron.

I propose that Celan attempts — through the medium of the poem — to translate the indelible Auschwitz tattoo into a divine menetekel. In this way, the ciphers that once marked an individual for death in the camps can be turned against the aggressor and used to pronounce the aggressor's guilt and immediate punishment by death. To do this, the cauterized inscription which we hear in the second fragment has to give way to a menetekel that is visible only to the one for whom it is intended. This shift from visible to invisible is projected in the two words that constitute the third fragment: 'findet, / verliert' [finds, / loses]. But it is the adverb 'schroff' [rough, harsh, abrupt] that opens the fourth and final fragment that describes *how* the transition from Auschwitz number to Babylonian menetekel will take place.

The inscription of 'schroff' in the final fragment challenges the adverb 'bedenkenlos' that has governed the poem so far, by introducing the possibility of the realization of justice and healing into the poem. As an adverb it qualifies the way the menetekel is read: 'schroff / liest sich, minutenlang, / die schwere, / schimmernde / Weisung' [rough / spells out, over minutes, / the heavy, / glimmering / directive]. To understand the full implication of this 'rough' reading, we need to be sensitive to the unique etymological properties of the word. The eighteenth-century German philologist Johann Christoph Adelung describes the word's acoustic development: 'It [schroff] appears in Italian without the sibilant [Zischlaut] as 'ruvido' [rough, coarse], and in Bavaria as 'roppet' [mangy, rough]. 'Rufe' [scab], the rough crust of a wound, is similarly related'.[241] The sibilant (in German 'Zischlaut') in 'schroff' is represented by the first three letters 'sch'. The 'Zisch' of 'ein Zischen' [a sizzing] is also a sibilant. According to Adelung's etymological calculation, 'schroff' marks the mid-point of an historical three-part acoustic diminution in sibilance from 'Zischen' [sizzing] to 'schroff' [rough] to 'Rufe' [scab]. The same three-part reduction in sibilance can be identified in the poem, which also moves from the sound of cauterization on human skin in 'Zischen', to its reduction and repair in 'schroff', and finally to its total absence and healing in 'Rufe'. The 'Rufe' or 'scab' that would indicate the sealing and healing of the wound is not visible in the poem, except in its acoustic and consonantal presence within 'schroff'. Like the menetekel, the 'Rufe' remains outside of human expression, the invisible sign of divine justice, retribution, and restoration. Like the menetekel, the invisible 'Rufe' repairs the wound and completes the process of healing.

The move from visible wound to invisible scab, and from visible identification number to invisible menetekel, posits the realization of justice through poetry just outside of language, in the silence and whiteness that surrounds human discourse.

It suggests that as something akin to divine justice is realized through poetry, and the more successfully trauma is healed, the more poetry will exist outside of inscribed and spoken language, and the less there will be to read. Celan's work has often been read as a writing-into-silence, as during the 1950s and 1960s his poems grow shorter, more difficult, and less lyrical. As discussed in chapter two, this has encouraged readers to perceive the poet's suicide as the poet's final act of poetry, in which he inscribes the poem that is more powerful than any other, but that contains no words. In the light of my reading of these two poems — and of my examination of poetry's approximation of divine justice — an alternative argument is possible. Namely that the growing silence of these poems, their increased brevity and difficulty, could instead be the mark of a poetry that is incrementally successful at bringing about some sort of healing, some sort of justice. The extent to which the poem successfully invokes divine justice is the extent to which it writes itself out of existence.

The violence perpetrated on Belshazzar has the curious quality of being both divine and mythic. The divine violence of the menetekel's inscription — that makes his death a certainty — throws him into physical dissolution. But Belshazzar's actual death occurs later that night as an act of mythic violence when he is murdered. The biblical narrative mentions this as if in passing. We are not told who was responsible, and it does not seem to matter. Belshazzar's death has the curious quality of being both bloodless and bloody. The death of Belshazzar and the subsequent ascension of Darius the Mede provide a perfect example — in two distinct, consecutive movements — of how divine justice destroys law and mythic violence founds it. The mythic violence that kills Belshazzar is not the violence that destroys the State and the rule of law. This occurs when the writing appears on the wall. The killing of Belshazzar is an act that establishes a new State or States, as Belshazzar's kingdom is divided between the Medes and the Persians. It is the moment when, as Benjamin puts it, myth 'bastardizes' divine violence and makes it comprehensible to mankind.[242] Any justice that can be achieved through poetry will similarly be dual in nature. If the poem momentarily achieves absolute justice through the application of divine violence in the moment of reading and understanding or perhaps comprehension, then this will manifest itself less perfectly and less completely as mythic violence when translated to visible or audible language.

Poetic Justice

The threat of damning critical judgment hangs over any cultural undertaking in the post-Holocaust world. An artistic project that takes the Holocaust as its subject, as in the case of Peter Weiss's *Investigation*, will necessarily be examined for any possible ways it perpetuates, transfigures, or removes the horror of the event, thereby creating further injustice for the victims. For instance, Adorno is unsparing in his critique of Arnold Schoenberg's 'A Survivor from Warsaw' (1947), a short piece for narrator, men's chorus, and orchestra: 'The victims are turned into works of art, tossed out to be gobbled up by the world that did them in. The so-called artistic rendering of the naked physical pain of those who were beaten down with rifle butts contains, however distantly, the possibility that pleasure can be squeezed from it'.[243] This was probably not Schoenberg's aim. It is instead the unintended result of a desire to make the horror evident to those who were not present at the time. Where post-Holocaust art seeks justice, restitution, and reparation, as it is morally obligated to, it will also stumble upon the problem of reproducing or representing the Holocaust.

In the wake of Germany's most comprehensive attempt to bring those responsible for running the camps at Auschwitz-Birkenau to justice according to German law, the question as to whether post-Holocaust art facilitates the pursuit and realization of justice re-asserts itself. Given the perceived failure of the trial, the question is whether art can bring about justice where law was unable to. Is justice as made possible through the writing and reading of literature of comparable worth to the justice sought in conventional legal trials? This is the role of poetry after Frankfurt, and it is to this that the three poems discussed in this chapter respond. Robert Cohen writes that Peter Weiss was aware of the need to bring perpetrators to justice after the Holocaust, 'but also of the impossibility of having literature perform such a gesture'.[244] *The Investigation* appears to relinquish its critical prerogative, and to instead devote itself to the representation of testimonial material. It refuses the critical distance that would allow for the possibility of contemplation and judgment, such that the play becomes a continuation, of sorts, of the Holocaust itself. Celan's cryptic critique of the play in the poem 'ALL YOUR SEALS BROKEN OPEN?' is meant to demonstrate that the mythic violence of the Holocaust — adopted as a means of procuring justice in the trial and reproduced in the play — requires a radically other form of violence in order for justice in the wake of the Holocaust to become possible.

In discussions of law and literature, it is common to perceive literature as a less powerful form of law, a law that requires the reader to suspend his or her normal critical faculties, and to submit to literature's fictional jurisdiction. This is the position that Peter Schneck adopts in his book on legal conflict and literary representation in North America: 'Like the law it sets out to criticize, literature's legitimacy as a rhetoric of evidence rests on the specific legality of literary fiction, a law of literature, to which the text and its readers must comply. To put it simply, literature can become evidence only if it presumes — and if its readers accept the presumption of — a literary jurisdiction and juridical authority existing prior to literature itself and regulating its representation of truth and justice'.[245] As Schneck goes on to concede, the law of literature is not a legal law, and any juridical power of literary authority is imaginary and transient.[246] The weakness of this notion of literature as law lies above all in its narrow conception of literature as being essentially representational. The justice aimed for by poetry — as exemplified in Celan's work — not only lies beyond any legal framework. It also lies beyond the communicative, or representational, function of language.

Justice in poetry is therefore not easy to identify. There is no *res poetica*, or poetical product, as there is a *res judicata* at the conclusion of a conventional trial. But something of justice can be realized through poetry when it is read attentively for what lies just outside of its expression. In response to the mythic violence of genocide — but also of the law and of theatrical representation — the poem achieves divine justice through the figure of the menetekel. Celan's poems not only share with the menetekel a conception of language that refuses or resists the reduction of language to its representational function. They also share a mode of expression that is not limited to what can be seen and read by a sighted individual. What one sees and reads of the menetekel — and of Celan's poetry — may depend on the reader's guilt, or on the reader's ethical disposition, or on the reader's ability 'to interpret dreams, to uncover dark utterances, and to reveal hidden things'.[247] The violence of Celan's poetry and of the menetekel is not indiscriminate. They both destroy law and annihilate limits, they bring about expiation and strike the guilty, but they do so 'without bloodshed'.[248] The justice of poetry — to the extent that it succeeds in harnessing and deploying divine violence — is therefore 'the most just, the most historic, the most revolutionary, the most decidable, the most deciding'.[249] And yet that part of justice will often lie just outside of our reach as readers. Like divine justice, poetic justice does not entirely 'lend itself to any human determination, to any knowledge of decidable 'certainty' on our part'.[250]

Any understanding will therefore either be divinely inspired, as is the case in Daniel's reading of the writing on the wall, or an educated and sensitive guess, as demonstrated by Derrida's retrospective projection of what Benjamin might have made of the Final Solution, had he lived to both survive and witness it. Even then, there will always be an element of uncertainty and in-conclusion. In law, as Felman notes, a crime that is historically unprecedented can still be litigated, understood, and judged in a discipline of precedents.[251] But poetry is a discipline of non-precedents, of that which occurs unexpectedly and uniquely. There is in poetry always the chance of an impossible reprieve and unlikely forgiveness, just as there is that unpunished crimes will finally be punished.

Notes to Chapter 3

1. Dante Alighieri, *Dante Alighieri's Divine Comedy, Italian Text and Verse Translation*, vol. 1, *Inferno*, trans. by Mark Musa (Bloomington: Indiana University Press, 1996), p. 306, xxxii, v. 12. 'So that speaking might not diverge from doing'. This quotation figured as an epigraph in the drafts for Celan's 1963 collection *Die Niemandsrose* (Paul Celan, *Die Niemandsrose*, ed. by Heino Schmull, with the assistance of Michael Schwarzkopf (Frankfurt a.M.: Suhrkamp, 1996), p. 5).
2. Shoshana Felman and Dori Laub, *Testimony: Crisis of Witnessing in Literature, Psychoanalysis, and History* (New York: Routledge, 1992), p. xix.
3. I use the word 'Holocaust' to be understood. As Primo Levi and others have pointed out, it is philologically inaccurate in its description of the collective crime perpetrated by the National Socialists and their allies in Europe during the 1930s and 1940s, as it comes from the Greek adjective 'holocaustos' [completely burned] and loosely describes the sacrificial doctrine of the Torah. Alternative and more pertinent terms might include the Hebrew 'שואה' [shoah] meaning 'devastation' or 'catastrophe' and 'חורבן' [khurban], initially used to refer to the destruction of the Second Temple in 70.
4. Shoshana Felman, *The Juridical Unconscious. Trials and Traumas in the Twentieth Century* (Cambridge: Harvard University Press, 2002), p. 107. Orig. emphasis.
5. Ibid.
6. Ibid.

7. Steiner, 'A Terrible Exactness', 709.
8. The Frankfurt trial was officially called the 'Criminal Case against Mulka and Others'. Robert Karl Mulka was an 'SS-Hauptsturmführer'. As adjutant to the Auschwitz camp commandant Rudolf Höss between 1942 and 1943, he was the highest ranking of the defendants remaining when the trial began.
9. Peter Weiss, *Die Ermittlung. Oratorium in 11 Gesängen* (Frankfurt a.M.: Suhrkamp, 1965).
10. Felman, *The Juridical Unconscious*, p. 106.
11. German courts had regained their legal autonomy from the occupying allied forces in 1950. The last remaining allied constraints on the German courts to practice German law were lifted in May 1955 (Devin O. Pendas, *The Frankfurt Auschwitz Trial, 1963–1965. Genocide, History, and the Limits of the Law* (New York: Cambridge University Press, 2006), p. 14).
12. Fritz Bauer, 'Zu den Naziverbrecher-Prozessen', *Stimme der Gemeinde: Zum kirchlichen Leben, zur Politik, Wirtschaft und Kultur*, 15.18 (1963), 563–74 (563). After Frankfurt, two further trials focused on prosecuting those responsible for running the camps at Auschwitz-Birkenau. The last of these came to a close in 1968. As Windham puts it: 'Neither got much press' (Scott Windham, 'Peter Weiss's *Die Ermittlung*: Dramatic and Legal Representation and the Auschwitz Trial', in *Re-examining the Holocaust through Literature*, ed. by Aukje Kluge and Benn E. Williams (Newcastle upon Tyne: Cambridge Scholars Publishing, 2009), pp. 29–60 (p. 33)).
13. Pendas, *The Frankfurt Auschwitz Trial*, p. 6. This is in contrast to how the Nuremberg trials functioned, where the atrocities committed at Auschwitz were counted as 'war crimes'. Whilst such terminology perhaps resulted from failing to understand the nature of the camps, whose operation had little to do with war, it did allow for the effective prosecution of those responsible for atrocities committed there.
14. Sonja Boos, *Speaking the Unspeakable in Postwar Germany: Toward a Public Discourse on the Holocaust* (Ithaca: Cornell University Press, 2014), p. 182.
15. Hannah Arendt, 'Introduction', in Bernd Naumann, *Auschwitz. A Report on the Proceedings Against Robert Karl Mulka and Others Before the Court at Frankfurt*, trans. by Jean Steinberg (New York: Praeger, 1966), pp. xi–xxx (pp. xxi–xxii).
16. Pendas, *The Frankfurt Auschwitz Trial*, p. 14; Rebecca Wittmann, *Beyond Justice: The Auschwitz Trial* (Cambridge: Harvard University Press, 2005), p. 17; Boos, *Speaking the Unspeakable*, p. 182.
17. Gerhard Neubert and Heinrich Bischoff had their cases suspended for health reasons (Pendas, *The Frankfurt Auschwitz Trial*, p. 1).
18. Ernst Bloch, *Gesamtausgabe*, 16 vols (Frankfurt a.M.: Suhrkamp, 1959–1972), IX, p. 551.
19. Giorgio Agamben, *Remnants of Auschwitz: The Witness and the Archive*, trans. by Daniel Heller-Roazen (New York: Zone, 1999), p. 18.
20. Boos, *Speaking the Unspeakable*, p. 185.
21. By contrast, Boos sees the trial as marking 'the institution of a sovereign West German judicial system' (ibid., p. 167). Wittmann asserts that the trial was a way for 'the newly independent, democratic West German government to demonstrate that it was capable on its own of coping with Nazi crimes' (Wittmann, *Beyond Justice*, p. 25).
22. Jacques Derrida, 'Force of Law: The "Mystical Foundation of Authority"', in Jacques Derrida, *Acts of Religion*, ed. by Gil Anidjar (New York: Routledge, 2002), pp. 230–98 (p. 268).
23. Walter Benjamin, 'Critique of Violence', in Walter Benjamin, *Selected Writings (Volume 1: 1913–1926)*, ed. by Marcus Bullock and Michael W. Jennings (Cambridge: The Belknap Press of Harvard University Press, 1996), pp. 236–52 (p. 241).
24. Derrida, 'Force of Law', p. 276.
25. Benjamin, 'Critique of Violence', p. 242.
26. Derrida, 'Force of Law', p. 275.
27. Ibid., p. 269.
28. It is likely that Celan read the essay, as there were at least two copies in his personal library, including the following edition: Walter Benjamin, 'Kritik der Gewalt', in Walter Benjamin, *Zur Kritik der Gewalt und andere Aufsätze* (Frankfurt a.M.: Suhrkamp, 1965) pp. 29–65. Celan dates this edition 'August 1965', which is when the Frankfurt trial comes to a close. See also Paul Celan, *La bibliothèque philosophique. Die philosophische Bibliothek*, ed. by Alexandra Richter,

Patrik Alac, and Bertrand Badiou, with a preface by Jean-Pierre Lefebvre (Paris: Éditions de la rue d'Ulm, 2004), p. 303.
29. Benjamin, 'Critique of Violence', p. 239.
30. Ibid., p. 249.
31. Benjamin provides two instances of divine justice: the 'true war' and the crowd's spontaneous judgment. In both cases, the result of violence is evident but the means leading to this result are beyond human comprehension (ibid., p. 252). Neither example is very convincing. The first evokes the expansionist war that will be waged by National Socialist Germany. The second evokes the spontaneous acts of public violence that marked National Socialism's beginnings. They might instead be said to constitute acts of mythic violence, whose mythic nature is obscured to the onlooker.
32. Derrida, 'Force of Law', p. 298.
33. Ibid.
34. Ibid.
35. Bernd Naumann, *Auschwitz. A Report on the Proceedings Against Robert Karl Mulka and Others Before the Court at Frankfurt*, trans. by Jean Steinberg, with an Introduction by Hannah Arendt (New York: Praeger, 1966), p. 4.
36. Hermann Langbein, *People in Auschwitz*, trans. by Harry Zohn (Chapel Hill: The University of North Carolina Press in association with The United States Holocaust Memorial Museum, 2004), p. 286.
37. Derrida, 'Force of Law', p. 244.
38. Peter Schneck, *Rhetoric and Evidence: Legal Conflict and Literary Representation in U.S. American Culture* (Berlin: De Gruyter, 2011), p. 11.
39. Hence Pascal's explanation that any attempt to trace the 'mystical foundation' to its founding principle 'annihilates' that founding principle (Derrida, 'Force of Law', p. 239).
40. Debórah Dwork and Robert Jan van Pelt, *Auschwitz: 1270 to the Present* (New Haven: Yale University Press, 1996), pp. 104 and 174.
41. Derrida, 'Force of Law', p. 257.
42. 'Wer das augenfällige Übel nicht bekämpft, verliert den Schutz des Unsichtbaren' (Celan, *Mikrolithen*, p. 48). Toward the end of his life, Celan wrote: 'Tu as guerroyé au lieu de combattre' [You skirmished instead of fighting], which perhaps indicates that the indirect means used by the poet to combat injustice were in some way inadequate (ibid., p. 57).
43. 'Wer nach Auschwitz mystifiziert, eskamotiert alles menschliche Leid' (ibid., p. 48).
44. Unpublished diary entry for Monday, 3 May 1965. Preserved at the German Literature Archive, Marbach a. N., Manuscript Department, Tagebuch 13 (26 April 1965–8 May 1965), D 90.1.3300, F 2390, 41. Three thousand corresponds to the number of those thought to have served in Auschwitz-Birkenau at the time.
45. Several newspaper articles relating to the conclusion of the Frankfurt trial were retained by Celan, and are preserved at the 'Unité de recherché Paul Celan', 'École normale supérieure', Paris. These include all relevant articles in the *Frankfurter Allgemeine Zeitung* (20 August 1965) and *Die Welt* (20 August; 25 August; 30 August 1965). Included among these is an article from *Die Welt*, dated 20 August, in which each defendant is profiled (p. 16). Stefan Baretzki — responsible for selecting Jews for the gas chambers on the ramp — is presented as an ethnic German native of Czernowitz. Born in 1919, he was almost an exact contemporary of Celan. Hannah Arendt would note that Baretzki's 'chief claim to notoriety in the camp was his ability to kill inmates with one blow of the hand' (Arendt, 'Introduction', p. xvi. For a brief biography see *Der Frankfurter Auschwitz-Prozess (1963–1965). Kommentierte Quellenedition*, ed. by Raphael Gross and Werner Renz, 2 vols (Frankfurt a.M.: Campus, 2013), II, p. 867). Baretzki committed suicide in June 1988.
46. Preserved at the 'Unité de recherché Paul Celan'.
47. Celan and Celan-Lestrange, *Correspondance*, I, p. 289. For further contemporary evaluations of the outcome of the trial see ibid., II, pp. 242–43.
48. Celan, *Die Gedichte*, p. 206.
49. Barbara Wiedemann, 'Kommentar', in Paul Celan, *Die Gedichte. Kommentierte Gesamtausgabe in*

einem Band, ed. by Barbara Wiedemann (Frankfurt a.M.: Suhrkamp, 2005), pp. 559–997 (pp. 743–44).

50. 'Ein Beinbruch des Kommandanten Höss? Die Verteidigung bezweifelt die Glaubwürdigkeit eines Zeugen', *Frankfurter Allgemeine Zeitung* (14 November 1964), 17–18 (p. 17). Räsänen proposes two other sources for Celan's poem: Stefan George's poem 'Entrückung', put to music in the fourth movement of Arnold Schoenberg's 'String Quartet No. 2', concludes with the line: 'Ich bin ein dröhnen nur der heiligen stimme' [I am but a droning of the holy voice]; Mandel'shtam's free verse poem 'Нашедший Подкову' [The Horseshoe Finder] includes the lines: 'Ни одно слово не лучше другого, / Земля гудит метафорой', which Celan translates as: 'Kein Wort ist besser als das andre, / die Erde dröhnt von Metaphern' [No word is better than the other, / the earth rumbles with metaphors] (Pajari Räsänen, *Counter-Figures. An Essay on Antimetaphoric Resistance: Paul Celan's Poetry and Poetics at the Limits of Figurality* (Helsinki: Dept. of Comparative Literature, University of Helsinki, 2007), p. 271).
51. *The Holy Bible*, p. 910, John 1. 14.
52. 'Die Aufklärer, die alles — genauer: das von ihnen als 'alles' bezeichnete — um sie her aufhellen, um umso besser im Dunkel bleiben zu können' (Celan, *Mikrolithen*, p. 51).
53. As Shmueli put it: 'for Celan, the Shoah never ended' (Ilana Shmueli, 'Paul Celans Judentum und Israel', in *Unverloren. Trotz Allem: Paul Celan-Symposion Wien 2000*, ed. by Hubert Gaisbauer, Bernhard Hain, and Erika Schuster (Vienna: Mandelbaum, 2000), pp. 288–303 (p. 299)). See also Felman and Laub for whom the historic trauma of the Second World War 'is essentially *not over*' and whose consequences 'are still actively *evolving*' (Felman and Laub, *Testimony*, p. xiv).
54. Felman, *The Juridical Unconscious*, p. 107.
55. For an early iteration of the play, called 'Frankfurt Extracts', see Peter Weiss, 'Frankfurter Auszüge', *Kursbuch*, 1 (1965), 152–88.
56. Joachim Kaiser, 'Plädoyer gegen das Theater-Auschwitz', *Süddeutsche Zeitung* (4–5 September 1965), 79–80 (80). Also quoted in Hermann Naber, 'Die "Ermittlung" in der Presse', *Die Zeit* (29 October 1965), 22 (22).
57. For the play's earliest translation into French see Peter Weiss, *L'instruction: oratorio en onze chants*, trans. by Jean Baudrillard (Paris: Seuil, 1966). In the play's first performance in France, at the Théâtre de la Commune at Aubervilliers — where it ran from March to May 1966 — a translation by André Gisselbrecht was used: Peter Weiss, ' "L'Instruction" (extraits)', trans. by André Gisselbrecht, *La Nouvelle Critique*, 172 (February 1966), 47–77. See also André Gisselbrecht, 'Peter Weiss: "L'Instruction" ', *La Nouvelle Critique*, 172 (February 1966), 42–46; André Gisselbrecht, 'Rencontre avec le théâtre documentaire — *L'Instruction* à Aubervilliers et ses suites', in *Peter Weiss à Paris. Actes du colloque international. Paris, du 16 au 19 janvier 1997*, ed. by Günther Schütz (Paris: Kime, 1998), pp. 77–85; and Nicole Zand, 'La création en France de «l'Instruction» de Peter Weiss. Auschwitz aujourd'hui', *Le Monde* (1 April 1966), 14.
58. Peter Weiss, *Die Ermittlung. Oratorium in 11 Gesängen*, with a DVD of the television broadcast (Frankfurt a.M.: Suhrkamp, 2008).
59. These newspaper cuttings, preserved at the 'Unité de recherche Paul Celan', include: Ernst Cramer, 'Peter Weiss und sein Auschwitz-Oratorium', *Die Welt* (6 November 1965), vii; Walter Jens, 'Die 'Ermittlung' in Westberlin', *Die Zeit* (29 October 1965), 20; Walter Jens, Dieter E. Zimmer, Hellmuth Karasek and Gerhard Schoenberner, 'Auschwitz auf der Bühne. Drei Fragen an fünf Intendanten', *Die Zeit* (29 October 1965), 19–20; Hellmuth Karasek, 'Die 'Ermittlung' in Stuttgart', *Die Zeit* (29 October 1965), 21; Hermann Naber, 'Die "Ermittlung" in der Presse', *Die Zeit* (29 October 1965), 22; Gerhard Schoenberner, 'Die 'Ermittlung' in München', *Die Zeit* (29 October 1965), 21; Peter Weiss, 'Peter Weiss erklärt', *Frankfurter Allgemeine Zeitung* (27 October 1965), 24; Dieter E. Zimmer, 'Die Lesung in der Volkskammer der DDR', *Die Zeit* (29 October 1965), 21.
60. Benjamin, 'Critique of Violence', p. 243.
61. Susan Sontag, 'Reflections on *The Deputy*', in *The Storm over the Deputy*, ed. by Eric Bentley (New York: Grove, 1964), pp. 117–23 (p. 118).
62. Ibid.
63. Weiss, *Die Ermittlung* (1965), p. 7.

64. Ibid. A reference to Rolf Hochhuth's play *The Deputy*, which premiered in 1963, and in which the concentration camp is staged in the fifth and final act (Rolf Hochhuth, *Der Stellvertreter. Ein christliches Trauerspiel*, with essays by Sabina Lietzmann, Karl Jaspers, Walter Muschg, Erwin Piscator, Golo Mann (Reinbek b. Hamburg: Rowohlt, 1976)).
65. Weiss, *Die Ermittlung*, p. 8.
66. Schoenberner, 'Die 'Ermittlung' in München', 21.
67. Martin Walser, 'Unser Auschwitz', *Kursbuch*, 1 (1965), 189–200 (190). This repeats and confirms Benjamin's observation from the early 1920s that 'the secret admiration of the public' is often aroused by the violence deployed by the 'great' criminals, without regard for the result of that violence (Benjamin, 'Critique of Violence', p. 239).
68. Weiss, *Die Ermittlung*, p. 8.
69. Peter Weiss, 'Notizen zum dokumentarischen Theater', in Peter Weiss, *Rapporte 2* (Frankfurt a.M.: Suhrkamp, 1971), pp. 91–104 (pp. 91–92). See also Peter Weiss, 'The Material and the Models. Notes Towards a Definition of Documentary Theater', *Theater Quarterly*, 1 (1971), 41–45.
70. See, for instance, the anonymous review of the performance at Aubervilliers: '*The Investigation* does not contain a single phrase that was not actually uttered at the trial in Frankfurt, where the author saw the murderers of Auschwitz brought to justice last year' ('"L'Instruction", de Peter Weiss', *Le Monde* (3–4 April 1966), 16).
71. See Robert Cohen, '1964: On March 13, in the middle of rehearsals for the premiere of *Marat/Sade*, Peter Weiss attends the Frankfurt Auschwitz trial', in *Yale Companion to Jewish Writing and Thought in German Culture 1096–1996*, ed. by Sander L. Gilman and Jack Zipes (New Haven: Yale University Press, 1997), pp. 722–28.
72. The articles were published in book form in German and in English translation (Bernd Naumann, *Auschwitz. Bericht über die Strafsache gegen Mulka und andere vor dem Schwurgericht Frankfurt* (Frankfurt a.M.: Athenäum, 1965); Bernd Naumann, *Auschwitz. A Report on the Proceedings Against Robert Karl Mulka and Others Before the Court at Frankfurt*, trans. by Jean Steinberg, with an Introduction by Hannah Arendt (New York: Praeger, 1966)). Heinrichsbauer first brought Weiss's use of Naumann's text to public attention (Jürgen Heinrichsbauer, 'In Sachen Weiss und andere. Oder: Missbrauch mit den Opfern des Grauens', *Der Arbeitgeber. Zeitschrift der Bundesvereinigung der Deutschen Arbeitgeberverbände*, 17.23/24 (1965), 735–38). Perry juxtaposes Naumann's reports and Weiss's play to identify Weiss's concentration of the material, and the amendment of vocabulary, grammar, and syntax (R. C. Perry, 'Historical Authenticity and Dramatic Form: Hochhuth's *Der Stellvertreter* and Weiss's *Die Ermittlung*', *Modern Language Review*, 64 (1969), 828–39).
73. Weiss, *Die Ermittlung*, p. 7.
74. Ibid., pp. 7–8.
75. Oliver Clausen, 'Weiss/Propagandist and Weiss/Playwright', *New York Times Magazine* (2 October 1966), 28–29, 124, 126, 128, 130–34 (134).
76. For problems relating to translation at the trial, see Langbein, *People in Auschwitz*, pp. 16–17.
77. Boos, *Speaking the Unspeakable*, pp. 176–77.
78. Agamben, *Remnants of Auschwitz*, p. 17.
79. Ibid. Agamben takes Primo Levi as exemplary of the 'superstes': 'his testimony has nothing to do with the acquisition of facts for a trial (he is not neutral enough for this, he is not a *testis*)' (ibid.).
80. Felman and Laub, *Testimony*, p. 6.
81. Naumann, *Auschwitz. A Report*, p. 416.
82. Weiss draws attention to the fragility of testimonial evidence, highlighting the moments at which a witness is unable to recollect or is uncertain about a detail: 'When I look at their faces / I find it hard to tell / whether I recognize them or not / But this man / looks familiar to me' (Weiss, *Die Ermittlung*, p. 17). Weiss also draws attention to one of the defense's tactics, which questioned the truth or accuracy of witness statements: 'What the witness is saying / is a mystery to me / I also don't understand / why the witness says / 5 or 6 / If he had said 5 / or if he had said 6 / then it would have been clear' (ibid., p. 22). As Boos puts it: 'Ultimately, there is only

testimony, which, independent of material evidence, accomplishes little' (Boos, *Speaking the Unspeakable*, p. 179).
83. Bednarek was found guilty of fourteen cases of murder and sentenced to life imprisonment. He was released in 1975 and died in 2001. For further details see Ernst Klee, *Auschwitz. Täter, Gehilfen, Opfer und was aus ihnen wurde. Ein Personenlexikon* (Frankfurt a.M.: Fischer, 2013), p. 39 and *Der Frankfurter Auschwitz-Prozess*, ed. by Gross and Renz, I, pp. 132 and 513–19.
84. Weiss, *Die Ermittlung*, p. 154.
85. Ibid., p. 157.
86. 'oratorio, *n.*', *OED Online*, March 2017, Oxford University Press, available at <http://www.oed.com/view/Entry/132208?redirectedFrom=oratorio>, [accessed 15 March 2017].
87. Katja Garloff, 'Peter Weiss's Entry into the German Public Sphere: On Diaspora, Language, and the Uses of Distance', *Colloquia Germanica*, 30.1 (1997), 47–70 (62). This also applies to the loud approbation voiced by the defendants that concludes the play (Weiss, *Die Ermittlung*, p. 210).
88. Luigi Nono, 'Musiche di scena per 'Die Ermittlung'' (1965) in Luigi Nono, *Complete Works for Solo Tape*, 2 CDs (Cologno Monzese: Stradivarius, 2006), CD 1, track 2.
89. See: Erika Salloch, 'The *Divina Commedia* as Model and Anti-Model for *The Investigation*', *Modern Drama*, 14.1 (1971), 1–12; Robert Cohen, *Understanding Peter Weiss* (Columbia: University of South Carolina Press, 1993), pp. 76–97; Garloff, 'Peter Weiss's Entry into the German Public Sphere', 59–60; Windham, 'Peter Weiss's *Die Ermittlung*', pp. 48–52.
90. Walser is highly critical of the tendency of reporters to draw on Dantean imagery to describe the conditions of the camps. 'To compare Auschwitz with Dante's inferno amounts almost to insolence. [...] The people in Auschwitz would have been stumped in a most horrific fashion, had they been obliged to recite for Dante, strolling by, the sins on account of which they were being tortured. With this torture to be followed only by extermination' (Walser, 'Unser Auschwitz', 190–91).
91. See Joseph Borkin, *The Crime and Punishment of I. G. Farben* (New York: The Free Press, 1978).
92. Robert Cohen, 'The Political Aesthetics of Holocaust Literature: Peter Weiss's 'The Investigation' and Its Critics', *History and Memory*, 10.2 (1998), 43–67 (61).
93. Sidra DeKoven Ezrahi, *By Words Alone: The Holocaust in Literature* (Chicago: University of Chicago Press, 1980), p. 40. See also Clausen, 'Weiss/Propagandist and Weiss/Playwright', 133. Bergman, who took over direction of the oratorio from a sick colleague, later said: 'Personally I deeply disliked the play from the beginning. I thought it was a form of pornography of violence [våldspornografi]. While working on it I revised my opinion. I understood that there was an almost insatiable will to truth in Peter Weiss and an uncompromising strength of character, a moral attitude' (Birgitta Steene, *Ingmar Bergman: A Reference Guide* (Amsterdam: Amsterdam University Press, 2005), p. 466).
94. Weiss, *Die Ermittlung*, p. 89.
95. Ian Hilton, *Peter Weiss: A Search for Affinities* (London: Oswald Wolff, 1970), p. 47.
96. Clausen, 'Weiss/Propagandist and Weiss/Playwright', 134.
97. Weiss's Marxist interpretation of Auschwitz, the Holocaust, and National Socialism has been the object of much criticism. Rosenfeld notes that 'far from exposing a profit motive for Auschwitz, the evidence all points the other way: to gratuitous waste and needless elimination of human resources' (Alvin H. Rosenfeld, *A Double Dying: Reflections on Holocaust Literature* (Bloomington: Indiana University Press, 1980), p. 157). See also Huyssen: 'Weiss never attempts to deal with the history and specificity of anti-Semitism in Germany. By blaming Krupp and IG Farben, Weiss subsumes the death of six million Jews to a universal Marxist critique of capitalism. Here Weiss comes dangerously close to depriving the victims of their personal and collective history and identity as Jews, and he just about instrumentalizes Auschwitz in order to advance a questionable interpretation of fascism as a necessary stage of capitalism' (Andreas Huyssen, *After the Great Divide: Modernism, Mass Culture, Postmodernism* (Bloomington: Indiana University Press, 1986), p. 111).
98. Lawrence L. Langer, *Admitting the Holocaust. Collected Essays* (New York: Oxford University Press, 1995), p. 98.
99. Cohen, 'The Political Aesthetics of Holocaust Literature', 45.

100. James E. Young, *Writing and Rewriting the Holocaust. Narrative and the Consequences of Interpretation* (Bloomington: Indiana University Press, 1988), p. 72.
101. Derrida, 'Force of Law', p. 296.
102. Clausen, 'Weiss/Propagandist and Weiss/Playwright', 132.
103. Ezrahi, *By Words Alone*, p. 40.
104. Derrida, 'Force of Law', p. 296.
105. Ibid.
106. The identification of the trial at Frankfurt and of Weiss's play as issues of pressing concern to Celan in the mid-1960s can help to identify the original context and emotional vectorization of a number of posthumously published aphorisms. For instance: 'im Feuille- und Meuchelton geschrieben' [written in feuille-tone and murderous tone] appears to describe the tenor of *The Investigation*, which is journalistic in its matter and murderous in its content; 'Er sagte 'j'adoube' und war überzeugt, 'j'accuse' geschrieben zu haben' [He said 'j'adoube' and was convinced he had said 'j'accuse'] might function as a specific reference to Weiss, where 'j'adoube' is what a chess player says when he or she wants to adjust a piece on its square without being required to move it; 'Die Krawattengesprächigen' [the talkative neckties] may describe the actors of the play, who in most productions wore dark suits and ties. For a comparison of the play with poetry see: 'Nicht das Versmässige, sondern das Unmässige, wo das Lyrische und das Tragische sich treffen oder einander überschneiden, macht das Gedicht zum Gedicht' [What makes a poem a poem is not the accommodation of verse, but what cannot be accommodated, where the lyrical and the tragic meet or cut across each other] (Celan, *Mikrolithen*, p. 53).
107. Weiss, 'Peter Weiss erklärt', 24.
108. Weiss, *Die Ermittlung*, pp. 7–8.
109. Ezrahi, *By Words Alone*, pp. 37–38.
110. Young, *Writing and Rewriting the Holocaust*, p. 70.
111. Peter Weiss, *The Investigation*, trans. by Jon Swan and Ulu Grosbard (New York: Atheneum, 1966), n. p.
112. This instance might be compared to Celan's evocation of the 'Königszäsur' [king-caesura] in the late poem 'Ich trink Wein' [I drink wine] (Celan, *Die Gedichte*, p. 363). Besides evoking Hölderlin's translations of Pindar, Fioretos notes that 'when drastically initialized' 'Königszäsur' becomes '*KZ*, the abbreviation for "concentration camp" — itself a concentrated name for that which remains incomparable' (Aris Fioretos, 'Preface', in *Word Traces. Readings of Paul Celan*, ed. by Aris Fioretos (Baltimore: The Johns Hopkins University Press, 1994), pp. ix–xxii (p. x)).
113. Celan, *Gesammelte Werke in sieben Bänden*, III, p. 186.
114. Celan and Celan-Lestrange, *Correspondance*, II, p. 558.
115. Celan, *Die Gedichte*, p. 230.
116. Oelmann, *Deutsche poetologische Lyrik nach 1945*, pp. 394–95.
117. Kluge, *Etymologisches Wörterbuch*, p. 305.
118. Abraham Sutzkever, 'Abraham Sutzkever on Poetry and Partisan Life', Youtube / The Yiddish Book Center, Jewish Public Library, Montreal, 24 May 1959, available at <https://www.youtube.com/watch?v=kofcyfycOFE>, [accessed 9 January 2015].
119. J. Feld, 'Dort wo die Zeder', in *Jüdisches Liederbuch* (Berlin: Jüdischer Verlag, 1930), pp. 110–11. See also Wiedemann, 'Kommentar', p. 589. Celan evokes 'the song of the cedar' in the poem 'Schwarze Flocken' [Black Flakes], which probably dates from 1944 (Celan, *Die Gedichte*, p. 19).
120. Ulrich Konietzny, ' "All deine Siegel erbrochen?" Chiffren oder Baumläufer im Spätwerk Paul Celans', *Celan-Jahrbuch*, 2 (1988), 107–20 (110).
121. *The Holy Bible*, p. 140, Numbers 19. 6.
122. *The Holy Bible*, p. 230, Judges 9. 15.
123. Luther, *Lutherbibel*, p. 189.
124. Derrida, 'Force of Law', p. 259.
125. See ibid., p. 288.
126. Benjamin, 'Critique of Violence', p. 252.
127. 'Tücke' appears in plural form in an unpublished aphorism composed at around the same time: 'Die Tücken — nicht: die Zacken — solcher Kronen' [The pitfalls — no: the jagged edges — of

such crowns] (Celan, *Mikrolithen*, p. 52). See also the short prose piece 'Eine Lanze' [A Lance] written in collaboration with Edgar Jené in Vienna in 1948, where 'Tücke' describes Surrealism: 'Voller Tücke ists und hat die Gabe sich zu verwandeln' [It is full of perfidy and knows how to change its form] (Paul Celan, *Prosa I. Zu Lebzeiten publizierte Prosa und Reden. Historisch-kritische Ausgabe*, ed. by Axel Gellhaus, Andreas Lohr, Heino Schmull and Rolf Bücher, vol. 15 of *Werke. Historisch-kritische Ausgabe. I. Abteilung: Lyrik und Prosa* (Frankfurt a.M.: Suhrkamp, 2014), p. 87).
128. Matthias Lexer, *Matthias Lexers Mittelhochdeutsches Taschenwörterbuch* (Stuttgart: S. Hirzel Verlag, 1986), p. 233.
129. The 'Germania Judaica, Cologne Library for the History of German Judaism' [Germania Judaica, Kölner Bibliothek für die Geschichte des deutschen Judentums] was a library founded in Cologne in 1959 by, among others, Heinrich Böll, Wilhelm Unger, and Paul Schallück. Its purpose was to teach the German public about the history and culture of German-speaking Judaism in a postwar culture still marked by anti-Semitism. Schallück was president of the Germania Judaica until 1962. See Alwin Müller-Jerina, *Germania Judaica, Kölner Bibliothek zur Geschichte des Deutschen Judentums. Die Entwicklung und Bedeutung einer wissenschaftlichen Spezialbibliothek* (Cologne: Greven, 1986).
130. Paul Celan, *Briefwechsel mit den rheinischen Freunden. Heinrich Böll, Paul Schallück und Rolf Schroers. Mit einzelnen Briefen von Gisele Celan-Lestrange, Ilse Schallück und Ilse Schroers*, ed. by Barbara Wiedemann (Berlin: Suhrkamp, 2011), pp. 337 and 455. See also Alan Frank Keele, *Paul Schallück and the Post-War German Don Quixote. A Case-History Prolegomenon to the Literature of the Federal Republic* (Bern: Herbert Lang, 1976), pp. 1–2.
131. Won by Ludwig Erhard's conservative CDU/CSU coalition on 19 September 1965.
132. Celan, *Briefwechsel mit den rheinischen Freunden*, pp. 33–39.
133. Cohen notes that 'most of Weiss's works after *Marat-Sade* [...] owe their structural and aesthetic concepts to the *Divine Comedy*' (Cohen, 'The Political Aesthetics of Holocaust Literature', 47). See also Hamida Bosmajian, *Metaphors of Evil: Contemporary German Literature and the Shadow of Nazism* (Iowa City: University of Iowa Press, 1979), pp. 166–82 and Arrigo V. Subiotto, 'Dante and the Holocaust: The Cases of Primo Levi and Peter Weiss', *New Comparison*, 11 (1991), 70–89.
134. Paul Gray, 'A Living World. An Interview with Peter Weiss', *Tulane Drama Review*, 11.1 (1966), 106–14 (108). Weiss singles out the pipe or tube as particularly evocative of the Holocaust: 'There are sculptures which are just a line of heavy tubes standing in a room, without any meaning. Part of Auschwitz is in that for me — a very heavy thing has happened which you say you can't understand' (ibid., pp. 108–10).
135. Ibid., p. 110.
136. Hilton notes that the number eleven is also incorporated into *Lusitanischer Popanz*, *Mockinpott*, and *Viet Nam Diskurs* (Hilton, *Peter Weiss*, p. 49).
137. Paul Celan, *Fadensonnen. Vorstufen — Textgenese — Endfassung*, ed. by Heino Schmull, Markus Heilmann, and Christiane Wittkop (Frankfurt a.M.: Suhrkamp, 2000), p. 46.
138. *The Holy Bible*, p. 49, Exodus 3. 8.
139. Celan, *Die Gedichte*, pp. 40–41.
140. For a more recent elaboration of the link between the 'Welle' [wave] and National Socialism see Anselm Kiefer, *Die Welle (The Wave)*, 1990, lead, clothes, steel wire, and ash on canvas, Seattle Art Museum, Seattle, WA.
141. Max Horkheimer and Theodor W. Adorno, *Dialectic of Enlightenment: Philosophical Fragments*, trans. by Edmund Jephcott, ed. by Gunzelin Schmid Noerr (Stanford: Stanford University Press, 2002), p. 140.
142. Ibid.
143. Ibid., pp. 140–41.
144. Martin Gilbert, *The Holocaust: A History of the Jews of Europe During the Second World War* (New York: Holt, Rinehart, and Winston, 1985), p. 365.
145. Weiss, *Die Ermittlung*, p. 149.
146. Walser, 'Unser Auschwitz', 191.
147. Ibid.

148. Theodor W. Adorno, *The Jargon of Authenticity*, trans. by Knut Tarnowski and Frederic Will (Evanston: Northwestern University Press, 1973). First published as *Jargon der Eigentlichkeit: zur deutschen Ideologie* (Frankfurt a.M.: Suhrkamp, 1964).
149. Adorno, *The Jargon of Authenticity*, p. 48.
150. Oelmann, *Deutsche poetologische Lyrik nach 1945*, p. 394.
151. Kluge, *Etymologisches Wörterbuch*, p. 122.
152. Paul Celan, *Paul Celan: Poems. A Bilingual Edition*, trans. by Michael Hamburger (New York: Persea, 1980), p. 119. 'The Straightening' [*Engführung*] was composed between 21 July 1957 and 3 November 1958.
153. Celan, *Gesammelte Werke in sieben Bänden*, III, p. 202.
154. Peter Weiss, *Meine Ortschaft* (Rostock: Volkstheater, 1965). It is unclear to what degree this claim reflects Weiss's partly Jewish origins — his father was born Jewish but became an Evangelical Protestant — and his Marxist convictions.
155. Ibid., p. 20.
156. Paul Celan, 'Briefe an Alfred Margul-Sperber', *Neue Literatur: Zeitschrift des Schriftstellerverbandes der Sozialistischen Republik Rumänien*, 26.7 (1975), 50–63 (57–58).
157. Celan, *Briefwechsel mit den rheinischen Freunden*, p. 323.
158. Jonathan Boyarin and Daniel Boyarin, 'Self-Exposure as Theory: The Double Mark of the Male Jew', *Rhetorics of Self-Making*, ed. by Debbora Battaglia (Berkeley: University of California Press, 1995), pp. 16–42 (pp. 28–29).
159. Horkheimer and Adorno argue that anti-Semitism is 'the reverse of genuine mimesis and has deep affinities to the repressed' (Horkheimer and Adorno, *Dialectic of Enlightenment*, p. 154).
160. Jean-Paul Sartre, *Réflexions sur la question juive* (Paris: Morihien, 1946), p. 27.
161. Vikki Bell, *Feminist Imagination: Genealogies in Feminist Theory* (London: Sage, 1999), p. 97.
162. Sartre, *Réflexions sur la question juive*, p. 15.
163. Lev Shestov, *Potestas Clavium*, trans. by Bernard Martin (Athens: Ohio University Press, 1968), p. 65. Celan possessed two editions of Boris de Schloezer's translation of *Potestas Clavium* into French, one from 1928, the other from 1967. Both contain numerous annotations in Celan's hand. For reproductions of these annotations see Celan, *La bibliothèque philosophique. Die philosophische Bibliothek*, pp. 607–19 and 619–24.
164. Felstiner implicitly identifies a parallel between Celan and Glatstein in their shared conviction that the traditional Jewish covenant with God is defunct (Felstiner, *Paul Celan: Poet, Survivor, Jew*, p. 151).
165. Jacob Glatstein, *I Keep Recalling. The Holocaust Poems of Jacob Glatstein*, trans. by Barnett Zumoff, with an Introduction by Emanuel S. Goldsmith (Brooklyn: Ktav, 1993), p. 220.
166. Ibid., pp. 212–13.
167. Ibid., pp. 244–45.
168. An unusual and ostentatious gesture because, as Calvin points out in his commentaries, not only did the king usually dine alone, but the city was then under siege (Jean Calvin, *Calvin's Old Testament Commentaries: The Rutherford House Translation*, ed. by D. F. Wright, D. F. Kelly, and N. M. de S. Cameron, 20 vols (Grand Rapids: Eerdmans, 1993–), XX, pp. 204 and 206).
169. *The Holy Bible*, p. 766, Daniel 5. 5.
170. תורה נביאים וכתובים = *Biblia Hebraica Stuttgartensia*, quae antea cooperantibus A. Alt, O. Eissfeldt, P. Kahle ediderat, R. Kittel; adjuvantibus H. Bardtke, W. Baumgartner, P. A. H. de Boer, O. Eissfeldt, J. Fichtner, G. Gerleman, J. Hempel, F. Horst, A. Jepsen, F. Maass, R. Meyer, G. Quell, Th. H. Robinson, D. W. Thomas; cooperantibus H. P. Rüger et J. Ziegler; ediderunt K. Elliger et W. Rudolph. Textum Masoreticum curavit H. P. Rüger; masoram elaboravit G. E. Weil. Editio quinta emendata opera A. Schenker (Stuttgart: Deutsche Bibelgesellschaft, 1997), p. 1395, Daniel 5. 26–28; *The Holy Bible*, p. 767.
171. Celan, *Fadensonnen. Vorstufen — Textgenese — Endfassung*, p. 46.
172. Glatstein, *I Keep Recalling*, pp. 4–5.
173. Cynthia Ozick, 'A Liberal's Auschwitz', in *The Pushcart Prize. Best of the Small Presses*, ed. by Bill Henderson (Yonkers: Pushcart Book Press, 1976), pp. 149–53 (p. 152).
174. Derrida, 'Force of Law', p. 294.

175. Benjamin, 'Critique of Violence', p. 252.
176. Derrida, 'Force of Law', p. 292.
177. Benjamin, 'Critique of Violence', p. 252.
178. Ibid., p. 250.
179. Charles R. Bambach, *Thinking the Poetic Measure of Justice: Hölderlin, Heidegger, Celan* (Albany: State University of New York Press, 2013), p. 180.
180. Windham, 'Peter Weiss's *Die Ermittlung*', p. 49. See also Jens, 'Die 'Ermittlung' in Westberlin', 20, and Schoenberner, 'Die 'Ermittlung' in München', 21.
181. Derrida, 'Force of Law', p. 255.
182. Ibid.
183. Ibid.
184. Ibid., p. 251.
185. Ibid.
186. Ibid.
187. Ibid., p. 252.
188. Ibid.
189. Paul Celan, 'Eingedunkelt', in Samuel Beckett, Karl Krolow, Wolfgang Koeppen, Hans Erich Nossack, Peter Weiss, Uwe Johnson, Wolfgang Hildesheimer, Nelly Sachs, Paul Celan, and Martin Walser, *Aus aufgegebenen Werken* (Frankfurt a.M.: Suhrkamp, 1968), pp. 149–61.
190. *The Holy Bible*, p. 766, Daniel 5. 5.
191. In Daniel, wise men are required to interpret what they cannot see. Nebuchadnezzar threatens to kill his wise men because they are unable either to recount the dream he has had and is unable to recall, or to interpret the dream (ibid., pp. 761–62, Daniel 2. 1–16).
192. *Biblia Hebraica Stuttgartensia*, p. 1393, Daniel 5. 2.
193. Ibid. 5. 5.
194. Ibid. 5. 1.
195. Ibid. 5. 5.
196. Ibid. 5. 11.
197. *Biblia Hebraica Stuttgartensia*, p. 1395, Daniel 5. 27.
198. *The Holy Bible*, p. 113, Leviticus 24. 19–20. See also Deuteronomy 19. 18–21.
199. Luther, *Lutherbibel*, p. 618, Daniel 5. 12.
200. Derrida, 'Force of Law', p. 246.
201. Celan, *Eingedunkelt*, p. 76.
202. *The Holy Bible*, p. 766, Daniel 5. 7.
203. Ibid. 5. 17.
204. Ibid. 5. 23.
205. The opening image of being forced down from the high wire comes from Celan's reading of Conrad's *Secret Agent*, as discussed in chapter one.
206. 'der dreimal hochbeschenkte' (Celan, *Eingedunkelt*, p. 65).
207. 'der Ungebändigte, / dreimal überschüttet / mit Gruss und Lebwohl' (ibid., p. 66).
208. 'Der Ungebändigte, drei- / mal überschattet mit Gaben' (ibid.).
209. Conrad, *Der Geheimagent*, p. 56.
210. Conrad, *The Secret Agent*, p. 48.
211. Celan, *Eingedunkelt*, p. 84.
212. *The Holy Bible*, p. 766, Daniel 5. 6.
213. *Biblia Hebraica Stuttgartensia*, p. 1393.
214. Ibid., Daniel 5. 12.
215. Badiou, 'D'une main — et d'une autre main —', p. 16.
216. Menasseh ben Israel, *De termino vitæ: libri tres. Quibus veterum rabbinorum, ac recentium doctorum, de hac controversia sententia explicatur* (Amstelodami: Typis & sumptibus authoris, 1639), p. 160.
217. See Fig. 3.2.
218. See Menasseh ben Israel, *La pierre glorieuse de Nabuchodonosor, ou, la fin de l'histoire au XVIIe siècle*, ed. by M. Hadas-Lebel and H. Méchoulan, trans. by H. Knafou, illustrations by Rembrandt (Paris: J. Vrin, 2007).

219. Celan, *Fathomsuns and Benighted*, p. 261.
220. 'Ziffer' [cipher] is also related to the Arabic 'مصفر' [musfir] meaning 'empty'. As we see in Rembrandt's painting, the disembodied hand of God is empty even as it writes.
221. William Shakespeare, *Shakespeare's History of Pericles, Prince of Tyre*, ed. by William J. Rolfe (New York: Harper, 1883), V.1, p. 100.
222. *Die Bibel: nach der Übersetzung Martin Luthers: mit Wortkonkordanz* (Stuttgart: Deutsche Bibelgesellschaft, 1987), p. 711, Isaiah 59. 13–14.
223. Luther, *Lutherbibel*, p. 433, Psalms 90. 12.
224. Celan, *Eingedunkelt*, p. 41.
225. Luther, *Lutherbibel*, p. 617.
226. Celan, *Eingedunkelt*, p. 47. 'Ausleuchten' can mean to light up or illuminate something, but in the theater is to light up with floodlights.
227. *Biblia Hebraica Stuttgartensia*, p. 1393, Daniel 5. 2.
228. Ibid., Daniel 5. 5.
229. 'den Umhergeworfenen, den Fahrenden, ~~oft Bestohlenen~~' (Celan, *Eingedunkelt*, p. 125). Composed on 9 and 10 April 1966.
230. *Grosse Konkordanz zur Lutherbibel* (Stuttgart: Calwer, 2001), pp. 521–22.
231. 'siedend zischt es aus unsern Fäusten: / eurer kleinen Träume schwüler / Tumult...' [seething it sizzes out of our fists: / your little dreams of sensuous / tumult...] (Celan, *Die Gedichte*, p. 384).
232. Homer, *Die Odyssee*, p. 118.
233. Conrad, *The Secret Agent*, p. 48; Conrad, *Der Geheimagent*, p. 56. See Fig. 3.3.
234. Zand, 'La création en France de «l'Instruction» de Peter Weiss', 14.
235. Peter Weiss, *Fluchtpunkt: Roman* (Frankfurt a.M.: Suhrkamp, 1962). Weiss fled Germany with his family in 1935 to find refuge in England, Prague, Switzerland and, from 1939, Sweden, where he would remain after the Second World War. Weiss had been a painter and a film-maker before he became a writer. In contrast to Celan, who continued to write in German after the Holocaust, Weiss first wrote in Swedish, and only returned to German with the composition and publication of *Der Schatten des Körpers des Kutschers* [The Shadow of the Body of the Coachman] in 1960 (Garloff, 'Peter Weiss's Entry into the German Public Sphere', 47).
236. Zand, 'La création en France de «l'Instruction» de Peter Weiss', 14. For the original German text see Weiss, *Fluchtpunkt*, p. 212.
237. Jean Améry (Hans Mayer), whose Jewish father was killed in action in the First World War, and who was brought up by his Roman Catholic mother, writes: 'I bear on my left forearm the Auschwitz number; it can be read more quickly than either the Pentateuch or the Talmud and yet it contains more detailed information. It also has more authority as a fundamental formula of Jewish existence. When I say "I am a Jew" to myself and to the world, and this includes those religious and nationally-minded Jews, who do not consider me to be one of them, then I mean by this the realities and possibilities that are contained in the Auschwitz number' (Jean Améry, *Jenseits von Schuld und Sühne: Bewältigungsversuche eines Überwältigten* (Munich: Szczesny, 1966), pp. 148–49). For Celan's annotations see Celan, *La bibliothèque philosophique. Die philosophische Bibliothek*, p. 459. See also Celan's note: 'Améry / Die Auschwitznummer und das Alte Testament' [Améry / The Auschwitz number and the Old Testament] (Celan, *Mikrolithen*, p. 121).
238. Weiss, *Fluchtpunkt*, p. 212.
239. Weiss, *Meine Ortschaft*, p. 18.
240. Weiss, *Die Ermittlung*, p. 34.
241. Johann Christoph Adelung, *Versuch eines vollständigen grammatisch-kritischen Wörterbuches der hochdeutschen Mundart, mit beständiger Vergleichung der übrigen Mundarten, besonders aber der oberdeutschen*, 5 vols (Brünn: Trassler, 1788), IV, p. 275.
242. Benjamin, 'Critique of Violence', p. 252.
243. Adorno, *Notes to Literature*, II, p. 88.
244. Cohen, 'The Political Aesthetics of Holocaust Literature', p. 56.
245. Schneck, *Rhetoric and Evidence*, p. 13.
246. Ibid., p. 17.

247. Daniel 5. 12.
248. Derrida, 'Force of Law', p. 288.
249. Ibid., p. 291.
250. Ibid.
251. Felman, *The Juridical Unconscious*, p. 108.

CHAPTER 4

Rembrandt, Mandel'shtam, and the Limits of Ekphrasis

> One or two illustrations might help us —
> *Geffe* — to take a fix on your position,
> anomalous as it is. Two Kokoschkas
> and one Rembrandt: Rembrandt's unfinished
> The Concord of the State, OK?[1]

I conclude this exploration of Paul Celan's unfinished poetics by examining a poem that has repeatedly been subject to interpretation and translation. In contrast to many of the texts by Celan examined so far in this book, 'EINKANTER: Rembrandt' — published in the posthumous collection *Schneepart* [*Snow-Part*] — is a completed poem authorized for publication by the poet.[2] It cannot therefore be said to be an example of the neglected margins of the oeuvre, of the sous-oeuvre. According to Werner Weber, it was this poem that Celan most valued in the weeks before his death in April 1970.[3] I examine this poem here to show how the development of an explicatory, critical tradition around a poem can sometimes prevent readers from perceiving the poem's unique, internal, self-sustaining logic.

The presence of Rembrandt's name in the opening line of 'EINKANTER' has led all previous commentators to see the text as an example of ekphrasis — a '*verbal representation of visual representation*'[4] — in which a particular image, or set of images, is referenced and in whole or in part reproduced through the medium of text. It is often thought that the evocation of a creator of visual art in an inscribed text necessarily indicates that a particular work of art is referenced or — as Timothy Bahti puts it — 'imagined' by the text before the reader.[5] To some degree this impulse is understandable. If we can be said to know Rembrandt, then it is through his paintings, drawings, and etchings. That is to say, we do not know Rembrandt at all, but know material traces of an artistic corpus attributed to an historical individual. It seems strange, though, to read Rembrandt's name, of all artists, as a definite indication of some reference, more or less hidden, to a work or works attributed to the painter. As André Malraux points out, Rembrandt's oeuvre is perhaps above all striking for the way that it asks questions about existence, rather than establishing definite and definitive truths: 'Rembrandt discovers the power to call things into question, so that models and spectators, the world itself, are all less triumphators than enigmas, and which occasionally, as with Shakespeare, succeeds in throwing time out of joint'.[6] The naming of Rembrandt in the opening line of this poem should therefore be approached with more circumspection than has so far been the case. The name does not necessarily indicate either the man or the corpus in the ways usually presumed. In addition to the ambiguity inherent in naming an individual is the fact that ekphrasis — if this is what is at issue in the poem — is always more than the simple 'speaking out' of its etymology, the re-production or re-creation of a known original, or parts of a known original, in a different medium. It may also involve the expression or revelation of things in the image (or images) previously unknown and perhaps unknowable. When a text speaks through ekphrasis, it not only 'speaks out' those things we know and recognize but also enounces parts of the original that have remained invisible and lost. To this point in time, critics of the poem have been mostly concerned with attributing specific paintings to the poem's poetic imagination, and to the moments of the poem's inspiration and subsequent creation. This not only tells us more about our increasing preference for representational images than about the unique logic of the poem itself. It also means that ekphrasis has been used to inhibit further interpretations of the poem.

Here, I explore the relation of the poem to Rembrandt and his painting in a way that goes beyond the limits of ekphrasis. I also show that there was a sustained and profound engagement on the part of the poet with the work of the painter that went beyond this single poem, and that was decisive in the development of Celan's poetics in the latter half of the 1960s. Celan repeatedly visited museums expressly to see Rembrandt's work, and often sent postcards to friends bearing representations of Rembrandt paintings.[7] When at the beginning of 1970, during the last months of his life, his childhood friend — and by that time lover — Ilana Shmueli asked for his photograph, Celan instead gave her a postcard of Rembrandt's Cologne self-portrait.[8] I argue that beyond these common gestures of appropriation and identification, an awareness of the ways in which Rembrandt manipulated oil paint, as well as the material qualities of oil paint, are crucial to a more intimate understanding of a number of Celan's later poems. 'EINKANTER' was composed on 20 July 1968, over two years after *Eingedunkelt* had been left unfinished and less than two years before Celan's death:

> EINKANTER: Rembrandt,
> auf du und du mit dem Lichtschliff,
> abgesonnen dem Stern
> als Bartlocke, schläfig,
>
> Handlinien queren die Stirn,
> im Wüstengeschiebe, auf
> den Tischfelsen
> schimmert dir um den
> rechten Mundwinkel der
> sechzehnte Psalm.[9]

Fig. 4.1. Rembrandt van Rijn, 'Selbstbildnis' [Self-Portrait], c.1665, oil on canvas, Wallraf-Richartz-Museum & Fondation Corboud, WRM 2526, Cologne. Photo: Rheinisches Bildarchiv Köln, rba_c019108.

> [VENTIFACT: Rembrandt,
> familiar with the light-slippe,
> thought away from the star
> as beardlock, on the temple,
>
> hand-lines cross the brow,
> in the desert drift, onto
> the table rock
> the sixteenth psalm glimmers
> around the right corner of
> your mouth.]

So much has been brought to the poem in the form of ekphrastic attributions since its publication in 1971 that it is impossible not to begin by engaging with and evaluating the work of other critics. Most notable among them is Barbara Wiedemann, who not only undertakes a close reading of Celan's Rembrandt poem,[10] but also provides detailed annotations for the poem in her single volume edition of Celan's poetry.[11] In both her article and annotations to the poem, Wiedemann states that Celan — or perhaps the poem itself — is mindful of two of Rembrandt's paintings: the late self-portrait that hangs in Cologne sometimes called 'Self-Portrait as Zeuxis'[12] and 'A Man Seated Reading at a Table in a Lofty Room', incorrectly attributed to Rembrandt during Celan's lifetime.[13] Celan first saw the self-portrait in November 1958, 'an acquaintance, that will accompany him for the rest of his life'.[14] He saw the second of these paintings at the National Gallery in London in both August 1967 and April 1968, and it is likely that he also saw it on his numerous previous visits to London.[15] According to Wiedemann, the catalyst that provokes these pictorial references and helps Celan articulate them in the poem is his reading of a geological dictionary in which the poet comes across the terms 'Tischfelsen' [table rock or mushroom rock] and 'Einkanter' [einkanter or ventifact].[16] Both terms describe geological phenomena common to desert environments. Wiedemann imagines the poet moving from these examples of desert geology to the memory of Jewish exile in the desert following the escape from Egypt and the crossing of the Red Sea, and asserts that the poem 'unexpectedly' begins to resemble a Jewish poem.[17] Any Jewish inspiration behind the poem or Jewish aspect of the poem cannot really be said to be 'unexpected'.[18] It is clear from the outset that the poem is informed and inspired if not by Judaism then at least by an acute sense of Jewishness and Jewish history. This is evident in terms such as 'Bartlocke, schläfig' [Beardlock, on the temple], 'Stern' [star], 'Wüstengeschiebe', [desert drift], and 'der sechzehnte Psalm' [the sixteenth psalm]. Added to this is Rembrandt's well-established affinity and interaction with the Jews of Amsterdam — whom he painted, etched, and drew — and his acquaintance, business dealings, and perhaps even friendship with prominent Jewish religious figures including Menasseh Ben Israel.[19] Then there is Celan's own increased engagement with Jewish traditions from the early 1960s and the creation of *Die Niemandsrose* [*The No-One Rose*].[20]

Wiedemann argues that once the Jewish character of certain elements of Celan's poem has been established, our perception of Rembrandt's self-portrait might be opened up to the character's Jewish traits — the furrows on his brow [Handlinien queren die Stirn] and the curls around his temple [Bartlocke, schläfig] calling to mind the outward appearance of a traditional, aging Jew.[21] When considered alongside other self-portraits from this period of Rembrandt's career, however, the painting does not stand out for any particularly Jewish characteristics. Both the creased brow and the tufts of hair shown emerging from under the painter's creamy colored beret — obscuring the top half of the painter's right ear as we look at it — are comparable to the brow and hair in the vast majority of the self-portraits from the 1650s onward. Neither can the clean-shaven face of the sitter be said to possess anything resembling a beard-lock or 'pe'ah'.[22]

The painting does stand out from other self-portraits of the time, but for reasons other than those proposed by Wiedemann. In terms of its execution, the paint is particularly thick and pastose, above all around the brow, but also across the beret and the golden colored shawl.[23] In this it is reminiscent of Rembrandt's 'Homer' in The Hague.[24] The painting also represents Rembrandt laughing, a common pose in his youth, but less common toward the end of his life.[25] The laugh (which x-radiographs show initially resembled a smile) has led to the consensus that the self-portrait also depicts one of the more renowned painters of Greek antiquity, namely Zeuxis. According to the Dutch painter Samuel Dirksz van Hoogstraten (1627–1678), an old woman came to Zeuxis to commission a painting of Venus-Aphrodite. Zeuxis accepted. When the old woman insisted on sitting for the painting herself, however, the painter 'split with laughter' and died.[26] This theory would explain the presence in the top left-hand corner of the canvas of a large nose, a small but protruding chin, and a complex arrangement of gold chains and ribbons that adorn Aphrodite's unarticulated bosom. The portrait is therefore striking not for depicting any particularly Jewish characteristics, but for depicting a painter (notice the knob of the maulstick) in the throes of suffocating laughter.

Celan may not have been aware of this interpretation as it was first published by Albert Blankert in 1973.[27] When Celan viewed the painting during his repeated trips to Cologne between 1954 and 1969,[28] it was commonly considered to date from the final years of Rembrandt's life, after the deaths of his second wife Hendrickje (1626–1663) and of his only son to survive into adulthood, Titus (1641–1668). As a result, it was said to show Rembrandt laughing in the face of imminent death. This led Max Eisler to state 'senility is in evidence here'[29] and Malraux to fantasize: 'when evening falls on the deserted studio, where his cumbersome masterpieces [ses chefs-d'oeuvre encombrants] are accumulating, he observes his sorry face in a mirror covered in shadow, drives everything earthly out of it, and throws resplendent glory at it, the Cologne *Portrait* that bursts into insane laughter'.[30] Although the figure in the painting doesn't really appear to burst into laughter — assuming instead an open-mouthed grin — it is possible that in his poem Celan intends to reference the insanity [Absinn] associated with this painting in 'Rembrandt [...] abgesonnen dem Stern'. Here, 'abgesonnen' could be said to indicate the past participle of the hypothetical verb 'absinnen, absann, abgesonnen' — 'to think or ponder away, to think away from, to think insanely'. The juxtaposition of 'ab-' [from] and 'sinnen' [think, ponder] begins to make sense (or perhaps 'ab-sense') when the etymology of 'sinnen' is pursued back to the Germanic root '*sinþa-' meaning journey, way, route, or passage.[31] 'Sinnen' is to think, to ponder, and to move in the process. It is to be in a different place when one has thought than when one began to think. 'Abgesonnen' therefore suggests not only the displacement of a madman's thought from the accepted norms of sanity, but also, more simply, some progress or advancement made in thought away from some object in space.

In this case, the object in relation to which thought defines itself is 'the star' [dem Stern]. As such, the star exerts a gravitational pull which incipient thought — whether considered or mad — must overcome in order to detach itself and to achieve the distinction and differentiation of thought. On the other hand, the light ('*Licht*schliff') and heat ('abge*sonnen*') that emanate from the star must overcome the interferences of external forces as they move away from their source. 'Abgesonnen' therefore captures the contradictory dynamics of a celestial body, achieving dissemination in light and heat, and resisting material dissemination through its gravitational force. Whether we read Rembrandt or the 'Lichtschliff' [light-slippe] with which he is familiar [auf du und du] as the object of 'abgesonnen', the poem draws the reader's attention to the persistent gravitational pull of Rembrandt's corpus, and to the particular terrestrial (as opposed to celestial) light of painting. The poem also reminds us of the extent to which this corpus is lost to us, the extent to which we cannot grasp the heat of human flesh that inspired it and that it seeks to imitate, and the oily wetness of the paint that Rembrandt moved about the canvas, perhaps especially when we turn from what Seamus Heaney calls the 'instantaneous thereness' of the painting itself to read this 'wordlogged poem'.[32]

If, for the time being, we pursue Wiedemann's ekphrastic method of comparison and identification between image and text, the most notable element of the self-portrait we might recognize in the poem is the hand-lines [Handlinien] that cross the brow [queren die Stirn]. Lines can be seen in the corrugated skin that crosses the painter's forehead, puckered into zigzags above the raised eyebrows, but this does not allow us to understand why such lines would be '*hand*-lines'. Some have tried to see in the hand-lines that run across the brow chiromantic or chirognomic potential, by which the future or the character of the portrayed individual can be read. Slightly more intriguing is the fact that in the X-ray image of the painting, the painting hand is visible to the left of the painter's head as we look at the canvas, holding a brush to the depicted canvas.[33] The hand appears as a clutch of thick white lines, lines that would have to cross the brow of Aphrodite as it paints her into existence.

Whether the lines that cross the brow refer to the creased forehead of Rembrandt as Zeuxis, or the old woman as Aphrodite, or to the now hidden but painted lines of the painting hand, lines possess a particular significance in painting, and by extension here in this poem. As Georges Didi-Huberman explains: 'If in painting, the stroke [le trait], the line [la ligne], constitute the privileged instruments of definition, it is precisely because they have the virtue of tracing limits, of separating'.[34] In painting, lines define, and in the process of definition, begin to extract themselves from their meaningless materiality, projecting themselves toward — although never actually reaching — the ideal of representation: 'The stroke, when it defines a form, is no longer, or at least almost no longer, the infinitesimal powder of wood charcoal that administers its particles upon a given surface, according to a more or less hit and miss course. It extracts itself from its material cause, but of course never entirely; it gives to itself, in a very intimate way, a sort of *anadyomene* birth'.[35] Although the materiality of Didi-Huberman's example is traced in charcoal and the lines crossing Rembrandt-Zeuxis's brow are modeled in oil paint on canvas, Didi-Huberman's reflection on the line also seems to capture the painted line's anadyomene birth. It is not only that the oil paint is wet and greasy on the canvas as Rembrandt manipulates it, recreating the wetness of the polluted sea in which Aphrodite is always 'anadyomene' (that is, always both 'emerging from' and 'immerging into'), but that at certain points — most notably at the left eyebrow as we look at the picture — Rembrandt has traced his own finger through the still wet paint to inscribe a line, defining the representation of the old man's eyebrow through the relative absence of paint, an absence that the paint's liquid, anadyomene presence makes possible.

If this is in part what 'Handlinien' intends, it would not be the only time that Celan seeks to articulate the painting of aging skin through the definition and limits of lines. In an early draft of the *Eingedunkelt* poem 'KANTIGE' [ANGULAR], composed in March 1966, he writes:

> Umdrängt von
> Unverlierbarem, umschlossen von
> erfahrenem Inkarnat[36]
>
> [Bound in to
> the inalienable, enclosed in
> experienced tones of flesh]

'Erfahrenes Inkarnat' denotes not only the skillful [erfahren] representation of painted skin, but also perhaps the painting of experienced or aged [erfahren] skin, the skin of an aging Rembrandt, or of a Zeuxis, or of his old woman sitter and, by extension, the aging of oil paint, which through its gradual deterioration continues to both depict and to mimic the deterioration of human flesh, whether young or old. The lines that define Rembrandt's painting not only cross the depiction of the painter's own forehead as corrugations, nor do they simply run through the now dried oil paint as inscriptions in paint — they also run horizontally across the painting in the craquelure of the thick and heavy layer of yellowish varnish, which robs the painted skin of its pink fleshiness, cloaking the entire image with the golden glow we now associate with Rembrandt's painted corpus.[37] The line 'Handlinien queren die Stirn' — even as we read it as an example of ekphrasis — calls us to go beyond the primitive identification of an ekphrastic referent and to read the lines of the poem and of the painting for more than their qualities of representation. Lines define not only the depiction of the subject and the manipulation of paint, but also the painting's material and historical reality. The line 'Handlinien queren die Stirn' points the reader beyond poetry, beyond any particular painting the reader might attribute to the poem's imagination, and toward the practice of painting and the particular material qualities of old and dried oil paint.

I now briefly draw back from Celan's Rembrandt poem to consider a short text written by Celan in May 1968, just two months before the creation of 'EIN-KANTER'. The text, which explicitly reflects on Rembrandt's self-portrait in Cologne, provides an opportunity to gauge more precisely the poetic and philosophical potential that Celan perceives in Rembrandt's oil paint:

> Je regarde l'autoportrait
> de Rembrandt (celui de Cologne),
> son regard et sa bouche
> distendus par les contingences,
> sa tête et un peu de son
> son [sic] manteau dorés par les
> contingences, rongés par elles, songés
> par elles, son bâton éclaboussé de deux
> gouttes, trois gouttes de cette
> même substance.
>
> 45 rue d'Ulm
> Paris, am 10. Mai 1968[38]

> [I am looking at the self-portrait
> by Rembrandt (the one in Cologne),
> his gaze and his mouth
> distended by contingencies,
> his head and a bit of his
> his [sic] cloak gilded by
> contingencies, eaten away by them, dreamt
> by them, his stick spattered with two
> splashes, three splashes of this
> same substance.
>
> 45 rue d'Ulm
> Paris, 10 May 1968]

In contrast to 'EINKANTER', in which there is no reference to a first person speaker, the 'je regarde' [I am looking] of Celan's French text firmly establishes its ekphrastic status. We know that Celan wrote this text with a color postcard representation of the Cologne self-portrait to hand. He had asked Ruth Kraft — fellow native of Bukowina and now resident in Cologne — to send it to him.[39] The distance of the poet from the materiality of the original painting, the reduction of the painting to the status of representable and represented image, the distortion to the painting's size, colors, and textures, as well as the rendition in ink of the oil paint's reticulations initially seem to persuade Celan to concentrate less upon the painting itself than on some notion of Rembrandt's biography that the self-portrait might be said to represent: 'his gaze and his mouth / distended by contingencies'. If we understand by contingency something that is such because of the effect of circumstances that could also not have occurred, not something that occurs necessarily because of the essence of the thing, then we could conclude that the contingencies that distend the lines of Rembrandt's gaze and mouth — the recent deaths of Hendrickje and Titus, his financial ruin, his fall from favor and out of fashion, the imminence of death — are what 'speak out' or define the painting. But the notion that there is more to this text than a simple ekphrastic reflection structured on the popular fictions of biography is suggested by the way that the tidy succession of rhyming, bi-syllabic past participles — 'dorés' [gilded], 'rongés' [eaten away], 'songés' [dreamt] — gives way to the muddy splashes of 'éclaboussé' [spattered, with echoes of both 'éclater' [burst, explode] and 'boue' [mud]] in the closing lines: 'his stick spattered with two / drops, three drops of this / same substance'. In hunting, the 'éclaboussure' once described the telltale drops of muddy water kicked up by the quarry in flight that the hunter used to identify its recent passage.[40] Here the spatterings are not only unintended traces of the painter's passage. They also serve to challenge what Didi-Huberman terms the 'tyrannical legislation' of the painting's distended lines.[41] They mark the point at which lines fail to represent, the point at which the line breaks, at which the poet can no longer say anything about the painted and varnished surface of the canvas. They mark the moment 'where speech is no longer able to describe, for example, the 'spattering' effect [l'effet 'éclaboussant'] of a pigment, where speech is simply not able to *take cognizance* of a surface splattered in colors [tachetée de couleurs]'.[42] The 'éclaboussures' that spatter Rembrandt's painted maulstick represent the failure of representation, but they also suggest that the text has reached the limits of ekphrasis. It is therefore significant that Celan does not specify the nature of the substance that is spattered on the maulstick, describing it instead as 'this same substance', even as he gives to understand that the substance of contingency par excellence is oil paint.

The insubstantiation of contingency into the wet paint that spatters the painter's maulstick reminds us of similarly improbable moments of materialization, of muddy incorporation, and of wet births. Didi-Huberman recounts that when Apelles painted the birth of Venus-Aphrodite, the painting was so life-like that Julian of Egypt warned: 'Move quickly away from the painting if you do not want to be splashed by the foam that drips down from her wrung out hair'.[43] In other words, 'the painting itself will be able to *spatter* [éclabousser] whosoever encounters or sees it'.[44] The 'écume' [foam, froth, scum — in Greek 'αφρός' [afrós]] from which Aphrodite materializes (in every sense) is the mixture of blood and sperm from Uranus's genitals, severed and thrown into the sea by his son Cronos. As Didi-Huberman explains: 'The foam would therefore be the very matter of a form in the process of becoming: it would somehow be water before Narcissus, water before it becomes totally calm again, cleansed of its purple and whitish froth and slick, water which is not yet dead flat, in which nothing can be *distinguished*'.[45] Despite Julian of Egypt's warning, there is no risk that Celan could be spattered by the two or three drops of paint that mark Rembrandt-Zeuxis's maulstick, given that he is removed in time and space not only from the greasy wetness of its creation, but also from the dried creation itself. The surface of the postcard upon which he sees the painting's representation is as smooth as the undisturbed water in which Narcissus will see and fall in love with his own reflection. It is this smoothness of surface that allows Celan to make out — to *distinguish* — Rembrandt Anadyomene, not emerging naked from the surf, spattered with the scum of froth, blood, and

REMBRANDT, MANDEL'SHTAM, AND THE LIMITS OF EKPHRASIS 205

FIG. 4.2. Follower of Rembrandt, 'A Man Seated Reading at a Table in a Lofty Room', late 17th century, oil on wood, National Gallery, London, NG3214. Bought, 1917.
© The National Gallery, London.

sperm, but hunched over, engaging the viewer, and laughing. The contingencies that distend his gaze and his mouth, that gild his head and part of his coat, that eat away at him, that dream at him, are materialized in paint, and are therefore always in the process of both miraculously bringing Rembrandt to life and matter-of-factly drowning him to death.

The second painting that Wiedemann draws into the intertextual orbit of 'EINKANTER', thought at one time to be by Rembrandt, is 'A Man Seated Reading at a Table in a Lofty Room'.[46] It is here that her interpretation begins to overlap with Theo Buck's more extensive investigation.[47] Both critics recount how in April 1968, three months before composing 'EINKANTER', Celan signs off a letter to his friend, the Swiss poet and translator Franz Wurm, by saying that he has recently revisited the National Gallery: 'Wiedergesehn in London [Saw again in London]: The man reading in a lofty room. O ja: reading. O ja: lofty'.[48] In response to Wurm's understandable puzzlement — 'Who & where is The man reading in a lofty room?'[49] — Celan explains, 'The reading one is a Rembrandt — I'll get a reproduction of it sent to me, and then it will clamber up to you'.[50] Although Celan sent Gisèle a postcard representation of 'A Man Seated Reading at a Table in a Lofty Room' in August 1967,[51] it appears that Wurm did not receive the promised postcard. Wiedemann and Buck nevertheless see this brief exchange as sufficient evidence to presume that Celan had this painting in mind when he composed 'EINKANTER' later that year. Wiedemann supports this claim by arguing that the heavy blockish table in the painting — of which little more than a silhouette can be seen, and upon which a large book and loose papers are piled up — is found in the poem's 'auf den Tischfelsen' [onto the table rock]. 'Tischfelsen', as most previous critics of this poem have pointed out, denotes a large rock the lower part of which has been eroded to leave a thin plinth supporting a much larger head.[52] Such rock formations being common in windswept, desert environments, Wiedemann again traces a line through the Jewish people's wandering in the desert to the image of a Torah pulpit upon which some traditions dictate that part of the sixteenth psalm should be inscribed, namely:

'שויתי יהוה לנגדי תמיד'

[I have placed God in front of me always][53]

or the abbreviated form 'תמיד' [always]. Wiedemann concludes that through the agency of Celan's poem, the aging Rembrandt of the self-portrait is transformed into a Jew reading in a lofty room.[54]

Buck makes similar claims for the importance of this picture to the poet's imagination (which he boldly and without evidence reconstructs). He states that Celan is attracted not only to the posture of the reader but also to 'the deeper dimension of a skeptical but perceptive assessment of life' supposedly evident in the reader's face, and to 'the reflection of a wandering, eternal Jew'.[55] It cannot be denied that the posture of the reader is something that appealed to Celan in April 1968 ('O ja: reading'), but Celan makes no mention of the way in which the reader might conceive of life, nor does he project a Jewish identity onto the reader, and there is nothing in the picture to support such an identification. In fact, once the picture has been scrutinized, the focus of both critics on the reading figure seems misdirected for two reasons. First, the head of the reader — so central to Buck's and to Wiedemann's explications, and of which little more than a silhouette is visible — is poorly (or as the Rembrandt Research Project puts it, 'summarily') painted.[56] Heads painted with the crudest marks can still possess what one contemporary British portraitist calls a 'directed gaze, and something else which seems sufficient to begin to hang character upon'.[57] The painter Francis Bacon intends something very similar when he speaks of some of the most beautiful painted images being made 'out of non-rational marks', out of 'a coagulation of non-representational marks', 'marks of the brush and the movement of paint on canvas' that in the best cases 'speak directly to us'.[58] Here, these 'non-rational' marks are too weak to capture the human head that by their approximating presence they nevertheless claim to communicate. The marks of the reading head do not 'speak directly to us'.

The second reason for which Buck's and Wiedemann's focus appears misplaced concerns the subject of the painting. Despite the title by which the painting is commonly known, a brief glance is enough to establish that the principal subject of the painting is not a man reading, but the bright sunlight pouring into the high dark room from two cross-barred windows and an open doorway in the top left side of the painting ('O ja: lofty').[59] The creamy sunlight is depicted cutting into the darkness of the interior in such a way that the irregular surface of the wall, as well as the shadows of the uneven glass cast upon the wall, are clearly visible. The primary focus of the painting on light represents a departure from Rembrandt's usual approach, as he tends to examine the way light relates to a human figure not to a mostly empty interior. It is nonetheless the light depicted in the painting — rather than the man reading or the reader's possible Jewishness — that Celan explicitly acknowledges in his letter to Wurm as he signs off: 'Als fiele das Licht ein' [as if the light were falling in], evoking the way the light falls diagonally from the top left-hand side of the picture down into the dark room, but also the way that light 'might come to mind' [einfallen].[60]

Adjusting our focus away from the human figure and toward the whitewashed wall and the light that is reflected against it does not require us to deny the potential proximity of this painting to the poem's imagination. To pursue Wiedemann's and Buck's ekphrastic model a little further, it is in this painting in particular that Rembrandt (let us for the moment presume, as Celan did, that this is Rembrandt's work) could be said to be on mutually familiar terms [auf du und du] with the 'Lichtschliff' [light-slippe].[61] The neologism 'Lichtschliff' is probably inspired by the common geological term 'Windschliff', which describes the product of a process through which wind-blown particles — usually of sand — polish [schleifen] one side of a rock or a stone over an extended period of time, creating a smooth surface. It is the same process through which a ventifact [Einkanter] is fashioned.[62] The attribution of the process of corrasion to light in 'Lichtschliff' suggests that the depicted light contains physical particles that imperceptibly wear the whitewashed plaster of the wall away.[63] The light with which Rembrandt is on such familiar terms is therefore not the light of photography or cinematography, nor even the light of chiaroscuro. Instead, it is the corrasive light of painting. It is this that the neologism 'light-slippe' attempts to express, where 'slippe' is a seventeenth- and eighteenth-century English noun, related to the Dutch 'slijpen' [to sharpen, polish], that describes the filings of steel worn away on a cutler's grindstone and deposited in the trough.[64] Rembrandt is on familiar terms with 'light-slippe', with light as powder, pigment, oil, and varnish. He is familiar with light as physical matter that has been 'thought-away' (or perhaps 'sunned-away') from the star [abgesonnen dem Stern]. This notion of light as gritty substance removes us perhaps as far as it is possible to be from the spectral 'white space' of cinema as perceived by Gilles Deleuze, for whom the 'unknown body' appears to materialize in the 'dancing seeds' and 'luminous dust' of the 'experimental night'.[65] It is instead the granular, erosive quality of light that fashions the 'ventifact', the 'desert drift' and the 'table rock', all of which are to be understood not only as symbolic or metaphorical references to particular paintings attributed to Rembrandt or to the passage of the Jewish people through the desert, as Buck and Wiedemann claim, but also as intimations in language of the material reality of Rembrandt's oil paint.

The closing reference of the poem to the sixteenth psalm might initially be thought to propose as concrete and definite a reference to an external text as the name Rembrandt does in the poem's opening line to an historical figure or oeuvre. Identification of the psalm by critics has been complicated by the slight inconsistencies in Hebrew and Greco-Roman systems of numbering the psalms.[66] The search for a definite reference that may or may not have been intended by the poet (or by the poem) has so far failed to take into account the significance of the verb that describes the sixteenth psalm's action:

> schimmert dir um den
> rechten Mundwinkel der
> sechzehnte Psalm
>
> [shimmers around the
> right corner of your mouth the
> sixteenth psalm.]

Friedrich Kluge reminds us that 'schimmern' was introduced into written German vernacular through Martin Luther's translation of psalm 68.14.[67] By looking at how Luther forges this verb from the Hebrew, we can begin to understand the quality of light the sixteenth psalm casts over the corner of the mouth and over the poem. The Hebrew reads:

אִם־תִּשְׁכְּבוּן בֵּין שְׁפַתָּיִם כַּנְפֵי יוֹנָה נֶחְפָּה בַכֶּסֶף וְאֶבְרוֹתֶיהָ בִּירַקְרַק חָרוּץ׃[68]

Literally this might be translated as: 'even if you [masculine plural] lie down between the ash heaps — the wings of the dove are covered with silver, its pinions with pale gold'. Luther renders this as: 'Wenn ihr zwischen den Hürden laget, so glänzte es wie der Taube Flügel, die wie Silber und Gold schimmern' [If you lay among the pens, then it would shine like wings of the dove, which gleam like silver and gold].[69] The Hebrew does not include direct equivalents to the pair of active verbs 'schimmern' [gleam] and 'glänzen' [shine]. The intimations of light in the Hebrew emanate from the 'wings of the dove' [כנפי יונה] that are 'covered in silver' [נחפה בכסף], and from the dove's 'pinions' [אברותיה] that are covered (the repetition of the verb being implicit) 'in pale-green gold' [בירקרק חרוץ]. The notion of shimmering asserts itself not only through the implied brilliance of the silver and gold that cover the dove's wings and pinions, but also through the unusual adjective that qualifies the gold. The word for 'pale green' [ירקרק] comes from the root 'ירק' meaning to grow green as of plants, but also indicates the greenish paling of the human face. Luther presumably obtains the notion of shimmering from the visual and acoustic repetition of the second and third radicals 'ר' and 'ק'. The silver and gold do not gleam with the constancy of the dove's wings, as implied in 'glänzen' [shine]. Instead, they glitter tremulously, flickering in and out of darkness. The particular light of 'schimmern' is further characterized by the unique qualities of the Hebrew 'חרוץ' [gold] instead of the more commonly used and less ambiguous 'זהב' [gold],[70] because 'חרוץ' is also homonymous with the adjective meaning 'sharp', 'diligent', or 'strict'.[71] The light that glimmers on the right corner of the mouth in 'EINKANTER' therefore betrays the grace and gratitude of the sixteenth psalm ('The lines are fallen unto me in pleasant places; yea, I have a goodly heritage')[72] but also perhaps the moral strictness and sharpness of the preceding psalm ('Lord, who shall abide in thy tabernacle? Who shall dwell in thy holy hill?').[73] Although I refrain from identifying a particular portrait in which a psalm could be said to 'shimmer' around the right corner of its mouth, we know from Rembrandt's method of painting that the representation of skin reflecting shimmering light is achieved with thicker, more pastose paint. The flesh colored paint that defines the 'Mundwinkel' [corner of the mouth] therefore stands in relative relief to the darker and thinner parts of the painting.[74] Celan's use of 'schimmern' to describe the action of the psalm is not an impressionistic device, nor does it invite the reader to identify a particular painting, nor is there any reason to assume with Buck that it describes 'a ray of utopian hope'.[75] More than any other word in the poem, 'schimmern' draws the reader's attention to the human and material qualities of painted flesh.

As we begin to establish the limits of ekphrasis in Celan's poem, we may be surprised to find that it has been our assumption of ekphrasis that has blinded us to the poem's central intertextual reference, the discovery of which can teach us exactly what it is in Rembrandt's work that appealed to Celan and that he sought to incorporate in this poem. The psalm that shimmers with a greenish pastose glow around the right corner of the mouth is a psalm that resists the attribution of particular paintings to the poem's imagination, that rejects the pretensions of attributive ekphrasis. The psalm referred to in Celan's poem is a poem by the Russian Jewish poet Osip Mandel'shtam, to whose memory Celan dedicated his 1963 collection of verse *Die Niemandsrose*, and with whom Celan so closely identified that in one poem he describes himself tearing off Mandel'shtam's limbs to put his own in their place.[76] In February 1937, less than two years before his death in a Soviet transit camp near Vladivostok, Mandel'shtam wrote the following poem:

Как светотени мученик Рембрандт,
Я глубоко ушел в немеющее время,
И резкость моего горящего ребра
Не охраняется ни сторожами теми,
Ни этим воином, что под грозою спят.

Простишь ли ты меня, великолепный брат,
И мастер, и отец черно-зеленой теми,
Но око соколиного пера
И жаркие ларцы у полночи в гареме
Смущают не к добру, смущают без добра
Мехами сумрака взволнованное племя.

8 февраля 1937 Воронеж[77]

Like Rembrandt, martyr of chiaroscuro,
I went deep into time that was growing numb,
But the sharpness of my burning rib
Is not guarded either by those guards,
Nor by this warrior, who sleep under the thunder-storm.

Forgive me, magnificent brother,
And master, and father of blackgreen darkness,
But the eye of the falcon feather
And the hot caskets in the harem of midnight
Trouble not for good, trouble without good
The agitated tribe with the furs of twilight.

8 February 1937. Voronezh

Once 'Как светотени' and 'EINKANTER' are juxtaposed, it becomes evident that they share a number of formal features. Both are divided into two slightly uneven stanzas — Celan's of four and six lines, Mandel'shtam's of five and six. In both poems Rembrandt's name appears at the end of the opening line, a naturally prominent position in prosody. It could also be argued that they share a common apostrophe to Rembrandt. Although this is not one of the nearly fifty Mandel'shtam poems translated into German by Celan,[78] it seems certain that Celan would have known this poem through its 1964 publication in *Собрание сочинений в двух томах*, which he possessed in his library.[79] Despite this cluster of circumstances, the two poems have never, as far as I can ascertain, been considered in each other's light. Once set alongside each other, Mandel'shtam's Rembrandt poem contaminates and haunts the poetic imagination of 'EINKANTER'. The pale green gold of the sixty-eighth psalm that shimmers around the right corner of the mouth in Celan's poem is also found glimmering darkly, like patina, in Mandel'shtam's text: 'великолепный брат, / И мастер, и отец черно-зеленой теми' [magnificent brother, / and master, and father of blackgreen darkness]. The sharpness of the glimmering gold felt through the Hebrew 'חרוץ' and the German 'schimmert' is the same sharpness [резкость] that pierces the first person speaker of the poem in the side: 'И резкость моего горящего ребра / Не охраняется ни сторожами теми, / Ни этим воином, что под грозою спят' [And the sharpness of my burning rib / Is not guarded either by those guards, / Nor by this warrior, who sleep under the thunder-storm]. Furthermore, Mandel'shtam's poem seems to resonate formally and thematically with the sixteenth psalm. Both 'Как светотени' and the sixteenth psalm consist of eleven verses, and where Mandel'shtam's first person voice pleads for forgiveness from Rembrandt ('Простишь ли ты меня, великолепный брат' [Forgive me, magnificent brother]), the singer of the psalm asks God for preservation:

'שמרני אל כי־חסיתי בך'

[Keep me, God, for I have sought refuge in you]).[80]

Perhaps that which draws Mandel'shtam's poem most unambiguously into the imagination of Celan's poem is the fact that the sixteenth psalm (or perhaps Mandel'shtam's poem) shimmers 'around the / right corner of the mouth' [um den / rechten Mundwinkel]. The 'corner of the mouth' calls to mind two crucial textual moments in Celan's prose oeuvre that are so closely related as to be almost indistinguishable from each other. The first dates from a text Celan wrote in early 1960 for a radio program on Mandel'shtam broadcast by Norddeutscher Rundfunk.[81] Describing Mandel'shtam's poetics, Celan writes: 'The poem is here the poem of the one who knows that he is speaking under the angle of inclination of his existence [unter dem Neigungswinkel seiner Existenz]'.[82] When on 22 October later that same year Paul Celan was awarded the Büchner Prize in Darmstadt, he described his own poetics in almost identical terms: 'This ever-yet of poems can only be found in a poem by one who does not forget that he speaks under the angle of inclination of his being [Neigungswinkel seines Daseins], the angle of inclination of his creatureliness [Neigungswinkel seiner Kreatürlichkeit]'.[83] Both Celan and Mandel'shtam speak under the angle of inclination [Neigungswinkel] of their existence and of their individual creatureliness. The 'Mundwinkel' [mouth-angle] around which the sixteenth psalm shimmers in Celan's poem is also the 'Neigungswinkel' [inclination-angle] under whose narrowness Mandel'shtam's first person speaker asks Rembrandt for forgiveness. As Mandel'shtam's poem advises us, the narrowness of this angle and the sharp pain of existence will pass just as they did for Rembrandt, not through healing but through death. Rembrandt is the 'martyr of chiaroscuro' because he dies into his work, martyring himself through his work to descend 'deep into time that was growing numb'. He becomes at one with the wetness of oil paint, dissolving himself into viscous light and time that will slowly dry, to signify, to exist, and perhaps to breathe beyond the individual death of his body. This time and flesh that grow numb, this paint that grows dry, will never again soften and liquefy. But for a time, perhaps for many centuries, the paint will mimic the liveliness, the porosity, the breathing, and the aging of human skin. As Elizabeth Jennings puts it in the closing lines of her poem 'Rembrandt's Late Self-Portraits': 'To paint's to breathe, / And all the darknesses are dared. You chose / What each must reckon with'.[84]

In his discussion on dialogue in Celan and Mandel'shtam, Michael Eskin projects a place for the poem, the poet, and the proleptic reader that he calls the 'un-space', in which 'interpersonal encounters that may have never taken place and might never take place in history may and indeed do take place poetically'.[85] What our reading of these Rembrandt poems demonstrates is that although there is a world of poetic possibility, it cannot be a permanently accessible utopia. It is a world in which the 'sharpness' of the speaker's burning rib is fleeting, where sharp pain passes into numbness, where bleeding wounds heal, where liquid pigment reverts to stone, where the quickness of life slowly solidifies into death. It is a descent into time growing numb, a solidification in which something lively and liquid has been taken hostage, a death in which part of life has been captured in its quickness and slowed down — agogically Étienne Souriau might say — so that it continues to sleep (with echoes of 'sleep' [Schlaf] in 'on the temple' [schläfig]) like those guards or this warrior, through the thunderstorm's 'plastic time'.[86]

The attempts of Wiedemann and Buck, amongst other commentators, to identify and explicate potential ekphrastic references in Celan's poem are understandable. The presence of Rembrandt's name in a European postwar poem must, it is thought, refer to at least one part of his now very visible corpus. But if we approach the role of Rembrandt in Celan's poem through the particular logic and method of oil painting itself, we become aware of a richer and deeper potential for ekphrastic interpretation, one that takes into account oil paint's material thickness and weight, the varying degrees of its tone and translucency, one that is mindful both of what a painting thrusts forward for us to see, and also of what it partially or wholly conceals. Oil paint applied to a surface will always to some degree, however small and apparently insignificant, inform, inflect, and qualify the final appearance of the painting, even if scrubbed out in the process of painting, or simply overpainted. Rembrandt would often paint on top of still wet paint, abdicating part of his prerogative of control, ceding mastery to the anadyomene ambiguities of oil paint. It is this living material reality of wet, drying, and dried paint, its natural and stubborn refusal to be simply representational, its insubstantiation of contingency, that has largely been kept out of the picture, so to speak, in readings of "EINKANTER." It is as if we might have had something to gain from preserving our understanding of Celan's engagement with Rembrandt from the often incoherent spatterings, stains, and contaminations of living and deteriorating paint that constitute Rembrandt's corpus. Celan's incorporation of Rembrandt into his published oeuvre is much more essential than the cultural reference it might initially appear to be. It is the human quality, the vitality, aging, and death of Rembrandt's oil paint, the terrestrial light and muddy weight of painted flesh that Celan's poem seeks to embody. We should therefore read J. D. McClatchy literally when he says that 'for most poets paintings are as primal, as "real" as the bread and wine on the table, as urgent as a dying parent or concealed lover in the next room'.[87] Rembrandt's painting should similarly be understood as an intimate, pressing, bodily presence in Celan's work.

Notes to Chapter 4

1. Geoffrey Hill, *The Triumph of Love* (Boston: Houghton Mifflin, 1998), p. 70.
2. Paul Celan, *Schneepart* (Frankfurt a.M.: Suhrkamp, 1971), p. 66.

3. Werner Weber, *Forderungen. Bemerkungen und Aufsätze zur Literatur* (Zurich: Artemis, 1970), p. 202. Weber reports that Celan wrote the poem out in front of him. Celan also sent manuscript copies of the poem to Nani Demus on 3 March 1970, and to Ilana Shmueli on 6 March 1970, to mark their respective birthdays (Wiedemann, 'Kommentar', p. 853).
4. James A. W. Heffernan, *Museum of Words. The Poetics of Ekphrasis from Homer to Ashbery* (Chicago: University of Chicago Press, 1993), p. 3.
5. Bahti, *Ends of the Lyric*, p. 182.
6. André Malraux, *La Métamorphose des dieux. L'Irréel* (Paris: Gallimard, 1974), p. 263.
7. The postcards include: 'The Jewish Bride' (c. 1667) sent from Amsterdam in May 1964 to Gisèle's cousins, Bernard and Anne de Veyrac (Celan and Celan-Lestrange, *Correspondance*, I, p. 380); also in May, to Paul Schallück, 'Jeremiah lamenting the destruction of Jerusalem' (1630) (Celan, *Briefwechsel mit den rheinischen Freunden*. p. 646); the 1648 etching 'Three Beggars at the Door of a House' to Peter Szondi and to Jean Bollack, also in May 1964 (Paul Celan and Peter Szondi, *Briefwechsel. Mit Briefen von Gisèle Celan-Lestrange an Peter Szondi und Auszügen aus dem Briefwechsel zwischen Peter Szondi und Jean und Mayotte Bollack*, ed. by Christoph König (Frankfurt a.M.: Suhrkamp, 2005), p. 202); 'A Bearded Man in a Cap' to Nelly Sachs from London in April 1968 (Paul Celan and Nelly Sachs, *Briefwechsel*, ed. by Barbara Wiedemann (Frankfurt a.M.: Suhrkamp, 1993), pp. 97–98).
8. Paul Celan and Ilana Shmueli, *Briefwechsel*, ed. by Ilana Shmueli and Thomas Sparr (Frankfurt a.M.: Suhrkamp, 2004), p. 234. After viewing the painting in October 1964, Celan noted: 'Rembrandt portrait / — i — / yes, I am eclipsed [ich bin überspielt] / I have lived, yes' (Celan, *Mikrolithen*, p. 612). See also Dischner, who states that Celan felt 'particularly drawn' to Rembrandt's self-portraits, and 'in viewing them often became melancholy' (Paul Celan and Gisela Dischner, *»Wie aus weiter Ferne zu Dir«. Paul Celan — Gisela Dischner. Briefwechsel. Mit einem Brief von Gisèle Celan-Lestrange*, ed. by Barbara Wiedemann, with Gisela Dischner (Berlin: Suhrkamp, 2012), p. 149).
9. Celan, *Die Gedichte*, p. 336.
10. Barbara Wiedemann, 'Zwischen Pestkreuz und Bocklemünd — Paul Celan in Köln', *Celan-Jahrbuch*, 9 (2007), 103–26.
11. Wiedemann, 'Kommentar', pp. 853–54.
12. Rembrandt van Rijn, 'Selbstbildnis' [Self-Portrait], c. 1665, oil on canvas, Wallraf-Richartz-Museum & Fondation Corboud, WRM 2526, Cologne. See Fig. 4.1.
13. Follower of Rembrandt, 'A Man Seated Reading at a Table in a Lofty Room', late 17th century, oil on wood, National Gallery, London, NG3214. Bought, 1917. See Fig. 4.2. The painting dates from after Rembrandt's death: 'Because of the manner of painting the work has to be seen as a fabrication in a style that the author conceived as being Rembrandtesque without taking any real account of the way Rembrandt worked. Its history can probably be traced back to 1749 and dating should not be looked for before the end of the 17th century' (J. Bruyn et al., *A Corpus of Rembrandt Paintings*, ed. by J. Bruyn, with the collaboration of L. Peese Binkhorst-Hoffscholte, trans. by D. Cook-Radmore, 6 vols (The Hague: Nijhoff, 1982–2015), I, p. 532).
14. Wiedemann, 'Zwischen Pestkreuz und Bocklemünd', 117.
15. A room by room guide to the National Gallery from 1966 indicates that this painting hung in room 12 (now room 30), which is where 'Belshazzar's Feast' (1635) — discussed in the previous chapter — also hung, along with other paintings by Rembrandt, Aelbert Cuyp, and Pieter de Hooch.
16. Wiedemann, 'Zwischen Pestkreuz und Bocklemünd', 119.
17. The Red Sea is properly the Reed Sea, in German 'Schilfmeer'. So there is the potential to slip acoustically and graphically from 'Schilf' [reed] to 'Schliff' [slippe] as it occurs in 'Lichtschliff' [light-slippe].
18. For Felstiner, the poem stems from late self-portraits (unspecified) and the 'tronie' (Dutch for 'face') known as 'A Bearded Man in a Hat' (NG 190). Felstiner suggests that the model for the painting was probably a Jew who had come to Amsterdam from Poland after the massacres of 1648 (Felstiner, *Paul Celan: Poet, Survivor, Jew*, p. 259).
19. See Erwin Panofsky, 'Rembrandt und das Judentum', *Jahrbuch der Hamburger Kunstsammlungen*, 18 (1973), 75–108.

20. Paul Celan, *Die Niemandsrose* (Frankfurt a.M.: S. Fischer, 1963). See Klaus Reichert, 'Hebräische Züge in der Sprache Paul Celans', in *Paul Celan*, ed. by Werner Hamacher and Winfried Menninghaus (Frankfurt a.M.: Suhrkamp, 1998), 156–69.
21. Wiedemann, 'Zwischen Pestkreuz und Bocklemünd', 119.
22. Curiously, one of the discrepancies highlighted between the radiographic image of the painting and its visible image concerns precisely the hair about the ears: 'In the X-radiograph the sitter's hair extends further to the right. A reserve to the left of the head suggests that originally a lock of hair was planned here' (Bruyn et el., *Corpus*, IV, p. 554).
23. 'The Cologne *Self-portrait* is unusually roughly and freely painted. The face is done with a heavily loaded brush in places, elsewhere with light dabbing movements and with an eye to the relief. The direction of the brushstrokes seems to take little account of the forms. For instance, a fairly arbitrary dab of paint has been placed over the nostril. The manner of painting is thus more concerned with suggesting light than with defining form. The broad, flowing strokes done with "juicy" paint have raised edges. At the same time the figure on the left is only cursorily delineated, with the lack of clarity increasing in the lower areas' (ibid.).
24. Malraux also juxtaposes the Cologne self-portrait and 'Homer' (Malraux, *La Métamorphose des dieux*, p. 283).
25. See Ernst van de Wetering, '*Rembrandt laughing*, c. 1628 — a painting resurfaces', *De Kroniek van het Rembrandthuis* (2007), 18–40.
26. Quoted in Bruyn et al., *Corpus*, IV, pp. 559 and 561.
27. Albert Blankert, 'Rembrandt, Zeuxis and ideal beauty', in *Album amicorum J. G. van Gelder*, ed. by J. Bruyn, J. A. Emmens, E. de Jongh and D. P. Snoep (The Hague: Martinus Nijhoff, 1973), pp. 32–39.
28. Wiedemann, 'Zwischen Pestkreuz und Bocklemünd', 103.
29. Max Eisler, *Der alte Rembrandt. Mit 44 Tafeln in Kupfertiefdruck* (Vienna: Druck und Verlag der Österreichischen Staatsdruckerei, 1927), p. 102.
30. Malraux, *La Métamorphose des dieux*, p. 284. The acoustic echo of 'Rembrandt' in 'encombrant' [cumbersome] is probably intentional.
31. Kluge, *Etymologisches Wörterbuch*, p. 710.
32. Seamus Heaney, *Sweeney's Flight* (London: Faber and Faber, 1992), p. vii.
33. Jan Białostocki, 'Rembrandt's « Terminus »', *Wallraf-Richartz-Jahrbuch. Westdeutsches Jahrbuch für Kunstgeschichte*, 28 (1966), 49–60 (52).
34. Georges Didi-Huberman, 'La couleur d'écume ou le paradoxe d'Apelle', *Critique: Revue générale des publications françaises et étrangères*, 42 (1986), 606–29 (617).
35. Ibid., 618.
36. Celan, *Eingedunkelt*, p. 157. The syntagm 'umdrängt von' recalls F. A. Leo's translation of *Macbeth*: 'Nun bin ich eingezwängt in Haft und Banden, / Umdrängt von Furcht und Zweifel' [But now I am cabin'd, cribb'd, confined, / Bound in to saucy doubts and fears] (William Shakespeare, 'Macbeth', trans. by F. A. Leo, in *Shakespeare's dramatische Werke nach der Uebersetzung von August Wilhelm Schlegel und Ludwig Tieck* (Berlin: Reimer, 1871), pp. 163–287 (III.4, p. 231)).
37. See Robert Lowell's poem 'Rembrandt': 'His faces crack... if mine could crack and breathe! / [...] We see, if we see at all, through a copper mist / the strange new idol for the marketplace' (Robert Lowell, *Collected Poems*, ed. by Frank Bidart and David Gewanter, assisted by DeSales Harrison (New York: Farrar, Straus and Giroux, 2003), p. 466).
38. Celan and Celan-Lestrange, *Correspondance*, II, p. 580.
39. Celan, *Mikrolithen*, p. 612. For a color reproduction of the postcard of the self-portrait see Fig. XVI in 'Dossier iconographique', in Celan and Celan-Lestrange, *Correspondance*, II, n. p.
40. Larousse, *Grand dictionnaire universel du XIXe siècle*, VII, p. 90.
41. Didi-Huberman, 'La couleur d'écume ou le paradoxe d'Apelle', 618.
42. Ibid., 610.
43. See Adolphe Reinach, *Textes grecs et latins relatifs à l'histoire de la peinture ancienne. Recueil Milliet* (1921; Paris: Macula, 1985), p. 339, §444.
44. Didi-Huberman, 'La couleur d'écume ou le paradoxe d'Apelle', 607.
45. Ibid., 612.

46. See Fig. 4.2. Recent appraisals of this painting have been severe: 'The attribution of [this painting] has not up to now been doubted. It has however only a superficial similarity to Rembrandt's early work. [...] The theme of a scholar in his room [...] is not uncommon in Rembrandt's circle. Yet the approach and the treatment of this theme are lacking in any refinement, and in every respect show an exaggeration aimed at effect — in the loftiness of the ill-defined room, in the chiaroscuro contrast between the silhouettes and the illuminated background, and in the perfunctory treatment of the forms seen in semi-darkness. The execution shows, as the x-ray confirms, a weak connection between brushwork and indication of form, and in this respect differs totally from Rembrandt's manner of painting' (Bruyn et al., *Corpus*, I, pp. 529–32).
47. Theo Buck, 'Bildreflexion, Lebensreflexion. Zu Paul Celans Gedicht *Einkanter: Rembrandt*', in *'Hinauf und Zurück / in die herzhelle Zukunft.' Deutsch-jüdische Literatur im 20. Jahrhundert. Festschrift für Birgit Lermen*, ed. by Michael Braun, Peter J. Brenner, Hans Messelken, and Gisela Wilkending (Bonn: Bouvier, 2000), pp. 325–51.
48. Paul Celan and Franz Wurm, *Briefwechsel*, ed. by Barbara Wiedemann and Franz Wurm (Frankfurt a.M.: Suhrkamp, 1995), pp. 140–41.
49. Ibid., p. 142.
50. Ibid., p. 144.
51. Celan and Celan-Lestrange, *Correspondance*, II, p. 110.
52. Celan probably encountered the term as follows: 'Free standing rocks are worn away [angeschliffen] at their base by blown sand, and transformed into mushroom or table rocks [Pilz- oder Tischfelsen]' (*Brockhaus-Taschenbuch der Geologie*, p. 135).
53. *Biblia Hebraica Stuttgartensia*, p. 1097, Psalms 16. 8.
54. An element of the painting that commentators of the poem neglect to mention is a series of three or four roughly square-shaped scratchings in the black paint of the lower third of the painting — each about an inch high — which reveal the red-orange wash underneath, and which might be said to bear a vague resemblance to Chinese characters. They are distinguishable only from a live viewing of the painting and would have been evident to Celan.
55. Buck, 'Bildreflexion, Lebensreflexion', p. 329.
56. The National Gallery is even less generous in its appraisal of the way the picture is painted: 'stylistic weaknesses — the fussy, literal-minded way in which details are incised in the paint, the clumsy drawing of the arch on the back wall, the contrast between the detailed draughtsmanship of the globes and books and the loose, almost careless treatment of the figure' (quoted in Buck, 'Bildreflexion, Lebensreflexion', p. 345).
57. E-mail correspondence with Anthony C. Connolly, Royal Society of Portrait Painters, 23 February 2011.
58. David Sylvester, *Interviews with Francis Bacon, with 94 illustrations* (London: Thames and Hudson, 1975), p. 58. Bacon is speaking specifically about Rembrandt's c. 1659 self-portrait at the Musée Granet, Aix-en-Provence. The attribution of this painting remains contested.
59. Not coincidentally, this is also the most heavily painted part. This is particularly evident when viewing the picture in the flesh, as it is only in the darker, lower third of the painting, painted with thinner paint, that the grain of the underlying wooden panel is visible.
60. The notion that Celan was particularly interested in Rembrandt's depiction of light is corroborated by Dischner, who viewed the Rembrandt paintings in the National Gallery with Celan (Celan and Dischner, *Briefwechsel*, p. 149).
61. Könneker sees 'auf du und du mit dem Lichtschliff' [familiar with the light-slippe] as highlighting Rembrandt's 'skillful execution of chiaroscuro technique, for which the artist is famous' (Sabine Könneker, *»Sichtbares, Hörbares«. Die Beziehung zwischen Sprachkunst und bildender Kunst am Beispiel Paul Celans* (Bielefeld: Aisthesis, 1995), p. 72). Pöggeler is closer to the mystery of the painter's light and Celan's conception of it, when he writes: 'There is at the very least a reference to Rembrandt's famous 'luminism', which exposes the radiance and the defiance of this world, but also its misery, to a light that irrupts as if it came from the other side [wie von jenseits]' (Otto Pöggeler, *Die Frage nach der Kunst. Von Hegel zu Heidegger* (Freiburg: Alber, 1984), p. 331). The British pop artist Peter Blake notes that the transparency of dried oil paint tends to increase with time, and that this results in a more pronounced contrast between dark and light

areas than originally intended (quoted in Jo Crook and Tom Learner, *The Impact of Modern Paints* (New York: Watson-Guptill, 2000), p. 44).
62. 'ventifact, n.' *OED Online*. March 2017. Oxford University Press, available at <http://www.oed.com/view/Entry/222229?redirectedFrom=ventifact>, [accessed 17 March 2017].
63. In contrast to corrosion, which in geology describes the destruction of rock or soil through the chemical and solvent action of water or other liquids, corrasion describes the wearing away of the surface of the earth through the movement of particles of inorganic matter transported by air, water, or glacial ice. See 'corrasion, n.2' *OED Online*. March 2017. Oxford University Press, available at <http://www.oed.com/view/Entry/41894?redirectedFrom=corrasion>, [accessed 17 March 2017].
64. The obsolete English noun 'slippe' is a cognate of the German 'Schliff' [grinding, sharpening, corrasion] ('† slip. *n*.5', *OED Online*. March 2017. Oxford University Press, available at <http://www.oed.com/view/Entry/181879?rskey=TzouFl&result=5&isAdvanced=false>, [accessed 17 March 2017]). The association of 'Einkanter', 'Lichtschliff', and 'Mundwinkel' is foreshadowed in 'PAU, SPÄTER' [PAU, LATER], a poem written in October 1965. An early version of this poem includes a reference to Waterlooplein, the central district of Amsterdam where both Rembrandt and Baruch Spinoza lived. The final version of the poem ends as follows: 'dass Baruch, der niemals / Weinende / rund um dich die / kantige, / unverstandene, sehende / Träne zurecht- / schleife' [that Baruch, the one / who never cries / may grind aright, / around you, the / angular, / misunderstood, seeing, / tear] (Celan, *Fadensonnen. Vorstufen — Textgenese — Endfassung*, p. 31). We are thus invited to perceive the grains (or slippe) from the lens (or tears) that Spinoza grinds [schleift] in his occupation as lens-grinder in the contemporaneous light-slippe [Lichtschliff] of Rembrandt's pigment.
65. Deleuze, *Cinéma 2. L'Image-temps*, p. 262.
66. Masoretic numbering divided psalm nine into two parts numbered nine and ten, thereby displacing the number of subsequent psalms by one. The Septuagint and Vulgate psalm sixteen would therefore correspond with psalm seventeen in the Hebrew tradition. Most critics agree that the sixteenth psalm referred to in Celan's poem is the Masoretic version, and not the Septuagint or Vulgate version. Buck, however, proposes that we should read the fifteenth psalm (Hebrew), and quotes it in full (Buck, 'Bildreflexion, Lebensreflexion', pp. 342–43). Wiedemann notes that the only complete Bible in Celan's possession was a Luther translation from 1897, in which the psalms are numbered according to the Hebrew system (Wiedemann, 'Zwischen Pestkreuz und Bocklemünd', 119–20).
67. Kluge, *Etymologisches Wörterbuch*, p. 650. This verse is sometimes recorded as 63. 13.
68. *Biblia Hebraica Stuttgartensia*, p. 1147, Psalms 68. 14.
69. Luther, *Lutherbibel*, p. 423. Compare to Buber's translation: ' — wollt liegen ihr zwischen den Hürden?! — , / Taubenflügel, silberüberspannt, / Gefieder dran aus grüngelbem Feinerz' (Martin Buber, *Die Schriftwerke* (Cologne: Hegner, 1962), p. 100).
70. Francis Brown, *The Brown-Driver-Briggs Hebrew and English Lexicon, with an appendix containing the Biblical Aramaic,* with the cooperation of S. R. Driver and Charles A. Briggs (1906; Peabody: Hendrickson, 2005), p. 262.
71. Ibid., pp. 358–59.
72. *The Holy Bible*, p. 492, Psalms 16. 6.
73. Ibid., p. 491, Psalms 15. 1.
74. That the raised paint of shimmering impasto around the right corner of the mouth stands in 'relief' to the lower and thinner paint of the darker areas of the face and background is particularly pertinent when one considers the etymology of 'relief'. Historically, it not only denotes the 'extent to which the top of a fortification rises above the ditch' or the 'manner or degree of variation in elevation of a part of the surface of the earth', but in one of its earliest known forms designates the Middle French for the contours of a person's mouth, of that which seems to project itself above and beyond the face ('relief, n.3' *OED Online*. March 2017. Oxford University Press, available at <http://www.oed.com/view/Entry/161918?rskey=CaqbGs&result=3&isAdvanced=false>, [accessed 17 March 2017]).
75. Buck, 'Bildreflexion, Lebensreflexion', p. 342.
76. See 'ES IST ALLES ANDERS' [EVERYTHING IS DIFFERENT], written between 5 June

1962 and 25 April 1963 (Celan, *Die Gedichte*, p. 162).
77. Osip Mandel'shtam, *Sobranie sochinenii*, ed. by G. P. Struve and B. A. Filippova, 3 vols (New York: Mezhdunarodnoe literaturnoe sodruzhestvo, 1967), I, pp. 249–50. Three other poems by Mandel'shtam explicitly mention Rembrandt: 'На Надеждинской улице' [On Nadezhdin Street] (ibid., I, pp. 303–05), 'Полночь в Москве' [Midnight in Moscow] (ibid., I, pp. 182–85), and 'Еще далеко мне до патриарха' [I'm still far from a patriarch] (ibid., I, pp. 174–75).
78. For Celan's translations of Mandel'shtam see Celan, *Gesammelte Werke in sieben Bänden*, V, pp. 47–161.
79. Osip Mandel'shtam, *Sobranie sochinenii*, ed. by G. P. Struve and B. A. Filippova, 2 vols (Washington: Inter-Language Literary Associates, 1964), II, p. 233.
80. *Biblia Hebraica Stuttgartensia*, p. 1096, Psalms 16. 1.
81. The program, called 'The Poetry of Osip Mandel'shtam', was broadcast on 19 March 1960. For the transcript see Paul Celan, 'Die Dichtung Ossip Mandelstamms', in Ossip Mandelstamm, *Im Luftgrab. Ein Lesebuch. Mit Beiträgen von Paul Celan, Pier Paolo Pasolini, Philippe Jaccottet, Joseph Brodsky*, ed. by Ralph Dutli (Zurich: Ammann, 1988), pp. 69–81. For commentary see Christine Ivanović, *Das Gedicht im Geheimnis der Begegnung: Dichtung und Poetik Celans im Kontext seiner russischen Lektüren* (Tübingen: Niemeyer, 1996), pp. 321–45.
82. Celan, 'Die Dichtung Ossip Mandelstamms', p. 70. Celan employed a similar formula in a letter to Brigitte and Gottfried Bermann Fischer, dated 22 November 1958: 'It tries this with the means made available to it by language that has passed through time, under the particular angle of inclination [Neigungswinkel] of its (that's to say my) existence. It tries to do this, amidst all the embellishments and euphemisms, in the most unadorned way possible. It speaks into the open, to that point where language can also lead to the encounter' (Paul Celan, 'Letter to Brigitte Bermann Fischer and Gottfried Bermann Fischer, 22 November 1958' in Gottfried Bermann Fischer and Brigitte Bermann Fischer, *Briefwechsel mit Autoren*, ed. by Reiner Stach and Karin Schlapp (Frankfurt a.M.: Fischer, 1990), p. 617 (p. 617)).
83. Celan, *Gesammelte Werke in sieben Bänden*, III, p. 197.
84. Elizabeth Jennings, *Growing-Points* (Cheadle Hulme: Carcanet New Press, 1975), p. 39.
85. Michael Eskin, *Ethics and Dialogue in the Works of Levinas, Bakhtin, Mandel'shtam, and Celan* (Oxford: Oxford University Press, 2000), p. 160.
86. Étienne Souriau, 'Time in the Plastic Arts', *The Journal of Aesthetics and Art Criticism*, 7.4 (1949), 294–307 (307).
87. J. D. McClatchy, *Poets on Painters. Essays on the Art of Painting by Twentieth-Century Poets* (Berkeley: University of California Press, 1988), xiii.

CONCLUSION

Reading Poetry, Reading Celan

> Come, roll the door-stone with me
> before the untaken tent.[1]

The term 'oeuvre', whether in English or French, is rarely if ever used to refer to the totality of an author's scriptural activity. Instead, it is usually limited to signifying those parts of the work that are publically visible and accessible. In French, the parts of a ship's hull which are visible to the eye, and on which the name of the ship is inscribed, are the 'oeuvres mortes' [dead works], the freeboard or topsides that lie above the waterline. Those parts of the hull submerged in the water and hidden from view are the 'oeuvres vives' [live or quick-works]. Although both the quick and the dead 'oeuvres' form part of the same structure and combine seamlessly for the ship to float, only the dead works are visible and recognizable. This is despite the fact that the ship depends on the integrity of those parts of the hull that are mostly submerged and out of sight, and which are most susceptible to corrosion, the accretion of organic and mineral matter, and accidental penetration.

Any correspondence between the visible and hidden parts of the ship's hull and the visible and hidden parts of the literary oeuvre breaks down almost as soon as it has been proposed. As soon as material is published, the non-oeuvre or the quick-work has the potential to become part of the dead work, part of the visible oeuvre. As Blanchot puts it: 'the "oeuvre" is only "oeuvre" when it becomes the open intimacy of someone who writes it and of someone who reads it, the space violently unfolded by the dispute between the ability to speak and the ability to understand'.[2] Publication makes the sous-oeuvre publically accessible, and the 'open intimacy' of reading makes it visible. But it is also possible that for the reader to become intimate with the live work of an author's production, for the quick-work to become dead work, for the sous-oeuvre to become oeuvre, that the entire oeuvre will have been shipwrecked, or 'violently unfolded', and with it distinctions between oeuvre and sous-oeuvre. The purpose of the sous-oeuvre is perhaps ultimately to break down all such distinctions. The patterns we make out in an author's textual production, the sea-worthy vessels identified and launched by critics, indicate a greater or lesser ability to hold on to, make sense of, and imaginatively amplify textual flotsam and jetsam.

The oeuvre consciously created and published by Celan during his lifetime — including the two collections of poems prepared by the author but published posthumously — is significantly different to the oeuvre now available to contemporary readers. It not only comprises new material, some of it repetitive and somewhat familiar, some of it radically different. It also includes new modes of expression, new forms of text, and a new grammar, vocabulary, and syntax, for which reading the original oeuvre does not prepare us. The presence of this changed oeuvre means that we cannot continue to read Celan as Celan intended his work to be read. The conditions of reading, of understanding, and of creating meaning have changed since Celan delivered the Büchner prize speech in October 1960, and more generally since the late 1950s and early 1960s when he composed the prose pieces that continue to be central reference points in critical examinations of his work.

Paul Celan's Unfinished Poetics aims to familiarize readers with some of the less fashionable, less frequented, less convenient portions of Celan's textual production. It includes poems from the unfinished *Eingedunkelt* cycle (1966), and from *Fadensonnen* (1968) and *Schneepart* (1971), as well as a translation from the late 1950s, and a rare poem written in French. It also includes verbal and non-verbal annotations, cut out newspaper articles, and hermetic aphorisms. Some of the poems examined here were authorized for publication by the poet, others were authorized under unique circumstances as examples of unfinished or abandoned work, and others never authorized for publication. This book asks what happens when the sous-oeuvre is allowed to contaminate the oeuvre. What happens when a poet whose completed poems are economical and precise in the extreme — one critic aptly calls them 'Giacomettian' — then becomes synonymous with textual excess, repetition, imperfection, incompletion, and mental illness, if not madness?

The book begins, in chapter one, with an examination of three of the ways in which the pre-text teaches us to read unfinished texts. Although the notion of the sous-oeuvre intends to draw attention to a broad range of texts that have been overlooked in favor of the established oeuvre, the pre-text offers a privileged point of entry into any exploration of the sous-oeuvre. This is not only because it contains text that is almost always overlooked, but also because it presents challenges to creating meaning that are rarely if ever encountered in intercourse with the completed text. Instead of importing modes of reading forged in encounters with the published oeuvre, the pre-text can be shown to operate in ways that are unique to its ateleological configuration. It is in the wake of the opening chapter that the three following chapters are conceived. Although these chapters engage primarily with texts that are mostly completed, and in some cases authorized for publication, these texts tend either to have been consigned to the shadows of Celan's oeuvre, or to have been subjected to critical approaches that have themselves become canonical, overshadowing the text itself. Each of these chapters invites the reader of Celan's poetry to import the same vigilance, ambition, and attention to detail required when negotiating the pre-text, to reading the oeuvre as a whole, whether published by the poet, or published posthumously and edited by others.

Celan's engagement with Mallarmé has often been considered to be of marginal importance, and Mallarmé's impact on Celan's conception of the tasks and possibilities of poetry as negligible. Celan himself is said to have rejected Mallarmé as a fetish of contemporary criticism. In chapter two, I go behind these critical conventions to re-examine the three discrete moments when Celan encounters Mallarmé's work. In 'The Meridian', Mallarmé provides the conceptual framework that allows Celan to realize 'the majesty of the absurd' that is poetry's essential step outside of visible and audible language. Later, thanks to the intermediary of Sartre, Mallarmé will appear to propose the possibility of a poetics of suicide. By identifying the ways that Sartre's exposition is intended as a hoax, not unlike Mallarmé's own 'Glorious Lie', we can begin to challenge the critical convention that sees Celan's suicide as the culmination of his poetic career, and as providing — posthumously — an overarching rationale for the oeuvre. In his lone translation of Mallarmé's rondel, the conflicting dynamics of appropriation and destruction are indicative of the complex relations between Celan and his forebear in difficulty.

In chapter three, I re-consider Celan's poetic production in the immediate aftermath of the Frankfurt Auschwitz trial and its representation as theater. Although the trial and Weiss's play were, respectively, the most important legal and theatrical events in the Federal Republic during the mid-1960s, Celan's possible response to them has never been considered. This is in part because the conventional signs betraying interest in the trial and the play are not in evidence. The sous-oeuvre encourages us to look beyond what is evident to that which hides just outside of conventional expression. It is only then that we will recognize a sustained attempt on the part of the poet to lend the writing of poems to the pursuit of justice, where both the trial and its theatrical representation not only fail to deliver justice, but compound and continue the initial crime. We are invited to see here something of Celan's dream of action, his desire for poetry to do more than is conventionally ascribed to it or expected from it. Here, there is a conception of what poetry can do that goes beyond what conventional criticism is willing to accord to it. There may even be something of a larger, ambitious, but unrealized project on the part of Celan to radically redesign the way poetry relates to society.

In chapter four I mainly examine a poem that has repeatedly been read and written about, unlike the poems discussed in the introduction, and chapters one and three. Here, though, I seek to challenge the canon of criticism that has grown up around the poem over the past nearly half-century, and which not only conditions the ways the poem is read and understood, but which has come to block out the singularity of the poem's expression. By looking beyond ekphrasis as a mode of interpretation, we can see how the poem asks not to be read as an isolated exploration, through inscribed language, of certain of Rembrandt's paintings. Instead, by allowing contingency and chance to govern our reading of poetry — in the same way that Rembrandt allowed the contingency and chance of oil paint to inflect his paintings — it becomes possible to conceive of a poetics that is always unfinished, always slightly out of our control, always surprising us in ways we never expected.

If, as shown in chapter two, an event such as Celan's suicide can be thought to constitute the culmination of the poetics that drove his oeuvre, then the investigation of the sous-oeuvre, as attempted in this book, should reveal alternative conceptions of poetry that run counter to, and seek to preserve the oeuvre from, any monolithic poetics. Celan's poetry is not only bound to his death, as readings of the oeuvre by itself might suggest. The sous-oeuvre reveals a still breathing, porous, unpredictable hinterland to the oeuvre — sometimes human, sometimes monstrous, sometimes familiar, sometimes radically unsettling — that not only subtends and informs the oeuvre, but which offers an alternative place for poetic and conceptual expression. The sous-oeuvre guarantees that Celan's poetics is always in the process of formation. The poetics that each chapter of this book explores and seeks to present is therefore not a coherent or unified one. It is instead a partial and fragmented poetics that should always remain unfinished. As Mandel'shtam said of Dante, so too it might be said of Celan, that his work is 'a device for catching the future'. It demands 'commentary *in futurum*'.[3]

The sous-oeuvre complicates the notion of a poet's oeuvre. It deliberately seeks to prevent the reader from reaching the comfort of consensus, the sense of having understood, of having brought the ways we perceive a given poet and his or her work to completion. It means to spoil any attempt to transform an author into a critical and cultural cliché, whose poetry is a product that can be comprehended and consumed. This constant re-evaluation of the oeuvre echoes the task of the reader as formulated by the late Werner Hamacher, for whom reading is 'not so much a collecting and storage, nor a recollecting and sublation, as an opening of language onto what remains unsaid in it'.[4] The sous-oeuvre represents the oeuvre as it opens itself onto what remains unsaid in it, and which will continue to announce itself as coming and as to come. When Hamacher says that the reading of a poem 'opens itself onto a coming that no intentional act can bring about', the same should also be said of the oeuvre, which can no longer be restricted to the collection of intentional acts ascribed to and authorized by the poet. The sous-oeuvre reminds us of the openness of the oeuvre, of the fact that it does not give back a pre-given reality but is constantly in the process of becoming.

A useful parallel and guide to reading Celan's oeuvre through its sous-oeuvre may be found in recent studies of the work of Emily Dickinson. Dickinson's works were unpublished in her lifetime, and presented idiosyncrasies not only in their material presentation — often in the form of hand sewn fascicles — but also in the disposition of text on the page, and in a partially invented punctuation, grammar, and syntax. When her work was first published in 1890, editorial conventions transformed the unique manuscript disposition of the poet's text into conventional lyric poems. This was despite the evident resistance of many of the texts to this type of translation. As Higginson, one of the editors at the time, notes: 'In many cases these verses will seem to the reader like poetry torn up by the roots, with rain and dew and earth still clinging to them'.[5] Recently, attention has been drawn to the ways that Dickinson's texts were tamed for public consumption by publishing and editing conventions. Virginia Jackson is perhaps foremost among those critics who have attempted to identify reading practices that preceded the practices of critical lyric reading. By returning to Dickinson's original texts, Jackson aims to go back 'to a moment before lyric reading was the only way to apprehend a poem', and to retrieve previous reading practices for the present.[6]

Here, I do not propose to go back to a moment that precedes lyric reading. Unlike Dickinson, Celan wrote and published poems highly conscious of their mode of presentation in print. This mode of presentation is written into the poems that make up the original oeuvre and criticism has consistently respected the integrity of this mode. Instead, I want to highlight the importance for readers to respond to current material realities, neither intended nor foreseen by the poet. For example, the accessibility of the sous-oeuvre in its many forms invites us to challenge Celan's own conception of the poem. Celan's poem, even as it incorporates fragmentation, incompletion, and ambiguity, does so within the parameters of both the completed poem and the poet's authorization. The prestige of the completed poem depends on its conceptual integrity, illustrated and guaranteed by conventional typography that sets the poem out in the uncontested space of the white page. It is this same separation of the poem from all other traces of text that allows de Man to pursue his paradoxical definition of the lyric as that which refuses lyric, but which makes lyric possible, in his reading of Baudelaire's most canonical poem, 'Correspondances'.[7] In short, modern lyric reading requires discrete poems. Exposure to the sous-oeuvre, however, and to the pre-text in particular, will alert us to alternative, messy, inconvenient ways that poetry subsists, outside the boundaries of the poem as set out on the page by conventional editorial practices. The sous-oeuvre requires us to draw back from lyric, from modern lyric reading, from poetry, and from the poem, and to develop a new sensitivity for the complex, sometimes inextricable, interplay of the intentional and unintentional in a poet's textual production.

It is therefore incumbent upon contemporary readers of Paul Celan's work to be alert to the new ways that the sous-oeuvre requires us to conceive of the task of reading. This will mean expanding what we understand by poetry, to include those traces that would normally be disregarded: those inscribed under medication; those that bear evidence of the poet's severe depression or even psychosis; those that are repetitive or otherwise redundant; those that inhere in the extra-linguistic, non-verbal realm; those that are so obscure that they resist reading and understanding; or simply those that are currently unfashionable. Reading Celan today, and perhaps even reading poetry *tout court*, means retrieving the messiness of literary production from what have become, as Jackson notes, 'purified terms'.[8] Susan Howe writes that Dickinson's manuscripts 'represent a contradiction to canonical social power, whose predominant purpose seems to have been to render isolate voices devoted to writing as a physical event of immediate revelation'.[9] Although Celan did not perceive his writing in this way, our current situation as readers now permits us to approach all his texts — whether finished or unfinished, authorized or unauthorized, poem or draft, verbal or non-verbal inscription — for the 'physical event' of their 'immediate revelation'.

An increased awareness of the sous-oeuvre will therefore have radical implications for the ways we understand the poem, poetry, and lyric. If, as de Man says, 'any text, as text, compels reading as its understanding',[10] then the moment we begin to read the unfashionable, inconvenient, and unfinished part of the poet's textual production, we have begun to transform what we understand by the poem, poetry, and lyric. Lyric, poetry, and the poem are not expansive, social, or generous terms. They are not signs of strength or ambition. They are calculating, in the sense that they reduce and harden the text in front of us. They cut the text down to a size that can be consumed if not comprehended. They interrupt the text's unruly desires, be it for transcendence or immanence. They make it less ephemeral, less liable to be taken from us. De Man notes that lyric is 'convenient',[11] in the literal sense that it makes things come together (from the Latin 'com-' together, and 'venire' to come). It is paradigmatic of the relationship of grammar, trope, and theme. It has conventional characteristics that include 'various structures and moments: specular symmetry along an axis of assertion and negation [...], the grammatical transformation of the declarative into the vocative modes of question, exclamation, address, hypothesis, etc., the tropological transformation of analogy into apostrophe or [...] the transformation of trope into anthropomorphism'.[12] The sous-oeuvre in general, but perhaps the pre-text in particular, exposes us to an inconvenient realm, where lyric does not manifest itself with the uniformity, unambiguousness, self-confidence, and self-composure that allows de Man to list its characteristics. It is perhaps when faced with the excesses of the pre-text and the ambiguities of the sous-oeuvre, that we best understand 'the defensive motion of understanding' that brings a notion such as 'lyric' — but also 'poetry' and 'the poem' — into play, as terms which define the object of reading and allow for 'the possibility of a future hermeneutics'.[13]

Paul Celan's Unfinished Poetics invites us to pre-empt this defensive motion of understanding. It asks us to relinquish claims on lyric, poetry, and the poem. It does not propose understanding as a defensive motion to secure what we have. Reading does not need to be about security. As Bahti says, 'all reading tries — it need not succeed, nor end with this, but it minimally tries — to understand the literary text'.[14] There is much more freedom here than might be supposed. Although all reading tries to understand the text, reading is also where we can lose ourselves, where we can respond to irrational impulses, where we are not actually required to create coherent responses or definitive interpretations. When reading in the sous-oeuvre — a more difficult proposition than reading poetry in any conventional sense — we may find we have no choice. Conventional literary texts provide directions to readers 'for both the co-constitutive reading activity and the specific effort at reading as interpretation and understanding'.[15] One of the defining features of the sous-oeuvre is that it provides fewer of these 'directions' for its potential reader. It is therefore incumbent upon the reader of the sous-oeuvre to discover his or her own directions, to fashion the object of reading in the encounter with the text, to respond to the particular temporality of a given textual constellation. The sous-oeuvre, and especially the pre-text, present the reader with text that may not have been prepared with the reader of literature in mind. It demands hitherto unseen, robust modes of reading.

To read poetry is therefore not just to read poems or to read lyric. It designates the practice of exposing one's reading eye to the textual in whatever ways it manifests itself, to create objects of reading as well as coherent patterns of meaning. Lukács defined lyric poetry as that which 'can create a protean mythology of substantial subjectivity out of the constitutive strength of its ignorance'.[16] The sous-oeuvre teaches the oeuvre to know, and denies it the ignorance that Lukács would assign to it. When read through the sous-oeuvre, the oeuvre becomes conscious of its illusion, its staging, its imaginary projection. Lukács projects a poetry in which 'only the great moment exists, the moment at which the meaningful unity of nature and soul or their meaningful divorce, the necessary and affirmed loneliness of the soul becomes eternal'.[17] The sous-oeuvre reveals the great moments of unity and of divorce to be illusions, and the comparison of the poem with the soul, repeated by Celan at various points, to be an outmoded anthropomorphism. I would like instead to propose poetry as the term that relates to all scriptural traces of an author, those consciously intended to be poetic or public, and those only ever intended as mundane or private. This will explode the unicity of the poem with its corresponding illusions of 'spatial enclosure', or 'an interior consciousness',[18] just as European prosody once shook itself free of the 'small area complete in itself' of the stanza.[19] In the sous-oeuvre, as in the pre-text, such enclosures, intensities, and units are not absent, but neither should they be considered the unique or major currencies of thought.

To read poetry in this sense will therefore mean that each reader will break away from the community of readers. It is to discover reading that restores to poetry something of its originary isolation, of the youthfulness that Ernest Bovet once associated with it, but also perhaps something of its awkwardness.[20] In his essay 'Philosophy of Toys', Baudelaire evokes the image of the child playing alone who, with little more than a chair, is able to imagine being in a moving horse-drawn carriage. The poet rebukes members of the public for whom art has become tailored to such a degree that they are no longer able to deploy their own imaginative and creative faculties. As Baudelaire puts it, they 'demand a physical and mechanical perfection from the theater' and 'simply cannot understand that a Shakespeare play can be just as impressive with barbarically simple props'.[21] As a readership becomes expert in a particular mode of reading, the object of reading will appear familiar even before it has been read. Any surprise that a modern reader may have experienced on first seeing a poem has long since given way to a prefabricated mental framework, into which the poem is placed before the reader has begun to read. We are used to considering poems as commodities, products prepared for the reader's consumption, quality-tested, and marked with the various stamps of authenticity — the author's name, the reputation of the press, the approval of critics. Ever since Hegel's elevation of the lyric as that which is most likely to further the spirit of the age, because it enables the pure representation of subjectivity, poetry or lyric has been considered a transcendent genre.[22] A restitution of the sous-oeuvre, and of the pre-text, dismantles the primacy of the completed poem and allows subversive modes of what de Man calls 'language power' to assert themselves.[23] These might be 'non-anthropomorphic, non-elegiac, non-celebratory, non-lyrical, non-poetic' or simply 'non-comprehension'.[24] What Baudelaire reminds us is that poetry is a practice that depends on the creative imagination of the reader, on his or her willingness to improvise and co-create poetry in the prosaic reality of the everyday. The central place accorded to the sous-oeuvre, and with it the pre-text, in *Paul Celan's Unfinished Poetics*, is meant to remind us that poetry, more than a perfect idea, is a continuous and imperfect practice.

Spring of 2020 will see the fiftieth anniversary of Celan's death at the age of forty-nine. It will mark the end of a lifetime after the lifetime, during which Celan's work, and the critical studies it has provoked, have established the German language poet as one of the most important European authors of the twentieth century. For literary fame and familiarity to be established, much of the oeuvre's unpredictability and strangeness will have been put to one side. The oeuvre hardens under the repetition of similar critical gestures and begins to acquire a shape and form that it was not created to have, but with which it will from that point on be identified. Parts of Celan's work, as published, read, translated, and taught, have acquired a canonical status they were never meant to have. When alive, Celan would refuse requests to include his most famous poem 'Todesfuge' or 'Deathfugue' in various anthologies, irritated by its success, which overshadowed his other works. Something of this hostility to canonization should now be projected onto the success of those few poems and prose texts elevated in recent years by literary critics, which have also had the unintended effect of narrowing the ways the oeuvre is approached and perceived. It is in the nature of contemporary literary criticism, as much concerned by its professional implications as by its purely literary and philosophical demands, to revisit texts examined by other critics. The poet's work might therefore be described as a landscape in which readers follow the tracks of previous readers, which over time become highways, with which the landscape then becomes synonymous. The accretion of critical works that examine a similar group of primary texts has lead to a hardening of the lines of approach, to the creation of tunnels if not funnels for thought, which permit rapid access, assessment, and egress. *Paul Celan's Unfinished Poetics* aims to remind us of the need to restore to the reading of poetry something of its original extension and wildness, of its essential insubmission and unpredictability, and of the ways that the study of literature will have to change to account for new textual realities.

Notes to the Conclusion

1. 'Komm, wälz mit mir den Türstein / vors Unbezwungene Zelt' (Celan, *Eingedunkelt*, p. 91).
2. Blanchot, *L'espace littéraire*, p. 35.
3. Osip Mandel'shtam, *Sobranie sochinenii*, 4 vols (Moscow: Art-Biznes Centr, 1994), III, p. 238.
4. Hamacher, 'The Second of Inversion', p. 256.
5. Thomas Wentworth Higginson, 'Preface', in Emily Dickinson, *Poems*, ed. by Mabel Loomis Todd and T. W. Higginson (Boston: Roberts, 1892), pp. iii–vi (pp. v–vi).
6. Virginia Jackson, *Dickinson's Misery: A Theory of Lyric Reading* (Princeton: Princeton University Press, 2005), p. 116.
7. Paul de Man, *The Rhetoric of Romanticism* (New York: Columbia University Press, 1984), pp. 243–62.
8. Jackson, *Dickinson's Misery*, p. 235.
9. Susan Howe, *The Birth-Mark: Unsettling the Wilderness in American Literary History* (Hanover: University Press of New England, 1993), p. 1.
10. de Man, *The Rhetoric of Romanticism*, p. 261.
11. Ibid.

12. Ibid.
13. Ibid.
14. Bahti, *Ends of the Lyric*, p. 10.
15. Ibid.
16. Georg Lukács, *The Theory of the Novel. A Historico-Philosophical Essay on the Forms of Great Epic Literature*, trans. by Anna Bostock (Cambridge: MIT, 1971), p. 63.
17. Ibid.
18. Jackson, *Dickinson's Misery*, p. 114.
19. Northrop Frye, 'Approaching the Lyric' in *Lyric Poetry. Beyond New Criticism*, ed. by Chaviva Hošek and Patricia Parker (Ithaca: Cornell University Press, 1985), pp. 31–37 (p. 34).
20. Ernest Bovet, *Lyrisme, épopée, drame: une loi de l'histoire littéraire expliquée par l'évolution générale* (Paris, A. Colin, 1911), p. 214.
21. Baudelaire, *Oeuvres complètes*, I, p. 583.
22. G. W. F. Hegel, *Aesthetics: Lectures on Fine Art*, trans. by T. M. Knox, 2 vols (Oxford: Clarendon Press, 1975), II, p. 971.
23. de Man, *The Rhetoric of Romanticism*, p. 262.
24. Ibid.

BIBLIOGRAPHY

Texts by Paul Celan

'Paul Celan: Vier Gedichte aus dem Französischen', in *Insel-Almanach auf das Jahr 1959* (Leipzig: Insel, 1958), pp. 31–33.
Die Niemandsrose (Frankfurt a.M.: S. Fischer, 1963).
Tagebuch 13 (26 April 1965–8 May 1965). Unpublished diary preserved at the German Literature Archive, Marbach a. N., Manuscript Department, D 90.1.3300, F 2390.
Tagebuch 18 (20 March 1966–22 April 1966). Unpublished diary preserved at the German Literature Archive, Marbach a. N., Manuscript Department, D 90.1.3305, F 2395.
'Eingedunkelt', in Samuel Beckett, Karl Krolow, Wolfgang Koeppen, Hans Erich Nossack, Peter Weiss, Uwe Johnson, Wolfgang Hildesheimer, Nelly Sachs, Paul Celan, and Martin Walser, *Aus aufgegebenen Werken* (Frankfurt a.M.: Suhrkamp, 1968), pp. 149–61.
Schneepart (Frankfurt a.M.: Suhrkamp, 1971).
'Briefe an Alfred Margul-Sperber', *Neue Literatur: Zeitschrift des Schriftstellerverbandes der Sozialistischen Republik Rumänien*, 26.7 (1975), 50–63.
Paul Celan: Poems. A Bilingual Edition, trans. by Michael Hamburger (New York: Persea, 1980).
'Die Dichtung Ossip Mandelstamms', in Ossip Mandelstamm, *Im Luftgrab. Ein Lesebuch. Mit Beiträgen von Paul Celan, Pier Paolo Pasolini, Philippe Jaccottet, Joseph Brodsky*, ed. by Ralph Dutli (Zurich: Ammann, 1988), pp. 69–81.
'Letter to Brigitte Bermann Fischer and Gottfried Bermann Fischer, 22 November 1958' in Gottfried Bermann Fischer and Brigitte Bermann Fischer, *Briefwechsel mit Autoren*, ed. by Reiner Stach and Karin Schlapp (Frankfurt a.M.: Fischer, 1990), p. 617.
Eingedunkelt: und Gedichte aus dem Umkreis von Eingedunkelt, ed. by Bertrand Badiou and Jean-Claude Rambach (Frankfurt a.M.: Suhrkamp, 1991).
Die Niemandsrose, ed. by Heino Schmull, with the assistance of Michael Schwarzkopf (Frankfurt a.M.: Suhrkamp, 1996).
'Eingedunkelt: Enfosquit', trans. by Jordi Ibáñez Fanés, *Reduccions, revista de poesia*, 65–66 (1996), 32–53.
'Eingedunkelt', trans. by Espen Stueland, *Vagant* [Bilag], 1 (1996), 3–8.
Die Gedichte aus dem Nachlass, ed. by Bertrand Badiou, Jean-Claude Rambach, and Barbara Wiedemann, with notes by Barbara Wiedemann and Bertrand Badiou (Frankfurt a.M.: Suhrkamp, 1997).
Der Meridian. Endfassung — Vorstufen — Materialien, ed. by Bernhard Böschenstein and Heino Schmull, assisted by Michael Schwarzkopf and Christiane Wittkop (Frankfurt a.M.: Suhrkamp, 1999).
Fadensonnen. Vorstufen — Textgenese — Endfassung, ed. by Heino Schmull, Markus Heilmann, and Christiane Wittkop (Frankfurt a.M.: Suhrkamp, 2000).
Gesammelte Werke in sieben Bänden, 7 vols (Frankfurt a.M.: Suhrkamp, 2000).
Selected Poems and Prose of Paul Celan, trans. by John Felstiner (New York: W. W. Norton, 2000).

Fathomsuns / Fadensonnen and Benighted / Eingedunkelt, trans. by Ian Fairley (Riverdale-on-Hudson: Sheep Meadow Press, 2001).

La bibliothèque philosophique. Die philosophische Bibliothek, ed. by Alexandra Richter, Patrik Alac, and Bertrand Badiou, with a preface by Jean-Pierre Lefebvre (Paris: Éditions de la rue d'Ulm, 2004).

Die Gedichte. Kommentierte Gesamtausgabe in einem Band, ed. by Barbara Wiedemann (Frankfurt a.M.: Suhrkamp, 2005).

Mikrolithen sinds, Steinchen: Die Prosa aus dem Nachlass. Kritische Ausgabe, ed. by Barbara Wiedemann and Bertrand Badiou (Frankfurt a.M.: Suhrkamp, 2005).

Eingedunkelt. Historisch-kritische Ausgabe, ed. by Rolf Bücher and Andreas Lohr, assisted by Hans Kruschwitz and Thomas Schneider, vol. 12 of *Werke. Historisch-kritische Ausgabe. I. Abteilung: Lyrik und Prosa* (Frankfurt a.M.: Suhrkamp, 2006).

Briefwechsel mit den rheinischen Freunden. Heinrich Böll, Paul Schallück und Rolf Schroers. Mit einzelnen Briefen von Gisèle Celan-Lestrange, Ilse Schallück und Ilse Schroers, ed. by Barbara Wiedemann (Berlin: Suhrkamp, 2011).

The Meridian. Final Version — Drafts — Materials, ed. by Bernhard Böschenstein and Heino Schmull, assisted by Michael Schwarzkopf and Christiane Wittkop, trans. by Pierre Joris (Stanford: Stanford University Press, 2011).

Corona. Selected Poems of Paul Celan, trans. by Susan H. Gillespie (Barrytown: Station Hill, 2013).

Breathturn into Timestead. The Collected Later Poetry, trans. by Pierre Joris (New York: Farrar, Strauss, and Giroux, 2014).

Prosa I. Zu Lebzeiten publizierte Prosa und Reden. Bonner Historisch-kritische Ausgabe, ed. by Axel Gellhaus, Andreas Lohr, Heino Schmull and Rolf Bücher, vol. 15 of *Werke. Historisch-kritische Ausgabe. I. Abteilung: Lyrik und Prosa* (Frankfurt a.M.: Suhrkamp, 2014).

——《策蘭詩選》trans. by Ming Meng, available at <http://www.douban.com/group/topic/6470140/>, [accessed 12 March 2016].

CELAN, PAUL, and GISÈLE CELAN-LESTRANGE, *Correspondance (1951–1970). Avec un choix de lettres de Paul Celan à son fils Eric*, ed. by Bertrand Badiou and Eric Celan, 2 vols (Paris: Seuil, 2001).

—— *Correspondencia (1951–1970). Con una selección de cartas de Paul Celan a su hijo Eric*, ed. by Bertrand Badiou and Eric Celan, preface by Francisco Jarauta, trans. by Mauro Armiño and Jaime Siles (Madrid: Siruela, 2008).

CELAN, PAUL, and GISELA DISCHNER, *»Wie aus weiter Ferne zu Dir«. Paul Celan — Gisela Dischner. Briefwechsel. Mit einem Brief von Gisèle Celan-Lestrange*, ed. by Barbara Wiedemann, with Gisela Dischner (Berlin: Suhrkamp, 2012).

CELAN, PAUL, and NELLY SACHS, *Briefwechsel*, ed. by Barbara Wiedemann (Frankfurt a.M.: Suhrkamp, 1993).

CELAN, PAUL, and ILANA SHMUELI, *Briefwechsel*, ed. by Ilana Shmueli and Thomas Sparr (Frankfurt a.M.: Suhrkamp, 2004).

CELAN, PAUL, and PETER SZONDI, *Briefwechsel. Mit Briefen von Gisèle Celan-Lestrange an Peter Szondi und Auszügen aus dem Briefwechsel zwischen Peter Szondi und Jean und Mayotte Bollack*, ed. by Christoph König (Frankfurt a.M.: Suhrkamp, 2005).

CELAN, PAUL, and FRANZ WURM, *Briefwechsel*, ed. by Barbara Wiedemann and Franz Wurm (Frankfurt a.M.: Suhrkamp, 1995).

Other Texts

ADELUNG, JOHANN CHRISTOPH, *Versuch eines vollständigen grammatisch-kritischen Wörterbuches der hochdeutschen Mundart, mit beständiger Vergleichung der übrigen Mundarten, besonders aber der oberdeutschen*, 5 vols (Brünn: Joseph Georg Trassler, 1788).

ADORNO, THEODOR W., *Negative Dialectics*, trans. by E. B. Ashton (New York: Seabury, 1973).
—— *The Jargon of Authenticity*, trans. by Knut Tarnowski and Frederic Will (Evanston: Northwestern University Press, 1973).
—— *Prisms*, trans. by Samuel and Shierry Weber (Cambridge: MIT Press, 1981).
—— *Notes to Literature*, trans. by Shierry Weber Nicholsen, 2 vols (New York: Columbia University Press, 1991–1992).
—— *Aesthetic Theory*, ed. by Gretel Adorno and Rolf Tiedemann, trans. by Robert Hullot-Kentor (Minneapolis: University of Minnesota Press, 1997).
AGAMBEN, GIORGIO, *Remnants of Auschwitz: The Witness and the Archive*, trans. by Daniel Heller-Roazen (New York: Zone, 1999).
ALIGHIERI, DANTE, *Dante Alighieri's Divine Comedy, Italian Text and Verse Translation*, vol. 1, *Inferno*, trans. by Mark Musa (Bloomington: Indiana University Press, 1996).
AMÉRY, JEAN, *Jenseits von Schuld und Sühne: Bewältigungsversuche eines Überwältigten* (Munich: Szczesny, 1966).
AMTHOR, WIEBKE, '11. Nachlass', in *Celan-Handbuch: Leben, Werk, Wirkung*, ed. by Markus May, Peter Gossens, and Jürgen Lehmann (Stuttgart: Metzler, 2008), pp. 132–40.
ARENDT, HANNAH, 'Introduction', in Bernd Naumann, *Auschwitz. A Report on the Proceedings Against Robert Karl Mulka and Others Before the Court at Frankfurt*, trans. by Jean Steinberg (New York: Praeger, 1966), pp. xi–xxx.
ARON, THOMAS, *Littérature et littérarité: un essai de mise au point* (Paris: Belles-Lettres, 1984).
BADIOU, BERTRAND, 'D'une main – et d'une autre main –. Préface', in Paul Celan and René Char, *Correspondance: 1954–1968. Avec des lettres de Gisèle Celan-Lestrange, Jean Delay, Marie-Madeleine Delay et Pierre Deniker. Suivie de la Correspondance René Char–Gisèle Celan-Lestrange (1969–1977)*, ed. by Bertrand Badiou (Paris: Gallimard, 2015), pp. 9–31.
BAHTI, TIMOTHY, *Ends of the Lyric* (Baltimore: Johns Hopkins University Press, 1996).
BALZAC, HONORÉ DE, *Das Chagrinleder*, trans. by Hedwig Lachmann (Leipzig: Insel, 1927).
—— *La Peau de Chagrin* (Paris: Garnier, 1967)
BAMBACH, CHARLES R., *Thinking the Poetic Measure of Justice: Hölderlin, Heidegger, Celan* (Albany: State University of New York Press, 2013).
BARTHES, ROLAND, *Oeuvres complètes*, ed. by Éric Marty, 5 vols (Paris: Seuil, 2002).
BATAILLE, GEORGES, 'René Char et la force de la poésie', *Critique*, 53 (1951), 819–23.
BAUDELAIRE, CHARLES, *Oeuvres complètes*, ed. by Claude Pichois and Jean Ziegler, 2 vols (Paris: Gallimard, 1975–1976).
BAUER, FRITZ, 'Zu den Naziverbrecher-Prozessen', *Stimme der Gemeinde: Zum kirchlichen Leben, zur Politik, Wirtschaft und Kultur*, 15.18 (1963), 563–74.
BAUMANN, GERHART, '"... durchgründet vom Nichts"', *Études germaniques*, 25.3 (1970) 276–90.
—— *Erinnerungen an Paul Celan* (Frankfurt a.M.: Suhrkamp, 1986).
BECKETT, SAMUEL, *Texts for Nothing*, trans. by Samuel Beckett (London: Calder & Boyars, 1974).
BECKETT, SAMUEL, KARL KROLOW, WOLFGANG KOEPPEN, HANS ERICH NOSSACK, PETER WEISS, UWE JOHNSON, WOLFGANG HILDESHEIMER, NELLY SACHS, PAUL CELAN, and MARTIN WALSER, *Aus aufgegebenen Werken* (Frankfurt a. M.: Suhrkamp, 1968)
BELL, VIKKI, *Feminist Imagination: Genealogies in Feminist Theory* (London: Sage, 1999).
BELLEMIN-NOËL, JEAN, 'L'infamilière curiosité', in *Leçons d'écriture, ce que disent les manuscrits*, ed. by Almuth Grésillon and Michaël Werner (Paris: Lettres Modernes, 1985), pp. 345–57.
BENJAMIN, WALTER, *Zur Kritik der Gewalt und andere Aufsätze* (Frankfurt a.M.: Suhrkamp, 1965).

―――*Illuminations*, ed. by Hannah Arendt, trans. by Harry Zohn (New York: Schocken, 1968).
―――'Critique of Violence', in Walter Benjamin, *Selected Writings (Volume 1: 1913–1926)*, ed. by Marcus Bullock and Michael W. Jennings (Cambridge: The Belknap Press of Harvard University Press, 1996), pp. 236–52.
BENN, GOTTFRIED, *Probleme der Lyrik* (Wiesbaden: Limes, 1951).
BENN, M. B., 'Anti-Pygmalion: An Apologia for Georg Büchner's Aesthetics', *The Modern Language Review*, 64.3 (1969), 597–604.
BIAŁOSTOCKI, JAN, 'Rembrandt's « Terminus »', *Wallraf-Richartz-Jahrbuch. Westdeutsches Jahrbuch für Kunstgeschichte*, 28 (1966), 49–60.
BIASI, PIERRE-MARC DE, 'Avant-propos', in Gustave Flaubert, *Carnets de travail*, ed. by Pierre-Marc de Biasi (Paris: Balland, 1988), pp. 7–14
―――'Préface', in Gustave Flaubert, *Carnets de travail*, ed. by Pierre-Marc de Biasi (Paris: Balland, 1988), pp. 15–119
―――'What is a Literary Draft? Towards a Functional Typology of Genetic Criticism', *Yale French Studies*, 89 (1996), 26–58.
תורה נביאים וכתובים = *Biblia Hebraica Stuttgartensia*, quae antea cooperantibus A. Alt, O. Eissfeldt, P. Kahle ediderat, R. Kittel; adjuvantibus H. Bardtke, W. Baumgartner, P. A. H. de Boer, O. Eissfeldt, J. Fichtner, G. Gerleman, J. Hempel, F. Horst, A. Jepsen, F. Maass, R. Meyer, G. Quell, Th. H. Robinson, D. W. Thomas; cooperantibus H.P. Rüger et J. Ziegler; ediderunt K. Elliger et W. Rudolph. Textum Masoreticum curavit H. P. Rüger; masoram elaboravit G. E. Weil. Editio quinta emendata opera A. Schenker (Stuttgart: Deutsche Bibelgesellschaft, 1997).
BLANCHOT, MAURICE, *Faux pas* (Paris: Gallimard, 1943).
―――*La part du feu* (Paris: Gallimard, 1949).
―――*L'espace littéraire* (Paris: Gallimard, 1955).
BLANKERT, ALBERT, 'Rembrandt, Zeuxis and ideal beauty', in *Album amicorum J. G. van Gelder*, ed. by J. Bruyn, J. A. Emmens, E. de Jongh and D. P. Snoep (The Hague: Nijhoff, 1973), pp. 32–39.
BLOCH, ERNST, *Gesamtausgabe*, 16 vols (Frankfurt a.M.: Suhrkamp, 1959–1972).
BOGUMIL, SIEGHILD, 'Zur Dialoggestalt von Paul Celans Dichtung, dargestellt am Gedicht "Stimmen" und seiner Spiegelung in "Landschaft" und "Wutpilger-Streifzüge"', *Celan-Jahrbuch*, 5 (1993), 23–52.
BONACCORSO, GIOVANNI, 'Problèmes de l'édition des manuscrits d'*Un coeur simple*', in Gustave Flaubert, *Un coeur simple*, ed. by Giovanni Bonaccorso and others (Paris: Société d'Édition 'Les Belles Lettres', 1983), pp. xiii–xlviii.
BONNEFOY, YVES, 'Paul Celan', in Yves Bonnefoy, *La Vérité de parole et autres essais* (Paris: Mercure de France, 1995), pp. 545–52.
BOOS, SONJA, *Speaking the Unspeakable in Postwar Germany: Toward a Public Discourse on the Holocaust* (Ithaca: Cornell University Press, 2014).
BORKIN, JOSEPH, *The Crime and Punishment of I. G. Farben* (New York: The Free Press, 1978).
BORMANN, ALEXANDER VON, 'Notgesang der Gedanken. Nachgelassene Gedichte von Paul Celan', Sender Freies Berlin, November 1991.
BOSMAJIAN, HAMIDA, *Metaphors of Evil: Contemporary German Literature and the Shadow of Nazism* (Iowa City: University of Iowa Press, 1979).
BOVET, ERNEST, *Lyrisme, épopée, drame: une loi de l'histoire littéraire expliquée par l'évolution générale* (Paris, A. Colin, 1911).
BOYARIN, JONATHAN, and DANIEL BOYARIN, 'Self-Exposure as Theory: The Double Mark of the Male Jew', *Rhetorics of Self-Making*, ed. by Debbora Battaglia (Berkeley: University of California Press, 1995), pp. 16–42.

BRAYMAN HACKEL, HEIDI, *Reading Material in Early Modern England: Print, Gender, and Literacy* (Cambridge: Cambridge University Press, 2005).
BRETON, ANDRÉ, 'A Tribute to Antonin Artaud' in André Breton, *Free Rein (La Clé des champs)*, trans. by Michel Parmentier and Jacqueline D'Amboise (Lincoln: University of Nebraska Press, 1996), pp. 77–79.
BREUER, DIETER, 'Introduction', in *Deutsche Lyrik nach 1945*, ed. by Dieter Breuer (Frankfurt a.M.: Suhrkamp, 1988), pp. 7–9.
BRIERLEY, DAVID, *"Der Meridian" — ein Versuch zur Poetik und Dichtung Paul Celans* (Frankfurt a.M.: Peter Lang , 1984).
Brockhaus-Taschenbuch der Geologie. Die Entwicklungsgeschichte der Erde. Mit einem ABC der Geologie (Leipzig: Brockhaus, 1955).
BROWN, FRANCIS, *The Brown-Driver-Briggs Hebrew and English Lexicon, with an appendix containing the Biblical Aramaic,* with the cooperation of S. R. Driver and Charles A. Briggs (1906; Peabody: Hendrickson, 2005).
BRUYN, J., et al., *A Corpus of Rembrandt Paintings*, with the collaboration of L. Peese Binkhorst-Hoffscholte, trans. by D. Cook-Radmore, 6 vols (The Hague: Nijhoff, 1982–2015).
BUBER, MARTIN, *Die Schriftwerke* (Cologne: Hegner, 1962).
BUCHELI, ROMAN, 'Work in progress. Zur Fortsetzung der historisch-kritischen Celan-Ausgabe', in *Neue Zürcher Zeitung* (8/9 October 1994), 69.
BÜCHNER, GEORG, *Sämtliche Werke und Briefe. Historisch-kritische Ausgabe mit Kommentar*, ed. by Werner R. Lehmann (Munich: Hanser, 1979).
BUCK, THEO, 'Bildreflexion, Lebensreflexion. Zu Paul Celans Gedicht *Einkanter: Rembrandt*', in *'Hinauf und Zurück / in die herzhelle Zukunft.' Deutsch-jüdische Literatur im 20. Jahrhundert. Festschrift für Birgit Lermen*, ed. by Michael Braun, Peter J. Brenner, Hans Messelken, and Gisela Wilkending (Bonn: Bouvier, 2000), pp. 325–51.
BUHR, GERHARD, *Celans Poetik* (Göttingen: Vandenhoeck und Ruprecht, 1976).
BÜNDE, FRAUKE, 'Mallarmé und Paul Celan: Einfahrt in das Gedicht *Hafen*', *Lendemains*, 73 (1994), 54–63.
BUSHELL, SALLY, *Text as Process: Creative Composition in Wordsworth, Tennyson, and Dickinson* (Charlottesville: University of Virginia Press, 2009).
CALVIN, JEAN, *Calvin's Old Testament Commentaries: The Rutherford House Translation*, ed. by D. F. Wright, D. F. Kelly, and N. M. de S. Cameron, 20 vols (Grand Rapids: Eerdmans, 1993–).
CAMUS, ALBERT, *Essais*, introduction by R. Quilliot, ed. by R. Quilliot and L. Faucon (Paris: Gallimard/Calmann-Lévy, 1965).
CARNEY, RAYMOND, 'Making the Most of a Mess', *Georgia Review*, 35.3 (1981), 631–42.
CAVELL, STANLEY, *The Claim of Reason: Wittgenstein, Skepticism, Morality, and Tragedy* (Oxford: Clarendon Press/Oxford University Press, 1979).
CÉARD, JEAN, and JEAN-CLAUDE MARGOLIN, *Rébus de la renaissance. Des images qui parlent*, 2 vols (Paris: Maisonneuve et Larose, 1986).
CERQUIGLINI, BERNARD, *In Praise of the Variant. A Critical History of Philology*, trans. by Betsy Wing (Baltimore: The Johns Hopkins University Press, 1999).
CERTEAU, MICHEL DE, *The Mystic Fable*, trans. by Michael B. Smith (Chicago: University of Chicago Press, 1992).
—— 'Reading as Poaching', in *Readers and Reading*, ed. by Andrew Bennett (New York: Longman, 1995), pp. 150–63.
CHABROL, HENRI, 'Chronic Hallucinatory Psychosis, *Bouffée Délirante*, and the Classification of Psychosis in French Psychiatry', *Current Psychiatry Reports*, 5.3 (2003), 187–91.
CHALFEN, ISRAEL, *Paul Celan. Eine Biographie seiner Jugend* (Frankfurt a.M.: Insel, 1979).
CIORAN, E. M., *Le mauvais démiurge* (Paris: Gallimard, 1969).

—— *Cahiers 1957–1972*, foreword by Simone Boué (Paris: Gallimard, 1997).
CLAUSEN, OLIVER, 'Weiss/Propagandist and Weiss/Playwright', *New York Times Magazine* (2 October 1966), 28–29, 124, 126, 128, 130–34.
CLIFFORD, WAYNE, *The Exile's Papers: Part Two: The Face as its Thousand Ships* (Erin: Porcupine's Quill, 2009).
COETZEE, J. M. 'In the Midst of Losses', *The New York Review of Books*, 48.11 (5 July 2001), available at <http://www.nybooks.com/issues/2001/07/05/>, [accessed 5 August 2015].
COHEN, ROBERT, *Understanding Peter Weiss* (Columbia: University of South Carolina Press, 1993).
—— '1964: On March 13, in the middle of rehearsals for the premiere of *Marat / Sade*, Peter Weiss attends the Frankfurt Auschwitz trial', in *Yale Companion to Jewish Writing and Thought in German Culture 1096–1996*, ed. by Sander L. Gilman and Jack Zipes (New Haven: Yale University Press, 1997), pp. 722–28.
—— 'The Political Aesthetics of Holocaust Literature: Peter Weiss's 'The Investigation' and Its Critics', *History and Memory*, 10.2 (1998), 43–67.
CONNOLLY, ANTHONY C., E-mail correspondence with author, 23 February 2011.
CONNOLLY, THOMAS C., 'Oils, Psalms, and Scum: Anadyomene Paint and the Limits of Ekphrasis in Paul Celan's "EINKANTER: Rembrandt"', *Modern Philology*, 111.4 (2014), 841–61.
—— '"Keine Schönschrift für Schulkinder": Towards a Poetics of the Pre-Text in Paul Celan's *Eingedunkelt*', *Compar(a)ison*, (2013 [2017]), 107–30.
CONRAD, JOSEPH, *Der Geheimagent. Eine einfache Geschichte*, trans. by G. Danehl (Frankfurt a.M.: Fischer, 1963).
—— *The Secret Agent. A Simple Tale* (Harmondsworth: Penguin, 1976).
CRAMER, ERNST, 'Peter Weiss und sein Auschwitz-Oratorium', *Die Welt* (6 November 1965), vii.
CROOK, JO, and TOM LEARNER, *The Impact of Modern Paints* (New York: Watson-Guptill, 2000).
DEBRAY-GENETTE, RAYMONDE, *Métamorphoses du récit: autour de Flaubert* (Paris: Seuil, 1988).
DELEUZE, GILLES, *Cinéma 2. L'Image-temps* (Paris: Minuit, 1985).
DELEUZE, GILLES, and FÉLIX GUATTARI, *A Thousand Plateaus. Capitalism and Schizophrenia*, trans. by Brian Massumi (Minneapolis: University of Minnesota Press, 1987).
DE MAN, PAUL, *The Rhetoric of Romanticism* (New York: Columbia University Press, 1984).
—— *The Resistance to Theory* (Minneapolis: University of Minnesota Press, 1986).
—— *Critical Writings 1954–1978*, ed. by Lindsay Waters (Minneapolis: University of Minnesota Press, 1989).
—— *The Post-Romantic Predicament* (Edinburgh: Edinburgh University Press, 2012).
DERRIDA, JACQUES, *Schibboleth pour Paul Celan* (Paris: Galilée, 1986).
—— 'This Is Not an Oral Footnote', in *Annotation and Its Texts*, ed. by Stephen A. Barney (Oxford: Oxford University Press, 1991), pp. 192–205.
—— 'Force of Law: The "Mystical Foundation of Authority"', in Jacques Derrida, *Acts of Religion*, ed. by Gil Anidjar (New York: Routledge, 2002), pp. 230–98.
—— 'Archive et brouillon: table ronde du 17 juin 1995', in *Pourquoi la critique génétique? Méthodes, théories*, ed. by Michel Contat and Daniel Ferrer. Paris: CNRS EDITIONS, 1998), pp. 189–209.
DIDI-HUBERMAN, GEORGES, 'La couleur d'écume ou le paradoxe d'Apelle', *Critique: Revue générale des publications françaises et étrangères*, 42 (1986), 606–29.
Die Bibel: nach der Übersetzung Martin Luthers: mit Wortkonkordanz (Stuttgart: Deutsche Bibelgesellschaft, 1987).

DWORK, DEBÓRAH; ROBERT JAN VAN PELT, *Auschwitz: 1270 to the Present* (New Haven: Yale University Press, 1996).
ECO, UMBERTO, *The Open Work*, trans. by Anna Cancogni (Cambridge: Harvard University Press, 1989).
'Ein Beinbruch des Kommandanten Höss? Die Verteidigung bezweifelt die Glaubwürdigkeit eines Zeugen', *Frankfurter Allgemeine Zeitung* (14 November 1964), 17–18.
EISLER, MAX, *Der alte Rembrandt. Mit 44 Tafeln in Kupfertiefdruck* (Vienna: Druck und Verlag der Österreichischen Staatsdruckerei, 1927).
ÉLUARD, PAUL, *Choix de poèmes 1914–1941* (Paris: Gallimard, 1942).
EMMERICH, WOLFGANG, 'Review of Paul Celan, *Eingedunkelt: und Gedichte aus dem Umkreis von Eingedunkelt,*', *Der Buchtip*, Radio Bremen, 7 December 1992.
ENGLUND, AXEL, *Still Songs: Music In and Around the Poetry of Paul Celan* (Farnham: Ashgate, 2012).
ESKIN, MICHAEL, *Ethics and Dialogue in the Works of Levinas, Bakhtin, Mandel'shtam, and Celan* (Oxford: Oxford University Press, 2000).
EZRAHI, SIDRA DEKOVEN, *By Words Alone: The Holocaust in Literature* (Chicago: University of Chicago Press, 1980).
FAIRLEY, IAN, 'In that Dark Durance: Paul Celan's *Eingedunkelt*', in Paul Celan, *Fathomsuns / Fadensonnen and Benighted / Eingedunkelt*, trans. by Ian Fairley (Riverdale-on-Hudson: Sheep Meadow Press, 2001), pp. 251–53.
FELD, J., 'Dort wo die Zeder', in *Jüdisches Liederbuch* (Berlin: Jüdischer Verlag, 1930), pp. 110–11.
FELMAN, SHOSHANA, *The Juridical Unconscious. Trials and Traumas in the Twentieth Century* (Cambridge: Harvard University Press, 2002).
FELMAN, SHOSHANA, and DORI LAUB, *Testimony: Crisis of Witnessing in Literature, Psychoanalysis, and History* (New York: Routledge, 1992).
FELSTINER, JOHN, *Paul Celan: Poet, Survivor, Jew* (New Haven: Yale University Press, 1995).
—— '"Here we go round the prickly pear" or "Your song, what does it know?" Celan vis-à-vis Mallarmé', in *Mallarmé in the Twentieth Century*, ed. by Robert Greer Cohn (Cranbury: Associated University Presses, 1998), pp. 203–11.
FENVES, PETER, 'The Genesis of Judgment: Spatiality, Analogy, and Metaphor in Benjamin's "On Language as Such and On Human Language"', in *Walter Benjamin: Theoretical Questions*, ed. by David S. Ferris (Stanford: Stanford University Press, 1996), pp. 75–93.
FERRER, DANIEL, 'Clementis's Cap: Retroaction and Persistence in the Genetic Process', *Yale French Studies*, 89 (1996), 223–36.
FERRER, DANIEL, and MICHAEL GRODEN, 'Post-Genetic Joyce', *Romanic Review*, 86.3 (1995), 501–12.
—— 'Introduction: A Genesis of French Genetic Criticism', in *Genetic Criticism: Texts and Avant-textes*, ed. by Jed Deppman, Daniel Ferrer, and Michael Groden (Philadelphia: University of Pennsylvania Press, 2004), pp. 1–16.
FIORETOS, ARIS, 'Preface', in *Word Traces. Readings of Paul Celan*, ed. by Aris Fioretos (Baltimore: The Johns Hopkins University Press, 1994), pp. ix–xxii.
FLYNN, THOMAS, 'Jean-Paul Sartre', *Stanford Encyclopedia of Philosophy* (Fall 2013 Edition), Edward N. Zalta (ed.), available at <https://plato.stanford.edu/archives/fall2013/entries/sartre/> [accessed 26 July 2017].
FONDANE, BENJAMIN, *Le Mal des fantômes*, ed. by Patrice Beray and Michel Carassou, assisted by Monique Jutrin, foreword by Henri Meschonnic (Lagrasse: Verdier, 2006).
FORDHAM, FINN, 'Introduction', in James Joyce, *Finnegans Wake*, ed. by Robbert-Jan Henkes, Erik Bindervoet, and Finn Fordham (Oxford: Oxford University Press, 2012), pp. vii–xxxiv.

FOUCAULT, MICHEL, *Language, Counter-Memory, Practice. Selected Essays and Interviews*, ed. by Donald F. Bouchard, trans. by Donald F. Bouchard and Sherry Simon (Ithaca: Cornell University Press, 1977).

—— *This Is Not a Pipe, with Illustrations and Letters by René Magritte*, trans. and ed. by James Harkness (Berkeley: University of California Press, 1983).

FRIEDMAN, MAURICE, 'Paul Celan and Martin Buber: The Poetics of Dialogue and 'The Eclipse of God'', *Religion & Literature*, 29.1 (1997), 43–62.

FRYE, NORTHROP, 'Approaching the Lyric' in *Lyric Poetry. Beyond New Criticism*, ed. by Chaviva Hošek and Patricia Parker (Ithaca: Cornell University Press, 1985), pp. 31–37.

GABLER, HANS WALTER, 'Introduction', in *Contemporary German Editorial Theory*, ed. by Hans Walter Gabler, George Bornstein, and Gillian Borland Pierce (Ann Arbor: University of Michigan Press, 1995), pp. 1–16.

GADAMER, HANS-GEORG, *Gesammelte Werke*, 10 vols (Tübingen: Mohr Siebeck, 1999).

GARLOFF, KATJA, 'Peter Weiss's Entry into the German Public Sphere: On Diaspora, Language, and the Uses of Distance', *Colloquia Germanica*, 30.1 (1997), 47–70.

GENETTE, GÉRARD, 'Ce que nous disent les manuscrits', *Le Monde* (17 November 1989), 31.

GIDE, ANDRÉ, and PAUL VALÉRY, *Correspondance, 1890–1942*, ed. by Peter Fawcett (Paris: Gallimard, 2009).

GILBERT, MARTIN, *The Holocaust: A History of the Jews of Europe During the Second World War* (New York: Holt, Rinehart, and Winston, 1985).

GISSELBRECHT, ANDRÉ, 'Peter Weiss: "L'Instruction"', *La Nouvelle Critique*, 172 (February 1966), 42–46.

—— 'Rencontre avec le théâtre documentaire — *L'Instruction* à Aubervilliers et ses suites', in *Peter Weiss à Paris. Actes du colloque international. Paris, du 16 au 19 janvier 1997*, ed. by Günther Schütz (Paris: Kime, 1998), pp. 77–85.

GLATSTEIN, JACOB, *I Keep Recalling. The Holocaust Poems of Jacob Glatstein*, trans. by Barnett Zumoff, with an Introduction by Emanuel S. Goldsmith (Brooklyn: Ktav, 1993).

GOLDTHORPE, RHIANNON, 'Mallarmé: Sartre's committed poet', in *Baudelaire, Mallarmé, Valéry. New essays in honour of Lloyd Austin*, ed. by Malcolm Bowie, Alison Fairlie, and Alison Finch (Cambridge: Cambridge University Press, 1982), pp. 222–41.

GOLL, CLAIRE, 'Ivan Golls Witwe: So war es', in *Die Goll-Affäre: Dokumente zu einer 'Infamie'*, ed. by Barbara Wiedemann (Frankfurt a.M.: Suhrkamp, 2000), pp. 684–91.

GRANDONE, SALVATORE, *Lectures phénoménologiques de Mallarmé* (Paris: Harmattan, 2011).

GRAY, PAUL, 'A Living World. An Interview with Peter Weiss', *Tulane Drama Review*, 11.1 (1966), 106–14.

GREETHAM, D. C., 'A history of textual scholarship', in *The Cambridge Companion to Textual Scholarship*, ed. Neil Fraistat and Julia Flanders (Cambridge: Cambridge University Press, 2013), pp. 16–41.

GRÉSILLON, ALMUTH, 'Slow: Work in Progress', *Word and Image*, 13.2 (1997), 106–23.

GROSS, RAPHAEL, and WERNER RENZ (eds.), *Der Frankfurter Auschwitz-Prozess (1963–1965). Kommentierte Quellenedition*, 2 vols (Frankfurt: Campus, 2013).

Grosse Konkordanz zur Lutherbibel (Stuttgart: Calwer, 2001).

HAMACHER, WERNER, 'The Second of Inversion. Movements of a Figure through Celan's Poetry', trans. by Peter Fenves, in *Word Traces: Readings of Paul Celan*, ed. by Aris Fioretos (Baltimore: The Johns Hopkins University Press, 1994), pp. 219–63.

HAMBURGER, MICHAEL, *The Truth of Poetry. Tensions in Modern Poetry from Baudelaire to the 1960's* (New York: Harcourt, Brace & World, 1970).

HARBUSCH, UTE, *Gegenübersetzungen. Paul Celans Übertragungen französischer Symbolisten* (Göttingen: Wallstein, 2005).

HÄRTER, ANDREAS, 'Präzision der Dunkelheit: Gedichte von Paul Celan aus dem Nachlass',

Evangelische Kommentare. Monatsschrift zum Zeitgeschehen in Kirche und Gesellschaft, 25.6 (1992), 371–72.
HARTMAN, GEOFFREY, *Saving the Text. Literature/Derrida/Philosophy* (Baltimore: The Johns Hopkins University Press, 1981).
HARTUNG, HARALD, 'Späte Flaschenpost. Gedichte aus dem Nachlass Paul Celans', *Frankfurter Allgemeine Zeitung* (8 October 1991), L15.
HAY, LOUIS, '"Le texte n'existe pas." Réflexions sur la critique génétique', *Poétique*, 62 (1985), 146–58.
HEANEY, SEAMUS, *Sweeney's Flight* (London: Faber and Faber, 1992).
HEFFERNAN, JAMES A. W., *Museum of Words. The Poetics of Ekphrasis from Homer to Ashbery* (Chicago: University of Chicago Press, 1993).
HEGEL, G. W. F., *Aesthetics: Lectures on Fine Art*, trans. by T. M. Knox, 2 vols (Oxford: Clarendon Press, 1975).
HEIDEGGER, MARTIN, *Gesamtausgabe*, 102 vols (Frankfurt a.M.: Klostermann, 1975–2014).
——*Poetry, Language, Thought*, trans. by Albert Hofstadter (New York: Harper & Row, 1975).
HEINRICHSBAUER, JÜRGEN, 'In Sachen Weiss und andere. Oder: Missbrauch mit den Opfern des Grauens', *Der Arbeitgeber. Zeitschrift der Bundesvereinigung der Deutschen Arbeitgeberverbände*, 17.23/24 (1965), 735–38.
HIGGINSON, THOMAS WENTWORTH, 'Preface', in Emily Dickinson, *Poems*, ed. by Mabel Loomis Todd and T. W. Higginson (Boston: Roberts, 1892), pp. iii–vi.
HILL, GEOFFREY, *The Triumph of Love* (Boston: Houghton Mifflin, 1998).
HILTON, IAN, *Peter Weiss: A Search for Affinities* (London: Oswald Wolff, 1970).
HOCHHUTH, ROLF, *Der Stellvertreter. Ein christliches Trauerspiel*, with essays by Sabina Lietzmann, Karl Jaspers, Walter Muschg, Erwin Piscator, Golo Mann (Reinbek b. Hamburg: Rowohlt, 1976).
HØEG, CARSTEN, 'Les syllabes longues par position en grec', *Acta Jutlandica: aarsskrift for universitetsundervisningen i Jylland*, 9.1 (1937), 183–96.
HÖLDERLIN, FRIEDRICH, *Sämtliche Werke: Grosse Stuttgarter Ausgabe*, ed. by Friedrich Beissner, 8 vols (Stuttgart: Cotta, 1946–1985).
——*Selected Poems and Fragments*, trans. by Michael Hamburger, ed. by Jeremy Adler (London: Penguin, 1998).
HOMER, *Die Odyssee*, trans. by Wolfgang Schadewaldt (Hamburg: Rohwohlt, 1958).
HORKHEIMER, MAX, and THEODOR W. ADORNO, *Dialectic of Enlightenment: Philosophical Fragments*, trans. by Edmund Jephcott, ed. by Gunzelin Schmid Noerr (Stanford: Stanford University Press, 2002).
HORN, PETER, *Die Garne der Fischer der Irrsee: Zur Lyrik von Paul Celan* (Oberhausen: Athena, 2011).
HOWE, SUSAN, *The Birth-Mark: Unsettling the Wilderness in American Literary History* (Hanover: University Press of New England, 1993).
HUYSSEN, ANDREAS, *After the Great Divide: Modernism, Mass Culture, Postmodernism* (Bloomington: Indiana University Press, 1986).
IVANOVIĆ, CHRISTINE, *Das Gedicht im Geheimnis der Begegnung: Dichtung und Poetik Celans im Kontext seiner russischen Lektüren* (Tübingen: Niemeyer, 1996).
JACKSON, H. J., *Marginalia: Readers Writing in Books* (New Haven: Yale University Press, 2001).
JACKSON, JOHN E., 'Traduire Celan: raisons d'un échec', *Colloquium Helveticum*, 3 (1986), 131–38.
JACKSON, VIRGINIA, *Dickinson's Misery: A Theory of Lyric Reading* (Princeton: Princeton University Press, 2005).
JACOB, MAX, *Visions infernales* (Paris: Nouvelle Revue Française, 1924).

JACOBS, CAROL, *Telling Time. Lévi-Strauss, Ford, Lessing, Benjamin, de Man, Wordsworth, Rilke* (Baltimore: The Johns Hopkins University Press, 1993).
JÄGER, LUDWIG, *Seitenwechsel. Der Fall Schneider/Schwerte und die Diskretion der Germanistik* (Munich: Fink, 1998).
JANZ, MARLIES, *Vom Engagement absoluter Poesie: Zur Lyrik und Ästhetik Paul Celans* (Frankfurt a.M.: Syndikat, 1976).
JEAN PAUL, *Werke*, ed. by Norbert Miller, 6 vols (Munich: Carl Hanser, 1959–1963).
JENNINGS, ELIZABETH, *Growing-Points* (Cheadle Hulme: Carcanet New Press, 1975).
JENNY, LAURENT, 'Genetic Criticism and Its Myths', *Yale French Studies*, 89 (1996), 9–25.
JENS, WALTER, 'Die 'Ermittlung' in Westberlin', *Die Zeit* (29 October 1965), 20.
JENS, WALTER, DIETER E. ZIMMER, HELLMUTH KARASEK, and GERHARD SCHOENBERNER, 'Auschwitz auf der Bühne. Drei Fragen an fünf Intendanten', *Die Zeit* (29 October 1965), 19–20.
JOHNSON, BARBARA, 'Philology: What is at Stake?', in *On Philology*, ed. by Jan Ziolkowski (University Park: Pennsylvania State University Press, 1990), pp. 26–30.
JOYCE, JAMES, *Ulysses*, trans. by Georg Goyert, 2 vols (Basel: Rhein-Verlag, 1928).
—— *Ulysses: A Critical and Synoptic Edition*, ed. by Hans Walter Gabler, with Wolfhard Steppe and Claus Melchior, 3 vols (New York: Garland, 1984).
—— *Ulysses: The Corrected Text*, ed. by Hans Walter Gabler, Wolfhard Steppe and Claus Melchior, preface by Richard Ellmann (London: Bodley Head, 1986).
KAFKA, FRANZ, *Sämtliche Erzählungen*, ed. by Paul Raabe (Frankfurt a.M.: Fischer, 1970).
KAISER, JOACHIM, 'Plädoyer gegen das Theater-Auschwitz', *Süddeutsche Zeitung* (4–5 September 1965), 79–80.
KARASEK, HELLMUTH, 'Die 'Ermittlung' in Stuttgart', *Die Zeit* (29 October 1965), 21.
KÄSTNER, ERHART, 'Wo Verschlüsselung ist, da ist Aufschluss. Aus Erhart Kästners Rede zur Verleihung des Bremer Literaturpreises an Paul Celan', *Frankfurter Allgemeine Zeitung* (31 January 1958), 10.
KEELE, ALAN FRANK, *Paul Schallück and the Post-War German Don Quixote. A Case-History Prolegomenon to the Literature of the Federal Republic* (Bern: Herbert Lang, 1976).
KIEFER, ANSELM, *Die Welle (The Wave)*, 1990, lead, clothes, steel wire, and ash on canvas, Seattle Art Museum, Seattle, WA.
KLEE, ERNST, *Auschwitz. Täter, Gehilfen, Opfer und was aus ihnen wurde. Ein Personenlexikon* (Frankfurt a.M.: Fischer, 2013).
KLIGERMAN, ERIC, *Sites of the Uncanny. Paul Celan, Specularity and the Visual Arts* (Berlin: De Gruyter, 2007).
KLUGE, FRIEDRICH, *Etymologisches Wörterbuch der Deutschen Sprache*, ed. by Walther Mitzka, assisted by Alfred Schirmer, 18th ed. (Berlin: De Gruyter, 1960).
KOELLE, LYDIA, *Paul Celans pneumatisches Judentum: Gott-Rede und menschliche Existenz nach der Shoah* (Mainz: Matthias-Grünewald, 1997).
KOJÈVE, ALEXANDRE, *Introduction to the Reading of Hegel. Lectures on the* Phenomenology of Spirit, assembled by Raymond Queneau, ed. by Allan Bloom, trans. by James H. Nichols (New York: Basic, 1969).
KONIETZNY, ULRICH, '"All deine Siegel erbrochen?" Chiffren oder Baumläufer im Spätwerk Paul Celans', *Celan-Jahrbuch*, 2 (1988), 107–20.
KÖNNEKER, SABINE, »*Sichtbares, Hörbares*«. *Die Beziehung zwischen Sprachkunst und bildender Kunst am Beispiel Paul Celans* (Bielefeld: Aisthesis, 1995).
KUNZE, ROLF-ULRICH, 'Nachlassverwaltung', *Stadtblatt Osnabrück* (March 1992), n. p.
LACOUE-LABARTHE, PHILIPPE, *La Poésie comme expérience* (Paris: Bourgois, 1986).
—— *Poetry as Experience*, trans. by Andrea Tarnowski (Stanford: Stanford University Press, 1999).

LANGBEIN, HERMANN, *People in Auschwitz*, trans. by Harry Zohn (Chapel Hill: The University of North Carolina Press in association with The United States Holocaust Memorial Museum, 2004).
LANGER, LAWRENCE L., *Admitting the Holocaust. Collected Essays* (New York: Oxford University Press, 1995).
LAO TSE, *Tao-Tê-King. Das heilige Buch vom Weg und von der Tugend*, trans. by Günther Debon (Stuttgart: Philipp Reclam Jun., 1961).
LAROUSSE, PIERRE, *Grand dictionnaire universel du XIXe siècle, français, historique, géographique, mythologique, bibliographique, littéraire, artistique, scientifique, etc.*, 17 vols (Paris: Administration du Grand dictionnaire universel, 1866–1890).
LAUTRÉAMONT, *Les Chants de Maldoror et autres textes*, ed. by Jean-Luc Steinmetz (Paris: Librairie Générale Française, 2001).
LE CALVEZ, ERIC, *Genèses flaubertiennes* (Amsterdam: Rodopi, 2009).
LEGGEWIE, CLAUS, *Von Schneider zu Schwerte: das ungewöhnliche Leben eines Mannes, der aus der Geschichte lernen wollte* (Munich: Hanser, 1998).
LEIRIS, MICHEL, *Journal 1922–1989* (Paris: Gallimard, 1992).
LERNOUT, GEERT, 'Continental editing theory', in *The Cambridge Companion to Textual Scholarship*, ed. by Neil Fraistat and Julia Flanders (Cambridge: Cambridge University Press, 2013), pp. 61–78.
LESKY, ALBIN, 'ΘΑΛΑΣΣΑ', *Hermes*, 78.3 (1943), 258–69.
LEUTNER, PETRA, *Wege durch die Zeichen-Zone. Stéphane Mallarmé und Paul Celan* (Stuttgart: Metzler, 1994).
LEVI, PRIMO, 'On Obscure Writing', in Primo Levi, *Other People's Trades* (New York: Summit, 1989), pp. 169–75.
LEXER, MATTHIAS, *Matthias Lexers Mittelhochdeutsches Taschenwörterbuch* (Stuttgart: S. Hirzel Verlag, 1986).
'"L'Instruction", de Peter Weiss', *Le Monde* (3–4 April 1966), 16.
LITTRÉ, ÉMILE, *Dictionnaire de la langue française*, 4 vols (Paris: Hachette, 1881–1882).
LOEB, PAUL S., 'Suicide, Meaning, and Redemption', in *Nietzsche on Time and History*, ed. by Manuel Dries (Berlin: De Gruyter, 2008), pp. 163–90.
LOUTH, CHARLIE, review of Paul Celan, *Selected Poems and Prose of Paul Celan*, trans. by John Felstiner (2000) and Paul Celan, *Fathomsuns / Fadensonnen and Benighted / Eingedunkelt*, trans. by Ian Fairley (2001), *Translation and Literature*, 11.1 (2002), 123–35.
LOWELL, ROBERT, *Collected Poems*, ed. by Frank Bidart and David Gewanter, assisted by DeSales Harrison (New York: Farrar, Straus and Giroux, 2003).
LUKÁCS, GEORG, *The Theory of the Novel. A Historico-Philosophical Essay on the Forms of Great Epic Literature*, trans. by Anna Bostock (Cambridge: MIT, 1971).
LUTHER, MARTIN, *Lutherbibel: Textfassung 1912* (Altenmünster: Jazzybee Verlag Jürgen Beck, 2016)
LYON, JAMES K., 'Paul Celan and Martin Buber: Poetry as Dialogue', *PMLA*, 86.1 (1971), 110–20.
MADER, HELMUT, 'Schweigsame Gedichte. "Atemwende" von Paul Celan', *Stuttgarter Zeitung* (11 October 1967), 35.
MALLARMÉ, STÉPHANE, 'Si tu veux nous nous aimerons', *La Plume* (15 March 1896), 173.
—— *Oeuvres complètes*, ed. by Henri Mondor and G. Jean-Aubry (Paris: Gallimard, 1945).
—— *Correspondance*, ed. by Henri Mondor, with Jean-Pierre Richard, 11 vols (Paris: Gallimard, 1959–1985).
—— *Poésies: Poésies, choix de vers de circonstance, poèmes d'enfance et de jeunesse*, preface by Jean-Paul Sartre (Paris: Gallimard, 1966).
—— *Oeuvres complètes*, ed. by Bertrand Marchal, 2 vols (Paris: Gallimard, 1998–2003).

——— *Divagations*, trans. by Barbara Johnson (Cambridge: The Belknap Press of Harvard University Press, 2007).
MALLARMÉ, STÉPHANE, and JACQUES SCHERER, *Le 'Livre' de Mallarmé: premières recherches sur des documents inédits*, preface by Henri Mondor (Paris: Gallimard, 1957).
MALRAUX, ANDRÉ, *La Métamorphose des dieux. L'Irréel* (Paris: Gallimard, 1974).
MANDEL'SHTAM, OSIP, *Sobranie sochinenii*, ed. by G. P. Struve and B. A. Filippova, 2 vols (Washington: Inter-Language Literary Associates, 1964).
——— *Sobranie sochinenii*, ed. by G. P. Struve and B. A. Filippova, 3 vols (New York: Mezhdunarodnoe literaturnoe sodruzhestvo, 1967).
——— *Sobranie sochinenii*, 4 vols (Moscow: Art-Biznes Centr, 1994).
MARCHAL, BERTRAND, 'Notices, notes et variantes', in Stéphane Mallarmé, *Oeuvres complètes*, ed. by Bertrand Marchal, 2 vols (Paris: Gallimard, 1998–2003), I, pp. 1135–1452.
MARIN, LOUIS, *On Representation*, trans. by Catherine Porter (Stanford: Stanford University Press, 2001).
MASSEIX, FRÉDÉRIC, 'L'insulinothérapie', *Soin, Étude et Recherche en Psychiatrie*, available at <http://www.serpsy.org/piste_recherche/choc/masseix_ choc.html>, [accessed 8 January 2015].
MAYER, HANS, *Umerzogene Literatur* (Berlin: Siedler, 1988).
MCCLATCHY, J. D., *Poets on Painters. Essays on the Art of Painting by Twentieth-Century Poets* (Berkeley: University of California Press, 1988).
MCGANN, JEROME J., *A Critique of Modern Textual Criticism* (Chicago: University of Chicago Press, 1983).
MEINECKE, DIETLIND, *Wort und Name bei Paul Celan: zur Widerruflichkeit des Gedichts* (Bad Homburg v. d. H.: Gehlen, 1970).
MELLINKOFF, RUTH, *Outcasts: Signs of Otherness in Northern European Art of the Late Middle Ages*, 2 vols (Berkeley: University of California Press, 1993).
MENASSEH BEN ISRAEL, *De termino vitæ: libri tres. Quibus veterum rabbinorum, ac recentium doctorum, de hac controversia sententia explicatur* (Amstelodami: Typis & sumptibus authoris, 1639).
——— *La pierre glorieuse de Nabuchodonosor, ou, la fin de l'histoire au XVIIe siècle*, ed. by M. Hadas-Lebel and H. Méchoulan, trans. by H. Knafou, illustrations by Rembrandt (Paris: Vrin, 2007).
MENDÈS, CATULLE, *Rapport sur le mouvement poétique français de 1867 à 1900. Rapport à M. le ministre de l'instruction publique et des beaux-arts, précédé de réflexions sur la personnalité de l'esprit poétique de France, suivi d'un dictionnaire bibliographique et critique et d'une nomenclature chronologique de la plupart des poètes français du XIXe siècle* (Paris: Imprimerie Nationale, 1903).
MENNINGHAUS, WINFRIED, *Paul Celan: Magie der Form* (Frankfurt a.M.: Suhrkamp, 1980).
MERCIER, ALAIN, *La Littérature facétieuse sous Louis XIII. 1610–1643. Une bibliographie critique* (Geneva: Droz, 1991).
MERRIMAN, JOHN M., *The Dynamite Club. How a Bombing in fin-de-siècle Paris Ignited the Age of Modern Terror* (Boston: Houghton Mifflin Harcourt, 2009).
MESCHONNIC, HENRI, 'On appelle cela traduire Celan', *Cahiers du chemin*, 14 (1972), 115–49.
——— *Pour la poétique II. Épistémologie de l'Écriture — Poétique de la traduction* (Paris: Gallimard, 1973).
——— 'L'Écriture de Satan', in Gustave Flaubert, *Bibliomanie et autres textes 1836–1839* (Paris: Jean-Cyrille Godefroy, 1982), pp. 5–11.
MICHAELIS, ROLF, 'Der beschriftete Ankerstein', *Die Zeit* (11 October 1991), L9.
MICHAUX, HENRI, 'Sur le chemin de la vie, Paul Celan...', *Études germaniques*, 25.3 (1970), 250.

MICHEL, WILHELM, *Das Leben Friedrich Hölderlins* (Bremen: Schünemann, 1949).
MILTON, JOHN, *The Works of John Milton, Historical, Political, and Miscellaneous* (London: Millar, 1753).
MONDOR, HENRI, *Vie de Mallarmé*, 2 vols (Paris: Gallimard, 1941–1942).
MÜLLER-JERINA, ALWIN, *Germania Judaica, Kölner Bibliothek zur Geschichte des Deutschen Judentums. Die Entwicklung und Bedeutung einer wissenschaftlichen Spezialbibliothek* (Cologne: Greven, 1986).
NABER, HERMANN, 'Die "Ermittlung" in der Presse', *Die Zeit* (29 October 1965), 22.
NAUMANN, BERND, *Auschwitz. Bericht über die Strafsache gegen Mulka und andere vor dem Schwurgericht Frankfurt* (Frankfurt a.M.: Athenäum, 1965).
—— *Auschwitz. A Report on the Proceedings Against Robert Karl Mulka and Others Before the Court at Frankfurt*, trans. by Jean Steinberg, with an Introduction by Hannah Arendt (New York: Praeger, 1966).
NERVAL, GÉRARD DE, *Selected Writings*, trans. by Richard Sieburth (London: Penguin, 1999).
NEUMANN, GERHARD, 'Die "absolute" Metapher. Ein Abgrenzungsversuch am Beispiel Stéphane Mallarmés und Paul Celans', *Poetica*, 3 (1970), 188–225.
NIETZSCHE, FRIEDRICH, *Also sprach Zarathustra: Ein Buch für Alle und Keinen (1883–1885)*, part 6, vol. 1 of Friedrich Nietzsche, *Werke: Kritische Gesamtausgabe*, ed. by Giorgio Colli and Mazzino Montinari (Berlin: De Gruyter, 1968).
NONO, LUIGI, 'Musiche di scena per 'Die Ermittlung" in Luigi Nono, *Complete Works for Solo Tape*, 2 CDs (Cologno Monzese: Stradivarius, 2006), CD 1, track 2.
NOUSS, ALEXIS, *Paul Celan: Les lieux d'un déplacement* (Lormont: Le Bord de l'eau, 2010).
OELMANN, UTE MARIA, *Deutsche poetologische Lyrik nach 1945: Ingeborg Bachmann, Günter Eich, Paul Celan* (Stuttgart: Hans-Dieter Heinz, 1980).
OLSCHNER, LEONARD MOORE, 'Dark Origins', *Times Literary Supplement* (13 October 2000), 9.
OVID, *The Metamorphoses of Ovid*, trans. by Mary M. Innes (Harmondsworth: Penguin, 1955).
OZICK, CYNTHIA, 'A Liberal's Auschwitz', in *The Pushcart Prize. Best of the Small Presses*, ed. by Bill Henderson (Yonkers: Pushcart Book Press, 1976), pp. 149–53.
PANOFSKY, ERWIN, 'Rembrandt und das Judentum', *Jahrbuch der Hamburger Kunstsammlungen*, 18 (1973), 75–108.
PEARSON, ROGER, *Mallarmé and Circumstance: The Translation of Silence* (Oxford: Oxford University Press, 2004).
—— *Stéphane Mallarmé* (London: Reaktion, 2010).
PENDAS, DEVIN O., *The Frankfurt Auschwitz Trial, 1963–1965. Genocide, History, and the Limits of the Law* (New York: Cambridge University Press, 2006).
PERRY, R. C., 'Historical Authenticity and Dramatic Form: Hochhuth's *Der Stellvertreter* and Weiss's *Die Ermittlung*', *Modern Language Review*, 64 (1969), 828–39.
POE, EDGAR ALLAN, *The Complete Works of Edgar Allan Poe*, ed. by James A. Harrison, 17 vols (New York: Crowell, 1902).
PÖGGELER, OTTO, *Die Frage nach der Kunst. Von Hegel zu Heidegger* (Freiburg: Alber, 1984).
—— *Spur des Worts: Zur Lyrik Paul Celans* (Freiburg: Alber, 1986).
PONGE, FRANCIS, *La fabrique du 'Pré'* (Geneva: Skira, 1971).
—— *Pratiques d'écriture, ou, L'inachèvement perpétuel* (Paris: Hermann, 1984).
PROUST, MARCEL, *À la recherche du temps perdu*, ed. by Jean-Yves Tadié, 4 vols (Paris: Gallimard, 1987–1989).
RABATÉ, JEAN-MICHEL, *James Joyce and the Politics of Egoism* (Cambridge: Cambridge University Press, 2001).
RÄSÄNEN, PAJARI, *Counter-Figures. An Essay on Antimetaphoric Resistance: Paul Celan's Poetry and Poetics at the Limits of Figurality* (Helsinki: Dept. of Comparative Literature, University of Helsinki, 2007).

REICHERT, KLAUS, 'Hebräische Züge in der Sprache Paul Celans', in *Paul Celan*, ed. by Werner Hamacher and Winfried Menninghaus (Frankfurt a.M.: Suhrkamp, 1998), 156–69.
REIMANN, ARIBERT, *Eingedunkelt für Alt-Solo* (Mainz: Schott, 1995).
REINACH, ADOLPHE, *Textes grecs et latins relatifs à l'histoire de la peinture ancienne. Recueil Milliet* (1921; Paris: Macula, 1985).
REY, WILLIAM H., *Poesie der Antipoesie: moderne deutsche Lyrik: Genesis, Theorie, Struktur* (Heidelberg: Stiehm, 1978).
ROBB, GRAHAM, *Unlocking Mallarmé* (New Haven: Yale University Press, 1996).
ROSANOW, M. N., *Jakob M. R. Lenz, der Dichter der Sturm- und Drangperiode: sein Leben und seine Werke*, trans. by C. von Gütschow (Leipzig: Schulze, 1909).
ROSENFELD, ALVIN H., *A Double Dying: Reflections on Holocaust Literature* (Bloomington: Indiana University Press, 1980).
ROUSTANG, FRANÇOIS, 'On Reading Again' in *The Limits of Theory*, ed. by Thomas M. Kavanagh (Stanford: Stanford University Press, 1989), pp. 121–38.
RÜHMKORF, PETER, 'Das lyrische Weltbild der Nachkriegsdeutschen' in *Bestandsaufnahme. Eine deutsche Bilanz 1962. Sechsunddreissig Beiträge deutscher Wissenschaftler, Schriftsteller und Publizisten*, ed. by Hans Werner Richter (Munich: Desch, 1962), pp. 447–76.
RYAN, JUDITH, 'Monologische Lyrik: Paul Celans Antwort auf Gottfried Benn', *Basis: Jahrbuch für deutsche Gegenwartsliteratur*, 2 (1971), 260–82.
SAGÉ, SVEN, 'Celans Gedichte: Zauberstab', *Treffpunkt* (23 November 1991), n. p.
SALLOCH, ERIKA, 'The *Divina Commedia* as Model and Anti-Model for *The Investigation*', *Modern Drama*, 14.1 (1971), 1–12.
SANSY, DANIÈLE, 'Marquer la différence: l'imposition de la rouelle aux XIIIe et XIVe siècles', *Médiévales*, 41 (2001), 15–36.
SARTRE, JEAN-PAUL, *L'être et le néant. Essai d'ontologie phénoménologique* (Paris: Gallimard, 1943).
——*Réflexions sur la question juive* (Paris: Morihien, 1946).
——*Baudelaire*, with a foreword by Michel Leiris (Paris: Gallimard, 1947).
——'Mallarmé 1842–1898', in *Les Écrivains célèbres*, ed. by Raymond Queneau, 3 vols (Paris: Lucien Mazenod, 1951–1953), vol. 3, pp. 148–51.
——*Saint Genet: comédien et martyr* (Paris: Gallimard, 1952).
——*Les mots* (Paris: Gallimard, 1964).
——'Mallarmé 1842–1898', in Stéphane Mallarmé, *Poésies: Poésies, choix de vers de circonstance, poèmes d'enfance et de jeunesse*, preface by Jean-Paul Sartre (Paris: Gallimard, 1966), pp. 5–15.
——*L'idiot de la famille: Gustave Flaubert de 1821–1837*, 3 vols (Paris: Gallimard, 1971).
——'Mallarmé (1842–1898), in Jean-Paul Sartre, *Situations, IX, mélanges* (Paris: Gallimard, 1972), pp. 191–201.
——'L'engagement de Mallarmé', *Obliques*, 18/19 (1979), 169–94.
——*Mallarmé: la lucidité et sa face d'ombre*, ed. by Arlette Elkaïm-Sartre (Paris: Gallimard, 1986).
SCHOENBERNER, GERHARD, 'Die 'Ermittlung' in München', *Die Zeit* (29 October 1965), 21.
SCHMIDT, ARNO, *Zettel's Traum: 1963–69* (Stuttgart: Stahlberg, 1970).
SCHNECK, PETER, *Rhetoric and Evidence: Legal Conflict and Literary Representation in U.S. American Culture* (Berlin: De Gruyter, 2011).
SCHNEIDER, HANS ERNST. See 'SCHWERTE, HANS'.
SCHOLEM, GERSHOM G., *Major Trends in Jewish Mysticism* (New York: Schocken, 1954).
SCHWAB, CHRISTOPH THEODOR, 'Aus dem Berichte von Christoph Theodor Schwab', in *Der kranke Hölderlin: Urkunden und Dichtungen aus der Zeit seiner Umnachtung*, ed. by Erich Trummler (Munich: Recht, 1921), pp. 107–18.

SCHWARZ, HANS, 'Lied und Licht', in *Festschrift für Jost Trier zu seinem 60. Geburtstag am 15. Dezember 1954*, ed. by Benno von Wiese and Karl Heinz-Borck (Meisenheim am Glan: Westkulturverlag Anton Hain, 1954), pp. 434–55.

SCHWERTE, HANS (HANS ERNST SCHNEIDER), 'Die deutsche Lyrik nach 1945', *Der Deutschunterricht*, 14.3 (1962), 47–59.

SCOTT, CLIVE, *French Verse-Art. A Study* (Cambridge: Cambridge University Press, 1980).

SHAKESPEARE, WILLIAM, *Shakespeare's History of Pericles, Prince of Tyre*, ed. by William J. Rolfe (New York: Harper, 1883).

—— 'Macbeth', trans. by F. A. Leo, in *Shakespeare's dramatische Werke nach der Uebersetzung von August Wilhelm Schlegel und Ludwig Tieck* (Berlin: Reimer, 1871), pp. 163–287.

SHESTOV, LEV, *Potestas Clavium*, trans. by Bernard Martin (Athens: Ohio University Press, 1968).

SHMUELI, ILANA, 'Paul Celans Judentum und Israel', in *Unverloren. Trotz Allem: Paul Celan-Symposion Wien 2000*, ed. by Hubert Gaisbauer, Bernhard Hain, and Erika Schuster (Vienna: Mandelbaum, 2000), pp. 288–303.

SIEBURTH, RICHARD, 'Introduction', in Friedrich Hölderlin, *Hymns and Fragments*, trans. by Richard Sieburth (Princeton: Princeton University Press, 1984), pp. 3–43.

SIPE, DANIEL, 'Mallarmé et l'écriture du corps', *Nineteenth-Century French Studies*, 35.2 (2007), 367–83.

SONTAG, SUSAN, 'Reflections on *The Deputy*', in *The Storm over the Deputy*, ed. by Eric Bentley (New York: Grove, 1964), pp. 117–23.

SOURIAU, ÉTIENNE, 'Time in the Plastic Arts', *The Journal of Aesthetics and Art Criticism*, 7.4 (1949), 294–307.

SPINOZA, BENEDICTUS DE, *Éthique*, ed. by Bertrand Pautrat (Paris: Seuil, 1999).

SPIRE, ANTOINE, 'Préface', in Alexis Nouss, *Paul Celan: Les lieux d'un déplacement* (Lormont: Le Bord de l'eau, 2010), pp. 7–17.

STEENE, BIRGITTA, *Ingmar Bergman: A Reference Guide* (Amsterdam: Amsterdam University Press, 2005).

STEINER, GEORGE, 'A Terrible Exactness', *Times Literary Supplement* (11 June 1976), 709–10.

—— *On Difficulty and Other Essays* (Oxford: Oxford University Press, 1978).

SUBIOTTO, ARRIGO V., 'Dante and the Holocaust: The Cases of Primo Levi and Peter Weiss', *New Comparison*, 11 (1991), 70–89.

SUTHERLAND, KATHRYN, 'Anglo-American editorial theory', in *The Cambridge Companion to Textual Scholarship*, ed. by Neil Fraistat and Julia Flanders (Cambridge: Cambridge University Press, 2013), pp. 42–60.

SUTZKEVER, ABRAHAM, 'Abraham Sutzkever on Poetry and Partisan Life', Youtube/ The Yiddish Book Center, Jewish Public Library, Montreal, 24 May 1959, available at <https://www.youtube.com/watch?v=kofcyfycOFE>, [accessed 9 January 2015]

SYLVESTER, DAVID, *Interviews with Francis Bacon, with 94 illustrations* (London: Thames and Hudson, 1975).

SZONDI, PETER, *Schriften*, ed. by Wolfgang Fietkau, 2 vols (Frankfurt a.M.: Suhrkamp, 1978).

—— 'Lecture de *Strette*. Essai sur la poésie de Paul Celan', in *Poésies et poétiques de la modernité. Traduction française de textes de Peter Szondi sur Mallarmé, Paul Celan, Walter Benjamin, Bertolt Brecht*, ed. by Mayotte Bollack (Lille: Presses universitaires de Lille, 1981), pp. 165–99.

—— *On Textual Understanding and Other Essays*, trans. by Harvey Mendelsohn (Minneapolis: University of Minnesota Press, 1986).

—— *Celan Studies*, trans. by Susan Bernofsky with Harvey Mendelsohn (Stanford: Stanford University Press, 2003).

Tarn, Nathaniel, *The Embattled Lyric: Essays and Conversations in Poetics and Anthropology* (Stanford: Stanford University Press, 2007).
Terras, Victor, and Karl S. Weimar, 'Mandelstam and Celan: A Postscript', *Germano-Slavica*, 2 (1976–1978), 353–70.
The Holy Bible Containing the Old and New Testaments, Translated out of the Original Tongues and with the Former Translations Diligently Compared and Revised. King James Version 1611 (New York: American Bible Society, 1980).
Thomson, Alex, *Adorno: A Guide for the Perplexed* (London: Continuum, 2006).
Tiffany, Daniel, *Toy Medium: Materialism and Modern Lyric* (Berkeley: University of California Press, 2000).
Trummler, Erich (ed.), *Der kranke Hölderlin: Urkunden und Dichtungen aus der Zeit seiner Umnachtung* (Munich: Recht, 1921).
Valéry, Paul, *Oeuvres*, ed. by Jean Hytier, 2 vols (Paris: Gallimard, 1957–1960).
Varende, Jean De La, *Man d'Arc* (Paris: Grasset, 1939).
Voswinckel, Klaus, *Paul Celan: verweigerte Poetisierung der Welt: Versuch einer Deutung* (Heidelberg: Stiehm, 1974).
Wahrig, Gerhard, *Deutsches Wörterbuch*, ed. by Renate Wahrig-Burfeind (Gütersloh: Bertelsmann, 2001).
Walser, Martin, 'Unser Auschwitz', *Kursbuch*, 1 (1965), 189–200.
Weber, Werner, *Forderungen. Bemerkungen und Aufsätze zur Literatur* (Zurich: Artemis, 1970).
Weinrich, Harald, 'Kontraktionen: Paul Celans Lyrik und ihre Atemwende', *Neue Rundschau*, 79.1 (1968), 112–21.
Weiss, Peter, *Fluchtpunkt: Roman* (Frankfurt a.M.: Suhrkamp, 1962).
—— 'Frankfurter Auszüge', *Kursbuch*, 1 (1965), 152–88.
—— *Die Ermittlung. Oratorium in 11 Gesängen* (Frankfurt a.M.: Suhrkamp, 1965).
—— *Meine Ortschaft* (Rostock: Volkstheater, 1965).
—— 'Peter Weiss erklärt', *Frankfurter Allgemeine Zeitung* (27 October 1965), 24.
—— *L'instruction: oratorio en onze chants*, trans. by Jean Baudrillard (Paris: Seuil, 1966).
—— '"L'Instruction" (extraits)', trans by André Gisselbrecht, *La Nouvelle Critique*, 172 (February 1966), 47–77.
—— *The Investigation*, trans. by Jon Swan and Ulu Grosbard (New York: Atheneum, 1966).
—— 'Notizen zum dokumentarischen Theater', in Peter Weiss, *Rapporte 2* (Frankfurt a.M.: Suhrkamp, 1971), pp. 91–104.
—— 'The Material and the Models. Notes Towards a Definition of Documentary Theater', *Theater Quarterly*, 1 (1971), 41–45.
—— *Die Ermittlung. Oratorium in 11 Gesängen*, with a DVD of the television broadcast (Frankfurt a.M.: Suhrkamp, 2008).
Weissmann, Dirk, 'Poésie, Judaïsme, Philosophie. Une histoire de la réception de Paul Celan en France: des débuts jusqu'à 1991' (doctoral thesis, University of Paris — III, 2003), available at <publikationen.ub.uni-frankfurt.de/oai/container/index/docId/12414>, [accessed 12 March 2016].
Wellek, René, *History of Modern Criticism: 1750–1950*, 8 vols (New Haven: Yale University Press, 1955).
Wetering, Ernst Van De, 'Rembrandt laughing, c. 1628 — a painting resurfaces', *De Kroniek van het Rembrandthuis* (2007), 18–40.
Wiedemann, Barbara (ed.), *Paul Celan, die Goll-Affäre: Dokumente zu einer 'Infamie'* (Frankfurt a.M.: Suhrkamp, 2000).
—— 'Kommentar', in Paul Celan, *Die Gedichte. Kommentierte Gesamtausgabe in einem Band*, ed. by Barbara Wiedemann (Frankfurt a.M.: Suhrkamp, 2005), pp. 559–997.

——'Zwischen Pestkreuz und Bocklemünd — Paul Celan in Köln', *Celan-Jahrbuch*, 9 (2007), 103–26.
WINDHAM, SCOTT, 'Peter Weiss's *Die Ermittlung*: Dramatic and Legal Representation and the Auschwitz Trial', in *Re-examining the Holocaust through Literature*, ed. by Aukje Kluge and Benn E. Williams (Newcastle upon Tyne: Cambridge Scholars Publishing, 2009), pp. 29–60.
WITTGENSTEIN, LUDWIG, *Philosophische Untersuchungen / Philosophical Investigations*, trans. by G. E. M. Anscombe (New York: Macmillan, 1964).
WITTMANN, REBECCA, *Beyond Justice: The Auschwitz Trial* (Cambridge: Harvard University Press, 2005).
WOLFE, THOMAS, *Von Zeit und Strom. Eine Legende von Hunger des Menschen in der Jugend*, trans. by Hans Schiebelhuth, 2 vols (Berlin: Rowohlt, 1936).
YEATS, W. B., *The Poems*, ed. by Richard J. Finneran (New York: Macmillan, 1989).
YOUNG, JAMES E., *Writing and Rewriting the Holocaust. Narrative and the Consequences of Interpretation* (Bloomington: Indiana University Press, 1988).
ZAND, NICOLE, 'La création en France de «l'Instruction» de Peter Weiss. Auschwitz aujourd'hui', *Le Monde* (1 April 1966), 14.
ZARIFOPOL-JOHNSTON, ILINCA, *Searching for Cioran*, ed. by Kenneth R. Johnston (Bloomington: Indiana University Press, 2009).
ZIMMER, DIETER E., 'Die Lesung in der Volkskammer der DDR', *Die Zeit* (29 October 1965), 21.
ŽIŽEK, SLAVOJ, *Less than Nothing. Hegel and the Shadow of Dialectical Materialism* (London: Verso, 2012).

INDEX

abyss 29 n. 119, 48, 102–03, 127
Adelung, Johann Christoph 181
Adler, Alfred 95
Adorno, Theodor 94, 159, 163, 192 n. 159
 Aesthetic Theory 85–86
 'Cultural Criticism in Society' 22–23
 Jargon of Authenticity 160
 Notes to Literature 81 n. 72, 182–83
Agamben, Giorgio 139, 148, 188 n. 79
Alighieri, Dante 150, 157, 184 n. 1, 189 n. 90,
 191 n. 133, 221
allegory 68–69, 71–73, 97–99, 101
Allemann, Beda 31
Améry, Jean [Hans Mayer] 194 n. 237
Amthor, Wiebke 17–18
annotation 16, 22, 27 n. 68, 31, 34, 39, 41, 68–69,
 71–73, 76–77, 83 n. 141, 95–96, 104–05, 111–12,
 172, 180, 192 n. 163, 194 n. 237, 199, 219
anti-Semitism 127–28, 157–59, 162–64, 168, 189 n. 97,
 191 n. 129, 192 n. 159
Apollinaire, Guillaume 111
archive 1, 3, 25 n. 21, 31, 33–34, 37, 39, 44, 61, 78, 95,
 143, 153
Arendt, Hannah 138–39, 186 n. 45, 188 n. 72
Aron, Thomas 24 n. 10
Artaud, Antonin 27–28 n. 83
aspect 46–48, 52
Auschwitz-Birkenau 22–23, 138–39, 141–44, 148–53,
 158–62, 168, 171, 176, 179–81, 183, 185 n. 8,
 185 n. 12, 185 n. 13, 186 n. 44, 187 n. 57,
 187 n. 59, 188 n. 70, 188 n. 71, 189 n. 90,
 189 n. 97, 191 n. 134, 194 n. 237
Auschwitz number [die Auschwitznummer] 181,
 194 n. 237

Bachmann, Ingeborg 126
Bacon, Francis 207, 215 n. 58
Badiou, Bertrand 173
Bahti, Timothy 50, 196, 223
Balzac, Honoré de 95, 131 n. 73
Bambach, Charles 167
Barthes, Roland 67
Bataille, Georges 76–77
Baudelaire, Charles 38, 85, 96, 99, 112, 129 n. 17, 222, 224
Baudrillard, Jean 187 n. 57
Baumann, Gerhart 86
Beckett, Samuel 3, 15

becoming 15, 24, 39, 204, 221
Beissner, Friedrich 30, 32
Bell, Vikki 163
Bellemin-Noël, Jean 53
Benjamin, Walter 57, 152
 'Critique of Violence' 140–42, 156, 187 n. 60, 166–
  68, 182, 184, 185 n. 28, 186 n. 31, 188 n. 67
 'The Task of the Translator' 120–22, 124–27
Benn, Gottfried 80 n. 57, 82 n. 93, 85, 88
Benn, M. B. 129 n. 15
Bergman, Ingmar 150, 189 n. 93
Bermann Fischer, Brigitte and Gottfried 217 n. 82
Biasi, Pierre-Marc de 34, 36–37, 76, 78
Bible:
 Daniel 165, 168–69, 171–73, 175–77, 179, 182, 184,
  193 n. 191
 Deuteronomy 193 n. 198
 Exodus 121–22, 135 n. 218, 158
 Isaiah 176
 Judges 155–56
 Leviticus 169
 Numbers 190 n. 121
 Psalms 20–21, 53, 176, 197, 199, 206, 208–11, 216 n. 66
Biblical figures:
 Aaron 122, 155
 Abimelech 155–56
 Belshazzar 165, 168–69, 171–73, 175–77, 179, 182
 Daniel 165, 169, 171–73, 175, 177, 184
 Gideon 155–56
 Jotham 155–56
 Moses 121–22, 155
 Nebuchadnezzar 169, 193 n. 191
Blake, Peter 215 n. 61
Blanchot, Maurice 104, 112, 133 n. 162
 Faux pas 96–97
 La part du feu 96, 98–101
 L'espace littéraire 131 n. 91, 218
Blankert, Albert 200
Bloch, Ernst 139
body 3, 5, 20, 22, 24 n. 10, 45–48, 51, 53, 61, 71, 76,
 88, 92, 99, 101, 111, 113–14, 117–18, 133 n. 144,
 141, 153, 161, 173, 194 n. 220, 194 n. 235, 201,
 208, 211–12
Bogumil, Sieghild 130 n. 43
Bollack, Jean 30–31, 213 n. 7
Böll, Heinrich 191 n. 129
Bonaccorso, Giovanni 44

Bonnefoy, Yves 111
'Bonner Arbeitsstelle für die Celan-Ausgabe' 4, 31
Boos, Sonja 139, 147–48, 185 n. 16, 185 n. 21, 188–89 n. 82
Bormann, Alexander von 8
Bourdin, Martial 69
Bovet, Ernest 224
Boyarin, Daniel and Jonathan 163
Brentano, Clemens 109
Breton, André 27–28 n. 83
Breuer, Dieter 130 n. 43
Brierley, David 130 n. 43
Buber, Martin 88, 129 n. 28, 216 n. 69
Bucheli, Roman 39, 79 n. 8
Buchenwald 143
Bücher, Rolf 40, 42
Büchner, Georg:
   Dantons Tod 87–88, 94
   Lenz 88–89, 92–94, 100, 129 n. 29
   Leonce und Lena 87
Buck, Theo 206–09, 212, 215 n. 56, 216 n. 66
Buhr, Gerhard 130 n. 43
Bünde, Frauke 130 n. 42
Bushell, Sally 35–37, 53, 78

Calvin, Jean 192 n. 168
Camus, Albert 96, 101, 133 n. 143
Carney, Raymond 42
Cavell, Stanley 46, 48
Cazalis, Henri, 98, 106, 132 n. 111
Celan, Eric 16, 19, 25 n. 16, 25 n. 21, 27 n. 76
Celan, Paul:
   aphorisms 23, 29 n. 113, 143–44, 186 n. 42, 187 n. 52, 190 n. 106, 190 n. 127, 219
   correspondence 3, 17, 20, 91, 143, 157, 162, 206–07, 217 n. 82
   poems:
      'All deine Siegel erbrochen? Nie' [All your seals broken open? Never] 82 n. 109, 154–68, 183
      'Bedenkenlos' [Unthinking] 176–82
      'Bei Brancusi, zu zweit' [At Brancusi's, à deux] 23
      'Blitzgeschreckt' [Frightened by lightning] 23
      'Das am Gluteisen hier' [The hot branding iron here] 17
      'Das Nach-Fadensonnen-Poem' [The After-Fathomsuns-Poem] 24–25 n. 13
      'Das Seil' [The rope] 9, 17, 40–67, 69, 71
      'Die Atemlosigkeiten des Denkens' [The breathlessnesses of thinking] 104–09
      'Die leere Mitte' [The empty middle] 17
      'Ein Dröhnen' [A droning] 143–44, 187 n. 50
      'Einkanter: Rembrandt' [Ventifact: Rembrandt] 196–212, 216 n. 64
      '*Engführung*' [The Straightening] 5, 162, 192 n. 152
      'Es ist alles anders' [Everything is different] 216–17 n. 76
      'Füll die Ödnis' [Fill the wilderness] 11–15
      'Gegenlicht' [Counterlight] 29 n. 113
      'Gesang der fremden Brüder' [Song of foreign brothers] 180
      'Ich trink Wein' [I drink wine] 190 n. 112
      'Je regarde l'autoportrait de Rembrandt' [I am looking at the self-portrait by Rembrandt] 203–06, 219
      'Kantige' [Angular] 202
      'Keine Sandkunst mehr' [No more sand-art] 94
      'Kleide die Worthöhlen aus' [Dress the word-hollows] 82 n. 104
      'Lindenblättrige Ohnmacht' [Linden-leafed unconsciousness] 20–21
      'Mit dem rotierenden' [With the rotating] 29 n. 117
      'Mit uns' [With Us] 179
      'Nach dem Lichtverzicht' [Having forsworn the light] 17
      'Oder es kommt' [Or perhaps] 1, 6, 7, 24 n. 1
      'Pau, später' [Pau, later] 216 n. 64
      'Schwarze Flocken' [Black Flakes] 190 n. 119
      'Todesfuge' [Deathfugue] 158, 225
      'Todtnauberg' [Todtnauberg] 28 n. 108
      'Und mit dem Buch aus Tarussa' [And with the book from Tarussa] 111
      'Unter ein Bild' [Under a picture] 23
      'Vom Hochseil' [From the highwire] 171–76
      'Vor Scham' [For shame] 10
      'Wirfst du' [Will you throw] 225 n. 1
   prose:
      'Ansprache anlässlich der Entgegennahme des Literaturpreises der freien Hansestadt Bremen' [Speech on the occasion of the reception of the literature prize of the free Hanseatic city of Bremen] 8, 85, 190 n. 113
      'Der Meridian' [The Meridian] 1, 4–5, 8, 22, 24 n. 4, 26 n. 60, 31, 38–39, 71, 86–94, 112, 127–28, 129 n. 29, 162, 211, 219–20
      'Die Dichtung Ossip Mandelstamms' [The Poetry of Osip Mandel'shtam] 217 n. 81
      'Eine Lanze' [A Lance] 190–91 n. 127
      'Eingedunkelt' [prose poem] 29 n. 113
      'Gespräch im Gebirg' [Conversation in the Mountain] 94
   unpublished diary entries 26 n. 55, 28 n. 93, 28 n. 94, 143, 186 n. 44
   translations:
      'Rondel' 22, 112–13, 119–28, 219–20
      'Vier Gedichte aus dem Französischen' [Four poems from the French] 135 n. 214
   works:
      Atemwende [Breath-Turn] 4, 25 n. 18
      Die Niemandsrose [The No-One Rose] 184 n. 1, 199, 209
      Eingedunkelt [Indarkened] 3–4, 8–11, 15–20, 22,

27 n. 77, 29 n. 113, 29 n. 117, 30, 32–33,
37–38, 40, 56–57, 60, 76, 95, 154, 168, 197,
202, 219
  Fadensonnen [*Thread-Suns*] 24–25 n. 13, 191 n. 137,
  192 n. 171, 219
  Schneepart [*Snow-Part*] 196, 219
other:
  aggression 3, 16, 25 n. 16, 25 n. 17, 27 n. 76,
    29 n. 117, 154
  as reader and annotator 9–10, 12–15, 22, 26 n. 55,
    27 n. 68, 28 n. 105, 39, 69–77, 83 n. 141,
    83 n. 145, 95–96, 99–100, 104–05, 109, 111–12,
    132 n. 109, 133 n. 162, 134 n. 186, 145, 170,
    172, 178, 180–81, 185–86 n. 28, 192 n. 163,
    193 n. 205, 194 n. 237, 215 n. 52, 219
  as translator 42, 119–28, 187 n. 50, 217 n. 78
  hospitalization and treatment for mental illness 3,
    9–10, 14, 16–21, 25 n. 15, 25 n. 16, 25 n. 17,
    26 n. 55, 27 n. 77, 95, 131 n. 73, 134 n. 183,
    154, 168, 219
  neologisms 18, 20, 29 n. 113, 155–56, 169, 207–08
  on relation of 'Kunst' [art] and 'Dichtung' [poetry]
    9, 86–90, 100
  on the poem [Gedicht] 26 n. 47, 37–40, 49–50,
    86, 88, 93, 190 n. 106, 211
  press cuttings 143–45, 153, 186 n. 45, 187 n. 59,
    219
  relation to suicide 16, 22, 27 n. 76, 89, 95–96,
    99–100, 104, 109, 111–12, 128, 133 n. 162,
    134 n. 183, 134 n. 184, 134 n. 185, 182,
    220–21
  relations with Fischer Verlag 25 n. 18, 217 n. 82
  relations with Suhrkamp Verlag 25 n. 18
  use of geological terms 93, 105–06, 109,
    133 n. 164, 134 n. 175, 134 n. 186, 142–43,
    199, 207–08, 212, 215 n. 52, 216 n. 63
Celan-Lestrange, Gisèle 3, 16, 19, 20, 23, 25 n. 16,
  25 n. 17, 25 n. 21, 29 n. 117, 42, 52, 81 n. 86, 95,
  109, 131 n. 73, 143, 154, 206, 213 n. 7
Cerquiglini, Bernard 33–34, 81 n. 66
Certeau, Michel de 2, 4, 45, 62, 72, 76
Chabrol, Henri 25 n. 15
Char, René 76, 122
Cioran, Emil 16, 25 n. 17, 111
'Encounters with Suicide' 95–96
circle 44, 90, 102–03, 105, 113–14, 116–19, 121, 123–
  28, 135 n. 92, 136 n. 234, 150, 159, 162
Clausen, Oliver 147, 189 n. 93
Clifford, Wayne 27 n. 67
Coetzee, J. M. 2, 134 n. 182
Cohen, Robert 150–51, 183, 188 n. 71, 189 n. 89,
  191 n. 133
comma 47–50, 123, 179–80
Connolly, Anthony C. 215 n. 57
Conrad, Joseph, *The Secret Agent* 69–75, 83 n. 145, 95,
  170, 172–73, 178, 180, 193 n. 205

Contat, Michel 35
Cramer, Ernst 187 n. 59
Czernowitz 28 n. 109, 164, 186 n. 45

dampness 19–21, 28 n. 108, 125, 201–02, 204, 211–12
Danehl, G. 73
death 2, 3, 5, 18, 20–21, 30, 32, 48, 61, 67–68, 73, 78,
  83 n. 129, 85, 87, 92–93, 96, 98–99, 101–05, 109,
  111, 121, 128, 129 n. 29, 131 n. 91, 133 n. 148,
  134 n. 183, 139–40, 142, 144, 149, 154, 158–61,
  164–65, 176, 179–82, 189 n. 97, 196–97, 200, 203–
  04, 206, 209, 211–12, 213 n. 13, 218, 220, 225
Debray-Genette, Raymonde 38, 69
definitive version [endgültige Fassung] 4, 22, 28 n. 90,
  32, 34, 36–37, 39–52, 54–57, 61–62, 67, 72, 77,
  134 n. 187, 172–73, 216 n. 64
Delay, Jean 3
Deleuze, Gilles 81 n. 91, 109, 208
de Man, Paul 68, 99, 119, 127, 222–24
Demus, Nani 213 n. 3
depression 16–20, 134 n. 183, 222
Derrida, Jacques:
  'Archive et brouillon' 33
  'Force of Law' 140–43, 152–53, 166–68, 171, 184,
    190 n. 124, 190 n. 125
  Schibboleth pour Paul Celan 10–11
  'This is Not an Oral Footnote' 72–73
Dickinson, Emily 35, 221–22
Didi-Huberman, Georges 201–02, 204
Die Frankfurter Allgemeine Zeitung 4, 144, 147, 153,
  186 n. 45, 187 n. 59
difficulty 2, 4, 8–10, 17, 22, 25 n. 17, 32–34, 53, 57, 61,
  73, 76–77, 82 n. 104, 85, 91, 97, 106, 111–12, 124,
  137–39, 147–48, 149, 152, 154–55, 160, 166, 173,
  182, 220, 222–23
Dischner, Gisela 213 n. 8, 215 n. 60
draft 3, 17, 21, 30, 32, 34–36, 40, 42, 53, 63–67, 86, 98,
  105, 107, 114, 184 n. 1, 202, 222
du Bouchet, André 122

Eco, Umberto 32–33
Eichmann, Adolf 146, 159
Eisler, Max 200
ekphrasis 23, 196–97, 202, 204, 209, 220
Éluard, Paul 9, 26 n. 47
Emmerich, Wolfgang 4, 18
Englund, Axel 25 n. 14
Eskin, Michael 211–12
etymology 14, 19, 27 n. 69, 42, 51, 76, 103, 117–18,
  123–25, 138, 142, 148, 156, 161, 166, 175, 179, 181,
  184 n. 3, 197, 200–01, 204, 216 n. 64, 216 n. 74,
  223
excess 9, 20, 33, 35, 50, 52, 78, 117, 123, 219, 223
Ezrahi, Sidra DeKoven 150, 152–53

Fairley, Ian 11–12, 14–15, 18, 28 n. 95, 175
Federal Republic of Germany 14, 23, 137, 142, 145, 152, 157, 158, 183, 220
Felman, Shoshana 137–38, 145, 148, 184, 187 n. 53
Felstiner, John 8–10, 14, 16, 27 n. 67, 134 n. 185, 135 n. 217, 192 n. 164, 213 n. 18
Fénéon, Félix 83 n. 143
Fenves, Peter 126
Ferrer, Daniel 36, 40, 44, 52–53
Fioretos, Aris 190 n. 112
Flaubert, Gustave 34, 37–38, 44, 76, 78, 96
Fondane, Benjamin 46
Foucault, Michel 27 n. 73, 44
fragment 8, 30, 32, 39–42, 44–48, 50–52, 57, 60, 69, 78, 90, 94–96, 106, 109, 111–12, 121–22, 127, 138, 156, 160–61, 172–73, 177, 179–81, 221–22
Frankfurt Auschwitz Trial [Criminal Case against Mulka and Others] 23, 137–53, 155–63, 165–68, 171, 173, 176, 179, 183, 185 n. 8, 185 n. 12, 185 n. 21, 186 n. 45, 186 n. 47, 188 n. 71, 188 n. 72, 188 n. 76, 188–89 n. 82, 190 n. 106, 220
    Baretzki, Stefan 142, 186 n. 45
    Bauer, Fritz 138
    Bednarek, Emil 149, 189 n. 83
    Bischoff, Heinrich 185 n. 17
    Boger, Wilhelm 144, 146
    Hofmeyer, Hans 148
    Kaduk, Oswald 146
    Mulka, Robert Karl 185 n. 8
    Neubert, Gerhard 185 n. 17
free-reading 36, 41, 78
Friedman, Maurice 129 n. 28
Frye, Northrop 226 n. 19

Gabler, Hans Walter 21, 30, 35, 41
Gadamer, Hans-Georg 5, 8, 10–11, 15
Garloff, Katja 149, 189 n. 89, 194 n. 235
genesis 4, 22, 38–39, 41, 44, 49, 52–53, 56–57, 67–69, 77–78
Genet, Jean 96
genetic criticism 18, 22, 30, 34–38, 40–41, 44–47, 52–53, 57, 60–61, 67–69, 77–78, 82 n. 114
Genette, Gérard 35
genocide 139, 147, 184
genreader 34–35, 52
George, Stefan 135 n. 222, 187 n. 50
Géricault, Théodore 29 n. 125
German Academy for Language and Literature [Deutsche Akademie für Sprache und Dichtung] 24 n. 4
Germania Judaica, Cologne Library for the History of German Judaism [Germania Judaica, Kölner Bibliothek für die Geschichte des deutschen Judentums] 157, 191 n. 129
German Literature Archive [Deutsches Literaturarchiv],
Marbach am Neckar 3, 6–7, 13, 26 n. 53, 26 n. 55, 27 n. 68, 28 n. 93, 54–55, 63–66, 69–70, 74–75, 95, 107–08, 110, 170, 178, 186 n. 44
Giacometti, Alberto 219
Gide, André 9, 90
Gillespie, Susan H. 11–12, 14–15, 18
Gisselbrecht, André 187 n. 57
Glatstein, Jacob 163–65, 192 n. 164
Goethe, Johann Wolfgang von 24 n. 4, 129 n. 29
    The Sorrows of Young Werther 98
Goll, Claire 39, 86, 134 n. 180
Goll, Yvan 39, 85, 134 n. 180
Goyert, Georg 10, 95
Greetham, D. C. 81 n. 75
Grésillon, Almuth 30, 34, 53, 68–69, 80 n. 38
Groden, Michael 36, 41
Grosbard, Ulu 147, 153
Gruppe 47: 157
Guattari, Félix 81 n. 91

Hackel, Brayman 73, 83 n. 140
Hamacher, Werner 17, 29 n. 113, 82 n. 104, 221
Hamburger, Michael 92, 128 n. 1, 192 n. 152
Harbusch, Ute 90–92, 122, 130 n. 42, 130 n. 43, 134 n. 183, 135 n. 217, 135 n. 222
Härter, Andreas 8
Hartman, Geoffrey 3
Hartung, Harald 4, 16
Harvey, Pauline 109
Hay, Louis 34
Heaney, Seamus 201
Hegel, Georg Wilhelm Friedrich 140
    Aesthetics: Lectures on Fine Arts 224
    The Phenomenology of Spirit 103
Heidegger, Martin 9, 28 n. 108, 29 n. 119, 39, 86, 89, 102, 117, 160
Heinrichsbauer, Jürgen 188 n. 72
hermeneutics 22, 34–38, 40, 223
Higginson, Thomas Wentworth 221
highways 5, 225
Hill, Geoffrey 196, 212 n. 1
Hilton, Ian 191 n. 136
Hochhuth, Rolf 188 n. 64, 188 n. 72
Høeg, Carsten 80 n. 64
Hölderlin, Johann Christian Friedrich 18, 21, 29 n. 119, 30, 32–33, 51, 109, 122, 128 n. 1, 190 n. 112
Holocaust 18, 23, 128, 137–46, 149–53, 156, 159, 163–64, 166–68, 171, 173, 177, 182–83, 184 n. 3, 189 n. 97, 191 n. 133, 191 n. 134, 194 n. 235
Homer, *The Odyssey* 10, 12–15, 27 n. 68, 95, 161
Hoogstraten, Samuel Dirksz van 200
Horkheimer, Max, *Dialectic of Enlightenment* 159, 163, 192 n. 159
Horn, Peter 16–17, 134 n. 183
Howe, Susan 222

Huppert, Hugo 23
Huret, Jules 92
Huyssen, Andreas 189 n. 97

Ibáñez Fanés, Jordi 26 n. 61
intertextuality 10–11, 14–15, 90, 94, 206, 209
invisible 2, 14, 38, 49–50, 94, 120, 138, 156, 175–76, 181, 197
Ivanović, Christine 217 n. 81

Jackson H. J. 83 n. 161
Jackson, John E. 136 n. 224
Jackson, Virginia 221–22
Jacob, Max 18–19
Jacobs, Carol 57, 120
Jahnn, Hans Henny 95
Janz, Marlies 130 n. 43
Jean-Aubry, Gérard 96, 131 n. 90
Jean Paul 28 n. 105, 47
Jené, Edgar 23, 191 n. 127
Jennings, Elizabeth 211
Jenny, Laurent 34–35, 76, 78
Jens, Walter 151, 187 n. 59, 193 n. 180
jewish 23, 28 n. 109, 30, 76, 94, 111, 126, 139–40, 151–52, 155–56, 163–67, 172–73, 179–80, 186 n. 45, 189 n. 97, 192 n. 154, 192 n. 164, 194 n. 237, 199–200, 206–09, 213 n. 7, 213 n. 18
Johnson, Barbara 33, 50, 68
Joris, Pierre 18, 26 n. 60
Joubert, Joseph 95
Joyce, James 34, 114
    Finnegans Wake 28 n. 86, 31, 34
    Ulysses 10, 21, 26 n. 55, 30, 95
justice:
    divine violence 140–42, 156, 158, 165–69, 171, 173, 176, 181–82, 184
    mythic violence 140–42, 156, 161, 166–68, 182–84, 186 n. 31
    poetic justice 23, 138, 145, 167–68, 173, 175–76, 181–84, 186 n. 42, 220
    relation to law 137, 139–48, 156, 159, 161, 165–68, 171, 182–84, 185 n. 11

Kafka, Franz 16
    'In the Penal Colony' 60–62, 67, 73, 76, 83 n. 126, 84 n. 163
Kahler, Erich 111
Kaiser, Joachim 187 n. 56
Kant, Immanuel 129 n. 29, 140
Karasek, Hellmuth 187 n. 59
Kästner, Erhart 85
Kiefer, Anselm 191 n. 140
Kierkegaard, Søren 167
Klee, Ernst 189 n. 83
Klee, Paul, 'Ad Marginem' 49
Kleist, Heinrich von 129 n. 17

Kligerman, Eric 23
Kluge, Friedrich 19, 155, 208
Koelle, Lydia 130 n. 43
Kojève, Alexandre 103
Konietzny, Ulrich 155
Könneker, Sabine 215 n. 61
Kraft, Ruth 203
Kunze, Rolf-Ulrich 8

Lacoue-Labarthe, Philippe 5, 17, 122
Langbein, Hermann 186 n. 36, 188 n. 76
Langer, Lawrence L. 189 n. 98
Lanzmann, Claude 138
Lao Tse 83 n. 141, 95
Larousse, Pierre 24 n. 11, 82 n. 101, 214 n. 40
Laub, Dori 137, 148, 187 n. 53
Laurent, Méry 112, 126, 128
Lautréamont, Le Comte de, *The Songs of Maldoror* 113
Le Calvez, Eric 38
Leiris, Michel 27 n. 76
Le Monde 35, 95, 180
Lenz, Jakob Michael Reinhold 89, 129 n. 29
Leo, F. A. 214 n. 36
Lernout, Geert 35
Lesky, Albin 27 n. 69
Leutner, Petra 91
Levi, Primo 111, 184 n. 3, 188 n. 79, 191 n. 133
literature 3, 10, 23–24, 24 n. 4, 24 n. 10, 30–31, 33–37, 40–41, 50, 77–78, 82 n. 114, 85, 87–88, 92–101, 104, 106, 109, 111, 120, 128, 138, 157, 165, 183, 223, 225
Littré, Émile 130 n. 65
Lohr, Andreas 40, 42
Louth, Charlie 4
love 113, 115, 116, 119–21, 124–26, 128, 197, 204, 212
Lowell, Robert 214 n. 37
Lukács, Georg 223–24
Luther, Martin 121, 156, 171, 177, 179, 208–09, 216 n. 66
Lyon, James K. 129 n. 28
lyric 51, 88, 155, 182, 190 n. 106, 221–24

Mader, Helmut 130 n. 42
madness 21, 32, 87, 114, 165, 167, 200–01, 219
Malebranche, Nicolas 90
Mallarmé, Stéphane 1, 8, 22, 40, 50, 83 n. 143, 85–88, 90–106, 109, 111–16, 119, 121–22, 125–28, 129 n. 10, 130 n. 42, 131 n. 86, 131 n. 90, 131 n. 91, 132 n. 109, 133 n. 144, 219–20
    correspondence 90, 98, 101, 106, 131 n. 90, 132 n. 110, 132 n. 111
    poems:
        'Au seul souci de voyager' [To the sole goal of sailing] 134 n. 186
        'Billet' [Note] 135 n. 193

'Cantique de Saint-Jean' [Canticle of Saint John] 133 n. 170
'Éventail' [Fan] 136 n. 237
'Hérodiade' 106, 134 n. 186
'Le pitre châtié' [The clown chastised] 106
'Les fleurs' [The Flowers] 99
'Le sonneur' [The Bell-Ringer] 95
'Le tombeau de Charles Baudelaire' [The tomb of Charles Baudelaire] 99
'Le vierge, le vivace et le bel aujourd'hui' [The virgin, the vivacious and the beautiful today] 100–01, 106
'M'introduire dans ton histoire' [To introduce me into your tale] 133 n. 170
'Renouveau' [Renewal] 105–06
'Ses purs ongles très haut...' [Her pure nails very high...] 109
'Si tu veux nous nous aimerons' [If you will we will love each other] 22, 112–28, 134 n. 187, 134 n. 189, 135 n. 217
'Toute l'âme résumée' [The whole soul resumed] 114
'Un coup de dés' [A throw of the dice] 31–32, 87, 93–94
'Victorieusement fui le suicide beau' [The beautiful suicide victoriously fled] 99
prose:
  'Action restreinte' [Restricted Action] 101, 114
  'Ballets' [Ballets] 73, 117–18
  'Crise de vers' [Crisis of verse] 50, 135 n. 200, 135 n. 201, 135 n. 202, 135 n. 203, 135 n. 204
  '«Erechtheus», Tragédie par Swinburne' [«Erechtheus», Tragedy by Swinburne] 93
  'Hamlet' 132 n. 109
  Igitur 97–101, 103, 106, 114, 131 n. 91
  'La musique et les lettres' [Music and Letters] 69, 97
  'Le Démon de l'analogie' [The Demon of Analogy] 123
  'Le Livre' [The Book] 92, 97, 104, 111, 130 n. 57
  'Le Livre, instrument spirituel' [The book, spiritual instrument] 130 n. 54
  'Mimique' [Mimic] 130 n. 61
  'Pauvre enfant pâle' [Pale Poor Child] 99
  'Richard Wagner, rêverie d'un poëte français' [Richard Wagner, a French poet's revery] 101
  'Sur la philosophie dans la poésie' [On philosophy in poetry] 130 n. 64
  'Sur l'évolution littéraire' [On literary evolution] 130 n. 53
  'Sur l'explosion à la chambre des députés' [On the explosion in the Chamber of Deputies] 132 n. 130
  'Villégiatures' [Holidays in the country] 130 n. 46
  'Villiers de L'Isle-Adam' 101
works:
  Les mots anglais 135 n. 212
  Poésies 22, 95–96, 100, 105, 112, 134 n. 175, 134 n. 186
Malraux, André 196, 200, 214 n. 24, 214 n. 30
Mandel'shtam, Osip 23, 91, 187 n. 50, 209–11, 217 n. 77, 217 n. 78, 217 n. 81, 221
manuscript 3, 11, 26 n. 55, 28 n. 93, 30–35, 40–42, 44, 52, 61, 68, 76, 99, 108, 132 n. 132, 134 n. 187, 186 n. 44, 213 n. 3, 221–22
Marchal, Bertrand 98
Margul-Sperber, Alfred 162
Marin, Louis 49
Mauthausen 143
Mayer, Hans 24 n. 5, 88, 130 n. 42
McClatchy, J. D. 212
McGann, Jerome 41
Meinecke, Dietlind 130 n. 42
Menasseh ben Israel 175, 193 n. 218, 199
Mendès, Catulle 98
menetekel 154, 158, 162, 165, 168–69, 171, 173, 175–77, 179, 181–82, 184
Menninghaus, Winfried 130 n. 43
Mercier, Alain 24 n. 10
Merriman, John M. 83 n. 142
Meschonnic, Henri 19–20, 24 n. 10, 34, 85, 122
Michaelis, Rolf 4, 18, 21
Michaux, Henri 111
Michel, Wilhelm 109
Milton, John 18
Ming Meng 26–27 n. 61
Mondor, Henri 96–97, 131 n. 90
Montaigne, Michel de 140
Müller-Jerina, Alwin 191 n. 129

Naber, Hermann 187 n. 56, 187 n. 59
National Socialism 21, 148, 151, 153, 158–59, 186 n. 31, 189 n. 97, 191 n. 140
Naumann, Bernd 141, 147, 153, 160, 188 n. 72
Nerval, Gérard de 112, 114
Nietzsche, Friedrich, *Also sprach Zarathustra* 46–48, 81 n. 90
Nono, Luigi 149
non-verbal 41, 69, 73, 77, 219, 222
Nouss, Alexis 111
Nuremberg trials 137, 140, 185 n. 13

Oelmann, Ute Maria 130 n. 43, 155, 162
Olschner, Leonard 1, 4
Ovid (Publius Ovidius Naso) 89, 129 n. 15
Ozick, Cynthia 166

palimpsest 32–33, 51
Panofsky, Erwin 213 n. 19
Pascal, Blaise 90, 98, 140, 186 n. 39
Pearson, Roger 134 n. 188, 135 n. 193

Pendas, Devin 139, 185 n. 11, 185 n. 16, 185 n. 17
Perry, R. C. 188 n. 72
philology 33, 36, 68–69, 82 n. 114, 181, 184 n. 3
plagiarism 39, 86, 153, 157, 162
Plato, *Phaedo* 109
Poe, Edgar Allan 41
  'Marginalia' 81 n. 86
  'The Purloined Letter' 68–69, 97
poetry 1–2, 4–5, 8–9, 17–18, 21–24, 39–40, 47, 49, 51, 77, 85–88, 90–92, 94, 98–99, 102–04, 106, 111–12, 115, 119, 123–24, 128, 133 n. 162, 137–38, 143–44, 167–68, 181–84, 190 n. 106, 199, 202, 217 n. 81, 218–25
Pöggeler, Otto 28 n. 108, 85, 88, 94, 130 n. 43, 215 n. 61
Ponge, Francis 35
pre-text 21–22, 30–42, 44–47, 49–50, 52–53, 56–57, 60, 62, 67–69, 71, 73, 76–78, 92, 219, 222–24
prosody 80 n. 63, 83 n. 129, 87, 114–15, 135 n. 222, 210, 224
Proust, Marcel 21, 30
psychosis 16–20, 25 n. 15, 222

Queneau, Raymond 96, 132 n. 132

Rabaté, Jean-Michel 34–35, 52
Radway, Janice 69
Rambach, Jean-Claude 25 n. 21, 27 n. 77
Räsänen, Pajari 187 n. 50
reader 1–3, 5, 8–12, 14–17, 22, 24, 28 n. 105, 30–37, 39–42, 44–52, 56, 60–62, 68–69, 71–73, 76–78, 88, 91–94, 97, 100, 104, 112, 115–16, 118–19, 121–22, 126–27, 135 n. 217, 137–38, 143, 146–47, 149–51, 153, 155, 165–68, 173, 175, 182–84, 193 n. 205, 196, 199, 201–02, 205–07, 209, 211–12, 218–25
Reichert, Klaus 214 n. 20
Reimann, Aribert 25 n. 14
Rembrandt van Rijn 23, 196–97, 199, 216 n. 64, 217 n. 77
  'A Bearded Man in a Hat' 213 n. 7, 213 n. 18
  'A Man Seated Reading at a Table in a Lofty Room' [attributed] 199, 213 n. 13, 213 n. 15, 215 n. 46, 215 n. 54, 215 n. 56, 215 n. 59
  'Belshazzar's Feast' 174–76, 179, 194 n. 220, 213 n. 15
  'Homer' 200, 214 n. 24
  'Jeremiah lamenting the destruction of Jerusalem' 213 n. 7
  'Self-Portrait' [Musée Granet] 215 n. 58
  'Self-Portrait as Zeuxis' 198–99, 213 n. 8, 213 n. 12, 214 n. 22, 214 n. 23, 214 n. 24, 214 n. 39
  'The Jewish Bride' 213 n. 7
  'Three Beggars at the Door of a House' 213 n. 7
repetition 2, 14, 23, 34, 47, 49, 56, 67–68, 86, 96, 101, 103, 106, 109, 113–19, 121–25, 127–28, 140, 142–43, 147, 151, 153, 156, 158, 160–61, 163, 167, 169, 175, 188 n. 67, 196–97, 200, 209, 219–20, 224–25
resistance 8–10, 33, 40, 53, 67, 76–77, 99, 104, 111, 121–22, 124, 137, 146–48, 157, 166, 184, 201, 209, 221–22
Resnais, Alain 23
Rey, William H. 130 n. 42
Rimbaud, Arthur 85, 111–12
Robb, Graham 97, 116, 126
Rosanow, M. N. 129 n. 29
Rosenfeld, Alvin H. 189 n. 97
Roustang, François 68
Rühmkorf, Peter 85
Runge, Philipp Otto 109
Ryan, Judith 81–82 n. 93

Sachs, Nelly 3, 213 n. 7
Sachsenhausen 143
Sainte Anne [hospital] 3, 9–10, 16, 21, 25 n. 16, 27 n. 83, 95, 112, 131 n. 73, 168
Sakel, Manfred 20, 28 n. 109
Salloch, Erika 189 n. 89
Sartre, Jean-Paul 22, 35, 92, 112, 127–28, 132 n. 138, 220
  Being and Nothingness 102–03
  'L'engagement de Mallarmé' 99, 131 n. 86
  'Mallarmé 1842–1898' 95–106, 111–12, 131 n. 91
  Réflexions sur la question juive 163
Sattler, D. E. 32
Schadewaldt, Wolfgang 10, 12, 14–15, 27 n. 69, 95, 180
Schallück, Paul 157, 162, 191 n. 129, 213 n. 7
Scherer, Jacques 92
Schiebelhuth, Hans 95
Schiller, Friedrich 87
Schmidt, Arno 35
Schneck, Peter 142, 183
Schoenberg, Arnold 182–83, 187 n. 50
Schoenberner, Gerhard 187 n. 59, 193 n. 180
Schopenhauer, Arthur 96
Schulze-Rohr, Peter 145
Schwab, Christoph Theodor 18
Schwarz, Hans 125
Schwerte, Hans 85, 128 n. 3
Scott, Clive 134 n. 190
Shakespeare, William 126–27, 176, 197, 214 n. 36, 224
shaking 36, 72–73, 76, 84 n. 163, 98
Shestov, Lev, *Potestas Clavium* 163, 176, 192 n. 163
Shmueli, Ilana 187 n. 53, 197, 213 n. 3
Sieburth, Richard 32–33
silence 18, 39–40, 48, 50, 62, 76–77, 80 n. 63, 86–87, 90, 93–94, 96–97, 100, 112–13, 116–24, 157, 181–82
Sipe, Daniel 133 n. 144
Sontag, Susan 146
soul 39–40, 45–48, 90, 93, 116, 164, 166, 224

Souriau, Étienne 212
sous-littérature 24 n. 10
sous-oeuvre 2–4, 8, 10–11, 14–15, 18, 21–22, 24 n. 10, 77, 94, 112, 120–21, 124, 128, 138, 196, 218–24
Spinoza, Baruch 46, 216 n. 64
Spire, Antoine 134 n. 184
Starobinski, Jean 154
Steiner, George 1–2, 8, 85, 111, 137
Struve, Gleb 91
Stueland, Espen 26 n. 61
Sutherland, Kathryn 79 n. 16, 82 n. 117
Sutzkever, Abraham 155
Swan, Jon 153
Szondi, Peter 5, 8, 28 n. 105, 30–31, 42, 45, 127, 213 n. 7

Tadié, Jean-Yves 21, 30
Tarantino, Quentin 173
Tarn, Nathaniel 132 n. 138
telos 22, 36–38, 40–42, 52, 67
thanatic process 68
Tiffany, Daniel 129 n. 17
time 5, 11, 14, 20, 32–34, 36, 40, 44, 46, 61, 67, 69, 76–77, 80 n. 64, 86, 91, 99, 103, 106, 109, 114, 117, 128, 134 n. 184, 151, 161–62, 167, 176, 197, 204, 207, 210–12, 215 n. 61, 217 n. 82, 225
trace 2, 4, 30–31, 36–40, 42, 44–45, 51–53, 60, 62, 68–69, 71, 73, 76–78, 91–95, 99, 101, 104, 124, 134 n. 175, 143, 153, 165, 176, 196, 202, 204, 222, 224
Trakl, Georg 85
translation 1, 6–7, 10–12, 14–15, 17–18, 22, 24 n. 1, 24 n. 10, 26 n. 60, 26–27 n. 61, 27 n. 67, 29 n. 119, 31, 42, 50, 52, 54, 57, 69, 71, 73, 82 n. 118, 83 n. 145, 89, 92, 95, 112–13, 115, 117, 119–28, 131 n. 73, 134 n. 186, 134 n. 187, 135 n. 217, 136 n. 224, 145, 147–48, 153, 156, 175–77, 179–82, 187 n. 50, 187 n. 57, 188 n. 72, 188 n. 76, 190 n. 112, 192 n. 163, 196, 206, 208, 210, 214 n. 36, 216 n. 66, 216 n. 69, 217 n. 78, 219–21, 225
Trummler, Erich 18
Tübingen Celan Edition [Tübinger Celan-Ausgabe] 31–32, 40, 79 n. 10
typescript 3, 11, 31–32, 35, 110

underlining 27 n. 68, 71, 73, 77, 95, 99, 104, 109, 132 n. 109, 133 n. 162, 153
unfinished 3–5, 10, 15, 18, 20–22, 24, 25 n. 14, 30–33, 36–37, 40, 45, 48, 52, 57, 67, 69, 88, 92, 97, 99, 101, 111, 121, 128, 134 n. 186, 154, 175, 179, 196–97, 219–22
Unger, Wilhelm 191 n. 129
'Unité de recherche Paul Celan, École normale supérieure', Paris 186 n. 45, 186 n. 46, 187 n. 59

Unseld, Siegfried 3, 31

Valéry, Paul 9, 30, 39, 60
van de Wetering, Ernst 214 n. 25
Van Gogh, Vincent 29 n. 124
Varende, Jean de la 135 n. 211
Verhoeven, Paul 146
Villiers de L'Isle Adam, Auguste 101, 132 n. 110
voice 10–12, 25 n. 14, 28 n. 86, 67, 76–77, 80 n. 63, 88–90, 92, 105, 118, 146, 149, 151, 156, 165, 187 n. 50, 211, 222
Voswinckel, Klaus 130 n. 43

Walser, Martin 3
  'Unser Auschwitz' 146, 160, 188 n. 67, 189 n. 90
Weber, Werner 196, 213 n. 3
Weinrich, Harald 130 n. 42
Weiss, Peter 3, 23, 145, 188 n. 71, 191 n. 133, 191 n. 134, 191 n. 136, 192 n. 154, 194 n. 235
  Die Ermittlung [*The Investigation*] 23, 138, 145–62, 165–68, 180–83, 185 n. 12, 187 n. 57, 187 n. 59, 188 n. 70, 188 n. 72, 188 n. 82, 189 n. 87, 198 n. 89, 189 n. 93, 189 n. 97, 190 n. 106, 193 n. 180, 220
  Fluchtpunkt [*Vanishing Point*] 180–81
  'Frankfurter Auszüge' [Frankfurt Extracts] 187 n. 55
  interviews 147, 151–52, 157–58
  Meine Ortschaft [*My Place*] 162, 181
  'Notizen zum dokumentarischen Theater' [Notes on documentary theater] 147
  'Peter Weiss erklärt' [Peter Weiss explains] 153, 187 n. 59
Weissmann, Dirk 135–36 n. 223
Wellek, René 100, 131 n. 80
Wertheimer, Jürgen 31
whiteness 39, 48–49, 61, 91–94, 105, 119, 123, 125, 128, 175–76, 181, 208, 222
Wiedemann, Barbara 144, 155, 190 n. 119, 199–201, 206–08, 212, 216 n. 66
Windham, Scott 185 n. 12, 189 n. 89, 193 n. 180
Wittgenstein, Ludwig, *Philosophische Untersuchungen* 46, 52
Wittmann, Rebecca 185 n. 16, 185 n. 21
Wolfe, Thomas, *Of Time and the River* 10, 17, 95
Woolf, Virginia 73
Wurm, Franz 206–07

Yeats, W. B. 38
Young, James E. 151, 153

Zand, Nicole 187 n. 57, 194 n. 234, 194 n. 136
Zeuxis 200–02, 204
Zimmer, Dieter E. 187 n. 59
Zohn, Harry 120, 122
Zola, Émile 35

www.ingramcontent.com/pod-product-compliance
Lightning Source LLC
LaVergne TN
LVHW061250060426
835507LV00017B/1989